Mastering Payroll

—Paying wages, withholding, depositing and reporting taxes, correct use of government forms.

by Debera J. Salam, CPP
Director
Payroll Information and Process Services
Ernst & Young LLP

Debera J. Salam, CPP, is currently Director of Payroll Information and Process Services for Ernst & Young LLP, and has over 25 years of experience in payroll management and consulting on compliance issues. She is the author of *Principles of Payroll Administration* and *The Payroll Practitioner's Compliance Handbook: Year-End and Quarterly Reporting* (both published by Thomson Reuters/WG&L, New York, NY), The Ernst & Young Payroll Resource Library, published by Wolters Kluwer/Aspen Publishers, and contributing editor of *The General Ledger*. As one of the country's leading authors on payroll, Ms. Salam serves on the advisory boards of the American Institute of Professional Bookkeepers and Research Institute of America's *Payroll Guide*. She provides payroll training and consulting to private companies at seminars and conferences nationwide.

ISBN 978-1-884826-58-0

INTRODUCTION

Upon completing this course, you should be able to:

1. Carry out the basic payroll function, including paying wages, withholding, depositing and reporting taxes, and preparing federal forms.
2. Understand basic reporting of wages and taxes for Forms 940, 941, 944, 945, W-2, W-3, and 1099.
3. Make journal entries for the payroll distribution, payroll-related expenses, payroll liabilities, and remittance of employer taxes.

NOTE: Dated material, such as Social Security tax rates, is based on 2013 information and incorporates legislative changes enacted through January 31, 2013.

If you take the optional open-book Final Examination at the end of this workbook, return the answer sheet to AIPB and achieve a grade of at least 70, you will receive an AIPB *Certificate of Completion.*

Mastering Payroll covers everything you need to know for the payroll portion of the *Certified Bookkeeper* examination. Applicants for certification who pass the Final Examination will also receive a *Certificate of Completion* and, after being certified, be eligible to register seven (7) CPECs.

To get the most out of the course, this is the procedure the course recommends:

1. Read the concise narrative that begins at each section.
2. Read the section narrative again. The second time, cover the solution to each illustrative problem and try to figure it out. Actually write it out. Regardless of how easy or difficult it may seem, simply trying to solve it and checking your answer against the correct solution will help you learn a great deal.

3. Take Quiz #1 at the end of each section to see what you have learned and need to review.

4. Take Quiz #2 at the end of each section to master any points previously missed.

Finally, please take a moment to fill out and send in the brief "Course Evaluation" at the back of your workbook (whether or not you take the final). It will help AIPB to improve this and other courses.

AIPB recommends continuing with *Mastering Payroll II—From Benefits, Business Expenses and Sick Pay to Disability and Workers' Comp* and the excellent reference material listed in the "Bibliography" (page 185).

AIPB wants to thank the people whose hard work contributed to this course, including Supervisory Editor, L. G. Schloss, Department of Accounting and Law, Iona College (Ret.), New Rochelle, New York; Technical Editor, Lisa Miedich, payroll technical researcher and editor, Colorado Springs, CO; Joanne Brodsky for proofreading; and Carol Lovelady, Lovelady Consulting, Roswell, Georgia, for typesetting.

Thank you, enjoy the course and congratulations on taking a major step toward advancing your professional knowledge and career.

Certified Bookkeeper Applicants

The best way to study for the certification exam is to take each section's quizzes over and over until you can answer questions quickly and comfortably—and know why the answer is correct. If you have trouble with a question, or know the answer, but not why it is correct, review the related material. Write answers on a separate sheet, wherever possible, to avoid seeing them each time you take the quiz.

CONTENTS

Section 1

EMPLOYEES V. NONEMPLOYEES

Introduction

There are six categories of workers:

1. Common-law employees
2. Statutory employees
3. Statutory nonemployees
4. Independent contractors
5. Individuals referred by a temporary help agency
6. Leased employees

Only the first two categories are covered by unique tax and reporting requirements included in the complex process known as payroll. The other four groups are paid as an ordinary disbursement. (Individuals referred by a temporary help agency or leasing company are generally employees of the agency.)

Definition of Each Category

Each category is briefly defined next:

1. **Common-law employees.** Under IRS guidelines, individuals are considered common-law employees when they meet the "common law" test. This test determines whether the employer exercises control over an employee in the following areas:

    - Who performs the work.
    - What will be done.
    - How it will be done.
    - When it will be done.

See Form SS-8 in the Appendix for the measures the IRS uses to determine common law employment for purposes of federal income and employment tax withholding and IRS Publication 1779, *Independent Contractor or Employee?* Both are available at *www.irs.gov*.

Workers who meet the common-law test are considered employees. Length of employment has no bearing. If the common-law test is met, the individual is considered an employee *even if the employment relationship lasts for only one hour.*

However, because some parts of the common-law test are broad and open to interpretation, employers are allowed to use other guidelines, "safe harbors," or "Section 530 provisions" for determining whether an individual is an independent contractor, including common industry practice, past Internal Revenue Service (IRS) rulings and audits, and prior court decisions.

2. **Statutory employees.** A statutory employee includes the following:

   - A driver who distributes beverages (other than milk) or meat, vegetables, fruit, or bakery products; or who picks up and delivers laundry or dry cleaning, and is the employer's agent or is paid by commission.

   - A full-time life insurance sales agent whose principal activity is selling life insurance or annuity contracts, or both, primarily for one carrier (rather than as an independent agent selling for many carriers).

   - Certain homeworkers who work with materials or goods supplied by the employer, meet specifications given by the employer and must return the goods or materials to an employer or person named by the employer.

   - A full-time traveling or in-city salesperson whose principal activity is to submit orders to the employer from wholesalers, retailers, contractors, operators of hotels, restaurants, or similar establishments. The goods sold must be merchandise for resale or supplies used in the operation of the buyer's business.

   Payments made to statutory employees are not subject to federal income tax withholding, but they are subject to FICA (Social Security and Medicare) tax withholding and federal unemployment tax. For state unemployment insurance, check your state laws; most states exempt payments to full-time commissioned life insurance salespeople.

3. **Statutory nonemployees.** A statutory nonemployee is compensated based on sales and other achievements, not by the hour. The employer must provide statutory nonemployees with a contract explaining that they will not be treated as employees for the purposes of federal income tax withholding and FICA tax.

   Statutory nonemployees include the following:

   - **Direct sellers.*** Direct sellers are people engaged in (1) selling consumer products in the customer's home or place of business other than a permanent retail establishment; (2) selling consumer products to any buyer on a buy-sell basis, or any similar basis prescribed by IRS regulations, for resale in the home or at a place of business other than in a permanent retail establishment; or (3) newspaper distributors, carriers and directly related businesses (such as those who collect payment for the distributors or carriers).

     NOTE: These individuals may be categorized as nonstatutory employees only if (a) "substantially all" of their compensation is based on sales or performance (not on hours worked), and (b) the performance-based pay arrangement and the fact the individual will not be treated as an employee for federal tax purposes is stipulated in a written agreement.

   - **Licensed real estate agents.** A licensed real estate agent is an individual engaged in appraisal activities connected with real estate sales if he or she earns compensation based on sales or other achievements.

   - **Companion sitters.** A companion sitter provides personal attendance, companionship, or household services for children or the elderly and disabled. A referral agency is not considered the sitter's employer if it receives only a referral or placement fee and does not receive or pay the sitter's salary. A companion sitter not employed by an agency is generally considered to be self employed for federal employment and withholding tax purposes.

   Payments to statutory nonemployees are exempt from federal income tax withholding, FICA (Social Security or Medicare) tax and federal unemployment tax.

---

*For a more detailed explanation of direct sellers, see IRS Publication 334.

4. **Independent contractors.** An independent contractor is an individual or business that controls the methods and means of the work performed and bears the risk of financial gain or loss. The independent contractor must provide to the payer a *taxpayer identification number (TIN)*, which may be a Social Security number (SSN) or an *employer identification number* (EIN). Individuals receiving U.S.-source income and who are not eligible for an SSN are assigned an individual taxpayer identification number (ITIN).

5. **Individuals referred by a temporary help agency.** If the client contracts with an agency to use its employees for a specified amount of time, usually during peak-volume periods or to replace employees absent due to illness or vacation, this is a temporary help agency. Payment is made to the agency as an ordinary disbursement. Because the agency is the individual's employer, the agency is responsible for withholding federal, state and FICA taxes and for paying federal and state unemployment taxes. However, if the agency fails to pay its employees or fails to pay or withhold employment taxes properly, the client firm may be liable for the unpaid amount. The client firm and the temporary help agency are jointly responsible for compliance with wage-hour laws. In addition, certain temporary employees may be eligible for fringe benefits that are provided by the client company.

6. **Leased employees.** Some firms use a leasing agency, or professional employer organization (PEO), to reduce the costs of employee turnover and related payroll and administrative expenses. The agency is the employer and assumes responsibility for recruitment, wage and tax reporting and personnel recordkeeping. The client firm can hire or terminate leased individuals as it chooses. It pays the PEO as an ordinary disbursement. However, if the PEO fails to pay its employees or to appropriately withhold and deposit employment taxes, the client firm may be required to do so. The client firm and the PEO are jointly responsible for compliance with wage-hour laws. The client firm also may, under certain circumstances, be required to provide fringe benefits to its leased employees.

   NOTE: Many state taxing authorities do not recognize the PEO as the employer for state unemployment insurance purposes. Contact your state taxing authority for more information.

The Difference Between Employees and Independent Contractors

The IRS discourages employers from treating employees as independent contractors so that they can evade payment of FICA and other employment taxes. Under federal wage-hour law, an individual is presumed to be an employee unless the employer can prove otherwise.

Similarly, if employees leave a firm to become consultants, but continue to provide to the firm the same services that they did as employees, the IRS generally considers them employees—not independent contractors. Here again, the IRS seeks to prevent employers from evading payroll taxes and withholding by treating employees as independent contractors.

If an employer is unsure whether an individual is an independent contractor, it may obtain a written determination from the IRS with respect to its federal employment and withholding tax obligations by submitting Form SS-8 (see the Forms Appendix at the end of the workbook [page 187]). This is a 20-question evaluation that the IRS uses to determine the individual's worker status. While awaiting the IRS's decision, the employer should treat individuals in question as employees and pay them through the payroll system.

NOTE: Independent contractors also may complete an SS-8 if they believe that they are employees. If the workers' SS-8 indicates an employment relationship, the IRS may audit the employer's employment tax records.

Paying Employees v. Independent Contractors

Employees are paid wages, such as salaries, fees, bonuses, commissions, and vacation, retirement or other pay. Wages also may include suggestion awards, gift certificates, stock, life insurance, termination or overtime pay and reimbursed employment-agency fees. Only wages are subject to employment tax withholding and reporting requirements, which include federal income, FICA, federal and state unemployment insurance, state and local income tax withholding, and other taxes. Employers report an employee's annual wages and withheld federal taxes on Form W-2 and employment tax returns such as the Form 941 or 944. In addition, an employer may be required to file state and local employment and withholding tax returns and to pay for workers' compensation insurance.

Payments to independent contractors or "nonemployee compensation" are covered by a different set of tax and reporting rules. When annual compensation for an independent contractor is $600 or more, it is reported on a Form 1099-MISC. If the independent contractor fails to submit a TIN, or the IRS otherwise requires it, backup withholding tax is required on payments made to the independent contractor as a way of ensuring payment of federal income tax on nonwage payments. The federal backup tax rate for 2013 is 28%.

NOTE: Current law does not provide for voluntary withholding of backup tax from independent contractors. Thus, do not withhold backup tax unless the law requires it.

Consequences

The cost of erroneously classifying employees as independent contractors can be substantial and is assessed by a number of different federal and state agencies including the IRS, the U.S. Department of Labor and various state agencies such as state workforce agencies. Under the Internal Revenue Code (IRC), *intentional* misclassification may result in criminal charges against an employer.

However, even *unintentional* misclassification may have serious consequences. Employers can be assessed 100% of the FIT and FICA taxes that they fail to withhold. If certain requirements are met, the tax assessment for unintentional misclassification is reduced to 1.5% of the wage amount for failure to withhold federal income tax and 20% of the FICA tax that should have been withheld from the employee's wages. An employer that realizes it misclassified an employee can pay these lower penalties by reporting its mistake on Form 941-X, *Adjusted Employer's Quarterly Federal Tax Return or Claim for Refund.*

An employer that does not realize it misclassified an employee and also fails to file a Form 1099 for the worker may be penalized 3% of the total wages paid to the individual (for failure to withhold FIT) and 40% of FICA not withheld (in addition to paying 100% of the employer FICA tax).

Additional Employee Rights

Employee rights also are protected by wage-hour law, civil rights laws that prohibit discrimination in pay based on race, sex, age, or other nonjob-related factors, and immigration law. Effective in 2014, employers with 50 or more employees are also required to provide employees with minimum, affordable health insurance or pay a federal excise tax.

QUIZ 1 EMPLOYEES V. NONEMPLOYEES

Problem I.

Classify the individual in each problem as one of the following:

- employee
- statutory employee
- statutory nonemployee
- independent contractor
- temporary help agency referral
- leased employee

1. WidgeCo is a manufacturer. When the factory air conditioner breaks down, WidgeCo pays Gene to repair it. Gene sends his assistant to complete the job. How should WidgeCo classify Gene?

   ____

2. Mary, WidgeCo's receptionist, will be out for two weeks on vacation. The company offers the temporary job to her daughter Ellen. How should WidgeCo classify Ellen?

   ____

3. WidgeCo is preparing to take annual physical inventory. To help with the extra work, it calls Hire-a-Temp. Hire-a-Temp sends Jack on the one-week assignment. How should WidgeCo classify Jack?

   ____

4. WidgeCo is offered a two-year government contract. To do the work, WidgeCo will require the skills of an engineer and three technicians for the two-year period. It signs a contract with Aerospace Executive Services, which sends prospects for WidgeCo to interview. WidgeCo decides to hire Jose, an engineer, and three qualified technicians. It negotiates salaries with all four and reserves the right to fire them if they do not work out. Aerospace will pay them and handle payroll administration. How should WidgeCo classify them?

   ____

5. FoodCo pays Lisa to prepare flower baskets for each of its 20 stores across the city. FoodCo provides the materials for the baskets and pictures of what the flower baskets are to look like. Lisa makes the baskets in her home. How should FoodCo classify Lisa?

____

6. Jack goes door-to-door selling vacuum cleaners for VacCo. He is paid a 2% commission for each vacuum cleaner that he sells. How should VacCo classify Jack?

____

Problem II.

Fill in the blanks.

1. Name the six categories of workers:

   1. ______________________________
   2. ______________________________
   3. ______________________________
   4. ______________________________
   5. ______________________________
   6. ______________________________

2. If an employee-leasing or temporary help agency fails to withhold or deposit withholding taxes for its employees, it can become the responsibility of the ____________ ____________ to pay these taxes.

3. An independent contractor must supply the client firm with its ____________ ____________ ____________, which may be either a(an) ____________ or a(an) ____________.

4. When annual nonemployee compensation equals or exceeds $____________, it must be reported to the IRS.

5. Nonemployee compensation is reported on Form ____________.

6. Wages are subject to special federal requirements including federal income tax withholding, FICA tax withholding and federal ____________ tax.

Problem III.

Multiple choice. Circle the correct answer.

1. On which form are wages reported?

a. 1099-MISC
b. W-2
c. W-4
d. SS-8

2. If an employer wants a written determination from the IRS on a worker's status, which form should it submit?

a. SS-8
b. W-2
c. 1099-MISC
d. W-4

3. If an employer unintentionally misclassifies an employee as an independent contractor and files Form 1099-MISC, the tax assessment for failure to withhold federal income tax is equal to:

a. 20% of the wage amount
b. 1.5% of the wage amount
c. 3% of the wage amount
d. 40% of the wage amount

4. Nonemployee compensation is reported on Form:

a. W-2
b. W-4
c. SS-8
d. 1099-MISC

5. When the common-law test is met, an individual is considered:

a. an employee
b. an independent contractor
c. a leased employee
d. a temporary help agency referral

QUIZ 1 Solutions and Explanations

Problem I.

1. independent contractor

2. employee
Length of employment has no bearing on an individual's status.

3. temporary help agency referral

4. leased employees
The agency is the employer, but WidgeCo has the right to hire or fire these individuals as it wishes.

5. statutory employee

6. statutory nonemployee

Problem II.

1. In any order: (1) independent contractors, (2) employees, (3) temporary help agency referrals, (4) leased employees, (5) statutory employees, (6) statutory nonemployees

2. client firm

3. taxpayer identification number; SSN, EIN

4. $600

5. 1099-MISC

6. unemployment

Problem III.

1. b
2. a
3. b
4. d
5. a

QUIZ 2 EMPLOYEES V. NONEMPLOYEES

Problem I.

Classify the individual in each problem as one of the following:

- employee
- statutory employee
- statutory nonemployee
- independent contractor
- temporary help agency referral
- leased employee

1. ArnCo is asked to repair a car requiring body work. It sends the car to body-work specialist Jake down the street. How should ArnCo classify Jake?

 ____

2. ArnCo repairs automobiles. When tune-up expert Matthew is injured and must be out of work for two months, his brother John agrees to work in his place. How should ArnCo classify John?

 ____

3. Jim sells china on a full-time basis to hotel and restaurant chains for ChinaCo. Most sales are made at ChinaCo's showrooms. How should ChinaCo classify Jim?

 ____

4. After a fire, ArnCo asks Rent-a-Temp to send a crew for a week to repaint its burned-out shop. How should ArnCo classify the work crew?

 ____

5. ArnCo is asked to prep five cars for next year's Amazon Racing Classic. The job will require specialized mechanics for the next 12 months. ArnCo calls Automotive Technicians Limited and interviews several candidates. It selects four technicians, working out different compensation packages with each one. They will remain employees of Automotive Technicians Limited, which will also pay them. How should ArnCo classify the four technicians?

 ____

6. Sheila provides in-home care for an elderly woman that includes preparing meals, bathing, and daily walks. She is not an employee of the agency who referred her.

____

Problem II.

Fill in the blanks.

1. Employer payments to employees are called _______________.

2. Employer payments to independent contractors are made as ordinary _______________.

3. A taxpayer identification number supplied by an independent contractor may be either an individual's _______________ _______________ number or a company's _______________ _______________ number.

4. If an employer wishes to obtain a written determination from the IRS regarding an individual's status, it can submit Form _______________.

5. While an employer is waiting for a written determination of an individual's status from the IRS, it should treat the individual as (a, an) _______________.

Problem III.

Multiple choice. Circle the correct answer.

1. Payments made to independent contractors are reported on which of the following forms?

   a. W-2 b. SS-8 c. W-4 d. 1099-MISC

2. If an employer unintentionally misclassifies an employee as an independent contractor and also fails to file Form 1099-MISC, the tax assessment for failure to withhold FICA tax is equal to what percentage of the employee's portion of Social Security and Medicare tax?

   a. 1.5% b. 20% c. 3% d. 40%

3. A 1099-MISC must be filed when nonemployee compensation equals or exceeds:

a. $50 b. $150 c. $600 d. $1,000

4. The form filed with the IRS to determine if an individual is an employee or independent contractor is called the:

a. SS-4 b. SS-5 c. SS-8 d. 1099

5. For 2013, if a nonemployee fails to provide a TIN and is paid $600 or more for the year, what is the required backup withholding tax rate that the employer must use?

a. 1.5% b. 28% c. 3% d. 25%

QUIZ 2 Solutions and Explanations

Problem I.

1. independent contractor
2. employee
   Length of employment has no bearing on an individual's status.
3. statutory employee
4. temporary help agency referral
5. leased employees
6. statutory nonemployee

Problem II.

1. wages
2. disbursements
3. Social Security, employer identification
4. SS-8
5. employee

Problem III.

1. d
2. d
3. c
4. c
5. b

Section 2

FEDERAL AND STATE WAGE-HOUR LAW

Introduction

Normally, compensation is determined by prevailing rates, the free market and negotiations between employers and employees. However, federal and state wage-hour laws require that employees in most businesses receive *minimum wage* and *overtime pay*. Payment frequency and method (e.g., check or direct deposit) are regulated by the states.

Who Must Comply with Federal Wage-Hour Law?

Most companies, regardless of size, are required to comply with a number of federal regulations when paying employees. These regulations primarily are contained in the Fair Labor Standards Act of 1938 (FLSA), which is enforced by the U.S. Department of Labor, Wage and Hour Division. Employers covered by the FLSA are required to pay a minimum hourly wage and overtime rate to all covered employees. The FLSA defines the hours of work for which employees must be paid.

Many small companies have had to pay substantial penalties and back wages because they mistakenly believed that their size caused them to be exempt from federal wage-hour law.

Federal Minimum Wage

The federal minimum wage has stayed at $7.25 per hour since July 24, 2009.

Employers are not required to pay the minimum wage to the following individuals:

1. **Tipped employees.** Under federal law, the minimum hourly rate that employers must pay to certain tipped employees, after applying the maximum allowable "tip credit," is $2.13 per hour. However, after adding the employee's tips for the week to the employee's regular pay for the week (at $2.13 per hour) the average hourly rate for the week must at least

equal the applicable minimum wage—$7.25 per hour effective July 24, 2009. If the employee's average hourly pay falls below the minimum wage in any workweek, the employer is required to pay the difference.

> **EXAMPLE 1:** Mary earns $300: $214.80 in tips + $85.20 regular earnings ($2.13 per hour × 40 hours). Assuming that the federal minimum wage is $7.25 per hour, Mary need not be paid more because her average hourly rate for the workweek exceeds the federal minimum ($300/40 = $7.50).

> **EXAMPLE 2:** Assume the same facts as in Example 1 except that Mary's tip income for the workweek is $132.00, and her total earnings are $217.20 ($132.00 + $85.20). Her employer must pay her an additional $72.80 for the workweek. To compute: $7.25 per hour federal minimum wage × 40 hours = $290.00 minimum pay for the week – $217.20 actually earned = $72.80 still owed to Mary by her employer.

2. **Computer professionals.** Because of the overtime implications, certain computer professionals must be paid at least $27.63 per hour or $455 per week in order to be exempt from the overtime requirement.

3. **Recipients of the opportunity wage.** New employees under age 20 who qualify for the opportunity wage need not be paid the federal minimum rate of $7.25 per hour. They can be paid only $4.25 per hour for the first 90 consecutive calendar days of employment provided that employers do not hire them to displace current employees or to reduce current employees' work hours for the sole purpose of hiring workers eligible for the opportunity wage.

NOTE: The state minimum wage may be higher or lower than the federal minimum. A covered business must pay the higher rate. Additionally some states do not recognize certain federal exceptions, such as the tip credit.

> **PROBLEM 1:** Major Manufacturers, Inc. is a covered employer under the FLSA, and hires an employee on November 15, 2012. What is the minimum wage it must pay the employee?

> **SOLUTION 1:** $7.25 per hour.

Firms covered by the FLSA must also observe federal overtime and child labor laws. However, to shield some small businesses from the financial burden of the minimum wage and overtime requirements, there is a system of exemption known as the "enterprise test." Under the enterprise test, FLSA coverage is determined by a firm's gross annual sales. Most firms under the minimum sales threshold are exempt from federal minimum wage and overtime requirements. However, firms above the threshold must abide by these requirements.

For businesses that began operations after March 31, 1990, determining coverage is fairly simple. The firm need only check its annual sales against Figure 2-2 (page 20).

But for businesses operating before March 31, 1990, determining coverage is more complex. If a firm was subject to federal wage-hour law under the old enterprise test (in effect before April 1, 1990) (Figure 2-1), but is no longer covered under the new enterprise test, the firm is exempt from paying the federal minimum wage in effect on or after April 1, 1990. However, it must continue to pay the minimum wage and overtime rate required under the old law ($3.35).

Figure 2-1
Old Enterprise Coverage Test*

For businesses that began operations before April 1, 1990

Type of company	**Must comply with FLSA if gross annual sales are:**
Dry Cleaners	$0.00 or more
Construction Companies	$0.00 or more
Schools	$0.00 or more
Hospitals	$0.00 or more
Nursing Homes	$0.00 or more
Retail Enterprises	$362,500 or more
Nonretail Enterprises	$250,000 or more

*Coverage in any calendar quarter is determined by the total sales made or business done in the four previous calendar quarters.

Figure 2-2
New Enterprise Coverage Test*

For businesses that began operations on or after April 1, 1990

Type of company	Must comply with FLSA if gross annual sales are:
Dry Cleaners	$500,000 or more
Construction Companies	$500,000 or more
Schools	$0.00 or more
Hospitals	$0.00 or more
Nursing Homes	$0.00 or more
Retail Enterprises	$500,000 or more
Nonretail Enterprises	$500,000 or more

*Coverage in any calendar quarter is determined by the total sales made or business done in the four previous calendar quarters.

PROBLEM 2: In 1989, SamCo, a construction company had, and continues to have, gross annual sales of $300,000. Does the firm have to comply with the FLSA in 2013?

SOLUTION 2: Yes. Because SamCo was in business before April 1, 1990, and it was covered under the old enterprise test, it must comply with the FLSA in 2013—regardless of gross annual sales—and pay the minimum wage in effect prior to April 1, 1990 ($3.35). Had SamCo begun operations after March 31, 1990, it would not be required to pay minimum wage under the FLSA until its gross annual sales exceed $500,000.

Enterprise v. Individual Employee Coverage

Even when an enterprise is not covered by federal wage-hour law, some of its individual employees may be. Detailed information can be obtained from the U.S. Department of Labor, Wage and Hour Division.

"Mom and Pop" Shops

The enterprise test is only one way to determine if a firm's employees are exempt from federal wage-hour law. Employers also may be exempt from the requirement to pay minimum wage and overtime if they are "mom and pop" shops—family-owned and -operated businesses that employ only family members.

NOTE: Unless a business knows that it qualifies for exemption, it should assume that it must comply with federal wage-hour law.

Other minimum wage and overtime exemptions include:

- **Exemption by special certificate.** An employer may obtain a certificate that allows it to pay less than minimum wage to certain employees by applying to the U.S. Department of Labor, Wage and Hour Division, for a special certificate. Certificates may be issued for retail, service or agricultural employees, for those employed by institutes of higher learning and for some apprentices, learners, messengers, handicapped persons, and full-time students.

- **Outside salespersons.** An employee who meets the definition of "outside salesperson" (see Section 3) is exempt from the minimum wage and overtime provisions of the FLSA.

State Wage-Hour Law

In addition to the FLSA, most employers must comply with similar state laws. In general, state laws may regulate the frequency of payment, when a terminated employee must be paid, the method of payment, the requirement for a pay stub, recurring notices concerning rate of pay, and other pay and related practices such as the proper treatment of unclaimed wages (*escheat law*, see below), and whether unused vacation must be paid at termination, in addition to minimum wage and overtime pay.

> **EXAMPLE:** SamCo in Louisiana terminates an employee. Louisiana law requires that terminated employees be paid on or before the next regular payday not to exceed 15 days of the termination date or be subject to penalties.

Unclaimed Wages (Escheat Law)

Special problems arise when employees do not cash their paychecks. Many states have an *escheat* (pronounced es-cheat) *law*, which requires that an individual's unclaimed assets or property—including wages—be submitted to the appropriate state agency after a certain time period.

PROBLEM 3: Manhattan Distributors, Inc., New York City, mails Carl his final paycheck on January 4, 2013 in the amount of $2,000 but it is returned. The company then sends Carl two notices (required by state law for unclaimed wages in excess of $1,000) that it is holding his check, but these are also returned by the US Postal Service as nondeliverable. Despite numerous attempts, the check cannot be delivered to Carl, and Manhattan Distributors is unable to find his current address. Under New York law, unclaimed wages and an unclaimed property report are due to the state by May 1 (March 10 for general corporations) of the third year. What should the company do?

SOLUTION 3: The company must turn over Carl's final paycheck to the state by March 10, 2016. In New York, as in any state that has an escheat law, an employer may not keep an employee's unclaimed wages. (Certain notification requirements exist.)

Federal Law v. State Law

An employer subject to both federal and state laws must observe the law that is most favorable to the employee.

Where a pay practice is regulated only by state law or only by federal law, the employer must observe that law. For instance, although federal law is silent in such matters as when a terminated employee must be paid, many states regulate these practices. The employer must then observe its state's law.

PROBLEM 4: Mississippi has no state minimum wage law. Can a Biloxi manufacturer covered by the FLSA pay any minimum wage it chooses?

SOLUTION 4: No. Because the firm is covered by the FLSA, its employees must be paid at least $7.25 per hour effective July 24, 2009.

Detailed information on state laws affecting payroll and unclaimed funds may be obtained from your state's department of taxation or department of labor.

QUIZ 1 FEDERAL AND STATE WAGE-HOUR LAW

Problem I.

Indicate the applicable minimum wage that must be paid in each of the following situations. Assume the employer is covered by federal and state minimum wage laws.

1. On November 15, 2013, an employee works in Tennessee, which has no state minimum wage. $________________

2. On October 31, 2013, an employee works in Georgia, which has a state minimum wage of $5.15 per hour. $________________

3. On December 2, 2013, an employee works in Ohio, which has a state minimum wage for large employers of $7.85 per hour. $________________

4. On December 2, 2013, an employee works in Washington, which has a minimum wage of $9.19 per hour. $________________

5. On July 15, 2013, an employee works in Mississippi, which has no state minimum wage. $________________

Problem II.

Fill in the blanks.

1. The FLSA is silent on matters concerning the method and ________________ of wage payments.

2. Generally, businesses that began operations after March 31, 1990, must comply with the FLSA if gross annual sales exceed $________________.

3. State laws covering the treatment of unclaimed wages are called ________________ laws.

4. Four kinds of employees are exempt from the federal minimum wage. Name two (answers may be more than one word):
   1.____________________ 2.____________________

5. Name five kinds of businesses operating prior to April 1, 1990, that are covered by the FLSA regardless of their annual sales (answers may be more than one word):

1. ______________ 2. ______________ 3. ______________
4. ______________ 5. ______________

6. Name five kinds of employees who may qualify for a special certificate for the payment of a sub-minimum wage:

1. ______________ 2. ______________ 3. ______________
4. ______________ 5. ______________

Problem III.

Multiple choice. Circle the correct answer.

1. The federal law that governs minimum wage and overtime requirements is called:

a. Equal Pay Act
b. Fairness in Pay Act
c. ERISA
d. Fair Labor Standards Act

2. Assume that a nursing home began operations on April 1, 1988. The nursing home is covered by the FLSA under the enterprise coverage test if its sales for the year exceed:

a. $0 b. $362,500 c. $250,000 d. $500,000

3. The federal minimum wage effective July 24, 2009, is:

a. $5.15 b. $7.25 c. $5.85 d. $6.55

4. Retail enterprises in operation before April 1, 1990, are covered by the FLSA if their gross annual sales exceed:

a. $250,000 b. $362,500 c. $500,000 d. $450,000

5. Nonretail enterprises in operation before April 1, 1990, are covered by the FLSA if their gross annual sales exceed:

a. $250,000 b. $362,500 c. $500,000 d. $450,000

QUIZ 1 Solutions and Explanations

Problem I.

1. $7.25
   This is the current federal minimum wage. Tennessee has no minimum wage.

2. $7.25
   The federal minimum wage of $7.25 (effective July 24, 2009) is more favorable to employees than the Georgia minimum wage of $5.15.

3. $7.85
   The Ohio minimum wage of $7.85 is higher than the federal minimum wage of $7.25 (effective July 24, 2009).

4. $9.19
   The federal minimum wage is $7.25 (effective July 24, 2009), so Washington's minimum wage is higher.

5. $7.25
   The federal minimum wage is $7.25 (effective July 24, 2009). Mississippi has no minimum wage.

Problem II.

1. frequency

2. $500,000

3. escheat

4. tipped employees, computer professionals, recipients of the opportunity wage and outside salespersons

5. schools, hospitals, nursing homes, dry cleaners, construction companies

6. apprentices, learners, messengers, handicapped persons, full-time students

Problem III.

1. d

2. a

3. b

4. b

5. a

QUIZ 2 FEDERAL AND STATE WAGE-HOUR LAW

Problem I.

Indicate the applicable minimum wage that must be paid in each of the following situations. Assume that the employer is covered by federal and state minimum wage laws.

1. On February 15, 2013, an employee works in South Carolina, which has no state minimum wage. $______________
2. On January 2, 2013, an employee works in the Virgin Islands, which has a minimum wage of $4.30 per hour for small businesses. $______________
3. On February 28, 2013, an employee works in Hawaii, which has a state minimum wage of $7.25 per hour. $______________
4. On November 15, 2013, an employee works in Oregon, which has a state minimum wage of $8.95 per hour. $______________
5. On October 15, 2013, an employee works in Massachusetts, which has a state minimum wage of $8.00 per hour. $______________

Problem II.

Fill in the blanks.

1. The federal law governing minimum wage and overtime pay is the ______________ ______________ ______________ ______________ ______________ ______________.
2. The FLSA is enforced by the U.S. Department of Labor, ______________ ______________ ______________ Division.
3. States may regulate the ______________ and frequency of payment, as well as the minimum wages, overtime and proper handling of unclaimed wages.
4. A nonretail business established before April 1, 1990, must comply with federal wage-hour law if its annual gross sales exceed $______________.

5. One kind of employer not required to comply with the FLSA is a "mom and pop" shop, which describes a ______________-owned and -operated business that employs only ______________ members.

6. Which two kinds of employers are not required to pay the federal minimum wage (answers may be more than one word)?
   1. ______________________________
   2. ______________________________

7. Three kinds of establishments in operation on and after April 1, 1990, that are covered by the FLSA regardless of their annual sales volume are (answers may be more than one word):
   1. ______________ 2. ______________ 3. ______________

Problem III.

Multiple choice. Circle the correct answer.

1. A dry cleaner that began operations on May 1, 1991, is covered by the FLSA under the enterprise test if its gross annual sales exceed:

   a. $0 b. $362,500 c. $500,000 d. $250,000

2. An example of a business not likely to be covered by the FLSA is:
   a. a family-owned restaurant that employs only family members
   b. a husband and wife partnership that employs nonfamily members
   c. a plumbing company with annual sales of $600,000
   d. a small family business with limited stockholders who are not family members

3. Assuming that a retail establishment began operations in 1995 and that its gross annual sales in each year of business were $600,000, what is the minimum rate of pay this business must pay its employees effective July 24, 2009?

   a. $5.85 b. $0 c. $7.25 d. $6.55

4. A retail enterprise that began operations after March 31, 1990, is covered by the FLSA if its annual gross sales volume per year exceeds:

   a. $250,000 b. $362,500 c. $500,000 d. $450,000

5. Which of the following enterprises are covered by the FLSA only if they meet and annual sales volume test?

   a. schools b. nursing homes c. department stores d. hospitals

QUIZ 2 Solutions and Explanations

Problem I.

1. $7.25
   This is the current federal minimum wage effective July 24, 2009. South Carolina has no minimum wage.

2. $7.25
   The federal minimum wage of $7.25 effective July 24, 2009 is more favorable to Virgin Islands employees than $4.30 per hour.

3. $7.25
   The federal minimum wage is $7.25 (effective July 24, 2009), so the Hawaii minimum wage is the same as federal.

4. $8.95
   The federal minimum wage is $7.25 (effective July 24, 2009), so the Oregon minimum wage of $8.95 is more favorable to employees.

5. $8.00
   The federal rate is $7.25 (effective July 24, 2009), so the Massachusetts minimum wage of $8.00 is more favorable to employees.

Problem II.

1. Fair Labor Standards Act of 1938

2. Wage and Hour

3. method

4. $250,000

5. family, family

6. Family-owned and -operated businesses that employ only family members

   and

   businesses that are exempt under the enterprise test

7. Schools, hospitals, nursing homes

Problem III.

1. c

2. a

3. c
   The minimum wage of $7.25 (effective July 24, 2009) must be paid because the enterprise as a whole is covered by the FLSA's minimum wage and overtime pay provisions.

4. c

5. c

Section 3

PAYING EMPLOYEES UNDER FEDERAL LAW

Introduction

The following rules for paying employees are based only on *federal law*. Individual states or localities may have different laws.

When Has an Employee Earned Wages Under Federal Law?

Federal law is specific about when employees are entitled to wages. In general, an employee must be paid for all principal activities and activities necessary to the performance of those principal activities.

1. **Travel time.** Whether or not employees must be paid for their travel time depends on the nature of the travel. Following are the general rules that apply:

   (A) **Home to work travel.** In general, home to work travel is not considered working time, even if employees drive a company vehicle to their home. However, if the employer agrees to pay its employees for this commuting time, this time need not be considered for the purpose of determining if overtime pay (1½-times-regular-pay) is owed.

   There are two circumstances under which an employer is required to pay employees for their home to work travel:

   (1) An employee who is on 24-hour call takes a company vehicle home for the specific purpose of responding to emergency calls. For instance, a plumber takes the company truck home for the specific purpose of responding to after-hour emergencies.

   (2) After returning home from their regular shift and normal worksite, employees are called to work at a job site that is not their normal place of work. Under this circumstance, the travel from home to the remote job site and from the remote job site to home is considered hours worked, and employees must be paid for this time.

(B) **Travel that is all in a day's work.** If employees travel from one job site to another during their normal shift, they must be paid for this travel time. However, travel from home to the first work site and from the last work site to home is not considered working time, and employees need not be paid for this travel.

PROBLEM 1: Employee Juanita is an engineer for BuildCo. She leaves her home and goes directly to the office of a BuildCo client, ShopCo. From ShopCo's office she goes to another client's office, ParkCo, and from ParkCo's office she goes to another client's office, PropCo. Juanita leaves PropCo's office at the end of the day and goes directly home. What portion of Juanita's travel time, if any, does not have to be compensated?

SOLUTION 1: Juanita's travel from home to the first client site, ShopCo, and from the last client's site, PropCo, to home is not compensable. However, her travel from ShopCo's office to ParkCo's and from ParkCo's office to PropCo's office is considered hours worked, and she must be paid for this travel time.

(C) **Travel outside the normal commuting area.** From time to time employees may be asked to travel directly from their home to a remote job site that is outside their normal commuting area. In other words, the job site is a significant distance from the employee's normal place of work. If an overnight stay is not required, the travel from home to the remote job site is considered hours worked and must be compensated. At the employer's option, the employee's travel time may be reduced by the amount of time it normally takes the employee to travel from home to the normal job site.

PROBLEM 2: Employee Richard is asked to travel directly from his home in Houston to a temporary job site in Galveston (a round-trip commute of two hours). Richard works eight hours in Galveston and returns home the same night. It normally takes Richard 30 minutes per day to travel round trip between home and work. How many hours must Richard be compensated for?

SOLUTION 2: Because no overnight stay was required, the time that Richard travels round trip from Houston to Galveston (2 hours) is considered hours worked, and he must be paid for this travel time. At his employer's option, Richard's normal commuting time of 30 minutes may be deducted from the 2 hours of travel for the day. Richard must be paid for a total of 9.5 hours for the day (2 hours travel time + 8 hours worked – ½ hour normal commute time).

(D) **Overnight travel as a passenger on a public conveyance.** When employees travel to a remote job site and an overnight stay is required, only the portion of travel time that occurs during employees' normal working hours is considered working time. It is important to note that "normal working hours" are defined as the hours during the day that employees normally work and not the *days of the week* they normally work. Hence, if an employee normally works from 9:00 A.M. to 5:00 P.M., Monday through Friday, any travel that occurs on Saturday or Sunday between the hours of 9:00 A.M. and 5:00 P.M. is considered working time, even though the employee normally does not work on these days.

PROBLEM 3: Susan normally works from 9:00 A.M. to 5:00 P.M., Monday through Friday. Susan's employer sent her to a trade show. She takes a 3:00 P.M. flight on Sunday from her home in New York City and arrives in Chicago at 7:00 P.M. Susan spends the night in Chicago and on Monday morning takes a cab to the trade show where she begins work at 7:00 A.M. She returns to the airport at 4:00 P.M. and arrives home two hours later. For how many hours must Susan be compensated for Sunday and Monday?

SOLUTION 3: Because Susan normally works between 9:00 A.M. and 5:00 P.M., the hours she spent in flight between 3:00 P.M. and 5:00 P.M. (2 hours) on Sunday are compensable. The time spent in travel after 5:00 P.M. is not compensable because Susan is normally off work at 5:00 P.M. Because Susan arrived at the trade show at 7:00 A.M., she must be compensated for all hours between 7:00 A.M. and 5:00 P.M. on Monday (10 hours). Her total compensable time for Sunday and Monday is 12 hours (2 hours on Sunday and 10 hours on Monday).

2. **Showering and changing clothes at work.** Employees that are required to shower and change clothes at the work site must be compensated for this time.

PROBLEM 4: MetCo requires all employees to shower and change before leaving the work site. Does it have to pay employees for the time spent showering and changing?

SOLUTION 4: Yes. However, if the company offered space for showering and changing merely as a convenience to employees, it does not have to pay them for this time.

3. **Nonproductive time on the job.** Employees must be paid for hours spent on the job even if they are not working. Hours that employees are required to remain at the work site and are substantially restricted from engaging in personal activities are considered "hours worked" even if employees do nothing during that time.

   PROBLEM 5: Dave makes widgets. He must have each widget inspected before making the next one. One morning, the inspector keeps him waiting an hour. Must Dave be paid for the hour he waited to work?

   SOLUTION 5: Yes, because he was required to remain at the work site during the nonproductive hour.

   PROBLEM 6: Employee Felicia is on call for the weekend. She can stay home or go anywhere within beeper distance. Must she be paid for the on-call time?

   SOLUTION 6: No, because she is not required to be at the work site and is not "substantially restricted from engaging in personal activities."

4. **Docking pay for employee misconduct.** An employee who is otherwise entitled to overtime pay under the law may not be docked pay if docking reduces the employee's wages for the workweek to an average hourly rate that is below the federal minimum.

   PROBLEM 7: Simon is paid $7.80 per hour. Employer policy is to dock employees one hour for each five minutes that they are late for work. Simon reports five minutes late to work one day during the workweek. Can the employer dock him?

   SOLUTION 7: Yes, provided that Simon receives an average hourly wage for all hours worked in the workweek that at least equals the federal minimum ($7.25 per hour effective July 24, 2009). Remember that some states may have higher minimums.

Federal Standards for Overtime Pay

Employees must be paid at least 1½ times their regular hourly rate of pay for every hour that they *actually work* over 40 hours in a *workweek*. The additional ½-times-regular-pay makes this *premium pay*. The total 1½-times-regular-pay is called *overtime pay*. Overtime rates do not have to exceed 1½ times the regular rate of pay under federal law, even though some employers pay higher rates as required under their union contract or company policy. And there is no federal requirement to pay overtime when employees work more than eight hours in a day. (Note that some states, such as California do require that overtime be paid for hours over a daily maximum.)

Exceptions to this minimum overtime-pay rule are made for employees of federal, state and city governments and the health care industry. (Employers may obtain specific details from their local Wage and Hour office.)

PROBLEM 8: Marie's regular rate of pay is $7.70 per hour. What is her minimum premium rate under federal law?

SOLUTION 8: $3.85. To calculate:

$7.70 (Marie's regular rate of pay) ÷ 2 = $3.85 premium rate

When determining whether an employee is entitled to overtime pay, an employer need not include paid time-off such as paid vacations, holidays or sick days. Overtime rates are required only when an employee actually reports for work more than 40 hours in the workweek.

PROBLEM 9: Michael is to be paid for 48 hours in one week that includes eight hours for a day he was out sick. Does he have to be paid overtime for the extra eight hours?

SOLUTION 9: No. Michael is not due any overtime pay because he actually worked only 40 hours.

Of course, some employers can and do have more generous overtime pay policies than those required by federal law.

The Workweek

Workweek is defined under federal law as *any 7 consecutive days or 168 consecutive hours*. Although the workweek does not have to be Monday through Sunday, it must be consistent, employees must be made aware of it, and an employer may not continually change it to avoid paying overtime.

Computing Overtime Pay for Salaried, Nonexempt Employees

To determine the regular hourly rate of pay for a salaried, nonexempt employee, multiply the gross pay by the number of annual pay periods, then divide by the total hours of scheduled work in the year.

Gross pay	×	annual pay periods	÷	total hours worked in yr.* = hourly rate
$XXX	×	52 (weekly)	÷	total hours worked in yr. = hourly rate
$XXX	×	26 (biweekly)	÷	total hours worked in yr. = hourly rate
$XXX	×	24 (semimo.)	÷	total hours worked in yr. = hourly rate
$XXX	×	12 (monthly)	÷	total hours worked in yr. = hourly rate

*(generally 2,080 for full time employees)

NOTE: An easier way to calculate hourly rates for weekly or biweekly periods is simply to divide gross weekly pay by weekly hours or to divide gross biweekly pay by biweekly hours.

PROBLEM 10: Mai-Lee is paid $480 per week for a 40-hour workweek. What is her premium rate of pay for overtime work?

SOLUTION 10: $6.00. To calculate:

$480 weekly pay × 52 weeks = $24,960 per year

$24,960 ÷ 2,080 hours per yr. (40 hours × 52 weeks) = $12 per hr.

$12 ÷ 2 = $6, Mai-Lee's hourly, premium rate of pay

PROBLEM 11: Ted's normal workweek is 35 hours. His biweekly salary is $800. What is Ted's premium rate of pay for overtime work?

SOLUTION 11: $5.72. To calculate:

$800 biweekly pay × 26 biweekly payments = $20,800 per year

$20,800 ÷ 1,820 hours per yr. (35 hrs × 52 wks) = $11.43 per hr
$11.43 ÷ 2 = $5.72, Ted's hourly, premium rate of pay

NOTE: Ted's employer has a 35-hour workweek. Under federal law, Ted need not be paid for hours worked between 36 and 40 hours provided that his pay for the week divided by the hours he worked at least equals the federal minimum wage of $7.25 per hour effective July 24, 2009. (This is referred to as the Klinghoffer rule.)

When "Make-up Time" Is Unlawful

Joe needs a few hours off next week. He offers to work a few extra hours this week to make up the time. How must he be paid?

Under federal law, each workweek stands alone. An employer cannot transfer overtime hours from one week to another week to avoid paying overtime. If Joe works overtime this week, he must be paid overtime for this week. Unlawful "make-up time" practices designed to avoid paying higher overtime rates may result in back pay and penalties should the employer undergo a Wage and Hour Division investigation. Exceptions to rules on compensatory time off apply to employees of federal, state and municipal employers.

PROBLEM 12: Jane needs to take a personal day during the second week of the month, so she works only 32 hours that week. To avoid losing pay, she will work on her day off during the first week for a total of 48 hours. Under federal law, is she due any overtime pay?

SOLUTION 12: Yes. Jane must be paid overtime for the extra eight hours she works during the first week. However, her employer does not have to pay her for the eight hours she does not work during the second week.

Which Employees Are Entitled to Overtime Pay?

Employees who must be paid overtime under federal law are called *nonexempt*. Employees who do not have to be paid for overtime are called *exempt*. Whether or not an employee is exempt from the overtime pay requirements is unrelated to the employer's size. And an employee may be covered by federal wage-hour law even though the employer is not. This may occur when the individual employee is engaged in interstate commerce, a very broadly defined qualification. For instance, a cashier in a New York store who accepts a customer's credit card issued by a New Jersey bank is considered to be engaged in interstate commerce. That is why in today's workplace most employees are protected by federal wage-hour law.

Federal law provides four categories of employees who are exempt from overtime pay. (Note that some states do not recognize some of these federal provisions. For state wage-hour purposes check with a competent labor law attorney before making determinations on an employee's exempt status.)

Note that a job title does not automatically make an employee exempt from overtime pay. Duties, responsibilities and salary determine an employee's eligibility for overtime pay.

Categories of Exempt Employees

Executive. Primary duty is management of a company or department. Supervises two or more employees and has the power to hire and fire. Minimum salary: $455 per week (in American Samoa $380 per week).

Administrative. Performs and is actively responsible for the establishment and enforcement of company policy and general business operations, regularly assists company owners or executives in the general supervision of the business and has the authority and freedom to make important business decisions or work is directly related to academic instruction or training for a school system, educational establishment or institution. Minimum salary: $455 per week (in American Samoa $380 per week).

Professional. Performs work of an advanced type in a field of science or learning. Work must be varied as well as intellectual or creative and require analysis, discretion, and judgment. Minimum salary: $455 per week (in American Samoa $380 per week). Computer system professionals meet the definition of an exempt "professional employee." In addition, hourly paid computer system professionals are exempt from overtime during weeks in which their average hourly rate is greater than $27.63 per hour. A computer professional is defined as any employee who is a computer systems analyst, computer programmer, software engineer, or similarly skilled worker whose primary duty is:

(a) the application of systems analysis techniques and procedures, including consulting with users to determine hardware, software or system functional specifications;

(b) the design, development, documentation, analysis, creation, testing, or modification of computer systems or programs, including prototypes, based on and related to user or systems design specifications;

(c) the design, documentation, testing, creation, or modification of computer programs related to machine operating systems; or

(d) a combination of a–c.

Outside salespersons. Regularly and customarily work away from the employer's place of business while making sales calls. Sales representatives who spend most of their time in the office selling by phone (telemarketers) are not considered outside salespersons. There are no federal minimum salary requirements for outside salespersons.

Employers who have specific questions should contact the nearest U.S. Department of Labor (DOL) Wage and Hour Division office, and give appropriate details. Also, a more elaborate explanation of exempt v. nonexempt employees is provided in Publication 1281, "Regulations, Part 541, Defining Administrative, Executive, Professional, or Outside Sales," available through local federal Wage and Hour Division offices.

NOTE: For executive, administrative and professional categories, an employee who is compensated at least $455 per week, or $100,000 per year with a $455 per week guarantee, exclusive of board, lodging or other facilities, and whose primary duties consist of those specified, will be considered by the DOL as having met the requirements. Even if an employee is not paid $100,000 or more in a calendar year, the overtime exemption will apply retroactively in that calendar year if the employee's wages reach $100,000 in the last payroll period of the calendar year or anytime in January of the following year.

QUIZ 1 PAYING EMPLOYEES UNDER FEDERAL LAW

Problem I.

Calculate the gross wages under the FLSA due employees in each of the following cases. Assume that they do not work for federal, state or city governments or in health care and are nonexempt.

1. Max is paid $8.50 per hour. During the first week in March he is paid for 36 hours on the job and receives paid time off for 8 hours that he is out sick.
   Gross pay for the week: $______________

2. Mike is paid $400 per week for a 40-hour workweek. One week he works 1 hour over his normal schedule.
   Gross pay for the week: $______________

3. Juanita is paid $300 per week for a 35-hour workweek. One week she works 1 hour over her normal schedule.
   Gross pay for the week: $______________

4. Renee is paid $7.25 per hour. In one biweekly pay period, she works 32 hours during week 1 and 48 hours during week 2.
   Gross pay for the biweekly period: $______________

5. Adam is paid $8.10 per hour. He works 16 continuous hours at the beginning of one workweek and another 16 continuous hours at the end of the same week for a total of 32 hours.
   Gross pay for the week: $______________

6. Joe normally works from 7:00 A.M. to 3:00 P.M., Monday through Friday. On Sunday, Joe flies from his home in Indianapolis to New York City on a job assignment. He arrives at the airport at 2:00 p.m. and arrives in New York City two hours later. From Monday through Friday of the same workweek, Joe works 40 hours. Assume that Joe's regular rate of pay is $10.00.
   Gross pay for the week: $______________

Problem II.

Fill in the blanks.

1. Federal law requires that employees be paid for all ____________ activities of a job and all activities ______________ to the performance of those principal activities.

2. Under federal law, employees must be paid at least ________________ times their regular rate of pay for all overtime hours.

3. Overtime pay is required for each hour that a nonexempt employee works over ________________ in the workweek.

4. A workweek is defined as any ________________ consecutive days or ________________ consecutive hours.

5. Generally, to be exempt from overtime pay under federal law, an employee must be in one of four specific categories. Name them:
   1. ____________ 2. ____________ 3. ______________ 4. ____________

6. Whether or not an employee is exempt depends upon three key job factors. Name them: 1. ______________ 2. ______________ 3. ______________

7. A job ________________ does not automatically determine whether an employee is exempt.

Problem III.

Multiple choice. Circle the correct answer. Assume that the employees are nonexempt.

1. What is the overtime rate of an employee paid $9.50 per hour?

   a. $14.25 b. $9.50 c. $19.00 d. $4.75

2. What is the hourly premium rate of pay of an employee paid $9.50 per hour?

   a. $14.25 b. $9.50 c. $19.00 d. $4.75

3. What is the hourly rate of pay of an employee who is paid $350 per week for a 40-hour workweek?

a. $8.75 b. $4.38 c. $5.85 d. $13.13

4. What is the hourly rate of pay of an employee who earns $300 per week for a 35-hour workweek?

a. $7.50 b. $8.57 c. $3.46 d. $3.87

5. To be exempt from federal requirements for overtime pay, what is the minimum that a "professional" employee must be paid per week?

a. $170 b. $455 c. $152 d. $134

QUIZ 1 Solutions and Explanations

Problem I.

1. $374.00
To calculate:

36 hours + 8 hours = 44 hours

44 hours × $8.50 per hour = $374.00 gross pay for the week

There is no overtime pay for the 4 hours paid over 40 hours because he actually worked only 36 hours during the week. (The other 8 hours were paid time off for illness.)

2. $415.00
To calculate:

$400 per week × 52 weeks = $20,800 per year

$20,800 ÷ 2,080 hrs per year (40 hours × 52 weeks) = $10.00 per hr

$10.00 per hour regular pay × 1½ (overtime rate) = $15.00 (rounded) for 1 hour of overtime + $400 weekly pay = $415.00 gross pay

3. $300.00
To calculate:

$300 per week ÷ 36 hours = $8.33 per hour

$8.33 per hour is greater than minimum wage of $7.25 (effective July 24, 2009). No pay is due for the additional 1 hour of work. Had the employee worked more than 40 hours, overtime pay at 1½ times the regular rate of $8.33 would be due for all hours worked over 40.

NOTE: State law may require pay for hours worked between 36 and 40 in the work week.

4. $609.04
To calculate:

Week 1: 32 hours × $7.25 = $232.00

Week 2: 48 hours × $7.25 = $348.00

8 hours overtime × $3.63 premium pay ($7.25 ÷ 2) = $29.04 premium pay

$29.04 premium pay + $348.00 base pay = $377.04 gross pay in week 2

$232 (week 1) + $377.04 (week 2) = $609.04 total biweekly gross pay for the period

5. $259.20
To calculate:

32 hours × $8.10 per hour = $259.20 gross pay

There is no requirement under federal law that an employee be paid overtime for working more than eight hours in a day.

6. $415
To calculate:

Because Joe normally works between 7:00 A.M. and 3:00 P.M., he must be paid for 1 hour of travel time on Sunday (2:00 P.M. to 3:00 P.M.). The 40 hours worked on Monday through Friday plus the 1 hour of travel time on Sunday is a total of 41 hours. 41 hours × $10 = $410. 1 hour overtime × $5 = $5. $410 + 5 = $415.

Problem II.

1. principal, necessary
2. 1½
3. 40
4. seven, 168
5. executive, administrative, professional, outside sales
6. duties, responsibilities, salary
7. title

Problem III.

1. a
[($9.50 ÷ 2) + $9.50] = $14.25

2. d
($9.50 ÷ 2) = $4.75

3. a
To calculate:

$350 per week × 52 weeks = $18,200 per year

$18,200 ÷ 2,080 hours per year (40 hours × 52 weeks) = $8.75 per hour

4. b
To calculate:

$300 per week × 52 weeks = $15,600 per year

$15,600 ÷ 1,820 hours per year (35 hours × 52 weeks) = $8.57 per hour

5. b

QUIZ 2 PAYING EMPLOYEES UNDER FEDERAL LAW

Problem I.

Calculate the gross wages due employees in each of the following cases. Assume that they do not work for federal, state or city governments or in health care and are nonexempt.

1. Susan is paid $8.00 per hour. One week she works 39 hours and also receives 8 hours' holiday pay.
   Gross pay for the week: $______________

2. Mike is paid $350 for a normal 40-hour workweek. One week he works 3 hours over his normal schedule.
   Gross pay for the week: $______________

3. John is paid $350 per week for a normal 35-hour workweek. One week he works 2 hours over his normal schedule.
   Gross pay for the week: $______________

4. Nancy is paid biweekly at a rate of $8.90 per hour. Nancy works 34 hours during the first week in the period and 44 hours during the second week in the period.
   Gross pay for the biweekly period: $______________

5. Ed is paid $8.85 per hour. One week he works 15 continuous hours on Monday and 14 continuous hours on Thursday for a total of 29 hours.
   Gross pay for the week: $______________

6. Employee Sally is an electrician for WattCo. On Monday, Sally left her home at 8:00 A.M. and arrived at Client A's office at 8:30 A.M. to install new wiring in the copy room. She left Client A's office at 9:30 A.M. and went directly to Client B's home to find a short in the electrical heating system. Without taking a lunch break, she then went to Client C's office, installed new wiring for its air conditioner and completed her work at 4:30 P.M. She left Client C's office and arrived home at 5:30 P.M. She worked 32 hours in her office completing paperwork the remainder of the workweek. Assume that Sally earns $12 per hour.
   Gross pay for the week: $______________

Problem II.

Fill in the blanks.

1. The additional half-time rate of pay due for overtime hours is known as the ______________ rate of pay.

2. Under federal law, an employee must be paid premium pay for all hours worked over ______________ in the workweek.

3. Three kinds of paid time-off that does not have to be included when calculating overtime pay are: 1. ______________ 2. ______________ 3. ______________

4. To be exempt from the overtime pay requirements as an "executive," the employee must be paid a weekly rate of at least $______________.

5. To be exempt from the overtime provisions of federal law, an employee paid in excess of ______________ per year can qualify as exempt.

6. Employees earn overtime pay only for hours ______________ worked in the workweek.

Problem III.

Multiple choice. Circle the correct answer.

1. What is the hourly rate for an employee paid $1,551.33 monthly for a 40-hour workweek?

   a. $4.62 b. $8.95 c. $7.25 d. $9.70

2. What is the premium rate for an employee earning $8.00 per hour?

   a. $4.00 b. $12.00 c. $16.00 d. $8.00

3. What is the hourly rate for an employee paid $400 for a 35-hour workweek?

   a. $4.62 b. $11.43 c. $10.61 d. $10.00

4. What is the minimum weekly pay that an executive employee must receive to qualify as exempt?

a. $455 b. $170 c. $152 d. $155

5. What is the hourly overtime rate required by federal law for a nonexempt employee normally paid $10.00 per hour?

a. $10.00 b. $15.00 c. $ 5.00 d. $20.00

6. What is the minimum weekly pay that an administrative employee must receive to qualify as exempt from the overtime provisions of federal law?

a. $150 b. $455 c. $155 d. $175

QUIZ 2 Solutions and Explanations

Problem I.

1. $376

   To calculate:

   39 hours worked + 8 hours holiday pay = 47 hours total

   47 hours × $8 per hour = $376 gross pay

   She is not entitled to overtime pay under federal law because she actually worked fewer than 40 hours in the workweek.

2. $389.39

   To calculate:

   $350 per week × 52 weeks = $18,200 per year

   $18,200 ÷ 2,080 hours per year (40 hours × 52 weeks) = $8.75 per hour

   $8.75 ÷ 2 = $4.38 per hour premium pay rate

   $4.38 + $8.75 = $13.13 overtime pay rate

   3 hours × $13.13 = $39.39 total overtime pay

   $39.39 + $350 = $389.39 gross pay

3. $350

   To calculate:

   $350 ÷ 37 hours = $9.46 per hour.

   $9.46 per hour is greater than the federal minimum wage of $7.25 per hour effective July 24, 2009. Therefore the employee need not be paid for the additional 2 hours. Had the employee worked over 40 hours, overtime pay at 1.5 times the regular rate of $10.00 (350 ÷ 35) would be due for all hours worked over 40.

   NOTE: State law may require pay for hours worked between 37 and 40 in the work week.

4. $712.00
   To calculate:

   Week 1: 34 hours × $8.90 per hour = $302.60

   Week 2: 44 hours × $8.90 = $391.60

   4 hours premium pay × $4.45 = $17.80

   $302.60 + $391.60 + $17.80 = $712.00 biweekly gross pay for the period

5. $256.65
   To calculate:

   29 hours × $8.85 per hour = $256.65

   Overtime pay is based on hours actually worked over 40 hours in the workweek. Overtime pay is not earned on a daily basis.

6. $480
   To calculate:

   Sally need not be compensated for her travel time from home to Client A's office nor for her travel time from Client C's office to home. Therefore, she is due pay for only 8 hours for Monday, 8:30 A.M. to 4:30 P.M. (8 hours + 32 hours = 40 hours. 40 hours × $12 = $480).

Problem II.

1. premium

2. 40

3. paid vacation, sick pay, holidays

4. $455

5. $100,000

6. actually

Problem III.

1. b

To calculate, use the formula:

Gross pay × number of annual pay periods ÷ hours worked in year = hourly rate

\$1,551.33 × 12 = \$18,615.96 per year ÷ 2,080 hours worked during the year (40 hours × 52 weeks) = \$8.95 hourly rate

2. a

To calculate:

\$8 ÷ 2 = \$4 per hour premium pay

3. b

To calculate:

$$\frac{\$400}{\text{35-hour workweek}} = \$11.43 \text{ per hour}$$

4. a

5. b

To calculate:

\$10 normal pay + \$5 premium pay = \$15 per hour overtime pay

6. b

Section 4

EMPLOYMENT RECORDS AND PAYROLL RECORDKEEPING

Introduction

From the time that employees are hired to their date of separation and beyond, employers are required by federal and state laws to obtain, prepare and retain a variety of records. An employer who is unable to present proper records upon request in an audit, investigation or lawsuit may be subject to substantial penalties. Sample forms are shown in the Forms Appendix at the end of this workbook (page 187).

Documentation Employers Must Obtain from New Employees

Under federal and state regulations, there are a number of documents that employers must obtain from employees or inspect at the time of hiring. The required records are:

1. **Social Security card.** The employer should inspect the employee's Social Security card to make sure that its records reflect the correct Social Security number for that employee. New employees who do not have a Social Security card must complete Form SS-5 (*Application for a Social Security Card*). Although an SS-5 may be obtained by calling the local Social Security office (or on the SSA website at *www.socialsecurity.gov)*, employers are advised to keep a supply on hand. Employers are permitted, but not required to make photocopies of Social Security cards, and may not force employees to make their Social Security cards available for inspection.

2. **Form W-4: Employee's withholding allowance certificate.** All employees must submit a completed, signed and dated W-4. The W-4 informs the employer which tax tables or rate schedules to use to determine the amount of federal income tax to withhold. It must be completed even if an employee wishes to have no federal income tax withheld.

3. **State exemption certificates**. Although most states impose an income tax, about half require employees to fill out a separate state withholding allowance certificate. If the state doesn't have its own form, the Form W-4 is used.

4. **Age certificates.** Federal and state child labor laws establish the minimum age at which young people can be hired for certain jobs. To avoid violations, employers should obtain an employment/age certificate from new hires who appear to be within two years of the legal age to work. For more information about state age certificates go to *www.dol.gov/dol/topic/youthlabor/workpermitsagecert.htm*.

   Employers are required to return age certificates to workers upon their termination.

5. **Form I-9.** All employees must complete and sign Form I-9. All employers, regardless of size, must complete their portion of the I-9, which is required under the Immigration Reform and Control Act of 1986 (IRCA). The law was enacted to reduce the number of undocumented workers in the United States.

   Under IRCA, employers are responsible for substantiating each employee's sworn statement and must request documents that prove both the employee's identity *and* authorization to work in the United States. The employee has the option of presenting any of the following documents. Following are *some* of the documents allowed.

List A **Documents Establishing Both Identity and Employment**	***List B*** **Documents that Establish Identity**	***List C*** **Documents that Establish Employment Authorization**
U.S. Passport or U.S. Passport card	Driver's license or ID card issued by a state or outlying possession of the United States provided it contains a photograph or information such as name, date of birth, gender, height, eye color, and address	Social Security Account Number card other than one that specifies on its face that the issuance of the card does not authorize employment in the United States
Foreign passport that contains temporary I-551 stamp or temporary I-551 printed notation on a machine-readable immigrant visa	ID card issued by federal, state or local government agencies or entities, provided it contains a photograph or information such as name, date of birth, gender, height, eye color, and address	Certification of Birth Abroad issued by the Department of State (Form FS-545)
Permanent Resident Card or Alien Registration Receipt Card (Form I-551)	U.S. Military card, draft record or Military dependent's ID card	Certificate of Report of Birth issued by the Department of State (Form DS-1350)
Employment Authorization Document that contains a photograph (Form I-766)	Voter's registration card	Original or certified copy of birth certificate issued by a State, county, municipal authority, or territory of the U.S. bearing an official seal
	School ID with a photograph	U.S. Citizen ID Card (Form I-197)
	U.S. Coast Guard merchant Mariner Card	Identification Card for use of Resident Citizen in the United States (Form I-179)

Employers should make and retain copies of all documents that applicants present.

> **PROBLEM 1:** Tony presents Apex, Inc. with a driver's license to substantiate information on his I-9. Is this document adequate for Tony's employment verification?
>
> **SOLUTION 1:** No. The driver's license proves only Tony's identity. The employer must also ask for a document proving his authorization to work in the United States—a Social Security card or birth certificate. Tony may also present a U.S. passport or Resident Alien card, which are proof of his identity and authorization to work.

Due date: If the employee is expected to work three or more days, the I-9 must be completed by the end of the third work day. If the employee is expected to work less than three days, the I-9 must be completed by the end of the first work day.

> **PROBLEM 2:** Employee Greg starts work on January 2. He is expected to work more than three days. By what date must his I-9 be completed?
>
> **SOLUTION 2:** By the evening of January 4.

Note: Several states require that employers additionally verify an individual's right to work in the U.S. through the federal e-Verify system.

Data Employers Are Required To Obtain and Retain

1. Employers should retain the following wage and tax information for each employee for payroll purposes:

   - ☐ Name
   - ☐ Address
   - ☐ Sex
   - ☐ Date of birth
   - ☐ Social Security number
   - ☐ State where employee's services are rendered

- ☐ Employee health coverage information including copays, employee contributions, covered services and drugs, and employer's cost for the employee's health plan
- ☐ Federal and state withholding allowance certificates (see Section 5 for more information on state certificates)
- ☐ Date hired
- ☐ Date terminated
- ☐ Salary or hourly rate of pay
- ☐ Regular hours of work and normal work schedule
- ☐ Date and time work begins and ends each day
- ☐ Employee's exempt status (whether or not the employee is entitled to overtime pay)
- ☐ Hours worked each day and workweek
- ☐ Daily or weekly straight time and overtime pay
- ☐ Total deductions from pay (itemized)
- ☐ Total pay for the pay period, quarter and year
- ☐ Date of payment
- ☐ Payroll period
- ☐ Wages subject to tax for the pay period, quarter and year
- ☐ Adjustments to pay
- ☐ Tax deductions from wages for the pay period, quarter and year
- ☐ Date taxes are collected if other than date of wage payment
- ☐ Total pay for the pay period, quarter and year, if different from wages subject to tax
- ☐ Total tax paid by the employer on behalf of employees

2. Many employers also keep the following data, updating it as needed:

- ☐ Job description
- ☐ Reason for termination
- ☐ Employment applications and resumes

Retaining Employment Records, Tax Returns and Tax Documents

Employers are required to retain tax returns, forms, supporting documents, and personnel records for different time periods, as mandated by federal and state law. These documents may be stored on paper, microfiche or microfilm for the periods specified.

For example, the following tax returns must be retained for at least four years from April 15th (or the next business day) following the tax year to which the return relates, according to IRS regulations: Form 941, Form 944, Form W-3, Form 1042-S, and Form W-2 (including those returned as undeliverable). The Form 940 must be retained at least 4 years from the due date of the return (e.g. January 31). Also keep state income tax and unemployment tax returns for at least four years from the filing date (some states require keeping these returns for a shorter or longer period).

> **Warning:** Federal regulations require a minimum period that records must be kept. However, employers are advised to retain payroll records for at least 15 years (the total period records are needed in the event of an audit assessment and subsequent appeals to abate penalties). Also, state regulations on record retention may preempt federal rules and require that records be kept for longer periods.

The table on page 58 shows how long each kind of document must be kept under various federal laws.

> **PROBLEM 3:** Max completes his W-4 on January 4, 2013. On February 1, he submits another W-4 with a different number of allowances. What should the employer do with Max's first W-4?

> **SOLUTION 3:** The employer must retain Max's first W-4 (the one submitted January 4, 2013) until April 15, 2018—four years after April 15, 2014.

Statutory Record Retention Requirements for Employment-Related Records

Type of document	IRS	Wage and Hour	EEOC[1]	Immigration
Payroll register (earnings/deductions)	4[2]	3	3	N/A
Timecards	N/A	3[3]	3	N/A
Hours worked reports	N/A	3[3]	3	N/A
Work schedules	N/A	2	N/A	N/A
Payroll tax records	4[2]	3	N/A	N/A
Tax deposit receipts	4[2]	3	N/A	N/A
I-9	N/A	N/A	N/A	3[4]
Copies of employment tax returns (940, 941, 943, 944, W-2, 1099)	4[2]	N/A	N/A	N/A
Documents substantiating employment tax returns	4[2]	N/A	N/A	N/A
W-2s (returned)	4[2]	N/A	N/A	N/A
W-4s	4[5]	3	N/A	N/A
Personnel files, including resumes and employment applications	4[2]	3	3	N/A
Canceled/voided checks	4[2]	3	N/A	N/A

1. Equal Employment Opportunity Commission.
2. Under IRS regulations, applicable records must be retained four years from April 15th following the tax year to which the document pertains. For example, a 2013 Form W-2 should be retained four years from April 15, 2014, or until at least April 15, 2018. Form 940 and state unemployment returns must be retained four years from the filing due date.
3. Timecards need to be retained for two years if a report of hours worked by date and week also is retained. Otherwise, daily and weekly hours records must be retained for three years.
4. I-9 forms should be retained three years from the date of hire, or one year from the date of termination, whichever is longer.
5. W-4s must be retained four years from the April 15 that follows the tax year that the W-4 was submitted.

QUIZ 1 EMPLOYMENT RECORDS AND PAYROLL RECORDKEEPING

Problem I.

For each of the following problems, fill in the date on which federal law permits the specified documents to be destroyed.

1. John is terminated on May 15, 2012. Until what date must his employer retain his personnel file? ______________

2. DrillCo's payroll register, dated August 17, 2012, contains details on employee wages, deductions and taxes withheld from pay. Until what date must DrillCo retain its payroll register? ______________

3. Mary submits a W-4 dated February 1, 2013, then submits a new W-4 on March 21, 2013. Until what date must Mary's employer retain her first W-4? ______________

4. WidgeCo completes an I-9 for new hire Mark on September 1, 1994. He is terminated on December 16, 2012. Until what date must WidgeCo retain his I-9? ______________

5. PlumbCo has daily timecards for the period ending March 15, 2013. Assuming PlumbCo has no other daily record of employees' work time, until what date must it retain the timecards? ______________

Problem II.

Fill in the blanks. Answers may be more than one word.

1. Employers must return an age certificate to an employee at ___________.

2. Upon hire, all new employees provide their employer with a Social Security card; a completed, signed and dated W-4; and documents that prove the employee's ___________ and ___________.

3. Name two documents that an employer may accept as proof of both an employee's identity and the authorization to work:
1. ________________ 2. ________________

4. The law designed to reduce the number of undocumented workers in the United States is known by the initials IRCA, which stand for (answer is five words):

____________ ____________ ____________ ____________ ____________

5. Name six forms/tax returns an employer must retain:

1. ____________________ 2. ____________________
3. ____________________ 4. ____________________
5. ____________________ 6. ____________________

Problem III.

Multiple choice. Circle the correct answer.

1. Which form must an employee complete to get a new or duplicate Social Security card?

a. W-4 b. W-2 c. SS-5 d. I-9

2. Which document must employees complete to show that they are authorized to work in the United States?

a. W-4 b. W-2 c. SS-5 d. I-9

3. Under IRS regulations, how long must an employer retain a W-2 returned by the post office as undeliverable?

a. 2 years b. 4 years c. 3 years d. 5 years

4. Under Wage and Hour Division regulations, how long must an employer retain an employment application?

a. 2 years b. 4 years c. 3 years d. 5 years

5. Which of the following documents may be used to substantiate only an employee's authorization to work under IRCA?

a. Social Security card
b. driver's license
c. draft card
d. student photo I.D.

QUIZ 1 Solutions and Explanations

Problem I.

1. April 15, 2017
   4 years from April 15, 2013

2. April 15, 2017
   4 years from April 15, 2013

3. April 15, 2018
   4 years from April 15, 2014

4. Through December 16, 2013
   1 year from the date of termination (see footnote 4 on page 58.)

5. March 15, 2013
   3 years per Wage and Hour rules

Problem II.

1. termination

2. identity, authorization to work

3. Any two of the following: (See Form I-9 in Appendix.)
   - U.S. Passport or U.S. Passport card
   - Permanent Resident Card
   - Alien Registration Receipt Card (Form I-551)
   - Foreign passport that contains temporary I-551 stamp
   - Foreign passport that contains temporary I-551 printed notation on a machine-readable immigrant visa
   - Employment Authorization Document that contains a photograph (Form I-766)
   - Form I-94 or Form I-94A
   - FSM or RMI Passport with Form I-94 or I-94A.

4. Immigration Reform and Control Act

5. Any six of the following (State laws may vary.):
   - Form I-9
   - Form 1099
   - Forms W-4 and W-2 including those returned as undeliverable
   - Form 941
   - Form 944
   - Form 940
   - state unemployment tax returns
   - state income tax returns.

Problem III.

1. c

2. d

3. b

4. c

5. a

QUIZ 2 EMPLOYMENT RECORDS AND PAYROLL RECORDKEEPING

Problem I.

For each of the following problems, fill in the date on which federal law permits the indicated documents to be destroyed.

1. ZapCo completes an I-9 for new hire Pete on September 1, 2011. He is terminated on March 15, 2013. Until what date must ZapCo retain Pete's I-9? ________________

2. ABC Inc. obtains a completed, signed W-4 from employee Martha on May 7, 2013, her date of hire. She terminates on June 28, 2013. Until what date must ABC retain Martha's W-4? ________________

3. WilCo's records substantiate taxable income calculations for employees' personal use of company cars for tax year 2012. Until what date must WilCo retain these records? ________________

4. BakeCo has daily timecards for the period ending September 30, 2013. Assuming that BakeCo also has weekly reports of hours worked, until what date must it retain the daily timecards under federal wage and hour law? ________________

5. ServeCo has tax year 2012 Forms W-2 that were returned as undeliverable. Until what date must it retain these forms? ________________

Problem II.

Fill in the blanks. Answers may be more than one word.

1. Name one document that proves only an employee's identity.
____

2. Name one document that proves only an employee's authorization to work. ________________

3. The requirement to complete an I-9 ________________ [is/is not] related to the employer's size.

4. Under IRS regulations, tax returns and documents that substantiate tax returns should be retained by an employer for four years, starting on ______________ of the year following the year that the records cover.

5. An employee requiring a new or duplicate Social Security card should complete Form ______________.

Problem III.

Multiple choice. Circle the correct answer.

1. EEOC regulations require employers to retain an employee's personnel file for at least:

   a. 1 year b. 2 years c. 3 years d. 5 years

2. The Immigration Reform and Control Act of 1986 requires that employers and employees complete which of the following forms?

   a. W-4 b. I-9 c. SS-5 d. W-2

3. Which document provides proof of both identity and authorization to work in the U.S. for I-9 purposes?

   a. Driver's license
   b. School ID
   c. Birth Certificate
   d. U.S. Passport

4. By when must you complete an I-9 for an employee who will be working for your firm for less than three days?

   a. noon of the employee's first day on the job
   b. end of the employee's first day on the job
   c. noon of the employee's third day on the job
   d. end of the employee's third day on the job

5. By when must you complete an I-9 for an employee who will be working for your firm for the indefinite future?

   a. end of the employee's first day on the job
   b. end of the employee's second day on the job
   c. end of the employee's third day on the job
   d. end of the employee's fourth day on the job

QUIZ 2 Solutions and Explanations

Problem I.

1. September 1, 2014
   3 years from the employee's date of hire of September 1, 2011 (see footnote 4 on page 58)

2. April 15, 2018
   4 years from April 15, 2014.

3. April 15, 2017
   4 years from April 15, 2013

4. September 30, 2015
   2 years from September 30, 2013 (see footnote 3 on page 58)

5. April 15, 2017
   4 years from April 15, 2013

Problem II.

1. driver's license (See the list on page 54.)

2. Social Security card (See the list on page 54.)

3. is not

4. April 15

5. SS-5
   This application for a new or duplicate Social Security card may be obtained by calling your local Social Security office or by downloading it from the SSA web site at *www.socialsecurity.gov.*

Problem III.

1. c
2. b
3. d
4. b
5. c

Section 5

EMPLOYEE DATA: FORM W-4 AND STATE WITHHOLDING ALLOWANCE CERTIFICATES

Introduction

The most critical area of the payroll function is withholding and depositing taxes. Penalties for employer violations of withholding requirements can be severe.

The Withholding Allowance Certificate

Income taxes are assessed by a number of government agencies, such as the IRS, and state, city, and local taxing authorities. In general, the amount withheld is determined by each employee's marital status and number of *allowances* claimed. For federal income tax withholding purposes, this information is documented for the employer by each employee on Form W-4, *Employee's Withholding Allowance Certificate*.

Who Must Submit Form W-4?

All employees must submit a W-4, including those who do not expect to owe federal income taxes for the year. Each certificate must be signed and dated. An electronic signature of the W-4 is allowed for federal purposes, but many states continue to require an original signed certificate.

1. **New employees.** New employees should complete a W-4 on their first day of work. Until it is submitted, the employer is required to withhold federal income tax as though the employee were single with zero allowances.

   PROBLEM 1: When Bill starts his new job, he fails to fill out a W-4. On his first payday he asks his employer to fill out a W-4 for him claiming married with four allowances. What should the employer do?

   SOLUTION 1: Until the employer has in its possession Bill's completed, dated and *signed* W-4, it should withhold federal income tax as if Bill were single with no allowances.

2. **Current employees who want to adjust withholding allowances.** Employees who want to increase or decrease the number of withholding allowances or change their marital status must complete and sign a new W-4. An employer should not alter an employee's federal income tax withholding without first obtaining a newly completed and signed W-4 from the employee.

PROBLEM 2: Juanita submits a W-4 when hired in August 2012, claiming single with one allowance. Is she required to submit a new W-4 in 2013?

SOLUTION 2: No. Juanita need not complete a new W-4 the following year unless there is a change in her withholding status.

PROBLEM 3: Henrietta submits a W-4 in 2013. In 2014, she has a baby. Is she required to submit a new W-4?

SOLUTION 3: No. Henrietta would submit a new W-4 only if she wishes to increase her withholding allowances. If she decides to keep her withholding allowances as is, she need not submit a new W-4.

Claiming Exempt from All Federal Income Tax Withholding

An employee who does not expect to owe any income tax may claim exempt from federal income tax withholding—but only if he or she did not owe federal income tax for the previous year and does not expect to owe taxes for the current year. Employees who claim exempt from federal income tax withholding must submit a new W-4 each year by February 15 or the next business day if February 15 falls on a weekend. If the employer has not received the new W-4 by this date, it is required to withhold federal income tax as though the employee claimed single with no allowances.

NOTE: The rules for claiming exemption from state income tax differ. Contact your state taxing authority for more information.

Employer Responsibility for Implementing Changes to a W-4

Employers are required to implement changes on a revised W-4 by the start of the first payroll period ending on or after the 30th day from the date that the W-4 is submitted. A new employee's W-4 takes effect with the first paycheck.

PROBLEM 4: Lou is paid semimonthly, on the 15th and end of the month. He submits a new W-4 to his employer on June 10. What is the date of the first paycheck that must reflect Lou's revised withholding allowances?

SOLUTION 4: Lou's employer must make sure that his withheld federal income tax is adjusted on his paycheck dated July 15. To calculate: 30 days from June 10 is July 10, and the first payroll period ending after July 10 is July 15.

Submitting Copies of the W-4 to the IRS

You are required to give original Forms W-4 to the IRS only upon request. When providing copies to the IRS, be sure to include the employer's identification number (EIN) on line 10 of the Form W-4. After the IRS has reviewed personal income returns, you may receive a "Lock-in" letter directing you to change (lock in) the number of exemptions by a specified date. If the employee disagrees with the number of exemptions in the Lock-in letter, that employee may send the IRS a W-4 with the number of exemptions he or she thinks should be accepted, accompanied by a written statement to support the claim.

If, while awaiting the IRS's decision on the appeal, the employee gives you a different W-4 containing more exemptions than the Lock-in letter specifies, you must use the number of exemptions in the Lock-in letter until the IRS decides the appeal. (See Treasury Decision 9196 for further details.)

NOTE: State-by-state rules for submitting copies of income tax withholding allowance certificates vary. Contact your state taxing authority for more information.

When an Employer Should Not Accept an Employee's W-4

An employer is responsible for rejecting a W-4 under the following circumstances:

1. **A W-4 that is incomplete.** If an employee fails to complete side 1 (side 2 is a worksheet for the employee and need not be completed) and sign and date the W-4, the employer must reject it.

   PROBLEM 5: Jake currently claims married with three allowances. He gives his employer a revised W-4 claiming five allowances but forgets to sign it. What should the employer do?

   SOLUTION 5: The employer should return the W-4 for signature and continue to withhold at the rate of married with three allowances.

2. **A W-4 that is altered with additions or deletions.** If the employee alters a W-4 by adding or deleting information, the employer must reject it. For example, a typical addition is a handwritten note from an employee that says: "Please withhold a flat $xxx from my paycheck." An example of a deletion is a line drawn through the perjury statement (by employees who believe that income tax is unconstitutional). Employers are required to reject any W-4 with additions or deletions.

3. **A W-4 that has information the employer knows to be false.** Under IRS regulations, employers are not responsible for the truthfulness or accuracy of information employees provide on a W-4. However, they are required to reject the W-4 if an employee tells them that the information is false.

Withholding Additional Taxes or a Flat Amount of Tax

Additional taxes. Occasionally, an employee may ask to have additional federal income taxes withheld. The employer may withhold an additional fixed dollar amount of tax, provided that the employee completed the sections of the Form W-4 concerning marital status and number of personal allowances.

A flat dollar amount or percentage of tax. An employer may not withhold a flat dollar amount, such as $100 per paycheck, or a flat percentage of tax, such as 10% of wages per paycheck (exceptions apply to supplemental wages). Flat amounts of withholding are not an option, regardless of the employee's reason for requesting them. (Withholding alternatives are covered in *Mastering Payroll II.*) However, employees who want a specific amount withheld can review the graduated tables and adjust their withholding allowances and then, if necessary, request an additional amount of federal income tax withholding, to obtain the federal income tax withholding that they want.

PROBLEM 6: Al is married and has one child. He earns $25,000 a year. Because he will have mortgage interest of $5,000 this year, he wants to reduce his federal income tax far below the amount normally withheld from someone earning $25,000. What should his employer do?

SOLUTION 6: Al's employer should tell him to complete the worksheet included with his Form W-4. He can take as many allowances as he needs to bring his withholding in line with his estimated federal income tax liability for the year.

PROBLEM 7: Review the two Forms W-4 on page 74. Which one should you reject as invalid? Why should you reject it?

SOLUTION 7: Accept "B." This is a valid W-4 on which the employee has requested additional withholding tax. Reject "A" because the employee has altered the form in order to request a flat $100 of withholding. The employee should complete a new W-4.

State Withholding Allowance Certificates

Most states have an income tax that employers must collect by withholding it from employees' wages. About half of these states use the federal W-4 data to calculate state income tax withholding; as a result, employers should be certain to check state requirements and use a state-specific form where one is required.

A.

Form **W-4** Department of the Treasury Internal Revenue Service

Employee's Withholding Allowance Certificate

▶ **Whether you are entitled to claim a certain number of allowances or exemption from withholding is subject to review by the IRS. Your employer may be required to send a copy of this form to the IRS.**

OMB No. 1545-0074

2013

1 Your first name and middle initial: Allen | Last name: Smith | 2 **Your social security number**: 655-55-5555

Home address (number and street or rural route): 1234 West Gate

3 ☐ Single ☐ Married ☐ Married, but withhold at higher Single rate.

Note. If married, but legally separated, or spouse is a nonresident alien, check the "Single" box.

City or town, state, and ZIP code: Houston, TX 77085

4 **If your last name differs from that shown on your social security card, check here. You must call 1-800-772-1213 for a replacement card.** ▶ ☐

5 Total number of allowances you are claiming (from line **H** above **or** from the applicable worksheet on page 2) 5 XXX

6 Additional amount, if any, you want withheld from each paycheck . . . . 6 $ 100.00

7 I claim exemption from withholding for 2013, and I certify that I meet **both** of the following conditions for exemption.

- Last year I had a right to a refund of **all** federal income tax withheld because I had **no** tax liability, **and**
- This year I expect a refund of **all** federal income tax withheld because I expect to have **no** tax liability.

If you meet both conditions, write "Exempt" here . . . . ▶ 7

Under penalties of perjury, I declare that I have examined this certificate and, to the best of my knowledge and belief, it is true, correct, and complete.

Employee's signature
(This form is not valid unless you sign it.) ▶ Allen Smith **Date** ▶ 3-18-2013

8 Employer's name and address (Employer: Complete lines 8 and 10 only if sending to the IRS.) | 9 Office code (optional) | 10 Employer identification number (EIN)

For Privacy Act and Paperwork Reduction Act Notice, see page 2. Cat. No. 10220Q Form **W-4** (2013)

B.

Form **W-4** Department of the Treasury Internal Revenue Service

Employee's Withholding Allowance Certificate

▶ **Whether you are entitled to claim a certain number of allowances or exemption from withholding is subject to review by the IRS. Your employer may be required to send a copy of this form to the IRS.**

OMB No. 1545-0074

2013

1 Your first name and middle initial: Allen | Last name: Smith | 2 **Your social security number**: 655-55-5555

Home address (number and street or rural route): 1234 West Gate

3 ☐ Single ☑ Married ☐ Married, but withhold at higher Single rate.

Note. If married, but legally separated, or spouse is a nonresident alien, check the "Single" box.

City or town, state, and ZIP code: Houston, TX 77085

4 **If your last name differs from that shown on your social security card, check here. You must call 1-800-772-1213 for a replacement card.** ▶ ☐

5 Total number of allowances you are claiming (from line **H** above **or** from the applicable worksheet on page 2) 5 0

6 Additional amount, if any, you want withheld from each paycheck . . . . 6 $ 30.00

7 I claim exemption from withholding for 2013, and I certify that I meet **both** of the following conditions for exemption.

- Last year I had a right to a refund of **all** federal income tax withheld because I had **no** tax liability, **and**
- This year I expect a refund of **all** federal income tax withheld because I expect to have **no** tax liability.

If you meet both conditions, write "Exempt" here . . . . ▶ 7

Under penalties of perjury, I declare that I have examined this certificate and, to the best of my knowledge and belief, it is true, correct, and complete.

Employee's signature
(This form is not valid unless you sign it.) ▶ Allen Smith **Date** ▶ 3-18-2013

8 Employer's name and address (Employer: Complete lines 8 and 10 only if sending to the IRS.) | 9 Office code (optional) | 10 Employer identification number (EIN)

For Privacy Act and Paperwork Reduction Act Notice, see page 2. Cat. No. 10220Q Form **W-4** (2013)

Never Give Tax Advice

Many employees ask their employer for assistance in completing the W-4, such as how many allowances to claim. But employers are not responsible for helping an employee determine the number of allowances to claim on the W-4. Employers may explain how to fill out a W-4 (which sections to complete, what information goes on each line, what the word "allowance" means, etc.). However, it is inadvisable to tell an employee *what* to claim. For example, suppose an employee asks: "How do I report that I'm married and have two children?" You can assist in this case. But if employees ask if they should claim their spouse as an allowance, they should be referred to their tax advisor or to the IRS. You also may suggest that employees obtain IRS Publication 505, *Tax Withholding and Estimated Tax*, IRS Publication 213, *You May Need To Check Your Withholding*, or IRS Publication 919, *How Do I Adjust My Tax Withholding?* These publications may be obtained at no charge from the IRS Website at *www.irs.gov.*

QUIZ 1 EMPLOYEE DATA: FORM W-4 AND STATE WITHHOLDING ALLOWANCE CERTIFICATES

Problem I.

Circle True or False for each of the following:

1. Bill starts work on August 1 at a branch office. Because he will be unable to submit his W-4 before the first payday, the head office may take his W-4 information over the phone for his first paycheck.

a. True b. False

2. Because Ralph claims 11 allowances on his W-4 on May 2, 2013, his employer must submit a copy of his Form W-4 to the IRS.

a. True b. False

3. Alicia is paid on the 15th and end of the month. She marries during the summer and submits a new W-4 on August 10 showing her marital status. Her check of September 15 must reflect this new withholding amount.

a. True b. False

4. Jane claims four allowances on her W-4 despite the fact that she is entitled to only two. Even though she never tells her employer the truth, the company still may be held liable for improper withholding.

a. True b. False

5. The day Michael is hired, he submits a W-4 claiming single with two allowances. He need not submit a new W-4 next year.

a. True b. False

Problem II.

Fill in the blanks. Answers may be more than one word.

1. If the IRS Lock-in letter shows Married and 1 allowance and Form W-4 shows Married and 0 allowances, which should the employer use to compute federal income tax withholding?

2. If the IRS Lock-in letter shows Single and 1 allowance and Form W-4 shows Married and 2 allowances, which should the employer use to compute federal income tax withholding?

3. Employees who claim exempt from federal income tax withholding must submit a new W-4 each year by [give month and day] ________________.

4. An employer must reject a W-4 that it knows to be false or that has any ________________ or ________________.

5. Employees may request ________________ [additional/flat] withholding on the W-4.

Problem III.

Multiple choice. Circle the correct answer.

1. Employees can claim exempt from federal income tax withholding if . . .
   a. they expect to owe no tax in the current tax year.
   b. they earn an average of less than $200 per week.
   c. they owed no tax last year.
   d. they owed no tax last year and will owe none this year.

2. At what rate should an employer withhold federal income tax when the employee fails to submit a W-4?
   a. single with 1 allowance
   b. married with 2 allowances
   c. single with 0 allowances
   d. married with 1 allowance

3. An employee who claims exempt from all federal income tax withholding must submit a new W-4 each year by:

a. January 1
b. February 1
c. January 31
d. February 15

4. An employer is not responsible for:

a. rejecting a W-4 that it knows to be false
b. rejecting a W-4 that is not signed
c. withholding at single and zero if there is no valid W-4
d. determining the accuracy of an employee's W-4

5. If an employee gives you a Form W-4 without signing it, how would you compute federal income tax withholding on the next paycheck assuming the employee's prior Form W-4 showed married and two allowances?

a. Withhold at 25%
b. Withhold at married and two allowances
c. Withhold at single and zero
d. Withhold at 35%

QUIZ 1 Solutions and Explanations

Problem I.

1. False
2. False
3. True
4. False
5. True

Problem II.

1. Use Married and 0 allowances because withholding is higher than the Lock-in letter.
2. Use Single and 1 allowance because the Lock-in letter requires more withholding than the Form W-4.
3. February 15 or the next business day if the 15th is on Saturday or Sunday
4. additions, deletions
5. additional

Problem III.

1. d
2. c
3. d
4. d
5. b

QUIZ 2 EMPLOYEE DATA: FORM W-4 AND STATE WITHHOLDING ALLOWANCE CERTIFICATES

Problem I.

Circle True or False for each of the following:

1. On the day she is hired, Greta claims exempt from federal income tax withholding. For every subsequent year that she wishes to remain exempt, she will have to complete a new W-4.

a. True b. False

2. Tony claims 10 allowances on his W-4. His employer must submit a copy of his W-4 to the IRS.

a. True b. False

3. When Juanita submitted a new W-4 to change her withholding from married with two allowances to married with three allowances, she forgot to sign the W-4. Her employer should withhold federal income tax as though she is single with zero allowances.

a. True b. False

4. Juan wants a flat $75 withheld for federal income tax from each paycheck. His employer may do this provided that Juan writes the amount on his W-4.

a. True b. False

5. Jim had a Form W-4 on file showing single and two allowances. He submitted a new Form W-4 claiming married and one allowance but did not sign the form. In the next payroll period his employer should withhold federal income tax using married and one allowance.

a. True b. False

Problem II.

Fill in the blanks. Answers may be more than one word.

1. An employer may explain to employees how to fill out the W-4, but should never give ________________ ________________.

2. Hans gives his employer a W-4 and says that even though he is entitled to two allowances he is taking four because he needs the extra cash. The employer should ________________ his W-4.

3. Employees may not claim exempt from federal income tax withholding unless they did not owe any tax in the ________________ year and do not expect to owe tax in the ________________ ________________.

4. When submitting a W-4 to the IRS, include the employer's ________________ on Line 10.

Problem III.

Multiple choice. Circle the correct answer.

1. Which of the following options is not available to employees on their Forms W-4?

   a. withholding additional tax
   b increasing the number of allowances
   c. withholding flat tax
   d. withholding no tax

2. A W-4 should be rejected for which of the following reasons:

   a. employee claims more than 10 allowances
   b. employee claims exempt from withholding
   c. employee alters the form
   d. employee revises the number of allowances on a new W-4

3. How long does an employer have to implement a revised W-4 ?

   a. 90 days b. 60 days c. 30 days d. 10 days

QUIZ 2 Solutions and Explanations

Problem I.

1. True
2. False
   Prior to 2005, this rule applied only if *more than* 10 allowances were claimed.
3. False
   The employer should reject the new W-4 and continue to withhold as before (married with two allowances).
4. False
   The W-4 may not be used to withhold a flat dollar amount or percentage of federal income tax withholding.
5. False
   The employer should return the W-4 to Jim for his signature, and continue to withhold at the rate of single with two allowances until Jim submits a fully completed—and signed—W4.

Problem II.

1. tax advice
2. reject
   An employer is responsible for rejecting a W-4 that it knows to be false. However, the employee may adjust the number of withholding allowances for a valid reason (e.g. the purchase of a house).
3. previous, current year
4. EIN (Employer Identification Number)

Problem III.

1. c
2. c
3. c

Section 6

HOW EMPLOYERS WITHHOLD AND DEPOSIT FEDERAL TAXES

Introduction

In general, the amount of federal income tax that an employer withholds from an employee's paycheck is determined by matching information provided on the employee's W-4 to withholding tables published in IRS Publication 15, *Circular E, Employer's Tax Guide*. This guide contains federal income tax withholding tables for the following year and other important tax information. A copy may be obtained from the IRS Website at *www.irs.gov*.

Getting Started

Both the employer and the employee must have a Taxpayer Identification Number (TIN) before federal income tax can be withheld. The employer needs a federal Employer Identification Number (EIN), obtained by submitting Form SS-4 (*Application for Employer Identification Number*). The employee needs a Social Security number (SSN) obtained by completing an SS-5 (*Application for Social Security Card*). Both TINs are needed to withhold federal income and FICA taxes and to deposit them with the IRS. Individuals receiving U.S. source income and who are not eligible for an SSN are assigned an individual taxpayer identification number (ITIN). Form W-7 is used to request an ITIN.

FICA (Social Security and Medicare tax)

Almost all U.S. employees, regardless of age, are required under the Federal Insurance Contributions Act (FICA) to pay Social Security and Medicare taxes. Among those exempt from Social Security and Medicare tax are children under 18 employed by their parents, nonresident aliens covered by a totalization agreement, and workers covered by the Railroad Retirement Tax Act. Employer and employee FICA tax is based on a percentage of annual wages. FICA is made up of two separate taxes: Old Age, Survivors, and Disability Insurance (OASDI), also referred to as Social Security, and Hospital Insurance (HI), also referred to as Medicare. For 2013, both employee and employer pay a rate of 1.45% for the HI or Medicare portion of FICA (total: 2.9%). Effective with wages paid in 2013, employers withhold an additional Medicare tax of .9% from wages in excess of $200,000. There is no employer match on this tax. Effective January 1, 2013 employees pay Social Security tax of 6.2% and employers pay 6.2%, for a combined rate of 12.4%. Certain state and local government municipalities are allowed to pay only the Medicare portion of FICA. For 2013, the Social Security wage ceiling is $113,700, an increase from the 2012 wage base of $110,100. There is no limit on the wages subject to the 1.45% Medicare tax or the .9% addition to Medicare tax that applies to wages over $200,000.

EXAMPLE: As of December 15, 2013, Gunther's year-to-date FICA taxable wages are $121,900. On December 26, 2013, he is to receive FICA taxable wages of $1,200. How much FICA tax will his employer withhold from his December 26 payment? Answer: $17.40.
To calculate:

OASDI tax: $125,500 (year-to-date wages) + $1,200 (wages on 12-26) = $126,700

OASDI wage limit for 2013 is $113,700, therefore no OASDI will be withheld from his December 26 payment.

There is no HI wage limit, therefore $1,200 × 1.45% = $17.40, the HI tax to be withheld from his December 26 payment. His year-to-date wages don't exceed $200,000 and the .9% additional Medicare tax doesn't apply.

PROBLEM 1: As of December 17, 2013, Mai-Lee was paid wages of $143,100. On December 24 she receives $1,500 in regular salary. How much FICA tax will her employer withhold from her December 24 payment?

SOLUTION 1: Answer: $21.75. To calculate:

OASDI tax: $143,100 (year-to-date wages) + $1,500 (wages on 12-26) = $144,600

OASDI wage limit for 2013 is $113,700, therefore no OASDI will be withheld from her December 24 payment.

> There is no HI wage limit. Therefore, $1,500 × 1.45% = $21.75, the HI tax to be withheld from her December 24 payment. Her year-to-date wages are less than $200,000 and the .9% additional Medicare tax doesn't apply.

Employers must withhold FICA tax from each employee, each year, regardless of the FICA tax withheld by a previous employer in the same year. When the withholding of an employee's FICA tax by two or more employers in the same year results in withholding that exceeds the Social Security limit, the employee may claim a refund on his or her personal tax return. Employers, however, are not entitled to a refund.

> **EXAMPLE:** From January through November 2013, Cornelia earns $114,000 from ACME, exceeding the 2013 OASDI wage limit of $113,700. In December, she leaves to work for WidgeCo where she earns $5,000 for the month. WidgeCo is required to withhold FICA tax of $382.50 on this $5,000 ($5,000 × 6.2% = $310 OASDI. $5,000 × 1.45% = $72.50 HI. $310 + $72.50 = $382.50), even though Cornelia reached her OASDI limit while still at ACME. However, she may claim a refund of the $310 Social Security tax (OASDI) overpayment ($5,000 × 6.2%) on her personal tax return. (No Medicare refund is due as there is no annual limit.) WidgeCo is not entitled to a refund of the employer's portion.

NOTE: The additional Medicare tax of .9% on wages in excess of $200,000 applies regardless of the employee's marital status on Form W-4. The employer also may not consider wages paid by another employer or an employee's other additional earnings when determining if the $200,000 threshold has been met.

Federal Income Tax Withholding (FITW)

A number of factors determine the amount of FITW on each employee's paycheck:

- **Employer pay period.** A pay period may be daily, weekly, biweekly, semimonthly, monthly, or annually, or any frequency that the employer chooses.
- **Employee marital status.** Federal withholding rates are different for single and married employees.

- **Employee personal allowances.** The number of allowances the employee claims on the W-4 affects federal income tax withholding for each period.
- **Employee federal taxable wages for the period.** This includes all wages, overtime, bonuses, taxable benefits, and other payments for the period subject to federal income tax withholding.
- **Supplemental Wages.** Employers may optionally withhold federal income tax at 25% if certain conditions are met. If supplemental wages for the year exceed $1 million, a flat tax rate of 39.6% (35% for 2012) applies, without regard to the employee's Form W-4 and regardless of whether the supplemental withholding rate of 25% was used in the calendar year.

Using this information, the employer locates the correct FITW amount from the withholding tables in the current year's IRS Publication 15, Circular E, *Employer's Tax Guide*. The tables for 2013 are reprinted, in part, on the following pages.

PROBLEM 2: Jack is paid $515 weekly. He claims married with two allowances on his W-4. How much federal income tax should be withheld from Jack's weekly pay?

SOLUTION 2: Refer to the weekly table for a married employee on page 90. In the lefthand column find the appropriate range of wages. The correct line to use is $510–$520. At the top of the page, find the column for "2" allowances. Where the wage range line and the allowance column meet is the correct amount to withhold for Jack: $21.00.

PROBLEM 3: Rita earns $1,267 biweekly and claims single with one allowance on her W-4. How much tax should be withheld from Rita's biweekly pay?

SOLUTION 3: Refer to the biweekly table for a single employee on pages 92 and 93. In the lefthand column find the correct wage range ($1,260–$1,280). At the top of page 93, find the column for "1" allowance. Where the wage range line and the allowance column meet is the correct withholding amount: $138.00.

Special Withholding Rules for Family Members

FITW is required from the wages of almost all employees, including the wages paid children or parents of company owners.

However, under the following circumstances, family employees are exempt from FICA tax:

- **Children under 18 employed by their parents.** Children, foster children and stepchildren employed by sole proprietorships owned by their parents are exempt from FICA tax. The exemption also applies to partnerships, but only if the child is related to both partners. Work performed by children for parents in other than the parent's trade or business, such as domestic work in the parent's home, is exempt from FICA until the child reaches age 21.
- **Parents employed by children.** Under certain conditions where domestic services are provided, parents employed by their children are exempt.

There is no exemption for a spouse, and there is no exemption for family members employed by a corporation.

NOTE: Different rules apply to federal unemployment tax. See page 113.

Federal Deposit Rules

Effective January 1, 2011 all federal tax deposits must be made under the IRS Electronic Federal Tax Payment System (EFTPS) program. An exception applies where the taxes are allowed to be paid with the return.

Electronic Payment of Taxes

Most all employers are required to make their employment tax (and other business) deposits by electronic funds transfer (EFT) through the IRS EFTPS program. Whether or not an employer is required to deposit their employment taxes by EFT depends on whether the tax payment is allowed to be made with the return.

Form 8109, Tax Deposit Coupon is no longer allowed.

For information on the EFTPS program, call 1-800-555-4477, or see the EFTPS Website at *www.eftps.gov*.

Publication 15—Married Persons, Weekly Payroll Period

MARRIED Persons—**WEEKLY** Payroll Period

(For Wages Paid through December 2013)

And the wages are–		And the number of withholding allowances claimed is—										
At least	But less than	0	1	2	3	4	5	6	7	8	9	10
		The amount of income tax to be withheld is—										
$ 0	$160	$0	$0	$0	$0	$0	$0	$0	$0	$0	$0	$0
160	165	0	0	0	0	0	0	0	0	0	0	0
165	170	1	0	0	0	0	0	0	0	0	0	0
170	175	1	0	0	0	0	0	0	0	0	0	0
175	180	2	0	0	0	0	0	0	0	0	0	0
180	185	2	0	0	0	0	0	0	0	0	0	0
185	190	3	0	0	0	0	0	0	0	0	0	0
190	195	3	0	0	0	0	0	0	0	0	0	0
195	200	4	0	0	0	0	0	0	0	0	0	0
200	210	5	0	0	0	0	0	0	0	0	0	0
210	220	6	0	0	0	0	0	0	0	0	0	0
220	230	7	0	0	0	0	0	0	0	0	0	0
230	240	8	0	0	0	0	0	0	0	0	0	0
240	250	9	1	0	0	0	0	0	0	0	0	0
250	260	10	2	0	0	0	0	0	0	0	0	0
260	270	11	3	0	0	0	0	0	0	0	0	0
270	280	12	4	0	0	0	0	0	0	0	0	0
280	290	13	5	0	0	0	0	0	0	0	0	0
290	300	14	6	0	0	0	0	0	0	0	0	0
300	310	15	7	0	0	0	0	0	0	0	0	0
310	320	16	8	1	0	0	0	0	0	0	0	0
320	330	17	9	2	0	0	0	0	0	0	0	0
330	340	18	10	3	0	0	0	0	0	0	0	0
340	350	19	11	4	0	0	0	0	0	0	0	0
350	360	20	12	5	0	0	0	0	0	0	0	0
360	370	21	13	6	0	0	0	0	0	0	0	0
370	380	22	14	7	0	0	0	0	0	0	0	0
380	390	23	15	8	0	0	0	0	0	0	0	0
390	400	24	16	9	1	0	0	0	0	0	0	0
400	410	25	17	10	2	0	0	0	0	0	0	0
410	420	26	18	11	3	0	0	0	0	0	0	0
420	430	27	19	12	4	0	0	0	0	0	0	0
430	440	28	20	13	5	0	0	0	0	0	0	0
440	450	29	21	14	6	0	0	0	0	0	0	0
450	460	30	22	15	7	0	0	0	0	0	0	0
460	470	31	23	16	8	1	0	0	0	0	0	0
470	480	32	24	17	9	2	0	0	0	0	0	0
480	490	33	25	18	10	3	0	0	0	0	0	0
490	500	34	26	19	11	4	0	0	0	0	0	0
500	510	35	27	20	12	5	0	0	0	0	0	0
510	520	36	28	21	13	6	0	0	0	0	0	0
520	530	38	29	22	14	7	0	0	0	0	0	0
530	540	39	30	23	15	8	0	0	0	0	0	0
540	550	41	31	24	16	9	1	0	0	0	0	0
550	560	42	32	25	17	10	2	0	0	0	0	0
560	570	44	33	26	18	11	3	0	0	0	0	0
570	580	45	34	27	19	12	4	0	0	0	0	0
580	590	47	35	28	20	13	5	0	0	0	0	0
590	600	48	37	29	21	14	6	0	0	0	0	0
600	610	50	38	30	22	15	7	0	0	0	0	0
610	620	51	40	31	23	16	8	1	0	0	0	0
620	630	53	41	32	24	17	9	2	0	0	0	0
630	640	54	43	33	25	18	10	3	0	0	0	0
640	650	56	44	34	26	19	11	4	0	0	0	0
650	660	57	46	35	27	20	12	5	0	0	0	0
660	670	59	47	36	28	21	13	6	0	0	0	0
670	680	60	49	38	29	22	14	7	0	0	0	0
680	690	62	50	39	30	23	15	8	0	0	0	0
690	700	63	52	41	31	24	16	9	1	0	0	0
700	710	65	53	42	32	25	17	10	2	0	0	0
710	720	66	55	44	33	26	18	11	3	0	0	0
720	730	68	56	45	34	27	19	12	4	0	0	0
730	740	69	58	47	35	28	20	13	5	0	0	0
740	750	71	59	48	37	29	21	14	6	0	0	0
750	760	72	61	50	38	30	22	15	7	0	0	0
760	770	74	62	51	40	31	23	16	8	1	0	0
770	780	75	64	53	41	32	24	17	9	2	0	0
780	790	77	65	54	43	33	25	18	10	3	0	0
790	800	78	67	56	44	34	26	19	11	4	0	0

Publication 15—Married Persons, Weekly Payroll Period (Page 2)

MARRIED Persons—WEEKLY Payroll Period

(For Wages Paid through December 2013)

And the wages are–		And the number of withholding allowances claimed is—										
At least	But less than	0	1	2	3	4	5	6	7	8	9	10
		The amount of income tax to be withheld is—										
$800	**$810**	$80	$68	$57	$46	$35	$27	$20	$12	$5	$0	$0
810	**820**	81	70	59	47	36	28	21	13	6	0	0
820	**830**	83	71	60	49	38	29	22	14	7	0	0
830	**840**	84	73	62	50	39	30	23	15	8	0	0
840	**850**	86	74	63	52	41	31	24	16	9	1	0
850	**860**	87	76	65	53	42	32	25	17	10	2	0
860	**870**	89	77	66	55	44	33	26	18	11	3	0
870	**880**	90	79	68	56	45	34	27	19	12	4	0
880	**890**	92	80	69	58	47	35	28	20	13	5	0
890	**900**	93	82	71	59	48	37	29	21	14	6	0
900	**910**	95	83	72	61	50	38	30	22	15	7	0
910	**920**	96	85	74	62	51	40	31	23	16	8	1
920	**930**	98	86	75	64	53	41	32	24	17	9	2
930	**940**	99	88	77	65	54	43	33	25	18	10	3
940	**950**	101	89	78	67	56	44	34	26	19	11	4
950	**960**	102	91	80	68	57	46	35	27	20	12	5
960	**970**	104	92	81	70	59	47	36	28	21	13	6
970	**980**	105	94	83	71	60	49	38	29	22	14	7
980	**990**	107	95	84	73	62	50	39	30	23	15	8
990	**1,000**	108	97	86	74	63	52	41	31	24	16	9
1,000	**1,010**	110	98	87	76	65	53	42	32	25	17	10
1,010	**1,020**	111	100	89	77	66	55	44	33	26	18	11
1,020	**1,030**	113	101	90	79	68	56	45	34	27	19	12
1,030	**1,040**	114	103	92	80	69	58	47	35	28	20	13
1,040	**1,050**	116	104	93	82	71	59	48	37	29	21	14
1,050	**1,060**	117	106	95	83	72	61	50	38	30	22	15
1,060	**1,070**	119	107	96	85	74	62	51	40	31	23	16
1,070	**1,080**	120	109	98	86	75	64	53	41	32	24	17
1,080	**1,090**	122	110	99	88	77	65	54	43	33	25	18
1,090	**1,100**	123	112	101	89	78	67	56	44	34	26	19
1,100	**1,110**	125	113	102	91	80	68	57	46	35	27	20
1,110	**1,120**	126	115	104	92	81	70	59	47	36	28	21
1,120	**1,130**	128	116	105	94	83	71	60	49	38	29	22
1,130	**1,140**	129	118	107	95	84	73	62	50	39	30	23
1,140	**1,150**	131	119	108	97	86	74	63	52	41	31	24
1,150	**1,160**	132	121	110	98	87	76	65	53	42	32	25
1,160	**1,170**	134	122	111	100	89	77	66	55	44	33	26
1,170	**1,180**	135	124	113	101	90	79	68	56	45	34	27
1,180	**1,190**	137	125	114	103	92	80	69	58	47	35	28
1,190	**1,200**	138	127	116	104	93	82	71	59	48	37	29
1,200	**1,210**	140	128	117	106	95	83	72	61	50	38	30
1,210	**1,220**	141	130	119	107	96	85	74	62	51	40	31
1,220	**1,230**	143	131	120	109	98	86	75	64	53	41	32
1,230	**1,240**	144	133	122	110	99	88	77	65	54	43	33
1,240	**1,250**	146	134	123	112	101	89	78	67	56	44	34
1,250	**1,260**	147	136	125	113	102	91	80	68	57	46	35
1,260	**1,270**	149	137	126	115	104	92	81	70	59	47	36
1,270	**1,280**	150	139	128	116	105	94	83	71	60	49	38
1,280	**1,290**	152	140	129	118	107	95	84	73	62	50	39
1,290	**1,300**	153	142	131	119	108	97	86	74	63	52	41
1,300	**1,310**	155	143	132	121	110	98	87	76	65	53	42
1,310	**1,320**	156	145	134	122	111	100	89	77	66	55	44
1,320	**1,330**	158	146	135	124	113	101	90	79	68	56	45
1,330	**1,340**	159	148	137	125	114	103	92	80	69	58	47
1,340	**1,350**	161	149	138	127	116	104	93	82	71	59	48
1,350	**1,360**	162	151	140	128	117	106	95	83	72	61	50
1,360	**1,370**	164	152	141	130	119	107	96	85	74	62	51
1,370	**1,380**	165	154	143	131	120	109	98	86	75	64	53
1,380	**1,390**	167	155	144	133	122	110	99	88	77	65	54
1,390	**1,400**	168	157	146	134	123	112	101	89	78	67	56
$1,400 and over		Use Table 1(b) for a **MARRIED person** on page 44. Also see the instructions on page 42.										

Publication 15—Single Persons, Biweekly Payroll Period

SINGLE Persons—BIWEEKLY Payroll Period

(For Wages Paid through December 2013)

And the wages are–		And the number of withholding allowances claimed is—										
At least	But less than	0	1	2	3	4	5	6	7	8	9	10
		The amount of income tax to be withheld is—										
$ 0	$105	$0	$0	$0	$0	$0	$0	$0	$0	$0	$0	$0
105	110	2	0	0	0	0	0	0	0	0	0	0
110	115	3	0	0	0	0	0	0	0	0	0	0
115	120	3	0	0	0	0	0	0	0	0	0	0
120	125	4	0	0	0	0	0	0	0	0	0	0
125	130	4	0	0	0	0	0	0	0	0	0	0
130	135	5	0	0	0	0	0	0	0	0	0	0
135	140	5	0	0	0	0	0	0	0	0	0	0
140	145	6	0	0	0	0	0	0	0	0	0	0
145	150	6	0	0	0	0	0	0	0	0	0	0
150	155	7	0	0	0	0	0	0	0	0	0	0
155	160	7	0	0	0	0	0	0	0	0	0	0
160	165	8	0	0	0	0	0	0	0	0	0	0
165	170	8	0	0	0	0	0	0	0	0	0	0
170	175	9	0	0	0	0	0	0	0	0	0	0
175	180	9	0	0	0	0	0	0	0	0	0	0
180	185	10	0	0	0	0	0	0	0	0	0	0
185	190	10	0	0	0	0	0	0	0	0	0	0
190	195	11	0	0	0	0	0	0	0	0	0	0
195	200	11	0	0	0	0	0	0	0	0	0	0
200	205	12	0	0	0	0	0	0	0	0	0	0
205	210	12	0	0	0	0	0	0	0	0	0	0
210	215	13	0	0	0	0	0	0	0	0	0	0
215	220	13	0	0	0	0	0	0	0	0	0	0
220	225	14	0	0	0	0	0	0	0	0	0	0
225	230	14	0	0	0	0	0	0	0	0	0	0
230	235	15	0	0	0	0	0	0	0	0	0	0
235	240	15	0	0	0	0	0	0	0	0	0	0
240	245	16	1	0	0	0	0	0	0	0	0	0
245	250	16	1	0	0	0	0	0	0	0	0	0
250	260	17	2	0	0	0	0	0	0	0	0	0
260	270	18	3	0	0	0	0	0	0	0	0	0
270	280	19	4	0	0	0	0	0	0	0	0	0
280	290	20	5	0	0	0	0	0	0	0	0	0
290	300	21	6	0	0	0	0	0	0	0	0	0
300	310	22	7	0	0	0	0	0	0	0	0	0
310	320	23	8	0	0	0	0	0	0	0	0	0
320	330	24	9	0	0	0	0	0	0	0	0	0
330	340	25	10	0	0	0	0	0	0	0	0	0
340	350	26	11	0	0	0	0	0	0	0	0	0
350	360	27	12	0	0	0	0	0	0	0	0	0
360	370	28	13	0	0	0	0	0	0	0	0	0
370	380	29	14	0	0	0	0	0	0	0	0	0
380	390	30	15	0	0	0	0	0	0	0	0	0
390	400	31	16	1	0	0	0	0	0	0	0	0
400	410	32	17	2	0	0	0	0	0	0	0	0
410	420	33	18	3	0	0	0	0	0	0	0	0
420	430	34	19	4	0	0	0	0	0	0	0	0
430	440	35	20	5	0	0	0	0	0	0	0	0
440	450	37	21	6	0	0	0	0	0	0	0	0
450	460	38	22	7	0	0	0	0	0	0	0	0
460	470	40	23	8	0	0	0	0	0	0	0	0
470	480	41	24	9	0	0	0	0	0	0	0	0
480	490	43	25	10	0	0	0	0	0	0	0	0
490	500	44	26	11	0	0	0	0	0	0	0	0
500	520	47	28	13	0	0	0	0	0	0	0	0
520	540	50	30	15	0	0	0	0	0	0	0	0
540	560	53	32	17	2	0	0	0	0	0	0	0
560	580	56	34	19	4	0	0	0	0	0	0	0
580	600	59	36	21	6	0	0	0	0	0	0	0
600	620	62	39	23	8	0	0	0	0	0	0	0
620	640	65	42	25	10	0	0	0	0	0	0	0
640	660	68	45	27	12	0	0	0	0	0	0	0
660	680	71	48	29	14	0	0	0	0	0	0	0
680	700	74	51	31	16	1	0	0	0	0	0	0
700	720	77	54	33	18	3	0	0	0	0	0	0
720	740	80	57	35	20	5	0	0	0	0	0	0
740	760	83	60	38	22	7	0	0	0	0	0	0
760	780	86	63	41	24	9	0	0	0	0	0	0
780	800	89	66	44	26	11	0	0	0	0	0	0

Page 50 **Publication 15 (2013)**

Publication 15—Single Persons, Biweekly Payroll Period (Page 2)

SINGLE Persons—**BIWEEKLY** Payroll Period

(For Wages Paid through December 2013)

And the wages are–		And the number of withholding allowances claimed is—										
At least	But less than	0	1	2	3	4	5	6	7	8	9	10
		The amount of income tax to be withheld is—										
$800	**$820**	$92	$69	$47	$28	$13	$0	$0	$0	$0	$0	$0
820	**840**	95	72	50	30	15	0	0	0	0	0	0
840	**860**	98	75	53	32	17	2	0	0	0	0	0
860	**880**	101	78	56	34	19	4	0	0	0	0	0
880	**900**	104	81	59	36	21	6	0	0	0	0	0
900	**920**	107	84	62	39	23	8	0	0	0	0	0
920	**940**	110	87	65	42	25	10	0	0	0	0	0
940	**960**	113	90	68	45	27	12	0	0	0	0	0
960	**980**	116	93	71	48	29	14	0	0	0	0	0
980	**1,000**	119	96	74	51	31	16	1	0	0	0	0
1,000	**1,020**	122	99	77	54	33	18	3	0	0	0	0
1,020	**1,040**	125	102	80	57	35	20	5	0	0	0	0
1,040	**1,060**	128	105	83	60	38	22	7	0	0	0	0
1,060	**1,080**	131	108	86	63	41	24	9	0	0	0	0
1,080	**1,100**	134	111	89	66	44	26	11	0	0	0	0
1,100	**1,120**	137	114	92	69	47	28	13	0	0	0	0
1,120	**1,140**	140	117	95	72	50	30	15	0	0	0	0
1,140	**1,160**	143	120	98	75	53	32	17	2	0	0	0
1,160	**1,180**	146	123	101	78	56	34	19	4	0	0	0
1,180	**1,200**	149	126	104	81	59	36	21	6	0	0	0
1,200	**1,220**	152	129	107	84	62	39	23	8	0	0	0
1,220	**1,240**	155	132	110	87	65	42	25	10	0	0	0
1,240	**1,260**	158	135	113	90	68	45	27	12	0	0	0
1,260	**1,280**	161	138	116	93	71	48	29	14	0	0	0
1,280	**1,300**	164	141	119	96	74	51	31	16	1	0	0
1,300	**1,320**	167	144	122	99	77	54	33	18	3	0	0
1,320	**1,340**	170	147	125	102	80	57	35	20	5	0	0
1,340	**1,360**	173	150	128	105	83	60	38	22	7	0	0
1,360	**1,380**	176	153	131	108	86	63	41	24	9	0	0
1,380	**1,400**	179	156	134	111	89	66	44	26	11	0	0
1,400	**1,420**	182	159	137	114	92	69	47	28	13	0	0
1,420	**1,440**	185	162	140	117	95	72	50	30	15	0	0
1,440	**1,460**	188	165	143	120	98	75	53	32	17	2	0
1,460	**1,480**	191	168	146	123	101	78	56	34	19	4	0
1,480	**1,500**	195	171	149	126	104	81	59	36	21	6	0
1,500	**1,520**	200	174	152	129	107	84	62	39	23	8	0
1,520	**1,540**	205	177	155	132	110	87	65	42	25	10	0
1,540	**1,560**	210	180	158	135	113	90	68	45	27	12	0
1,560	**1,580**	215	183	161	138	116	93	71	48	29	14	0
1,580	**1,600**	220	186	164	141	119	96	74	51	31	16	1
1,600	**1,620**	225	189	167	144	122	99	77	54	33	18	3
1,620	**1,640**	230	192	170	147	125	102	80	57	35	20	5
1,640	**1,660**	235	197	173	150	128	105	83	60	38	22	7
1,660	**1,680**	240	202	176	153	131	108	86	63	41	24	9
1,680	**1,700**	245	207	179	156	134	111	89	66	44	26	11
1,700	**1,720**	250	212	182	159	137	114	92	69	47	28	13
1,720	**1,740**	255	217	185	162	140	117	95	72	50	30	15
1,740	**1,760**	260	222	188	165	143	120	98	75	53	32	17
1,760	**1,780**	265	227	191	168	146	123	101	78	56	34	19
1,780	**1,800**	270	232	195	171	149	126	104	81	59	36	21
1,800	**1,820**	275	237	200	174	152	129	107	84	62	39	23
1,820	**1,840**	280	242	205	177	155	132	110	87	65	42	25
1,840	**1,860**	285	247	210	180	158	135	113	90	68	45	27
1,860	**1,880**	290	252	215	183	161	138	116	93	71	48	29
1,880	**1,900**	295	257	220	186	164	141	119	96	74	51	31
1,900	**1,920**	300	262	225	189	167	144	122	99	77	54	33
1,920	**1,940**	305	267	230	192	170	147	125	102	80	57	35
1,940	**1,960**	310	272	235	197	173	150	128	105	83	60	38
1,960	**1,980**	315	277	240	202	176	153	131	108	86	63	41
1,980	**2,000**	320	282	245	207	179	156	134	111	89	66	44
2,000	**2,020**	325	287	250	212	182	159	137	114	92	69	47
2,020	**2,040**	330	292	255	217	185	162	140	117	95	72	50
2,040	**2,060**	335	297	260	222	188	165	143	120	98	75	53
2,060	**2,080**	340	302	265	227	191	168	146	123	101	78	56
2,080	**2,100**	345	307	270	232	195	171	149	126	104	81	59
$2,100 and over		Use Table 2(a) for a **SINGLE person** on page 44. Also see the instructions on page 42.										

Publication 15 (2013) Page 51

When Deposits Are Due

Employers deposit their federal payroll taxes annually, quarterly, monthly, semi-weekly, or in one banking day.

Quarterly depositors (annual, monthly, and semiweekly depositors are discussed on pages 95–96). A liability for the quarter of less than $2,500 may be paid by credit/debit card, Electronic Funds Withdrawal (EFW), check or money order at the end of the quarter with Form 941. Employers with a deposit liability of $100,000 or more must make their deposits one business day from the day the liability is incurred. Note that federal tax deposits cannot be made using a debit or credit card or EFW.

NOTE: Different rules apply to Federal unemployment tax. See page 113.

Lookback period. Most employers are either monthly or semiweekly depositors—generally, the deposit status is fixed for an entire calendar year. An employer is a monthly or semiweekly depositor based on its deposit liabilities in the "lookback period." The Form 941 lookback period is the July 1–June 30 prior to the calendar year for which the deposit status is determined.

> **EXAMPLE:** An employer's deposit status for 2013 is based on Form 941 liabilities from the quarter beginning July 1, 2011, through the quarter ending June 30, 2012.

Employers with an accumulated 941 liability of more than $50,000 during the lookback period are semiweekly depositors for the next calendar year; those with an accumulated 941 liability of $50,000 or less in the lookback period are monthly depositors for the next calendar year.

New employers. A new employer is a monthly depositor until the end of the calendar year unless the one-business-day rule is triggered. For new employers, the lookback period may not be a full 12-month period.

> **EXAMPLE 1:** On July 1, 2011, NewCo opens for business. It accumulates 941 liabilities through June 30, 2012, of $120,000. As a new firm, NewCo is a monthly depositor through December 31, 2012. On January 1, 2013, it is a semiweekly depositor because its accumulated liability in the 12-month lookback period exceeded $50,000.

> **EXAMPLE 2:** StartCo opens for business on June 1, 2012, and accumulates through June 30, 2012 (a one-month lookback period), Form 941 liabilities of $90,000. As a new firm, StartCo is a monthly depositor until December 31, 2012. On January 1, 2013, StartCo becomes a semiweekly depositor because its accumulated liability during the lookback period, though only one month, exceeded $50,000.

Form 941-X. A 941-X adjustment filed during a lookback period is not used to determine the $50,000 threshold even if the 941-X corrects a 941 filed in a quarter during the lookback period.

> **EXAMPLE:** For the 12-month period ending June 30, 2012, HessCo files Forms 941 showing a FICA and FITW liability of $60,100. Because this liability is over $50,000, HessCo will be a semiweekly depositor in calendar year 2013. In August 2013, HessCo discovers that it overstated its FIT liability by $10,900 on the 2012 second quarter 941. To correct this, it files a Form 941-X for the 2012 second quarter claiming a credit for the 2012 $10,900 overstatement.
>
> *Result:* HessCo will continue to be a semiweekly depositor in 2013. Although the $10,900 credit puts it under the $50,000 threshold ($60,100 – $10,900 = $49,200), HessCo will remain a semiweekly depositor for 2013 because the deposit status is based on the unadjusted liability ($60,100). The $10,900 credit will be offset against the accumulated liability for the lookback period ending June 30, 2013, and therefore may affect HessCo's deposit status in calendar year 2014.

Annual depositors. Employers with an estimated annual tax liability of less than $1,000 are eligible to file Form 944, *Employer's Annual Federal Employment Tax Return*. The IRS notifies employers of their eligibility to file a 944, which requires annual filing of taxes. However, if at any point during the year the employer's accumulated employment tax liability exceeds $2,500, the employer must remit payments quarterly or monthly or under the semi-weekly rule, depending on the amount of the accumulated liability. Employers can opt out or opt into filing Form 944. Go to *www.irs.gov* for more information.

Monthly depositors. Monthly depositors (new employers or employers with an accumulated liability in the lookback period of $50,000 or less) are required to deposit payroll taxes no later than the 15th of the month following the month in which they incurred the liability. They remain monthly depositors for the entire calendar year even if their accumulated liability for the calendar year exceeds $50,000.

IMPORTANT: A Form 941 or 944 filer that incurs a liability of $100,000 or more at any time in the calendar year must make its deposit within one business day of incurring this liability—and becomes a semiweekly depositor for the remainder of the calendar year and for the next calendar year.

EXAMPLE: GrowCo is a monthly depositor for calendar year 2013. On Friday September 6, 2013, it pays wages that result in a deposit obligation of $110,000. GrowCo must make its deposit no later than Monday September 9, 2013. Effective September 6, 2013, through December 31, 2013 and for calendar year 2014, GrowCo is a semiweekly depositor.

PROBLEM 4: CorCo is a monthly depositor. On Monday, May 16, CorCo pays wages resulting in a deposit liability of $110,000. When is the deposit due?

SOLUTION 4: CorCo must make the $110,000 deposit no later than Tuesday, May 17. For the remaining calendar year and the following calendar year, all deposits must be made under the semiweekly deposit rule.

Semiweekly Depositors: The Wednesday/Friday rule. A semiweekly depositor (an employer that in the calendar year incurred a deposit obligation of $100,000 or more or an employer with an accumulated liability of more than $50,000 in the lookback period) must deposit taxes for wages paid on Wednesday, Thursday and/or Friday no later than the following Wednesday. Employment tax liabilities for wages paid on Saturday, Sunday, Monday, and/or Tuesday must be deposited no later than the following Friday. If a deposit liability of $100,000 or more is incurred, the deposit must be made within one business day.

EXAMPLE: PlumbCo, a semiweekly depositor, pays wages on Monday, May 3, that result in a deposit obligation of $104,000. It must make its deposit by Tuesday, May 4. On Monday, May 10, it pays wages resulting in a deposit obligation of $94,000. It must make this deposit by Friday, May 14.

PROBLEM 5: WoodCo, a semiweekly depositor, pays wages on Tuesday, September 4, resulting in a deposit obligation of $56,000. When is this deposit due?

SOLUTION 5: The deposit is due no later than Friday, September 7.

PROBLEM 6: WoodCo pays wages on Thursday, August 5, that result in a deposit obligation of $49,000. When is this deposit due?

SOLUTION 6: The deposit is due no later than Wednesday, August 11.

Deposit periods that bridge two quarters. Liabilities incurred on the last day of the last month of a quarter are treated as separate and distinct from liabilities incurred in the following quarter. In addition, a separate deposit must be made for each quarter, even if the liabilities are deposited on the same day.

EXAMPLE: On Wednesday, March 31, CraftCo incurs a payroll tax liability of $30,000. On Thursday, April 1, CraftCo incurs an additional payroll tax liability of $71,000. Both deposits are due on Wednesday, April 7. Two deposits are made on April 7—one showing Quarter 1 for $30,000 and another showing Quarter 2 for $71,000. Although the total liability at the close of business on Thursday, April 1, was in excess of $100,000, the one-business-day rule does not apply because the liability incurred at the end of the first quarter (March 31) represents a fixed and separate deposit obligation from that incurred in April.

PROBLEM 7: On Wednesday, September 30, CraftCo incurs a deposit obligation of $70,000. On Thursday, October 1, CraftCo incurs a deposit obligation of $40,000. When should the deposits be made?

SOLUTION 7: Because September 30 is the end of the quarter, the $70,000 deposit obligation is not added to the deposit obligation on October 1 for the purposes of determining the deposit due date. Thus, the one-business-day rule does not apply ($70,000 + $40,000 = $110,000). Instead, both deposits are made on Wednesday, October 7. One deposit of $70,000 is made for Quarter 3, and another deposit of $40,000 is made for Quarter 4.

Nonbusiness days. A nonbusiness day is Saturday, Sunday, or a federal legal holiday.* A federal legal holiday is considered to be a nonbusiness day if it is observed in the District of Columbia (e.g., Emancipation Day, April 16, 2013, which is a nonbusiness day simply because it is observed in the District of Columbia). State holidays are not considered federal legal holiday days for these purposes.

*For federal legal holidays in 2013, see the Glossary (page 180).

Annual, quarterly, monthly and one-business-day deposits. If the due date for an annual, quarterly, monthly or one-business-day deposit falls on Saturday, Sunday or a federal legal holiday, the deposit is due on the next business day (e.g. Emanicpation Day is a federal legal holiday).

Semiweekly deposits. When a nonbusiness day falls in a period following the period in which the liability was incurred, the due date for the deposit is extended by one day. For example, if a liability is incurred on a Wednesday, Thursday and/or Friday, and a nonbusiness day falls on the following Monday, Tuesday or Wednesday, the deposit due date is Thursday rather than Wednesday. If a liability is incurred on Saturday, Sunday, Monday, or Tuesday, and a nonbusiness day falls on Wednesday, Thursday and/or Friday, the deposit is due on the following Monday rather than Friday.

Safe harbor: A deposit is considered timely if the shortfall does not exceed the greater of $100 or 2% of the liability. The due date of the deposit shortfall depends upon the employer's deposit status. Monthly depositors must deposit any shortfall by the 941 due date; semiweekly and one-business-day depositors must deposit any shortfall on or before the first Wednesday or Friday (whichever is earlier) falling on or after the 15th of the month following the month in which the deposit should have been made, or, if earlier, the Form 941 due date. Note that the IRS discourages the routine use of the deposit shortfall rule. It is to be applied only under extreme circumstances.

Deposit status can change each year. Employers are responsible for determining their own deposit status. Therefore, employers should check their Forms 941/944 for the lookback period each year to make sure that their deposit frequency is correct. Firms making late deposits may be penalized even if it was caused by assignment of an incorrect deposit status by the IRS.

Completing the Electronic Payment Information

When making an electronic tax payment, it is important to supply accurate and complete information concerning the deposit.

"Type of Tax." Designate the kind of tax as—"941 or 944" for FICA and FITW; "940" for FUTA; "945" for backup tax; and so on.

"Tax Period." This refers to the quarter *when taxes were withheld* (usually the quarter in which wages were paid)—*not* the quarter in which the deposit was made.

If taxes were withheld between:	The appropriate "tax period" is:
January 1–March 31	1st quarter
April 1–June 30	2nd quarter
July 1–September 30	3rd quarter
October 1–December 31	4th quarter

EXAMPLE: ACME's wage payments on January 15 result in a federal deposit obligation of $2,500. As a monthly depositor, when would ACME make the deposit, and what information would it provide concerning the deposit?

The deposit would be made on February 15. The type of tax is "941" because ACME is depositing FICA tax and FITW. The tax period is "1st Quarter."

QUIZ 1 HOW EMPLOYERS WITHHOLD AND DEPOSIT FEDERAL TAXES

Problem I.

Calculate the amount of federal tax due in each case, assuming it is 2013.

1. From January through October 2013, XYZ Co. pays Susan wages of $114,700. On November 1, she resigns and is hired by ACME, which pays her $3,000 in regular salary for November and December. How much FICA tax must ACME withhold from Susan's wages in November and December? $______________

2. On July 15, FurCo pays wages of $200,000. It withholds from these wages total federal income tax of $30,000 and Medicare tax of $15,300. (All employees had previously reached the OASDI wage limit.) What is FurCo's total federal deposit obligation? $______________

3. On August 15, ZapCo pays wages of $300,000. Its employment tax liability includes withheld federal income tax of $45,000, employee and employer FICA of $22,950 and state income tax of $9,000. What is ZapCo's total federal deposit obligation?
$______________

4. As of November 15, 2013, Mark's year-to-date wages from All-Purpose, Inc. are $113,500. When, on November 30, 2013, All-Purpose pays Mark $600 in wages, how much FICA tax should it withhold? $______________

5. Between February 1 and February 15, GreenCo incurs a federal tax liability of $3,000. By the end of February, this liability has increased to $3,700. Assuming GreenCo is a monthly depositor, when should the $3,700 be deposited? ______________

6. An employer is a monthly depositor if its accumulated Form 941 liabilities for the lookback period were $______________ or less.

7. The lookback period for determining an employer's 941 deposit status for 2013 is ______________.

8. On Tuesday, June 3, SisCo, a semiweekly depositor, pays wages that result in a deposit obligation of $36,000. The deposit must be made no later than ________________.

9. On Wednesday, January 13, PiCo, a semiweekly depositor, pays wages that result in a deposit obligation of $43,000. Assuming that Monday, January 18, is a federal legal holiday, the deposit must be made no later than ________________.

10. For a deposit to be considered timely under the deposit rules, the deposit shortfall cannot exceed the greater of 2% or $________________.

Problem II.

Fill in the blanks. Answers may be more than one word.

1. Unless a family member claims exempt on Form W-4, no family member is automatically exempt from ________________.

2. Children under ________________ years of age may be exempt from FICA tax when employed in the trade or business of a parent or by a sole proprietorship owned by a parent.

3. If an employer has an accumulated liability of more than ________________ in the lookback period, it is a semiweekly depositor.

4. When paying federal taxes with the return, payment may be made by ______________, ______________, ______________ or ______________.

5. If an employer has an accumulated liability of $ ________________ or more, the deposit must be made within one business day.

Problem III.

Multiple choice. Circle the correct answer.

1. ACME paid wages on Friday, September 7, resulting in a federal deposit obligation of $4,500. This deposit must be made no later than (if the employer is a monthly depositor):

   a. October 15
   b. September 10
   c. September 12
   d. September 8

2. On which form does an employer apply for an EIN?

   a. SS-4 b. SS-5 c. W-4 d. W-2

3. Total undeposited federal tax for the month of February is $2,500. This deposit must be made no later than (assuming the employer is a monthly depositor):

   a. March 15 b. March 31 c. February 28 d. April 15

4. Employees are exempt from having further Social Security tax withheld for 2013 if:

   a. they are over age 65
   b. they had tax withheld on $113,700 in covered wages and worked for one employer the entire year
   c. they collect Social Security benefits
   d. they are over age 55

5. XYZ Co.'s accumulated deposit liability for the lookback period of July 1, 2011, to June 30, 2012, was $160,000. XYZ must deposit its payroll taxes in 2013 under which of the following deposit schedules?

   a. quarterly c. semiweekly
   b. monthly d. one banking day

6. CDE Inc. has a deposit liability of $35,000 on May 15. Under the deposit rules, how much of this liability must be deposited for it to be considered "timely filed?"

   a. $34,900 b. $34,300 c. $33,250 d. $35,000

7. Alco Inc., a semiweekly depositor, pays wages on Wednesday, March 31, resulting in a deposit obligation of $80,000. On Thursday, April 1, Alco Inc. pays additional wages that give rise to a deposit obligation of $30,000. When is the deposit of $110,000 due?

a. April 2 b. April 7 c. May 15 d. April 4

8. PubCo, a semiweekly depositor, pays wages on Wednesday, June 30, resulting in a deposit obligation of $23,000. Assuming that Monday, July 5 is a federal holiday, when is the deposit due?

a. Tuesday, July 6
b. Wednesday, July 7
c. Thursday, July 8
d. Friday, July 9

9. Effective in 2011, deposits are paid . . .

a. to the Federal Reserve Bank of Dallas.
b. electronically.
c. to a local bank.
d. by check or money order.

10. An employer filing its federal employment tax return annually uses Form . . .

a. 941
b. 945
c. 940
d. 944

QUIZ 1 Solutions and Explanations

Problem I.

1. $229.50

   Her year-to-date wages with XYZ Co. make no difference. ACME is required to withhold FICA tax as though no other wages were paid for the year. To calculate:

   $3,000 × 6.2% = $186.00 (OASDI Tax)

   $3,000 × 1.45% = $43.50 (HI Tax)

   $186 + $43.50 = $229.50 total FICA tax

2. $60,600

   To calculate:

   FITW/$30,000 + Medicare/$15,300 + employer matching contribution of Medicare/$15,300 = $60,600

3. $67,950

   To calculate:

   FITW/$45,000 + FICA/$22,950 = $67,950. State income tax is not included.

4. $21.10

   To calculate:

   OASDI tax:

   $113,500 (year-to-date FICA taxable wages) + $600 (FICA taxable wages on 11-15) = $114,100

   $114,100 (FICA taxable wages) – $113,700 (OASDI taxable wage limit) = $400 exempt from OASDI tax

   $600 payment – $400 exempt = $200 OASDI taxable

   $200 × 6.2% OASDI tax rate = $12.40 OASDI tax to be withheld

   HI tax: There is no HI wage limit. Therefore the entire $600 payment is HI taxable.

   $600 × 1.45% = $8.70 HI tax to be withheld

   $12.40 (OASDI) + $8.70 (HI) = $21.10 FICA tax on the $600 payment

   Year-to-date wages are less than $200,000, therefore the .9% additional Medicare tax doesn't apply.

5. March 15
   Monthly depositors that do not incur a deposit obligation of $100,000 or more make their deposits on the 15th of the month following the month that the liability was incurred.

6. $50,000

7. July 1, 2011, through June 30, 2012

8. Friday, June 6

9. Thursday, January 21
   Deposit is delayed by one day because of the federal legal holiday on Monday.

10. $100

Problem II.

1. FITW (Federal Income Tax Withholding)

2. 18

3. $50,000

4. debit/credit card, EFW, check or money order

5. $100,000

Problem III.

1. a

2. a

3. a

4. b

5. c
If the accumulated liability in the lookback period is more than \$50,000, the employer is a semiweekly depositor in the next calendar year.

6. b
\$35,000 × 2% = \$700. \$700 is greater than \$100 therefore the shortfall can be \$700. \$35,000 – \$700 = \$34,300.

7. b
March 31 is the end of the quarter, so the liability on April 1 is not added to the liability of March 31. Thus, the one-banking-day rule does not apply.

8. c
The federal legal holiday delays the deposit due date by one day.

9. b

10. d

QUIZ 2 HOW EMPLOYERS WITHHOLD AND DEPOSIT FEDERAL TAXES

Problem I.

Calculate the amount of federal tax due in each case, assuming it is 2013.

1. Darryl is paid $77,600 by WidgeCo, from January to August 2013. In September, he takes a job with LimbCo where he works through December and is paid $30,000 for the four months. How much FICA tax should LimboCo withhold from Darryl's pay? $________________
2. As of Monday, October 7, ACME has a federal tax obligation of $11,000. When is its deposit due under the semiweekly rule? ________________
3. As of November 29, 2013, Gary's year-to-date wages are $143,200. On December 15, 2013, he is paid $2,600. How much FICA tax should his employer withhold? $________________
4. Total undeposited payroll tax liabilities on Thursday, March 31, are $99,000. On Friday, April 1, wages are paid resulting in a deposit obligation of $2,000. Assuming that the employer is a semiweekly depositor, when must these deposits be made? ________________
5. An employer whose accumulated Form 941 liabilities for the lookback period are more than $50,000 is what type of depositor? ________________
6. The lookback period for determining an employer's Form 941 deposit status for 2013 is ________________.
7. On Thursday, August 8, ShopCo, a semiweekly depositor, pays wages that result in a deposit obligation of $41,500. The deposit must be made by ________________.
8. On Thursday, October 8, TransCo, a semiweekly depositor, pays wages that result in a deposit obligation of $28,000. Assuming that Monday, October 12, is a federal legal holiday, the deposit must be made by ________________.
9. For a deposit to be considered timely, the deposit shortfall can not exceed what amount? ________________
10. An employer may file Form 944 annually if its estimated annual employment tax liability is less than what amount? ________________

Problem II.

Fill in the blanks. Answers may be more than one word.

1. Family members over age 18 who work in the trade or business of an employer ________________ [are/are not] exempt from FITW.

2. Children, foster children, and stepchildren under age 18 who work in a trade or business of a parent ________________ [are/are not] exempt from FITW.

3. Children, foster children, and stepchildren under age 18 who work in a trade or business of a parent ________________ [are/are not] exempt from FICA withholding.

4. FICA stands for ________________.

5. A quarterly employment tax liability of less than $2,500 can be ________________.

Problem III.

Multiple choice. Circle the correct answer.

1. Effective January 1, 2013, the employee Social Security tax rate is:

   a. 4.2%　　b. 6.2%　　c. 1.45%　　d. 7.65%

2. The OASDI wage limit for 2013 is:

   a. $113,700　　b. $200,000　　c. $110,100　　d. $0

3. Which family employee is exempt from FICA?

   a. a 20-year-old child employed in a parent's trade
   b. a 17-year-old child employed in a parent's trade
   c. a 54-year-old mother employed by her son's textile shop
   d. a wife employed by her husband

4. Effective in 2011, which of the following is used for making federal tax deposits?

a. SS-4 b. SS-5 c. EFTPS d. 8109

5. LockCo's accumulated deposit liability for the lookback period of July 1, 2011, to June 30, 2012, was $45,000. LockCo must deposit its payroll taxes under which of the following deposit schedules for calendar year 2013?

a. eighth-monthly
b. monthly
c. semiweekly
d. one business day

6. Mega Corp., a semiweekly depositor, incurs a deposit liability on Wednesday, March 31, of $99,000. On Thursday, April 1, it incurs an additional liability of $5,000. When are these deposits due?

a. deposit $99,000 on Wednesday, April 7, and $5,000 on April 15
b. deposit $104,000 on Friday, April 2
c. deposit $99,000 on Thursday, April 8, and $5,000 on April 15
d. deposit $104,000 on Wednesday, April 7

7. StartCo, a semiweekly depositor, pays wages on Tuesday, November 9, resulting in a deposit obligation of $65,000. Assuming that Thursday, November 11, is a federal holiday, when is the deposit due?

a. November 10
b. November 12
c. December 15
d. November 15

8. Ace Inc., a semiweekly depositor, pays wages on Thursday, September 30, that gives rise to a deposit obligation of $72,000. On Friday, October 1, Ace Inc. pays additional wages that give rise to a deposit obligation of $30,000. When is the deposit of $102,000 due?

a. October 6
b. October 2
c. October 3
d. November 15

QUIZ 2 Solutions and Explanations

Problem I.

1. $2,295
His year-to-date wages with WidgeCo make no difference. LimbCo is required to withhold FICA tax as though no other wages were paid for the year. To calculate:

$30,000 × 6.2% = $1,860.00 (OASDI tax)

$30,000 × 1.45% = $435.00 (HI tax)

$1,860.00 + $435.00 = $2,295 FICA tax

2. Friday, October 11

3. $37.70
To calculate:

OASDI tax:

$143,200 (year-to-date FICA taxable wages) + $2,600 FICA taxable wages of 12-15) = $145,800

OASDI wage limit for 2013 is $113,700. Wages paid on December 15 are exempt from OASDI tax.

HI *tax*:

There is no HI wage limit, therefore:

$2,600 × 1.45% = $37.70

The year-to-date wages are less than $200,000, therefore the additional .9% Medicare tax doesn't apply.

4. The accumulated liability of $101,000 ($99,000 + $2,000) must be deposited no later than Wednesday, April 6. Because March 31 is the end of the first quarter, the $99,000 liability incurred on Thursday is a separate liability and is not combined with the liability of $2,000 incurred on Friday. Thus, the one-business-day rule does not apply.

5. semiweekly

6. July 1, 2011, to June 30, 2012
7. Wednesday, August 14
8. Thursday, October 15
9. The greater of 2% of the liability or $100
10. $1,000

Problem II.

1. are not
2. are not
3. are
4. Federal Insurance Contributions Act
5. Paid quarterly with Form 941.

Problem III.

1. b
2. a
3. b
4. c
5. b

6. d
The March 31 deposit liability falls at the end of the quarter. The April 1 liability would be treated as a separate liability. Thus, the one-business-day rule does not apply.

7. d
The employer is a semiweekly depositor. The deposit due date is delayed by one banking or business day because of the federal holiday.

8. a
Liabilities at the end of a quarter are not added to liabilities incurred at the beginning of the next quarter. Thus, the one-business-day rule does not apply.

Section 7
FEDERAL EMPLOYMENT REPORTING FORMS AND DUE DATES

Introduction

Employers are required to complete and file various forms and returns that are used to report employer and employee tax liabilities and to determine amounts for benefits such as Social Security, Medicare and unemployment insurance.

Federal Unemployment Tax (FUTA)

FUTA pays federal costs for administering the state unemployment insurance program. The state unemployment insurance trust funds provide benefits to workers who have lost their jobs. It is not a withholding tax—only employers pay it, not employees. (However, some states require that employees contribute toward the cost of state unemployment insurance.) (Under federal wage-hour law, employers are *prohibited* from deducting FUTA tax from employees' wages.) An employer that pays wages of $1,500 or more in any calendar quarter or employs at least one person for some part of any day in 20 weeks must pay FUTA tax. Exceptions include not-for-profit organizations, federal, state and local government entities, certain household employers, certain agricultural employers, and sole proprietorships that employ family members. Also, certain work performed for a child or spouse, or by a child under age 21 for a parent, is exempt from FUTA (including foster children, foster parents, stepchildren, and stepparents).

How to Calculate FUTA

Effective July 1, 2011, the maximum FUTA tax is 6.0% of the first $7,000 of taxable wages paid to each employee. An employer that makes timely payments to its state unemployment fund may be entitled to a maximum credit of up to 5.4%, reducing its federal tax rate to a minimum of 0.6%.[*] Employers may assume the minimum FUTA rate of 0.6% for deposits made in the first three quarters of the year. An employer that loses any portion of this 5.4% credit makes up the difference for the lost credit in its fourth and

* In 2012 a number of states lost a portion of the maximum FUTA credit of 5.4% because they failed to repay their federal unemployment insurance loans. The reductions in the FUTA credit appear on the 2012 Form 940, Schedule A.

final quarter deposit. There are two ways that an employer can lose this credit: First, by failing to make timely payments to its state unemployment insurance fund; second, by its state failing to timely repay a federal unemployment insurance loan (this credit reduction, if applicable, appears on Form 940, Schedule A.). See the sample FUTA form shown on pages 116–117 and the Form 940 instructions that begin on page 197.

NOTE: An employer that is exempt from state unemployment tax for any reason is liable for the entire 6.0% of FUTA unless also exempt from FUTA.

PROBLEM 1: ZapCo pays Charlie $11,000 for 2013. Assuming that ZapCo is entitled to the maximum FUTA credit, what is the FUTA tax for Charlie's wages?

SOLUTION 1: $42: To calculate:

$\$7{,}000 \times 0.6\% \text{ (or } 0.006) = \$42$

When Federal Unemployment Tax Is Paid

An employer's FUTA liability is computed quarterly.

- If the FUTA liability is more than $500, a deposit must be made by the last day of the month following the end of the quarter. (For exact dates, use the schedule in Figure 7-1 on page 120.)
- If the FUTA balance is $500 or less at the end of a quarter, it may be rolled over to the next quarter and subsequent quarters until the liability exceeds $500 or until January 31 of the following year, whichever comes first.
- If the FUTA liability is $500 or less at the end of the fourth quarter, the employer may pay its FUTA liability with Form 940 (the 940 is explained below).

PROBLEM 2: As of June 30, Sam's Construction Co. has a FUTA tax liability of $510. By what date must it pay FUTA tax?

SOLUTION 2: Its FUTA tax must be deposited no later than July 31.

Like FITW and FICA, FUTA taxes are deposited electronically. The type of tax is "940." If the amount owed is less than $500 at the end of the year, it can be paid by debit/credit card, EFW, or by check or money order with the Form 940.

Federal Employment Tax Returns

Form 940: Employer's Annual Federal Unemployment Tax Return (FUTA)

What it is. Form 940 is an annual return used to compute the employer's federal unemployment tax liability and to reconcile FUTA deposits made during the year. Every employer that incurred a FUTA tax liability must file a 940 with the IRS.

The IRS matches information on the 940 with information from each state's unemployment agency to ensure that the reported wages agree. Any discrepancy may provoke a response from the IRS and may result in tax assessments and penalties.

When it is due. The 940 is due on the last day of the month following December 31; in other words, on January 31 of the following year. If January 31 is a Saturday, Sunday or federal legal holiday, the return is due on the next business day. Employers that make all FUTA deposits on time during the year may extend the due date of the 940 to February 10 or the next business day. Permission is not required from the IRS for this extension.

The following example shows how the 940 is completed.

> **EXAMPLE:** PlumbCo, Brookview, Texas, paid $250,050 in wages in the fourth quarter of 2012, $70,000 of which was FUTA taxable. $50 represents group-term life insurance over $50,000 that is exempt from FUTA. The other $180,000 in payments were in excess of the FUTA limit. PlumbCo is entitled to the maximum FUTA credit. All employees live and work in Texas. To calculate PlumbCo's FUTA tax: $70,000 (FUTA taxable wages) × 0.006 (0.6%) = $420. To see how PlumbCo completes its Form 940, see pages 116 and 117. After reviewing the completed form, fill in the blank form on pages 118 and 119 to become familiar with using it.
>
> **NOTE:** You must complete Form 940, Schedule A (page 209) if you paid state unemployment tax in more than one state or had employment in a state that was subject to a FUTA credit reduction.

Completed Form 940 (Page 1)

Form **940 for 2012: Employer's Annual Federal Unemployment (FUTA) Tax Return** 1213 870112
Department of the Treasury -- Internal Revenue Service OMB No. 1545-0028

(EIN)
Employer identification number 88-8888888

Name (not your trade name) PLUMBCO

Trade name (if any)

Address 123 FALLING BROOK AVE

BROOKVIEW, TX 77777

Type of Return (Check all that apply.)
- [ ] **a.** Amended
- [ ] **b.** Successor employer
- [ ] **c.** No payments to employees in 2012
- [ ] **d.** Final: Business closed or stopped paying wages

Instructions and prior-year forms are available at www.irs.gov/form940.

Read the separate instructions before you complete this form. Please type or print within the boxes.

Part 1: Tell us about your return. If any line does NOT apply, leave it blank.

1a **If you had to pay state unemployment tax in one state only, enter the state abbreviation** . . . . **1a** TX

1b **If you had to pay state unemployment tax in more than one state, you are a multi-state employer** . . . . **1b** [ ] Check here. Complete Schedule A (Form 940).

2 **If you paid wages in a state that is subject to CREDIT REDUCTION** . . . . **2** [ ] Check here. Complete Schedule A (Form 940).

Part 2: Determine your FUTA tax before adjustments for 2012. If any line does NOT apply, leave it blank.

3 **Total payments to all employees** **3** 250050.00

4 **Payments exempt from FUTA tax** **4** 50.00

Check all that apply: **4a** [ ] Fringe benefits **4b** [X] Group-term life insurance **4c** [ ] Retirement/Pension **4d** [ ] Dependent care **4e** [ ] Other

5 **Total of payments made to each employee in excess of $7,000** **5** 180000.00

6 **Subtotal** (line 4 + line 5 = line 6) **6** 180050.00

7 **Total taxable FUTA wages** (line 3 – line 6 = line 7) (see instructions) **7** 70000.00

8 **FUTA tax before adjustments** (line 7 x .006 = line 8) **8** 420.00

Part 3: Determine your adjustments. If any line does NOT apply, leave it blank.

9 **If ALL of the taxable FUTA wages you paid were excluded from state unemployment tax, multiply line 7 by .054** (line 7 x .054 = line 9). Go to line 12 . . . . **9**

10 **If SOME of the taxable FUTA wages you paid were excluded from state unemployment tax, OR you paid ANY state unemployment tax late** (after the due date for filing Form 940), complete the worksheet in the instructions. Enter the amount from line 7 of the worksheet **10**

11 **If credit reduction applies,** enter the total from Schedule A (Form 940) **11**

Part 4: Determine your FUTA tax and balance due or overpayment for 2012. If any line does NOT apply, leave it blank.

12 **Total FUTA tax after adjustments** (lines 8 + 9 + 10 + 11 = line 12) **12** 420.00

13 **FUTA tax deposited for the year, including any overpayment applied from a prior year** **13** 420.00

14 **Balance due** (If line 12 is more than line 13, enter the excess on line 14.)
- If line 14 is more than $500, you must deposit your tax.
- If line 14 is $500 or less, you may pay with this return (see instructions) **14**

15 **Overpayment** (If line 13 is more than line 12, enter the excess on line 15 and check a box below.) **15**

► You **MUST** complete both pages of this form and **SIGN** it. Check one: [ ] Apply to next return. [ ] Send a refund.

CAA 2 9401 NTF 2577479 B9401 Copyright 2012 Greatland/Nelco – Forms Software Only Next ►

For Privacy Act and Paperwork Reduction Act Notice, see Form 940-V, Payment Voucher. Form **940** (2012)

Completed Form 940 (Page 2)

870212

Form **940** (2012) Page **2**

Name (not your trade name)	**Employer identification number (EIN)**
PLUMBCO	88-8888888

Part 5: Report your FUTA tax liability by quarter only if line 12 is more than $500. If not, go to Part 6.

16 **Report the amount of your FUTA tax liability for each quarter; do NOT enter the amount you deposited. If you had no liability for a quarter, leave the line blank.**

16a	**1st quarter** (January 1 – March 31) **16a**	
16b	**2nd quarter** (April 1 – June 30) **16b**	
16c	**3rd quarter** (July 1 – September 30) **16c**	
16d	**4th quarter** (October 1 – December 31). **16d**	

17 **Total tax liability for the year** (lines 16a + 16b + 16c + 16d = line 17) . . . . **17**   **Total must equal line 12.**

Part 6: May we speak with your third-party designee?

Do you want to allow an employee, a paid tax preparer, or another person to discuss this return with the IRS? See the instructions for details.

☐ **Yes.** Designee's name and phone number

Select a 5-digit Personal Identification Number (PIN) to use when talking to IRS

☒ **No.**

Part 7: Sign here. You MUST complete both pages of this form and SIGN it.

Under penalties of perjury, I declare that I have examined this return, including accompanying schedules and statements, and to the best of my knowledge and belief, it is true, correct, and complete, and that no part of any payment made to a state unemployment fund claimed as a credit was, or is to be, deducted from the payments made to employees. Declaration of preparer (other than taxpayer) is based on all information of which preparer has any knowledge.

Sign your name here

Print your name here: TED WELLS

Print your title here: OWNER

Date: 1-25-2013

Best daytime phone: 713 888-8888

Paid Preparer Use Only

Check if you are self-employed . . . . ☐

Preparer's name		PTIN	
Preparer's signature		Date	
Firm's name (or yours if self-employed)		EIN	
Address		Phone	
City	State	ZIP code	

CAA **2 9402** NTF 2577480 **B9402** Form **940** (2012)

Form 940—Page 1

Form **940 for 2012: Employer's Annual Federal Unemployment (FUTA) Tax Return** 850112

Department of the Treasury — Internal Revenue Service

OMB No. 1545-0028

Employer identification number (EIN) ☐☐ – ☐☐☐☐☐☐☐

Name *(not your trade name)*

Trade name *(if any)*

Address

Number Street Suite or room number

City State ZIP code

Type of Return
(Check all that apply.)

☐ **a.** Amended
☐ **b.** Successor employer
☐ **c.** No payments to employees in 2012
☐ **d.** Final: Business closed or stopped paying wages

Instructions and prior-year forms are available at *www.irs.gov/form940.*

Read the separate instructions before you complete this form. Please type or print within the boxes.

Part 1: Tell us about your return. If any line does NOT apply, leave it blank.

1a **If you had to pay state unemployment tax in one state only, enter the state abbreviation** . 1a ☐☐

1b **If you had to pay state unemployment tax in more than one state, you are a multi-state employer** . . . . 1b ☐ Check here. Complete Schedule A (Form 940).

2 **If you paid wages in a state that is subject to CREDIT REDUCTION** . . . . 2 ☐ Check here. Complete Schedule A (Form 940).

Part 2: Determine your FUTA tax before adjustments for 2012. If any line does NOT apply, leave it blank.

3 **Total payments to all employees** . . . . 3 ______ .

4 **Payments exempt from FUTA tax** . . . . 4 ______ .

Check all that apply: 4a ☐ Fringe benefits 4b ☐ Group-term life insurance 4c ☐ Retirement/Pension 4d ☐ Dependent care 4e ☐ Other

5 **Total of payments made to each employee in excess of $7,000** . . . . 5 ______ .

6 **Subtotal** (line 4 + line 5 = line 6) . . . . 6 ______ .

7 **Total taxable FUTA wages** (line 3 – line 6 = line 7) (see instructions) . . . . 7 ______ .

8 **FUTA tax before adjustments** (line 7 x .006 = line 8) . . . . 8 ______ .

Part 3: Determine your adjustments. If any line does NOT apply, leave it blank.

9 **If ALL of the taxable FUTA wages you paid were excluded from state unemployment tax, multiply line 7 by .054** (line 7 × .054 = line 9). Go to line 12 . . . . 9 ______ .

10 **If SOME of the taxable FUTA wages you paid were excluded from state unemployment tax, OR you paid ANY state unemployment tax late** (after the due date for filing Form 940), complete the worksheet in the instructions. Enter the amount from line 7 of the worksheet . . 10 ______ .

11 **If credit reduction applies,** enter the total from Schedule A (Form 940) . . . . 11 ______ .

Part 4: Determine your FUTA tax and balance due or overpayment for 2012. If any line does NOT apply, leave it blank.

12 **Total FUTA tax after adjustments** (lines 8 + 9 + 10 + 11 = line 12) . . . . 12 ______ .

13 **FUTA tax deposited for the year, including any overpayment applied from a prior year** . 13 ______ .

14 **Balance due** (If line 12 is more than line 13, enter the excess on line 14.)
- If line 14 is more than $500, you must deposit your tax.
- If line 14 is $500 or less, you may pay with this return. (see instructions) . . . . 14 ______ .

15 **Overpayment** (If line 13 is more than line 12, enter the excess on line 15 and check a box below.) . . . . 15 ______ .

► You **MUST** complete both pages of this form and **SIGN** it. Check one: ☐ Apply to next return. ☐ Send a refund.

Next ►

For Privacy Act and Paperwork Reduction Act Notice, see the back of Form 940-V, Payment Voucher. Cat. No. 11234O Form **940** (2012)

Form 940—Page 2

850212

Name (not your trade name) | Employer identification number (EIN)

Part 5: Report your FUTA tax liability by quarter only if line 12 is more than $500. If not, go to Part 6.

16 Report the amount of your FUTA tax liability for each quarter; do NOT enter the amount you deposited. If you had no liability for a quarter, leave the line blank.

16a 1st quarter (January 1 – March 31) . . . . **16a** ▪

16b 2nd quarter (April 1 – June 30) . . . . **16b** ▪

16c 3rd quarter (July 1 – September 30) . . . . **16c** ▪

16d 4th quarter (October 1 – December 31) . . . . **16d** ▪

17 Total tax liability for the year (lines 16a + 16b + 16c + 16d = line 17) **17** ▪ **Total must equal line 12.**

Part 6: May we speak with your third-party designee?

Do you want to allow an employee, a paid tax preparer, or another person to discuss this return with the IRS? See the instructions for details.

☐ **Yes.** Designee's name and phone number

Select a 5-digit Personal Identification Number (PIN) to use when talking to IRS

☐ **No.**

Part 7: Sign here. You MUST complete both pages of this form and SIGN it.

Under penalties of perjury, I declare that I have examined this return, including accompanying schedules and statements, and to the best of my knowledge and belief, it is true, correct, and complete, and that no part of any payment made to a state unemployment fund claimed as a credit was, or is to be, deducted from the payments made to employees. Declaration of preparer (other than taxpayer) is based on all information of which preparer has any knowledge.

✗ **Sign your name here**

Print your name here

Print your title here

Date / /

Best daytime phone

Paid Preparer Use Only

Check if you are self-employed . . . ☐

Preparer's name | PTIN

Preparer's signature | Date / /

Firm's name (or yours if self-employed) | EIN

Address | Phone

City | State | ZIP code

Page **2** | Form **940** (2012)

Form 941: Employer's Quarterly Federal Tax Return

What it is. The 941 is a federal employment return used to report quarterly wage and tax information. The IRS uses the 941 to reconcile the wages that an employer paid and the employment taxes that it withheld to the tax deposited for the quarter and the Forms W-2 filed for the year. The 941 also tells the IRS the periods in which the tax liabilities were incurred. The IRS and Social Security Administration (SSA) reconcile the 941 with Forms W-2/W-3 (see pages 122–124). Discrepancies between Forms W-2 and 941 may prove costly to the employer.

NOTE: Qualifying employers that have received authorization from the IRS may file Form 944, *Employer's Annual Federal Employment Tax Return* (see page 241).

Who must file it. All employers that withhold federal income and FICA tax must file Form 941 or 944. Exceptions apply to household employers that report with Form 1040, agricultural employers that file Form 943 or other employers that file unique federal employment tax returns.

When it is due. Form 941 is due on the last day of the month after the end of the quarter, as follows:

Figure 7-1
Schedule of Due Dates for Form 941 and Quarterly FUTA Deposit

Quarter	Quarter ending date	Due date for 941 and FUTA deposits of $500 or more	941 Due date with automatic 10-day extension**
Quarter 1	March 31	April 30	May 10
Quarter 2	June 30	July 31	August 10
Quarter 3	September 30	October 31	November 10
Quarter 4	December 31	January 31*	February 10*

*Also Form 940 due date. Note that Form 944 is due January 31 (or February 10) of the following year.

**The automatic 10-day extension applies only if all deposits were timely made and for the full amount.

Note the following:

- If the 940, 944, or 941 due date falls on a Saturday, Sunday or federal legal holiday, the return is due on the next business day.
- An employer who made all monthly, semiweekly, etc., federal tax deposits for the quarter on time may file the 941 on the 10th of the second month following the end of the quarter. Employers filing annual Form 944 have 10 days following January 31. Permission need not be obtained from the IRS for this 10-day extension. No other filing extensions are allowed for filing Forms 941 or 944.

Where to file it. Form 941/944 is filed with the IRS at the address indicated in the forms instructions. Electronic filing is also permitted.

Schedule B: Employer's Record of Federal Tax Liability

Only monthly depositors report their liabilities on Form 941, Line 16. Semiweekly and one-business-day depositors must complete Schedule B. When Schedule B is completed, the employer checks the third box on Form 941, Line 16, "you were a semiweekly depositor for the entire quarter."

> **EXAMPLE:** QuickCo, a semiweekly depositor, is preparing the 941 for the second quarter of 2012. Total wages and FICA (OASDI and HI) taxable wages are $90,000. Three employees are paid on the 15th and last day of each month. Each semimonthly payroll resulted in a FITW and FICA tax (OASDI and HI) liability of $5,347.50. Federal income tax withheld for the quarter was $20,115. A total of $32,085.00 was deposited for the quarter. To see how QuickCo would complete its second quarter 2012 Form 941 and Schedule B, see the filled-in forms on pages 122–124. After reviewing the completed forms, fill in the blank forms on pages 125–127 to become familiar with using them.

NOTE: Line 5a *and Line 5c* must be completed. Semiweekly depositors must complete Schedule B. Note that the 2013 Form 941 now includes Line 5d for the reporting of those wages paid to employees in excess of $200,000 and subject to the .9% additional Medicare tax.

Completed Form 941 (Page 1)

Form **941 for 2012: Employer's QUARTERLY Federal Tax Return** 1213 970112
(Rev. January 2012) Department of the Treasury -- Internal Revenue Service OMB No. 1545-0029

Employer identification number (EIN) 99-9999988
Name (not your trade name) QUICKCO
Trade name (if any)
Address 101 LUCKY LANE
BLACK JACK, NV 88888

Report for this Quarter of 2012 (Check one.)
- [ ] **1:** January, February, March
- [X] **2:** April, May, June
- [ ] **3:** July, August, September
- [ ] **4:** October, November, December

Prior-year forms are available at www.irs.gov/form941.

Part 1: Answer these questions for this quarter.

Line	Description	Box	Amount
1	**Number of employees who received wages, tips, or other compensation for the pay period including: Mar. 12 (Quarter 1), June 12 (Quarter 2), Sept. 12 (Quarter 3), or Dec. 12 (Quarter 4)**	1	3
2	**Wages, tips, and other compensation**	2	90000.00
3	**Income tax withheld from wages, tips, and other compensation**	3	20115.00
4	**If no wages, tips, and other compensation are subject to social security or Medicare tax**		☐ **Check and go to line 6.**

	Column 1		Column 2
5a **Taxable social security wages**	90000.00	x .104 =	9360.00
5b **Taxable social security tips**		x .104 =	
5c **Taxable Medicare wages & tips**	90000.00	x .029 =	2610.00

Line	Description	Box	Amount
5d	**Add Column 2 line 5a, Column 2 line 5b, and Column 2 line 5c**	5d	11970.00
5e	**Section 3121(q) Notice and Demand--Tax due on unreported tips** (see instructions)	5e	
6	**Total taxes before adjustments** (add lines 3, 5d, and 5e)	6	32085.00
7	**Current quarter's adjustment for fractions of cents**	7	
8	**Current quarter's adjustment for sick pay**	8	
9	**Current quarter's adjustments for tips and group-term life insurance**	9	
10	**Total taxes after adjustments.** Combine lines 6 through 9	10	32085.00
11	**Total deposits for this quarter, including overpayment applied from a prior quarter and overpayment applied from Form 941-X or Form 944-X**	11	32085.00
12a	**COBRA premium assistance payments** (see instructions)	12a	
12b	**Number of individuals provided COBRA premium assistance**		
13	**Add lines 11 and 12a**	13	32085.00
14	**Balance due.** If line 13 is more than line 13, enter the difference and see instructions.	14	
15	**Overpayment.** If line 13 is more than line 10, enter the difference		Check one: ☐ Apply to next return. ☐ Send a refund.

► **You MUST complete both pages of Form 941 and SIGN it.** Next ►

For Privacy Act and Paperwork Reduction Act Notice, see the Payment Voucher. Form **941** (Rev. 1-2012)

CAA 2 **9411** NTF 2576945 **B12941** Copyright 2012 Greatland/Nelco – Forms Software Only

Completed Form 941 (Page 2)

970212

Form **941** (Rev. 1-2012) Page **2**

Name (not your trade name)	**Employer identification number (EIN)**
QUICKCO	99-9999988

Part 2: Tell us about your deposit schedule and tax liability for this quarter.

If you are unsure about whether you are a monthly schedule depositor or a semiweekly schedule depositor, see Pub. 15 (Circular E), section 11.

16 Check one: ☐ **Line 10 on this return is less than $2,500 or line 10 on the return for the prior quarter was less than $2,500, and you did not incur a $100,000 next-day deposit obligation during the current quarter.** If line 10 for the prior quarter was less than $2,500 but line 10 on this return is $100,000 or more, you must provide a record of your federal tax liability. If you are a monthly schedule depositor, complete the deposit schedule below; if you are a semiweekly schedule depositor, attach Schedule B (Form 941). Go to Part 3.

☐ **You were a monthly schedule depositor for the entire quarter.** Enter your tax liability for each month and total liability for the quarter, then go to Part 3.

Tax liability: **Month 1** ______

Month 2 ______

Month 3 ______

Total liability for quarter ______ **Total must equal line 10.**

☒ **You were a semiweekly schedule depositor for any part of this quarter.** Complete Schedule B (Form 941): Report of Tax Liability for Semiweekly Schedule Depositors, and attach it to Form 941.

Part 3: Tell us about your business. If a question does NOT apply to your business, leave it blank.

17 If your business has closed or you stopped paying wages . . . . . ☐ Check here, and

enter the final date you paid wages ______ .

18 If you are a seasonal employer and you do not have to file a return for every quarter of the year . . . . . ☐ Check here.

Part 4: May we speak with your third-party designee?

Do you want to allow an employee, a paid tax preparer, or another person to discuss this return with the IRS? See instructions for details.

☐ Yes. Designee's name and phone number ______ ______

Select a 5-digit Personal Identification Number (PIN) to use when talking to the IRS. ______

☒ No.

Part 5: Sign here. You MUST complete both pages of Form 941 and SIGN it.

Under penalties of perjury, I declare that I have examined this return, including accompanying schedules and statements, and to the best of my knowledge and belief, it is true, correct, and complete. Declaration of preparer (other than taxpayer) is based on all information of which preparer has any knowledge.

▶ **Sign your name here** Ted Wells

Print your name here: TED WELLS

Print your title here: Owner

Date: 7-31-2012

Best daytime phone ______

2 9412 NTF 2576946 **B129412** Copyright 2012 Greatland/Nelco – Forms Software Only

Paid Preparer Use Only Check if you are self-employed . . . . ☐

Preparer's name		PTIN	
Preparer's signature		Date	
Firm's name (or yours if self-employed)		EIN	
Address		Phone	
City	State	ZIP code	

Completed Form 941 Schedule B

Schedule B (Form 941): Report of Tax Liability for Semiweekly Schedule Depositors

Department of the Treasury -- Internal Revenue Service

OMB No. 1545-0029 970311

Calendar Year 2012

Employer identification number 99-9999988

Name (not your trade name) QUICKCO

Report for this Quarter

- [ ] **1:** January, February, March
- [X] **2:** April, May, June
- [ ] **3:** July, August, September
- [ ] **4:** October, November, December

Use this schedule to show your TAX LIABILITY for the quarter; DO NOT use it to show your deposits. When you file this form with Form 941 or Form 941-SS, DO NOT change your tax liability by adjustments reported on any Forms 941-X. You must fill out this form and attach it to Form 941 or Form 941-SS if you are a semiweekly schedule depositor or became one because your accumulated tax liability on any day was $100,000 or more. Enter your daily tax liability on the numbered space that corresponds to the date wages were paid. See Section 11 in Pub. 15 (Circular E), Employer's Tax Guide, for details.

Month 1

Day	Amount	Day	Amount	Day	Amount	Day	Amount
1		9		17		25	
2		10		18		26	
3		11		19		27	
4		12		20		28	
5		13		21		29	
6		14		22		30	5347.50
7		15	5347.50	23		31	
8		16		24			

Tax liability for Month 1 10695.00

Month 2

Day	Amount	Day	Amount	Day	Amount	Day	Amount
1		9		17		25	
2		10		18		26	
3		11		19		27	
4		12		20		28	
5		13		21		29	
6		14		22		30	
7		15	5347.50	23		31	5347.50
8		16		24			

Tax liability for Month 2 10695.00

Month 3

Day	Amount	Day	Amount	Day	Amount	Day	Amount
1		9		17		25	
2		10		18		26	
3		11		19		27	
4		12		20		28	5347.50
5		13		21		29	
6		14	5347.50	22		30	
7		15		23		31	
8		16		24			

Tax liability for Month 3 10695.00

B11941B

1 941B1 NTF 2575997

Fill in your total liability for the quarter (Month 1 + Month 2 + Month 3) ▶

Total must equal line 10 on Form 941 or Form 941-SS.

Total liability for the quarter 32085.00

For Paperwork Reduction Act Notice, see separate instructions. CAA **Schedule B (Form 941)** (Rev. 6-2011)

Form 941 (Page 1)

Form **941 for 2013: Employer's QUARTERLY Federal Tax Return** 950113
(Rev. January 2013) Department of the Treasury — Internal Revenue Service OMB No. 1545-0029

Employer identification number (EIN) ☐☐ – ☐☐☐☐☐☐☐

Name *(not your trade name)* ________

Trade name *(if any)* ________

Address ________
Number Street Suite or room number
____
City State ZIP code

Report for this Quarter of 2013
(Check one.)

☐ **1:** January, February, March
☐ **2:** April, May, June
☐ **3:** July, August, September
☐ **4:** October, November, December

Instructions and prior year forms are available at *www.irs.gov/form941.*

Read the separate instructions before you complete Form 941. Type or print within the boxes.

Part 1: **Answer these questions for this quarter.**

Line	Description				Box
1	**Number of employees who received wages, tips, or other compensation for the pay period including:** ***Mar. 12*** **(Quarter 1),** ***June 12*** **(Quarter 2),** ***Sept. 12*** **(Quarter 3), or** ***Dec. 12*** **(Quarter 4)**				1
2	**Wages, tips, and other compensation**				2 .
3	**Income tax withheld from wages, tips, and other compensation**				3 .
4	**If no wages, tips, and other compensation are subject to social security or Medicare tax**				☐ **Check and go to line 6.**
		Column 1		**Column 2**	
5a	**Taxable social security wages**	.	× .124 =	.	
5b	**Taxable social security tips**	.	× .124 =	.	
5c	**Taxable Medicare wages & tips**	.	× .029 =	.	
5d	**Taxable wages & tips subject to Additional Medicare Tax withholding**	.	× .009 =	.	
5e	**Add Column 2 from lines 5a, 5b, 5c, and 5d**				5e .
5f	**Section 3121(q) Notice and Demand—Tax due on unreported tips** (see instructions)				5f .
6	**Total taxes before adjustments** (add lines 3, 5e, and 5f)				6 .
7	**Current quarter's adjustment for fractions of cents**				7 .
8	**Current quarter's adjustment for sick pay**				8 .
9	**Current quarter's adjustments for tips and group-term life insurance**				9 .
10	**Total taxes after adjustments.** Combine lines 6 through 9				10 .
11	**Total deposits for this quarter, including overpayment applied from a prior quarter and overpayment applied from Form 941-X or Form 944-X filed in the current quarter**				11 .
12a	**COBRA premium assistance payments** (see instructions)				12a .
12b	**Number of individuals provided COBRA premium assistance**				
13	**Add lines 11 and 12a**				13 .
14	**Balance due.** If line 10 is more than line 13, enter the difference and see instructions				14 .
15	**Overpayment.** If line 13 is more than line 10, enter the difference	.	Check one:	☐ Apply to next return.	☐ Send a refund.

▶ **You MUST complete both pages of Form 941 and SIGN it.** Next ▶

For Privacy Act and Paperwork Reduction Act Notice, see the back of the Payment Voucher. Cat. No. 17001Z Form **941** (Rev. 1-2013)

Form 941 (Page 2)

950213

Name (not your trade name) | Employer identification number (EIN)

Part 2: Tell us about your deposit schedule and tax liability for this quarter.

If you are unsure about whether you are a monthly schedule depositor or a semiweekly schedule depositor, see Pub. 15 (Circular E), section 11.

16 Check one: ☐ **Line 10 on this return is less than $2,500 or line 10 on the return for the prior quarter was less than $2,500, and you did not incur a $100,000 next-day deposit obligation during the current quarter.** If line 10 for the prior quarter was less than $2,500 but line 10 on this return is $100,000 or more, you must provide a record of your federal tax liability. If you are a monthly schedule depositor, complete the deposit schedule below; if you are a semiweekly schedule depositor, attach Schedule B (Form 941). Go to Part 3.

☐ **You were a monthly schedule depositor for the entire quarter.** Enter your tax liability for each month and total liability for the quarter, then go to Part 3.

Tax liability: Month 1 ______ .

Month 2 ______ .

Month 3 ______ .

Total liability for quarter ______ . **Total must equal line 10.**

☐ **You were a semiweekly schedule depositor for any part of this quarter.** Complete Schedule B (Form 941), Report of Tax Liability for Semiweekly Schedule Depositors, and attach it to Form 941.

Part 3: Tell us about your business. If a question does NOT apply to your business, leave it blank.

17 If your business has closed or you stopped paying wages . . . . ☐ Check here, and

enter the final date you paid wages ___/___/___ .

18 If you are a seasonal employer and you do not have to file a return for every quarter of the year . . ☐ Check here.

Part 4: May we speak with your third-party designee?

Do you want to allow an employee, a paid tax preparer, or another person to discuss this return with the IRS? See the instructions for details.

☐ Yes. Designee's name and phone number ______ ______

Select a 5-digit Personal Identification Number (PIN) to use when talking to the IRS. ☐☐☐☐☐

☐ No.

Part 5: Sign here. You MUST complete both pages of Form 941 and SIGN it.

Under penalties of perjury, I declare that I have examined this return, including accompanying schedules and statements, and to the best of my knowledge and belief, it is true, correct, and complete. Declaration of preparer (other than taxpayer) is based on all information of which preparer has any knowledge.

✗ **Sign your name here** ______

Print your name here ______

Print your title here ______

Date ___/___/___

Best daytime phone ______

Paid Preparer Use Only

Check if you are self-employed . . . ☐

Preparer's name		PTIN	
Preparer's signature		Date	/ /
Firm's name (or yours if self-employed)		EIN	
Address		Phone	
City	State	ZIP code	

Page **2** Form **941** (Rev. 1-2013)

Form 941 (Schedule B)

Schedule B (Form 941):

960311

Report of Tax Liability for Semiweekly Schedule Depositors

OMB No. 1545-0029

(Rev. June 2011) Department of the Treasury — Internal Revenue Service

(EIN)
Employer identification number ☐☐ – ☐☐☐☐☐☐☐

Name *(not your trade name)* ______________________

Calendar year ☐☐☐☐ (Also check quarter)

Report for this Quarter...
(Check one.)

☐ **1:** January, February, March
☐ **2:** April, May, June
☐ **3:** July, August, September
☐ **4:** October, November, December

Use this schedule to show your TAX LIABILITY for the quarter; DO NOT use it to show your deposits. When you file this form with Form 941 or Form 941-SS, DO NOT change your tax liability by adjustments reported on any Forms 941-X. You must fill out this form and attach it to Form 941 or Form 941-SS if you are a semiweekly schedule depositor or became one because your accumulated tax liability on any day was $100,000 or more. Write your daily tax liability on the numbered space that corresponds to the date wages were paid. See Section 11 in Pub. 15 (Circular E), Employer's Tax Guide, for details.

Month 1

1	.	9	.	17	.	25	.	Tax liability for Month 1 .
2	.	10	.	18	.	26	.	
3	.	11	.	19	.	27	.	
4	.	12	.	20	.	28	.	
5	.	13	.	21	.	29	.	
6	.	14	.	22	.	30	.	
7	.	15	.	23	.	31	.	
8	.	16	.	24	.			

Month 2

1	.	9	.	17	.	25	.	Tax liability for Month 2 .
2	.	10	.	18	.	26	.	
3	.	11	.	19	.	27	.	
4	.	12	.	20	.	28	.	
5	.	13	.	21	.	29	.	
6	.	14	.	22	.	30	.	
7	.	15	.	23	.	31	.	
8	.	16	.	24	.			

Month 3

1	.	9	.	17	.	25	.	Tax liability for Month 3 .
2	.	10	.	18	.	26	.	
3	.	11	.	19	.	27	.	
4	.	12	.	20	.	28	.	
5	.	13	.	21	.	29	.	
6	.	14	.	22	.	30	.	
7	.	15	.	23	.	31	.	
8	.	16	.	24	.			

Fill in your total liability for the quarter (Month 1 + Month 2 + Month 3) ▶
Total must equal line 10 on Form 941 or Form 941-SS.

Total liability for the quarter .

For Paperwork Reduction Act Notice, see separate instructions. Cat. No. 11967Q **Schedule B (Form 941)** (Rev. 6-2011)

Form 945: Annual Return of Withheld Federal Income Tax

What it is. Form 945 is used to report (1) backup tax under IRC Section 3406 and federal income tax withheld under IRC Section 3402(q); (2) amounts paid as retirement pay for service in the Armed Forces of the United States under IRC Section 3402; (3) certain annuities under IRC Section 3402(o)(1)(B); and (4) pensions, annuities, IRAs, and certain other deferred income under IRC Section 3405. Form 945 is never used to report either wages or nonqualified deferred compensation.

Who must file it. An employer must annually file Form 945 if it withholds backup tax under IRC §3406, or federal income tax from (1) gambling winnings under IRC Section 3402(q); (2) amounts paid as retirement pay for service in the Armed Forces of the United States under IRC Section 3402; (3) certain annuities under IRC Section 3402(o)(1)(B); and (4) pensions, annuities, IRAs, and certain other deferred income under IRC Section 3405.

If an employer has no Form 945 liability in a calendar year, then it is not required to file a 945 for that calendar year.

When it is due. Form 945 must be filed annually and postmarked by the end of the first month following the end of the calendar year (generally, January 31). The 2013 Form 945 must be filed by January 31, 2014 (February 10, 2014 if taxes deposited timely and for the full amount).

Depositing Form 945 taxes. Taxes reported on Form 945 and taxes reported on Form 941 are not combined for purposes of determining when either deposit is due, whether the one-business-day rule applies or whether any safe harbor is applicable. In addition, separate deposits must be made for taxes reported on Form 945 and taxes reported on Form 941.

> **Example:** On Tuesday, January 25, RaCorp, a semiweekly depositor for both 941 and 945 taxes, incurs a 941 deposit obligation of $99,500 and withholds backup tax of $600. The 945 deposit and the 941 deposit are due on Friday, January 28. Notice that although the combined 941 and 945 liabilities exceed $100,000, the one-business-day rule does not apply because 941 taxes are separate from 945 taxes. RaCorp must use separate EFT transmittals for each kind of tax.

Determining the deposit status. An employer determines its deposit status based on the accumulated 945 liabilities in the lookback period. The lookback period for 945 liabilities differs from the 941 lookback period. For 945 deposits, the lookback period is the second calendar year preceding the current calendar year. For example, an employer with $50,000 or less in accumulated 945 liabilities in 2011 will deposit its 945 taxes using the monthly rule in calendar year 2013 (see Section 6). Any monthly depositer who incurs a 945 liability of $100,000 or more is a semiweekly depositor for the remainder of the tax year and the following year.

Making the deposit. Employers making deposits of 945 taxes must designate tax type "945" when making the payment. ***Form 945 taxes must be deposited separately from Form 941 taxes.***

> **PROBLEM 3:** In 2013, DelCo deposits its 941 taxes under the semiweekly rule and its 945 taxes under the monthly rule. On Monday, March 18, it pays wages that result in a 941 deposit obligation of $30,000. On Tuesday, March 19, it withholds backup tax totaling $200. When are these deposits due?
>
> **SOLUTION 3:** DelCo must deposit $30,000 by Friday, March 22 (see Section 6). The backup tax of $200 is deposited on April 15.

Form W-2: Wage and Tax Statement

What it is. The W-2 is the employee's annual summary of taxable wages and taxes withheld. Employees file a copy of the W-2 with their federal and state income tax returns. Copies also are submitted by employers to the Social Security Administration (SSA) with a Form W-3 (transmittal form unless filing electronically). The SSA uses the W-2 to update the employee's retirement earnings account. The SSA also reconciles the W-2 amounts to the 941/944 amounts submitted to the IRS. An inaccurate EIN or employee SSN can result in reduced retirement benefits for the employee and penalties to the employer.

Who receives a W-2. A Form W-2 must be provided to the following:

- Any employee for whom the employer paid wages, withheld federal income or FICA tax or would have withheld income tax had the employee not claimed exempt from federal income tax withholding or claimed more than one withholding allowance. *This rule also applies to an employee who is a child of a sole proprietor.*

- Any employee to whom the employer made payments in cash, property or other benefits in exchange for services provided.
- Any employee for whom the employer received a statement from a third-party payer of sick or disability pay.
- Any former employees for whom the employer paid wages or individuals for whom the employer paid wages in anticipation of employment.

  NOTE: A W-2 is required even when taxes are not withheld and no matter how small the wage amount to report.

When it is due. Employees must receive Copy B, Copy C and Copy 2 of their W-2 by January 31 or the next available business day if January 31 falls on a weekend. Terminated employees must be given their W-2s by January 31 or 30 days from the day they request it, whichever comes first. Form W-2, Copy A, and Form W-3 (explained below) must be postmarked by the last day in February. If the due date falls on a weekend or federal legal holiday, it is due on the next business day.

NOTE: For employers filing their Forms W-2 with SSA electronically (i.e., via the Internet) the due date is extended to March 31.

NOTE: Some states specify a different due date for the employee Copy 2. Check with the appropriate state taxing authority. Employers with 250 or more Forms W-2 (or 250 or more Forms W-2c) at the end of the year must file W-2 (or W-2c) data with the SSA electronically. Most states require magnetic media or electronic filing of Forms W-2 Copy 1 if a certain threshold is met.

> **PROBLEM 4:** Edna terminates on August 30, 2013. On her last day of work she requests her 2013 W-2. By when must she receive it?
>
> **SOLUTION 4:** No later than September 30—30 days from the date of the request.
>
> **EXAMPLE:** Rod Runner, an employee of QuickCo, earned $25,000 in FIT and FICA (OASDI and HI) wages in 2012. FICA tax withheld was $1,050.00 and FITW was $3,750. His SSN is 666-66-6666. Rod Runner's completed W-2 is shown on page 131. After reviewing the completed W-2 on page 131, fill in the blank form on page 132 to become familiar with using it.

Completed Form W-2 (Rod Runner)

a Employee's social security no.	**Copy B--To Be Filed With Employee's FEDERAL Tax Return.** OMB No. 1545-0008	
b Employer identification number (EIN): 99-9999988	**1** Wages, tips, other comp.: 25000.00	**2** Federal income tax withheld: 3750.00
c Employer's name, address, and ZIP code: QUICKCO 101 LUCKY LANE BLACK JACK, NV 88888	**3** Social security wages: 25000.00	**4** Social security tax withheld: 1050.00
	5 Medicare wages and tips: 25000.00	**6** Medicare tax withheld: 362.50
	7 Social security tips	**8** Allocated tips
d Control number	**9**	**10** Dependent care benefits
e Employee's name, address, and ZIP code: ROD R. RUNNER 1402 Wolverine Desert, NV 88888	**11** Nonqualified plans	**12a** See instructions for box 12 (Code)
	13 Statutory employee ☐ Retirement plan ☐ Third-party sick pay ☐	**12b** (Code)
	14 Other	**12c** (Code)
		12d (Code)

15 State	Employer's state ID number	**16** State wages, tips, etc.	**17** State income tax	**18** Local wages, tips, etc.	**19** Local income tax	**20** Locality name
NV	6827-1	25000.00				

Form **W-2** **Wage and Tax Statement** **2012** 38-2099803 Department of the Treasury -- Internal Revenue Service

This information is being furnished to the Internal Revenue Service.

2 **BW2BC** NTF 2576749 **BW2EEBC** Copyright 2012 Greatland/Nelco – Forms Software Only

NOTE: When completing Form W-3, assume that wages were paid in more than one state and enter an "X" in box 15. Also be certain to check "Kind of Employer" at the top of the form. For-profit private employers check the box "None Apply." See page 134.

Extensions: To request a filing extension of Copy A of the W-2, complete IRS Form 8809. To request an extension of the date on which W-2 copies are due to employees, write a letter to the IRS—but expect to be refused.

Form W-2

22222	Void ☐	**a** Employee's social security number	**For Official Use Only ▶** **OMB No. 1545-0008**

b Employer identification number (EIN)	**1** Wages, tips, other compensation	**2** Federal income tax withheld
c Employer's name, address, and ZIP code	**3** Social security wages	**4** Social security tax withheld
	5 Medicare wages and tips	**6** Medicare tax withheld
	7 Social security tips	**8** Allocated tips
d Control number	**9**	**10** Dependent care benefits
e Employee's first name and initial · Last name · Suff.	**11** Nonqualified plans	**12a** See instructions for box 12 Code
	13 Statutory employee ☐ Retirement plan ☐ Third-party sick pay ☐	**12b** Code
	14 Other	**12c** Code
f Employee's address and ZIP code		**12d** Code

15 State · Employer's state ID number	**16** State wages, tips, etc.	**17** State income tax	**18** Local wages, tips, etc.	**19** Local income tax	**20** Locality name

Form **W-2** **Wage and Tax Statement** **2012**

Department of the Treasury—Internal Revenue Service

For Privacy Act and Paperwork Reduction Act Notice, see the separate instructions.

Cat. No. 10134D

Copy A For Social Security Administration — Send this entire page with Form W-3 to the Social Security Administration; photocopies are **not** acceptable.

Do Not Cut, Fold, or Staple Forms on This Page

Form W-3: Transmittal of Wage and Tax Statements

What it is. Form W-3 is both a transmittal form for sending W-2s to the SSA and an annual reconciliation of wage and tax information. W-3 data must equal the total of attached Forms W-2 and the Forms 941 filed for the year with respect to wages, tips, and other compensation, FICA taxable wages, FICA tax withheld, federal income tax withheld, and qualified retirement plan benefits reported in box 12 of Form W-2.

Who files it. All employers filing paper Forms W-2 with the SSA.

When it is due: The W-3 and accompanying Forms W-2, Copy A, are filed with the SSA by the last day of February. A W-3 is not used when filing Form W-2 data electronically. The due date for electronically submitted Forms W-2 is March 31. If the due date falls on a Saturday, Sunday or a federal legal holiday, they are due on the next business day.

Where to send it. It must be sent to the SSA Data Operations Center specified on the front of the form.

> **EXAMPLE:** QuickCo issued a total of 15 W-2s for tax year 2012. Total wages were $360,000. FITW was $82,800, Social Security wages were $325,000, and Social Security tax (at 4.2%) was $13,650. Medicare wages were $360,000, and Medicare tax (at 1.45%) was $5,220. Total Social Security wages reported on its 941s for the year were $325,000, and total Medicare wages reported on its 941s were $360,000. On page 134 is an example of how QuickCo completes Form W-3 for 2012. After reviewing the completed W-3 on page 134, fill in the blank form on page 135 to become familiar with using it.

Completed W-3 (QuickCo)

DO NOT STAPLE

33333	a Control number	**For Official Use Only ▶** **OMB No. 1545-0008**

b Kind of Payer (Check one) ▶ 941 [X] Military [ ] 943 [ ] 944 [ ] CT-1 [ ] Hshld. emp. [ ] Medicare govt. emp. [ ]

Kind of Employer (Check one) ▶ None apply [X] 501c non-govt. [ ] State/local non-501c [ ] State/local 501c [ ] Federal govt. [ ]

Third-party sick pay (Check if applicable) [ ]

c Total no. of Forms W-2 15	d Establishment number	1 Wages, tips, other compensation 360000.00	2 Federal income tax withheld 82800.00
e Employer identification number (EIN) 99-9999988		3 Social security wages 325000.00	4 Social security tax withheld 13650.00
f Employer's name QUICKCO		5 Medicare wages and tips 360000.00	6 Medicare tax withheld 5220.00
101 LUCKY LANE BLACK JACK, NV 88888 g Employer's address and ZIP code		7 Social security tips	8 Allocated tips
		9	10 Dependent care benefits
		11 Nonqualified plans	12a Deferred compensation
h Other EIN used this year		13 For third-party sick pay use only	12b
15 State NV	Employer's state ID number 6827-1	14 Income tax withheld by payer of third-party sick pay	
16 State wages, tips, etc. 360000.00	17 State income tax	18 Local wages, tips, etc.	19 Local income tax
Contact person		Telephone number	For Official Use Only
Email address		Fax number	**0 0 0 0/1034**

Under penalties of perjury, I declare that I have examined this return and accompanying documents and, to the best of my knowledge and belief, they are true, correct, and complete.

Signature ▶ Ted Wells Title ▶ Owner Date ▶ 2-27-2013

2 W3A NTF 2577027 Copyright 2012 Greatland/Nelco – Forms Software Only

Form **W-3 Transmittal of Wage and Tax Statements** **2012** 38-2099803 Department of the Treasury Internal Revenue Service

Send this entire page with the entire Copy A page of Form(s) W-2 to the Social Security Administration (SSA).
Photocopies are not acceptable. Do not send Form W-3 if you filed electronically with the SSA.
Do not send any payment (cash, checks, money orders, etc.) with Forms W-2 and W-3.

Form W-3

DO NOT STAPLE

33333	a Control number	For Official Use Only ▶ OMB No. 1545-0008

b **Kind of Payer** (Check one) ▶	941 ☐ / CT-1 ☐	Military ☐ / Hshld. emp. ☐	943 ☐ / Medicare govt. emp. ☐	944 ☐
Kind of Employer (Check one) ▶	None apply ☐ / State/local non-501c ☐	501c non-govt. ☐ / State/local 501c ☐	Federal govt. ☐	Third-party sick pay (Check if applicable) ☐

c Total number of Forms W-2	d Establishment number
1 Wages, tips, other compensation	2 Federal income tax withheld
e Employer identification number (EIN)	
3 Social security wages	4 Social security tax withheld
f Employer's name	
5 Medicare wages and tips	6 Medicare tax withheld
7 Social security tips	8 Allocated tips
9	10 Dependent care benefits
11 Nonqualified plans	12a Deferred compensation
g Employer's address and ZIP code	
h Other EIN used this year	
13 For third-party sick pay use only	12b
15 State	Employer's state ID number
14 Income tax withheld by payer of third-party sick pay	
16 State wages, tips, etc.	17 State income tax
18 Local wages, tips, etc.	19 Local income tax
Contact person	Telephone number
Email address	Fax number
For Official Use Only	

Under penalties of perjury, I declare that I have examined this return and accompanying documents and, to the best of my knowledge and belief, they are true, correct, and complete.

Signature ▶ Title ▶ Date ▶

Form **W-3** Transmittal of Wage and Tax Statements **2013** Department of the Treasury Internal Revenue Service

Send this entire page with the entire Copy A page of Form(s) W-2 to the Social Security Administration (SSA). Photocopies are not acceptable. Do not send Form W-3 if you filed electronically with the SSA.
Do not send any payment (cash, checks, money orders, etc.) with Forms W-2 and W-3.

Reminder

Separate instructions. See the 2013 General Instructions for Forms W-2 and W-3 for information on completing this form.

Purpose of Form

A Form W-3 Transmittal is completed only when paper Copy A of Form(s) W-2, Wage and Tax Statement, is being filed. Do not file Form W-3 alone. Do not file Form W-3 for Form(s) W-2 that were submitted electronically to the SSA (see below). All paper forms **must** comply with IRS standards and be machine readable. Photocopies are **not** acceptable. Use a Form W-3 even if only one paper Form W-2 is being filed. Make sure both the Form W-3 and Form(s) W-2 show the correct tax year and Employer Identification Number (EIN). Make a copy of this form and keep it with Copy D (For Employer) of Form(s) W-2 for your records. The IRS recommends retaining copies of these forms for four years.

E-Filing

The SSA strongly suggests employers report Form W-3 and Forms W-2 Copy A electronically instead of on paper. The SSA provides two free e-filing options on its Business Services Online (BSO) website:

- **W-2 Online.** Use fill-in forms to create, save, print, and submit up to 50 Forms W-2 at a time to the SSA.
- **File Upload.** Upload wage files to the SSA you have created using payroll or tax software that formats the files according to the SSA's *Specifications for Filing Forms W-2 Electronically (EFW2).*

W-2 Online fill-in forms or file uploads will be on time if submitted by March 31, 2014. For more information, go to *www.socialsecurity.gov/employer* and select "First Time Filers" or "Returning Filers" under "BEFORE YOU FILE."

When To File

Mail Form W-3 with Copy A of Form(s) W-2 by February 28, 2014.

Where To File Paper Forms

Send this entire page with the entire Copy A page of Form(s) W-2 to:

Social Security Administration
Data Operations Center
Wilkes-Barre, PA 18769-0001

Note. If you use "Certified Mail" to file, change the ZIP code to "18769-0002." If you use an IRS-approved private delivery service, add "ATTN: W-2 Process, 1150 E. Mountain Dr." to the address and change the ZIP code to "18702-7997." See Publication 15 (Circular E), Employer's Tax Guide, for a list of IRS-approved private delivery services.

For Privacy Act and Paperwork Reduction Act Notice, see the separate instructions.

Cat. No. 10159Y

QUIZ 1 FEDERAL EMPLOYMENT REPORTING FORMS AND DUE DATES

Problem I.

Indicate the due dates for each return or information statement.

1. Form 940, assuming the employer did not make FUTA deposits by the filing deadline. ________________
2. Date by which each current employee must receive copies of the W-2, Copy B. ________________
3. Form 941 for the second quarter, assuming the 10-day extension does not apply. ________________
4. Form W-3. ________________
5. Form 945. ________________

Problem II.

Indicate True or False for these statements.

1. A parent has no FUTA liability for an employed child regardless of the child's age.

   a. True b. False

2. A child has no FUTA liability for an employed parent regardless of the parent's age.

   a. True b. False

3. An employer with 10 employees has no FUTA liability.

   a. True b. False

4. The W-3 is filed with the IRS.

   a. True   b. False

5. The 940 report is filed annually.

   a. True   b. False

Problem III.

Multiple choice. Circle the correct answer.

1. An employer must deposit FUTA tax if the undeposited amount at the end of the quarter exceeds:

   a. $100   b. $500   c. $1,500   d. $3,000

2. A child employed by a parent is exempt from FUTA tax if under what age?

   a. 18   b. 16   c. 21   d. 19

3. Which of the following forms serves as the annual reconciliation of wage and tax information?

   a. 941   b. 940   c. W-2   d. W-3

4. Effective January 1, 2013, the maximum FUTA tax rate is:

   a. 5.4%   b. 6.0%   c. 0.6%   d. 7.65%

5. The FUTA wage limit for 2013 is:

   a. $106,800   b. $1,500   c. $7,000   d. $10,000

6. Backup withholding tax is reported as which kind of tax?

   a. 940   b. Sch. A   c. 941   d. 945

7. Form 944 is filed:

   a. quarterly   b. annually   c. monthly   d. semi-weekly

QUIZ 1 Solutions and Explanations

Problem I.

1. January 31
   For the previous tax year
2. January 31
   For the previous tax year
3. July 31
4. February 28 or 29 (unless filing Forms W-2 electronically)
   For the previous tax year
5. January 31 (or February 10 if all deposits were made timely)
   For the previous tax year

Problem II.

1. False
2. True
3. False
4. False
5. True

Problem III.

1. b
2. c
3. d
4. b
5. c
6. d
7. b

Quiz 2 FEDERAL EMPLOYMENT REPORTING FORMS AND DUE DATES

Problem I.

Choose among the following forms for each statement:

W-2-Copy B **940** **941** **W-2-Copy A** **945**

1. ______________ is used to report an employer's FUTA tax liability.
2. ______________ is used to report wage and tax information to employees.
3. ______________ is used to report wage and tax information to the IRS.
4. ______________ is used to report federal income tax withheld from nonwage income.
5. ______________ is used by the SSA to update an employee's retirement earnings account.

Problem II.

Indicate True or False for these statements.

1. Employers submit wage details by employee on a 940.

   a. True b. False

2. The maximum annual FUTA tax an employer pays in 2013 for each covered employee earning $7,000 or more is $42.

   a. True b. False

3. An employer that makes all federal tax deposits on time may file its W-3 on March 10.

   a. True b. False

4. Employers do not have to fill out a W-2 for employees who were paid wages but no federal income tax or Social Security tax was withheld.

   a. True b. False

5. If a due date for a federal return falls on a Saturday, Sunday or federal legal holiday, it is not due until the next business day.

   a. True b. False

Problem III.

Multiple choice. Circle the correct answer.

1. Effective January 1, 2013, the minimum FUTA rate is:

   a. 0.6% b. 5.4% c. 6.0% d. 7.65%

2. For an employer that did not make all its deposits on time, the due date for a second quarter 941 is:

   a. June 30
   b. July 31
   c. August 10
   d. August 15

3. An employer must pay FUTA tax quarterly if its quarterly liability exceeds:

   a. $1,500 b. $100 c. $500 d. $7,000

4. An employer's quarterly reconciliation of wage and tax data is made on a:

   a. 940 b. 941 c. W-2 d. W-3

5. Which of the following is not exempt from FUTA tax?

   a. a parent employed by a child over age 18
   b. a spouse employed by a spouse
   c. a stepparent employed by a child over age 21
   d. a child over age 21 employed by a parent

6. Which of the following forms is submitted annually?

   a. Form 8109
   b. Form 945
   c. Schedule B
   d. Form 941

QUIZ 2 Solutions and Explanations

Problem I.

1. 940
2. W-2, Copy B
3. 941
4. 945
5. W-2, Copy A

Problem II.

1. False
2. False
   $42.00 is the minimum tax.
3. False
4. False
5. True

Problem III.

1. a
2. b
3. c
4. b
5. d
6. b

Section 8
WHEN WAGES BECOME TAXABLE

Introduction

There is often a lapse of at least a week between the time wages are earned and the time they are actually paid. For instance, an employee who is paid biweekly works during week 1 and week 2 but is not paid until week 3.

Under IRS regulations, wages are taxable when *constructively received by* (actually made available to) employees, regardless of when earned. This is known as the principle of "constructive receipt."

PROBLEM 1: AccountCorp pays employees weekly. Employees who work from February 5 through February 9 are paid for this work on February 13. When are these wages subject to federal income tax withholding (FITW) and FICA withholding?

SOLUTION 1: On February 13. These wages are subject to FITW and FICA on the day that they are paid. Thus, taxes are withheld on February 13. The employer's FICA tax liability also is incurred on February 13, the day that wages are actually paid to employees.

Unclaimed Checks

Say that you prepare paychecks on December 27, 2013. However, some employees are on vacation and do not claim their checks until 2014. Are the wages taxable in 2013 or 2014?

The answer is 2013. Under the rule of constructive receipt, wages are constructively (actually) received when funds are available to employees without substantial limitation. If paychecks are available to employees, but they do not pick them up, wages are taxable on the day when they could have claimed the checks.

PROBLEM 2: Anthony is terminated on payday, December 27, 2013. Although his check is ready for him on that day, he does not pick it up until January 17, 2014. Should these wages be reported on Anthony's W-2 for 2013 or 2014?

SOLUTION 2: Generally speaking, the wages should be reported on Anthony's W-2 for 2013 because the paycheck was available to him in that year. It was his choice to take receipt on January 17, 2014.

PROBLEM 3: ABC Corp. failed to prepare a paycheck for new hire Margaret on December 31, 2013. The employer discovered the error on December 31, but did not prepare her paycheck until January 2, 2014. Should the company include these wages in Margaret's taxable income for 2013 or 2014?

SOLUTION 3: These wages should be included in her taxable income for 2014—the year in which they were made available to her.

Selecting the Correct Annual Tax Rate

The federal income tax and/or FICA tax rates and limits generally change every year. For instance, in 2012, employee OASDI was 4.2% of the first $110,100 in wages. For 2013, the rate is 6.2% of the first $113,700. The employer OASDI rate is 6.2% for 2012 and 2013.

Because the federal income tax and FICA tax rates and limits can and often do change every year, the rule of constructive receipt is particularly important at the end of the year.

EXAMPLE: Connie is paid $114,700 from January 1, 2013, through December 20, 2013. From December 20, 2013, to December 31, 2013, she earns $1,000 but is not paid until January 3, 2014. The $1,000 paid in 2014 is subject to Social Security tax, even though her last $1,000 in wages earned during 2013 exceeded the 2013 maximum OASDI wage limit of $113,700.

The rule of constructive receipt is important for another reason. Each employee's federal and state income tax liability is based on wages paid for the year. The higher the wage amount reported on an employee's W-2, the more federal and state income tax the employee likely owes.

PROBLEM 4: Edward's year-to-date FICA taxable wages on December 13, 2013, were $113,700. He earned an additional $500 from December 14 through December 31, but was not paid this $500 until January 3, 2014. How much of the $500 payment is subject to FICA (OASDI and HI)?

SOLUTION 4: The full $500 is subject to FICA (combined OASDI and HI taxes) because the wages were not received until 2014.

PROBLEM 5: Ricardo's year-to-date FICA taxable wages as of December 27, 2013, were $51,000. He earned an additional $500 from December 29 through December 31 but was not paid the $500 until January 3, 2014. What amount does the employer report on Ricardo's 2013 Form W-2: $51,000 or $51,500?

SOLUTION 5: The employer reports $51,000 for 2013 because the additional $500, though earned in 2013, was not paid until 2014.

Postdating and Backdating Paychecks

Because of the favorable or unfavorable effect that the rule of constructive receipt has on tax liability, employees and employers sometimes request that checks be either postdated or backdated.

EXAMPLE: Under company policy, employee bonuses are payable on December 31, 2013. To help highly paid employees defer federal income tax, the employer postdates these checks to January 3, 2014, but distributes them to employees on December 31, 2013. Under the rule of constructive receipt, these wages are taxable when made available to employees (2013), regardless of the date of the paycheck. Although a check date may seem to be proof of when wages were received, the IRS can easily detect postdating by reviewing bank transactions.

PROBLEM 6: Each January 15, HessCo pays bonuses for the previous year. All employees receiving a bonus reached their OASDI limit in 2013. To avoid withholding FICA on 2014 bonuses, HessCo backdates bonus checks to December 31, 2013, but distributes them to employees on January 15, 2014. Are these checks considered wages for 2013 or 2014?

SOLUTION 6: The date of the check does not alter the facts. Because bonus checks were not made available to employees until 2014, they must be treated as 2014 wages (subject to 2014 FICA and FITW rates).

Postponing Payment of Wages

Maureen is in a high income tax bracket in 2013 and expects to be in a lower income tax bracket in 2014. She asks her employer to pay her December 2013 wages in January 2014. What should the employer do?

Unless the company has a "formal deferred compensation plan," taxes should not arbitrarily be deferred by postponing wage payments.

> **EXAMPLE:** Wesley asks his employer to delay his November and December paychecks until January 2014. His employer agrees to delay payment of the $2,000, and he is paid in 2014 instead of 2013. Without a formal deferred compensation plan covering Wesley, his employer may be required to report and tax this $2,000 as though it were paid in 2013.

Salary Advances and Overpayments

Because wages are taxable when constructively received, regardless of when earned, a salary advance or overpayment of wages is taxable when paid to the employee, even though wages are not yet earned.

When an employee repays an overpayment or advance, his or her gross taxable wages will be reduced by the amount of the repayment *provided the repayment occurs in the same tax year as the advance.* If a salary advance is repaid in a year after the year in which the advance is paid, the repayment cannot be deducted from gross wages. Instead, the "claim-of-right rule" applies. Under the claim-of-right rule, complex reporting rules apply for both the employee and the employer. Speak to an accountant or legal advisor for more information.

> **EXAMPLE:** In July, Randy receives a salary advance of $500 less withheld taxes. Randy agrees to repay the advance by having it deducted from his August paycheck, which would normally be $1,500. His employer will withhold taxes on $1,000 in August ($1,500 less the repaid advance of $500).

QUIZ 1 WHEN WAGES BECOME TAXABLE

Problem I.

How much FICA would you withhold from the following wage payments?

1. John is paid biweekly. On January 11, 2013, he is paid $800 for the biweekly period December 24, 2012, to January 4, 2013. As of December 24, he has had year-to-date FICA tax withheld on wages of $113,100. How much FICA should be withheld from his $800 paycheck, and in which calendar year would it be withheld? $__________ year __________

2. When paychecks are distributed on December 31, 2012, Margaret is ill. She picks up her paycheck for $425 on January 2, 2013. As of December 31, 2012 she has had year-to-date FICA tax withheld on $145,300. How much FICA should be withheld from her $425 paycheck, and in which calendar year would it be withheld? $__________ year__________

3. On December 17, 2013, Jose receives a partial salary advance of $50 from which FITW and FICA are withheld. He repays it in full by having it deducted from his December 31, 2013, paycheck of $900. How much FICA should be withheld from the December 31 payment, assuming that Jose did not reach the OASDI limit in 2013 and that a Social Security withholding rate of 6.2% applies? $__________

4. On December 31, 2012, Tom receives a $500 paycheck postdated to January 2, 2013. How much FICA should be withheld assuming that he did not reach his FICA limit in 2012 or 2013, the Social Security withholding rate is 4.2% for 2012 and 6.2% for 2013, and in which calendar year would it be withheld?
   $__________ year __________

Problem II.

Fill in the blanks.

1. Under IRS regulations, wages are subject to tax when ______________ received.

2. Under the rule of constructive receipt, wages are taxable when funds are ______________ to employees.

3. Under the rule of constructive receipt, wages are taxable when ______________, regardless of when ______________.

4. A wage or salary advance repayment from which FITW and FICA was withheld is ______________ from gross wages before computing the amount of withholding when repaid in the same calendar year.

Problem III.

Multiple choice. Circle the correct answer.

1. The principle that governs when wages become taxable is:

   a. Generally Accepted Accounting Principal (GAAP)
   b. cash accounting
   c. accrual accounting
   d. constructive receipt

2. On December 31, 2012, Elmer received a paycheck dated January 2, 2013. The Social Security withholding wage rate applied to this payment is:

   a. 5.65% b. 6.2% c. 4.2% d. 7.65%

3. Wages earned in 2012, but paid in 2013 are subject to a Social Security withholding rate of:

   a. 5.65% b. 6.2% c. 4.2% d. 7.65%

QUIZ 1 Solutions and Explanations

Problem I.

1. $61.20 from 2013 wages
   Wages are taxable in the year paid—not the year earned.
   To calculate:

   OASDI: $800 × 6.2% = $49.60

   HI: $800 × 1.45% = $11.60

   $49.60 (OASDI) + $11.60 (HI) = $61.20

2. $6.16 from 2012 wages
   To calculate:

   $145,300 exceeds the 2012 OASDI wage limit of $110,100.

   There is no HI wage limit, therefore $425 × 1.45% = $6.16

3. $65.03
   To calculate:

   $900 – $50 (advance) = $850 (FICA taxable)

   OASDI: $850 × 6.2% = $52.70

   HI: $850 × 1.45% = $12.33

   $52.70 (OASDI) + $12.33 (HI) = $65.03

4. $28.25 from 2012 wages
   To calculate:

   $500 × 5.65% = $28.25

Problem II.

1. constructively
2. available
3. paid, earned
4. deducted

Problem III.

1. d
2. c
3. b

QUIZ 2 WHEN WAGES BECOME TAXABLE

Problem I.

How much FICA would you withhold from the following wage payments?

1. Jim is paid weekly. On January 4, 2013, he is paid $950 for the weekly period ending December 28, 2012. His year-to-date FICA taxable wages as of December 28, 2012 were $113,400. How much FICA should be withheld from his $950 paycheck?
   $_______________ year _______________

2. Evelyn's company pays wages on December 31, 2012. But she was on vacation and did not obtain her paycheck until January 2, 2013. The check is for $525. How much FICA should be withheld from this $525 if her 2012 year-to-date wages before the payment were $112,000, and in which calendar year would it be withheld? $_______________
   year _______________

3. On December 3, 2013, Juan is given a salary advance of $200, from which FICA and FITW are withheld. He cannot repay it until December 31, 2013. His December 31st wages before repayment are $2,000. How much FICA should be withheld from this $2,000, assuming that he did not reach the OASDI limit and the Social Security withholding rate is 6.2% on December 31, 2013? $_______________ year of withholding
   ____

4. On December 31, 2012, Ron picks up his paycheck of $400 postdated to January 2, 2013, per his request. How much FICA should be withheld from the $400, assuming that he reached the OASDI limit in 2012?
   $_______________ year of withholding _______________

Problem II.

Fill in the blanks.

1. The rule of constructive receipt is particularly important at the _______________ of the year.

2. Federal income tax and FICA tax are withheld from wages in the year that they are _______________ _______________ by employees.

3. Wages should not be deferred unless the employee is covered by a _______________ _______________ _______________ _______________.

Problem III.

Multiple choice. Circle the correct answer.

1. Parker receives a paycheck backdated to December 30, 2012, on January 3, 2013. What is the Social Security tax rate? _______________.

   a. 5.65% b. 4.2% c. 6.2% d. 7.65%

2. Constructive receipt is based on the principle that wages are taxable when:
   a. the employee earns the wages
   b. the check is dated
   c. the wages are made available
   d. the employer mails the paychecks

3. A payment of an advance is taxable when the employee:
   a. receives the advance
   b. earns the advance
   c. terminates
   d. repays the advance

QUIZ 2 Solutions and Explanations

Problem I.

1. $72.68 from 2013 wages
   To calculate:

   OASDI tax: $950 × 6.2% = $58.90

   HI tax: $950 × 1.45% = $13.78

   $58.90 (OASDI) + $13.78 (HI) = $72.68 FICA tax

2. $7.61 from 2012 wages
   To calculate:

   $525 × 1.45% = $7.61

   OASDI limit was $110,100 in 2012. Withhold Medicare tax only.

3. $137.70 from 2013 wages
   To calculate:

   $2,000 (wage payment) – $200 (repayment of advance) = $1,800

   OASDI tax: $1,800 × 6.2% = $111.60

   HI tax: $1,800 × 1.45% = $26.10

   $111.60 (OASDI) + $26.10 (HI) = $137.70 FICA tax

4. $5.80 from 2012 wages
   To calculate:

   OASDI limit was $110,100 for 2012. Withhold HI tax only.

   HI tax: $400 × 1.45% = $5.80

Problem II.

1. end

2. constructively received

3. formal deferred compensation plan

Problem III.

1. c
   The wages are taxable in the year actually received—in this case, 2013.

2. c

3. a

Section 9
OTHER REPORTING RULES

Introduction

State employment reporting requirements vary nationwide. There are also additional federal employment reporting requirements, as follows.

State Unemployment Reporting

Like the federal government, each state imposes an unemployment tax on employers. Unlike FUTA, however, state unemployment insurance (SUI) returns generally are filed quarterly, due by the end of the month following the end of the quarter. The tax rate varies by employer and is generally based on the employer's "unemployment experience"—the amount of benefits claimed against the employer's account weighed against the unemployment taxes paid and/or taxable payroll reported. Employers usually receive a notice from the state indicating their SUI tax rate for the year. The SUI taxable wage limit varies by state but is generally the same for all employers in the state. An employer's failure to pay timely the correct state unemployment tax may result in loss of some or all of its FUTA credit (up to 5.4%). In addition, employers in states that have failed to timely repay their federal unemployment insurance trust fund loans are subject to a FUTA credit reduction, effectively raising their FUTA tax.

Annual State Wage and Tax Returns

Like the federal government, most states that have an income tax require that a transmittal form (similar to the W-3) accompany copies of the state W-2 (Copy 1). Most states require employers to submit a copy of the state W-2 by the last day of February (several states extend the due date to March 31 if Forms W-2 are submitted electronically). The following are exceptions (for tax year 2012):

Due January 31: District of Columbia, Kentucky, Pennsylvania, Puerto Rico, and Wisconsin.

Due February 1: Nebraska.

No requirements (no state income tax): Alaska, Florida, Nevada, New Hampshire, South Dakota, Tennessee, Texas, Washington, and Wyoming.

State Due Dates for Employee Copies of the State W-2

All states, except those indicated below (for tax year 2012), require that employees receive copies of their state W-2 (Copy 2) by January 31, the same due date as the federal W-2.

Due February 15: Nebraska, New Jersey, New York, and West Virginia.

No requirements (no state income tax): Alaska, Florida, Nevada, New Hampshire, South Dakota, Tennessee, Texas, Washington, and Wyoming.

Form 1099 Reporting: Filing Requirements and Due Dates

Generally, the 1099 must be submitted to the IRS and the payee whenever payments totaling $600 or more are made for interest, fees, commissions, dividends, rents, royalties, annuities, pensions, profits, or other kinds of nonemployee compensation. It must be provided to recipients by January 31 following the year in which the amounts are paid. For example, Forms 1099 for 2012 were due to recipients by January 31, 2013.

The IRS must receive a copy of each 1099 by February 28 following the year it covers. If Forms 1099 are filed electronically (i.e., via the Internet), the due date is extended to March 31. Form 1096 is used to summarize and transmit copies of Forms 1099 to the IRS. A separate 1096 should be used for each *kind* of 1099 submitted and for each employer identification number. For example, one 1096 is used to file the 1099-MISC, another to file the 1099-DIV. Summary information on the 1096 should reconcile with the Forms 1099 attached. A return that is out of balance may provoke a response from the IRS and result in tax assessments and penalties.

Variations of Forms 1099

The following is a brief description of various Forms 1099:

Form 1099-MISC. Used to report payments of $600 or more for rents, commissions, fees, prizes and awards, royalties, and other nonemployee compensation. Also used to report wages and/or accrued vacation pay given to the estate of a deceased employee and "golden parachute" payments made to nonemployees.

1099-DIV. Used by all corporations and regulated investment companies to report distributions of:

- $10 or more in gross dividends and other distributions of stock;
- withheld foreign tax eligible for the recipient's foreign tax credit on dividends and other distributions of stock; or
- distributions made as part of a liquidation.

NOTE: Patronage dividends are reported on the 1099-PATR.

1099-INT. Used to report:

- interest of $10 or more paid on, or credited to, earnings from savings and loan associations, credit unions, bank deposits, corporate bonds, etc.;
- interest of $600 or more paid in the course of a trade or business;
- forfeited interest due to premature withdrawals of time deposits;
- foreign tax eligible for the recipient's foreign tax credit withheld and paid on interest; and
- payments of any interest to bearer of certificates of deposit.

1099-R. Used to report all distributions from profit-sharing and retirement plans and Individual Retirement Accounts (IRAs).

Electronic Media Reporting of Federal W-2 and 1099

An employer with 250 or more Forms W-2 (or W-2c) must submit them to the SSA electronically or on the Internet. Similarly, the IRS requires electronic reporting if filing 250 or more of each type of form (e.g. 1099-MISC). For Forms W-2 electronic reporting information visit the SSA's Website at *www.socialsecurity.gov*. For details on filing Forms 1099 electronically, see IRS Publication 1220, available on the IRS Website at *www.irs.gov*.

NOTE: Some states also require that Forms W-2 and 1099 be filed magnetically or electronically when a certain threshold is reached. Contact your state taxing authority for details.

QUIZ 1 OTHER REPORTING RULES

Problem I.

Mark the following statements True or False.

1. In all states, employers are required to submit copies of Form W-2 (Copy 1) to the state by February 28.

   a. True   b. False

2. State unemployment returns are filed annually with the state.

   a. True   b. False

3. A 1099-MISC is used to report professional fees paid to an employer's unincorporated attorney.

   a. True   b. False

Problem II.

Match the correct form with each description.

1099-DIV   **1099-MISC**   **1096**

1. Used to transmit copies of information statements to the IRS: ______________

2. Used to report dividends on stock: ______________

3. Used to report "golden parachute" payments to nonemployees: ______________

QUIZ 1 Solutions and Explanations

Problem I.

1. False
   There are many exceptions; see the list on pages 155–156.

2. False
   State unemployment tax returns are filed quarterly.

3. True

Problem II.

1. 1096

2. 1099-DIV

3. 1099-MISC

QUIZ 2 OTHER REPORTING RULES

Problem I.

Mark each statement True or False.

1. States must receive copies of state Forms W-2 (Copy 1) no later than February 1 following the year covered by the W-2.

   a. True b. False

2. A recipient of nonemployee compensation should receive a copy of the Form 1099 no later than February 28.

   a. True b. False

3. A 1099-R is used to report all distributions from a profit-sharing or IRA account.

   a. True b. False

4. State unemployment tax generally is paid quarterly.

   a. True b. False

5. The state unemployment tax rate is the same for all employers in the same state.

   a. True b. False

Problem II.

Indicate the due dates for each return.

1. Copy of the state W-2 in Wisconsin: ________________
2. Copy of the state W-2 to employees in New Jersey: ________________
3. Copy of the 1099-INT to the recipient: ________________
4. Copy of paper Form 1099-MISC to the IRS: ________________
5. Copy of paper 1096 to the IRS: ________________

QUIZ 2 Solutions and Explanations

Problem I.

1. False
   Due date varies by state.

2. False
   The correct date is January 31.

3. True

4. True

5. False
   State rates vary by employer due to experience, but state taxable wage limits are generally the same for a specific year for all employees working in the state.

Problem II.

1. January 31

2. February 15

3. January 31

4. February 28

5. February 28

Section 10
PAYROLL ENTRIES

Introduction

Each time an employer issues paychecks to its employees, it records in the payroll register the employee's gross wages or salary, withholding taxes, and other deductions (health insurance, contributions to pension plans, union dues, etc.). The appropriate entries, termed the "payroll distribution," are made in the proper general ledger accounts.

Payroll Distribution—The Payroll Register

Figure 10-1 on page 164 shows a payroll register. It illustrates the basic elements that are recorded in a payroll register and the details used to record entries to the proper general ledger accounts:

1. Date of payroll
2. Check number
3. Employee's name
4. Employee's Social Security number
5. Gross wages or salary
6. Social Security wages (OASDI)
7. Medicare wages (HI)
8. Federal taxes withheld
9. State and local taxes withheld
10. Other deductions
11. Net pay

Figure 10-2 on page 164 shows how a wage history record may be kept for each employee.

Figures 10-1 and 10-2

Figure 10-1
Payroll Register for Jones Electrical Supply Company

Week Ending January 11, 2013
Pay Date January 15, 2013

Ck#	Name	Soc. Sec. No.	Regular	Overtime	Gross	FITW	FICA tax OASDI	FICA tax HI	State tax	Health ins.	Dental ins.	Life ins.	Uniforms	Net
001	Robert Smith	222-22-7862	$ 500.00	$50.00	$ 550.00	$ 83.00	$ 34.10	$ 7.98	$17.00	$30.00			$5.00	$ 372.92
002	Shirley Black	333-33-3333	$ 600.00		$ 600.00	$ 90.00	$ 37.20	$ 8.70	$18.00	$25.00				$ 421.10
003	Mark Grow	444-44-4444	$ 900.00		$ 900.00	$297.00	$ 55.80	$13.05	$45.00	$40.00	$20.00	$30.00		$ 399.15
Company pay period totals			$2,000.00	$50.00	$2,050.00	$470.00	$127.10	$29.73	$80.00	$95.00	$20.00	$30.00	$5.00	$1,193.17

Figure 10-2
Employee Wage History for

Robert Smith SS# 222-22-7862
15 Main Street, Troy, NY 12017
As of January 15, 2013

Status: Single, 0 allowances

Pay period ending	Ck#	Regular	Overtime	Gross	FITW	FICA tax OASDI	FICA tax HI	State tax	Health ins.	Dental ins.	Life ins.	Uniforms	Net
1/11/13*	001	$ 500.00	$50.00	$ 550.00	$ 83.00	$34.10	$ 7.98	$17.00	$30.00			$ 5.00	$ 372.92
1/11/13	079	$ 500.00		$ 500.00	$ 75.00	$31.00	$ 7.25	$15.00	$30.00			$ 5.00	$ 336.75
1/11/13	103	$ 500.00		$ 500.00	$ 75.00	$31.00	$ 7.25	$15.00	$30.00			$ 5.00	$ 336.75
Employee QTD		$1,500.00	$50.00	$1,550.00	$233.00	$96.10	$22.48	$47.00	$90.00			$15.00	$1,046.42
Employee YTD		$1,500.00	$50.00	$1,550.00	$233.00	$96.10	$22.48	$47.00	$90.00			$15.00	$1,046.42

*The figures for this pay period appear above in the payroll register.

Payroll Distribution—Recording Journal Entries

Every payday, the employer makes two sets of journal entries: (1) journal entries to record employees' salary and deductions (the "payroll distribution"); and (2) entries to record the employer's payroll tax expenses such as FICA and FUTA. For illustration purposes we have combined Social Security and Medicare tax into one entry called "FICA." In practice, these two amounts are separately stated.

1. Entry for Employees' Salary and Deductions

The basic entry for payroll is (a) a debit to Salary Expense (gross wages) and a credit to *each* liability account for which deductions from pay were made (FICA Employee Payable, FITW Payable, Health Insurance Payable/Employee Contribution, Union Dues/Employee Contribution, etc.); and (b) a credit to Cash for net pay. The general format for this entry is:

Salary Expense	XXX	
Deductions (liability accounts)		XXX
Cash		XXX

Some employers allocate salary expense to particular departments, such as Office/Clerical or Sales and modify the basic entry accordingly:

Office/Clerical Salaries Expense	XXX	
Sales Salaries Expense	XXX	
Deductions (liability accounts)		XXX
Cash		XXX

Which Liability Accounts Are Used for Deductions? Of course, the actual entry does not say "Deductions." Instead, specific accounts are used, as follows:

FICA Employee Payable
FITW Payable
Health Insurance Payable/Employee Contribution
Union Dues Payable/Employee Contribution

NOTE: Employee FICA withheld ("FICA Employee Payable") is usually the first liability account listed in a payroll distribution.

EXAMPLE: On January 9, ABC Co. pays gross wages of $10,000 and withholds $765 for FICA and $2,000 for FITW. The correct entry is:

Salary Expense	10,000	
FICA Employee Payable		765
FITW Payable		2,000
Cash		7,235

2. *Recording the Employer's Salary Expense*

The employer's salary expenses include employer FICA tax, as well as FUTA and other payroll taxes. This expense is recorded at the same time as employee salary expense—on payday—but requires a separate entry: A debit to Payroll Tax Expense and a credit to the affected payable accounts. The general format for this entry is:

Payroll Tax Expense	XXX	
FICA Employer Payable		XXX
FUTA Payable		XXX
SUI Payable		XXX
Etc.		XXX

EXAMPLE: On February 15, 2013 ABC Co. pays two employees a total salary of $10,000 and withholds $765 in FICA tax from the employees' wages and $2,000 for federal income tax. It has a total FUTA liability of $80. Two entries are required:

1. The entry to record employees' payroll expense:

Salary Expense	10,000	
FICA Employee Payable		765
FITW Payable		2,000
Cash		7,235

2. The entry to record employer's payroll tax expense:

Payroll Tax Expense	845	
FICA Employer Payable		765
FUTA Payable		80

The employer's salary expense generally includes items other than taxes, such as employer contributions to health insurance. These nontax salary expenses are recorded in a separate journal entry, such as the following;

Health Ins. Expense/Employer Contr.		
Health Ins. Payable/Employer Contr.		

In some companies, this entry may also include the cost of vacation pay (Vacation Pay Expense), fringe benefits such as employer paid parking (Parking Expense), employer contributions to pension plans (Pension Expense), and so on.

Remitting Employee and Employer Taxes and Other Payments

On the date that an employer remits federal taxes, the following entry is recorded:

FICA Employee Payable	XXX	
FICA Employer Payable	XXX	
FITW Payable	XXX	
Cash		XXX

Each remittance to a separate agency requires a separate check and therefore a separate entry. For example:

FUTA Payable	XXX	
Cash		XXX
SIT[1] Payable	XXX	
Cash		XXX
SUI Payable	XXX	
Cash		XXX
Health Ins. Payable/Employee Contr.	XXX	
Health Ins. Payable/Employer's Share	XXX	
Cash		XXX
Pension Plan Trustee Payable	XXX	
Cash		XXX
Union Dues Payable/Employee Contr.	XXX	
Cash		XXX

1. State income tax.

EXAMPLE: On March 14, WidgeCo remits $765 for employee FICA withheld, $765 for employer FICA and $2,000 for FITW. The following entry is required:

FICA Employee Payable	765	
FICA Employer Payable	765	
FITW Payable	2,000	
Cash		3,530

Also on March 14, WidgeCo remits $100 for a group health insurance premium, including $50 contributed by employees through payroll deduction. This requires the following entry:

Health Ins. Payable/Employee Contr.	50	
Health Insurance Payable	50	
Cash		100

Putting It All Together

Now, go back to the payroll register in Figure 10-1 (page 164) and make the entries for the pay period ending January 11, 2013.

PROBLEM 1: Using the payroll register in Figure 10-1, what entries should Jones Electrical Supply Company make on payday?

SOLUTION 1: The required entries are as follows:

1. To record employee's salary expense:

Salary Expense/Office and Clerical	2,050.00	
FICA Employee Payable		156.83
FITW Payable		470.00
SIT Payable		80.00
Health Insurance Payable/Employee Contr.		95.00
Dental Insurance Payable/Employee Contr.		20.00
Life Insurance Payable/Employee Contr.		30.00
Uniforms Payable/Employee Contr.		5.00
Cash		1,193.17

2. To record Jones Electrical Supply's payroll expense for the payroll period ending January 11:

Payroll Tax Expense	156.83	
FICA Employer Payable		156.83

3. If an employer's FUTA rate is .6% and SUI rate is 3.5% the payroll expense entry would also include the following:

Payroll Tax Expense	84.05	
FUTA Payable		12.30
SUI Payable		71.75

Accruing Payroll Expenses[2]

Often, paydays do not coincide with an employer's accounting period. When this occurs, a company on the accrual basis must accrue its payroll for that period. (Businesses on a cash-basis cannot accrue their payroll.) The general format for an accrual is:

Salary Expense	XXX	
Salary Payable		XXX

EXAMPLE: PlumbCo distributes its final payroll on December 31, 2012. Wages total $4,000 ($1,000 each day). Employees will work additional days during the year—December 28–31—and will be paid for this work in January 2013. The accrual entry is:

Salaries Expense	4,000	
Salaries Payable		4,000

NOTE: Accrual-basis employers must also accrue other payroll expenses, such as employer FICA.

2. For a detailed understanding of accruals and deferrals, see AIPB's Home Study Course, *Mastering Accruals and Deferrals.*

QUIZ 1 PAYROLL ENTRIES

Problem I.

Write the correct journal entries for each transaction assuming it is 2013:

1. ACME pays gross wages of $2,000. FITW is $300; FICA is $153.

2. ACME makes a tax deposit representing FITW of $400, employee FICA tax withheld of $160 and employer FICA tax of $160.

3. ACME pays $3,000 to its office and clerical staff, $3,000 to its production staff and $1,500 to its sales staff. It withholds FICA tax of $563, FITW of $1,125 and contributions to health insurance premiums of $500.

Questions 4–6 are based on the following facts: Alice receives gross pay of $450. FICA withholding is $34.42, and FITW is $61 assuming it is 2013.

4. Calculate net pay.

5. Record the payroll entry for paying Alice.

6. Record the entry for her employer's payroll expense.

7. On November 15, 2013 WidgeCo paid gross wages of $2,100. What is the entry to record its FICA tax liability for the November 15 paycheck assuming none of the employees exceed the wage limit for Social Security wages?

Questions 8–11 are based on the following facts. Assume that it is 2013. The payroll for employees A and B is as follows:

	Employee A	Employee B
Gross wages	$650.00	$850.00
FICA withheld	49.72	65.02
FITW	116.00	173.00
SIT withheld	30.00	40.00
Health insurance/employee contr.	2.50	2.50

8. What is the net pay for employee A and for employee B?

9. What is the entry to record the payroll?

10. What is the entry to record the payroll expense for the employer's FICA tax?

11. What are the entries (a) to remit FICA and FITW to the IRS, and (b) to remit state withholding to the state income tax agency?

Problem II.

Indicate whether to "debit" or "credit" each account.

1. To record the FICA withheld from employees' pay, ______________ FICA Employee Withheld Payable and ______________ Salary Expense.

2. To record the entry for accrued salary, ______________ Salaries Payable and ______________ Salaries Expense.

3. To record an employer's FICA liability, ______________ Payroll Tax Expense and ______________ FICA Employer Payable.

Problem III.

Indicate if the following transactions or accounts represent an employee or employer expense.

1. FICA withheld from employees: ______________

2. Employee contributions to pension plan: ______________

3. FUTA Payable: ______________

4. FICA Employer Payable: ______________

5. Health Ins./Employee Contribution: ______________

QUIZ 1 Solutions and Explanations

Problem I.

1. Two entries are required:

a. To record employee's salary expense:

Salary Expense	2,000	
FICA Employee Payable		153
FITW Payable		300
Cash		1,547

b. To record employer's payroll tax expense:

Payroll Tax Expense	140	
FICA Employer Payable		140

2.

FICA Employee Payable	160	
FICA Employer Payable	160	
FITW Payable	400	
Cash		720

3. Two entries are required:

a. To record employee's salary expense:

Office/Clerical Salary Exp.	3,000	
Production Salary Exp.	3,000	
Sales Salary Exp.	1,500	
FICA Employee Payable		563
FITW Payable		1,125
Health Ins. Payable/Employee Contr.		500
Cash		5,312

b. To record payroll tax expenses:

Payroll Tax Expense	563	
FICA Employer Payable		563

4. $354.58
To calculate:

$450 gross – $34.42 FICA withheld – $61 FITW = $354.58 net

5. To record the payroll entry for paying Alice:

Salary Expense	450.00	
FICA Employee Payable		34.42
FITW Payable		61.00
Cash		354.58

6. To record employer's payroll expense for FICA:

Payroll Tax Expense	34.42	
FICA Employer Payable		34.42

7. To calculate employer's FICA tax liability on $2,100:

$2,100 × 0.0765 (7.65%, the FICA combined rate) = $160.65

To record employer's payroll tax expense for FICA:

Payroll Tax Expense	160.65	
FICA Employer Payable		160.65

8. To calculate net pay for employees A and B:

	Employee A	Employee B
Gross wages	$650.00	$850.00
FICA withheld	(49.72)	(65.02)
FITW	(116.00)	(173.00)
SIT Withheld	(30.00)	(40.00)
Health ins. contribution	(2.50)	(2.50)
Net pay	$451.78	$569.48

9. Entry to record the payroll:

Salary Expense	1,500	
FICA Employee Payable		114.74
FITW Payable		289.00
SIT Payable		70.00
Health Ins. Payable/Employee Contr.		5.00
Cash		1,021.26

10. Entry to record payroll tax expense for employer's share of FICA tax:

Payroll Tax Expense	114.74	
FICA Employer Payable		114.74

11. a. Entry to remit FICA and FITW to the IRS:

FICA Employee Payable	114.74	
FICA Employer Payable	114.74	
FITW Payable	289.00	
Cash		518.48

b. Entry to remit state income tax to the state income tax agency:

SIT Payable	70.00	
Cash		70.00

Problem II.

1. credit, debit
2. credit, debit
3. debit, credit

Problem III.

1. employee
2. employee
3. employer
4. employer
5. employee

QUIZ 2 PAYROLL ENTRIES

Problem I.

Write the journal entries for the following transactions assuming it is 2013:

1. Employer pays a health insurance premium of $3,000, of which $600 was contributed by employees through payroll deduction.

2. On November 15, 2013 ACME pays wages of $6,000. FICA withheld is $459; FITW is $1,200.

3. ACME makes a federal tax deposit including $800 for FICA withheld, $800 for employer FICA and $2,000 for FITW.

The following facts are for Questions 4–7. Assume that it is 2013. Your company has the following payroll:

Gross wages	$1,000.00
FICA withheld	76.50
FITW	217.00
SIT withheld	40.00
Health insurance contributions	7.00
Contributions to pension plan	50.00

4. What is the net pay?

5. What is the payroll distribution?

6. What is the entry to record remittance of the employee's pension contribution to the pension trustee?

7. What is the entry (a) to remit FICA and FITW to the IRS and (b) to remit state income tax to the state income tax agency?

Problem II.

Fill in the name of the appropriate accounts:

1. To record the deposit of FITW, credit ______________ and debit ______________.

2. To record the payment of wages, credit both liability (withholding) accounts and ______________, and debit ______________.

3. To record the employer's FICA tax expense on payday, credit ______________ and debit ______________.

QUIZ 2 Solutions and Explanations

Problem I.

1.

Health Insurance Payable/Employee Contrib.	600	
Health Insurance Payable/Employer's Share	2,400	
Cash		3,000

2. Two entries are required:

a. To record employee's salary expense:

Salary Expense	6,000	
FICA Employee Payable		459
FITW Payable		1,200
Cash		4,341

b. To record employer's payroll tax expense:

Payroll Tax Expense	459	
FICA Employer Payable		459

3.

FICA Employee Payable	800	
FICA Employer Payable	800	
FITW Payable	2,000	
Cash		3,600

4. To calculate net pay:

Gross wages	$1,000.00
FICA	(76.50)
FITW	(217.00)
SIT withheld	(40.00)
Health ins. employee contribution	(7.00)
Contributions to pension plan	(50.00)
Net pay	$ 609.50

5. Entry to record payroll:

Salary Expense	$1,000	
FICA Employee Payable		76.50
FITW Payable		217.00
SIT Payable		40.00
Health Ins. Payable/Employee Contr.		7.00
Pension Plan Trustee Payable		50.00
Cash		609.50

6. Entry to record remittance of the pension contribution to the pension trustee:

Pension Plan Trustee Payable	50.00	
Cash		50.00

7. a. Entry to record remittance of FICA and FITW to the IRS:

FICA Employee Payable	76.50	
FICA Employer Payable	76.50	
FITW Payable	217.00	
Cash		370.00

b. Entry to record remittance of state income tax to the state:

SIT Payable	40.00	
Cash		40.00

Problem II.

1. Cash, FITW Payable

2. Cash, Salary Expense

3. FICA Employer Payable, Payroll Tax Expense

GLOSSARY

Additional Medicare Tax: Effective in 2013 an additional Medicare tax of .9% on wages in excess of $200,000. There is no employer matching contribution.

Business day: Any day of the week that is not a legal federal holiday.

Circular E: Annual IRS Publication 15 released each December containing federal income tax withholding rates for the following year and other important employment tax information.

COBRA: This acronym stands for the Consolidated Omnibus Budget Reconciliation Act (COBRA). This law gives workers and their families who lose group health benefits under an employer plan as a result of termination (voluntary or involuntary), reduced hours, changing jobs, divorce, and other events, the right to continue coverage for a limited period of time. Separated employees may be required to pay up to 102% of what the plan cost while they were employed.

COBRA Premium Subsidy: An employee who was involuntarily terminated and was eligible for COBRA could receive a subsidy of up to 65% of COBRA health premiums, which the employer deducted in its invoices to the separated worker. The employer could claim a credit for the amount of the subsidy when it filed Form 941 or 945. Although the credit expired on May 31, 2010, it applied for 15 months, or generally through August 31, 2011.

Constructive receipt: When funds are actually made available to employees and they have access to them without substantial limitation.

EFTPS: Electronic Federal Tax Payment System—IRS system for remitting federal tax deposits by electronic funds transfer.

EIN: Employer Identification Number.

EFW2: The mandatory format used to electronically submit Form W-2 files to the SSA.

Employee: Under IRS guidelines, an individual is considered an employee when the employer exercises control over who will do the work, what the person will do, how it will be done, and when it will be done, and if the safe harbor rules do not apply (e.g., a past IRS audit, common industry practice).

Enterprise test: A method of determining exemptions from federal wage and hour law for businesses that do not exceed specified gross annual sales.

Escheat law: State laws requiring that an individual's unclaimed assets or property, including wages, be submitted to the appropriate state agency.

Exempt employees: Employees who are not covered by the overtime provisions of federal wage and hour law.

Federal legal holidays: For 2013, they are as follows [IRS Publication 509]:
January 1—New Year's Day
January 21—Birthday of Martin Luther King, Jr. and Inauguration Day
February 18—Presidents Day
April 16—District of Columbia Emanicpation Day
May 27—Memorial Day
July 4—Independence Day
September 2—Labor Day
October 14—Columbus Day
November 11—Veteran's Day
November 28—Thanksgiving Day
December 25—Christmas Day

FICA: Federal Insurance Contributions Act. See "Social Security tax" and "Medicare tax."

FIT: Federal income tax.

FITW: Federal income tax withholding.

Form 8109: Federal Tax Deposit Coupon—formerly used to deposit FICA, FITW, FUTA, and various nonpayroll taxes at an authorized financial institution. As of 2011, Form 8109 is no longer used.

Form 940: Employer's Annual Federal Unemployment Tax Return—used to compute the employer's annual federal unemployment tax (FUTA) liability and to report quarterly payments.

Form 941: Employer's Quarterly Federal Tax Return—the federal return used to report quarterly wage and tax information.

Form 944: Employers Annual Federal Tax Return—the federal return used by filers with less than $1,000 of federal employment tax liability in the previous year.

Form 945: Annual Return of Withheld Federal Income Tax—used to report backup tax and certain federal income tax withheld from nonwage income.

FORM 1099: Forms 1099—1099-MISC, 1099-DIV, etc.—are used to report different kinds of nonemployee income such as commissions, fees, royalties, and dividends.

Form I-9: Employment Eligibility Verification—required by IRCA (see below) for all employees hired after November 5, 1986, by firms of any size in the United States.

Form SS-4: Application for an Employer Identification Number (EIN).

Form SS-5: Application for a Social Security Number (SSN) and/or card.

Form SS-8: A 20-question evaluation that employers and workers may submit to the IRS for a determination on whether an individual is an employee or an independent contractor.

Form W-4: Federal Employee's Withholding Allowance Certificate—informs the employer, under penalty of perjury, which tax tables or rate schedules to use to determine the amount of federal income tax to withhold from an employee's wages.

Form W-2: Wage and Tax Statement—the employee's annual summary of total taxable wages paid and taxes withheld and certain fringe benefits totals.

Form W-3: Transmittal of Wage and Tax Statements—a form that serves both to transmit paper Forms W-2 to the SSA and as an employer's annual reconciliation of wage and tax information. This form is not used when W-2's are filed electronically.

Form W-7: Application for IRS individual taxpayer identification number—a form used by individuals to apply for an individual taxpayer identification number. See "ITIN."

FUTA: Federal Unemployment Tax Act—tax paid by for-profit private employers to the federal unemployment fund.

Gross-up: Process of calculating an employee's gross pay based on net pay and a formula for calculating taxable income when the employer pays the employee's share of taxes on a bonus or other payment.

HI tax: Hospital Insurance (also referred to as Medicare)—one of two kinds of insurance that make up FICA tax; the other is OASDI tax (see below).

Imputed income: Income from which no taxes have been withheld (such as group-term life, cash bonus or other compensation) that is added to an employee's next paycheck so that taxes may be collected on it.

Independent contractor: An individual or business that controls the methods and means of work performed.

IRCA: Immigration Reform and Control Act of 1986—enacted to reduce the number of undocumented workers in the United States.

IRS: Internal Revenue Service.

ITIN: Individual taxpayer identification number—used by individuals with U.S. source income who are not eligible for a Social Security number.

Lookback period: A 12-month period used by the IRS to determine an employer's deposit status. The 941 lookback period for 2013 is July 1, 2011, to June 30, 2012. The 945 lookback period for 2013 is January 1, 2011 to December 31, 2011.

Medicare tax: Federal insurance program. See "HI tax" and "Additional Medicare Tax."

MMREF: The mandatory format formerly used to submit Form W-2 files to the SSA magnetically. See "EFW2".

"Mom and Pop" shop: A term for a family-owned and operated business that employs only family members and therefore may be exempt from federal wage and hour law.

Nonexempt employees: Employees who are covered by the overtime provisions of federal law.

OASDI tax: Old Age, Survivors, and Disability Insurance—one of two kinds of federal insurance that make up FICA tax; the other is HI tax (see above).

Overtime pay: Defined under federal law as 1½-times an employee's regular rate of pay but may be higher based on company policy or union contract.

Premium pay: Under federal law the additional ½-times-regular-rate added to base pay to yield the hourly overtime rate.

Professional employee organization (PEO): Another term for an employee leasing company.

Safe harbor: An alternative procedure established by the IRS to simplify recordkeeping and tax computations.

Semiweekly rule: Tax deposit schedule—also known as the Wednesday/Friday rule.

Social Security tax: Tax on almost all U.S. employees, regardless of age, required under the Federal Insurance Contributions Act (FICA). Employers and employees pay this tax based on a percentage rate and taxable wage base.

SSA: Social Security Administration.

SIT: State income tax—used in entries that record payroll distribution and on check stubs.

SSN: Social Security Number.

Statutory employee: Drivers paid by commission, insurance agents who work for a single carrier and certain employees who work for an employer out of their home. A statutory employee's wage payments are not subject to FITW but are subject to FICA (Social Security and Medicare) tax withholding. See also "Statutory nonemployee."

Statutory nonemployee: Persons engaged in selling consumer products in the home or business other than a retail establishment or selling consumer products to any buyer on a buy-sell basis whose compensation is based on sales and other achievements (not an hourly rate), companion sitters for children, elderly, or disabled persons, and licensed real-estate agents who do appraisals and are paid by commission. The employer must provide statutory nonemployees with a contract explaining that they will not be treated as employees and FITW and FICA will not be withheld. See also "Statutory employee."

SUI: State unemployment insurance.

Taxpayer Identification Number (TIN): A Social Security Number (SSN) or Employer Identification Number (EIN).

TIN: See "Taxpayer Identification Number."

TTIN: Truncated taxpayer identification number allowed only on payee copy of certain payee information returns (e.g. Form 1099 series). For example, the SSN 999-99-9999 appears as XXX-XX-9999.

Workweek: Under federal law, any seven consecutive days or 168 consecutive hours. Although it need not be Monday through Sunday, it must be consistent, employees must be made aware of it, and it may not be continually changed to avoid paying overtime.

BIBLIOGRAPHY

Internal Revenue Service. "Circular E Employer's Tax Guide," Publication 15 (January 2013).

------. Publication 15-A, "Employer's Supplemental Tax Guide" (2013).

------. Publication 15-B, "Employer's Tax Guide to Fringe Benefits" (2013).

Payroll Management Guide, Commerce Clearing House, Inc. (2013).

Research Institute of America's Payroll Guide (2013).

Salam, Debera J. *Principles of Payroll Administration*, Thomson Reuters/WG&L, New York, NY (2013).

------. *The Payroll Practitioner's Compliance Handbook: Year-End and Quarterly Reporting*, Thomson Reuters/WG&L, New York, NY (2012–2013).

U.S. Department of Labor, Wage and Hour Division. See the U.S Department of Labor's web site, Wage-Hour Division.

Appendix

FORMS FOR MASTERING PAYROLL

CONTENTS

*2012 Form. The 2013 form was not available at the time of this update.

Form W-4 (Page 1)

Form W-4 (2013)

Purpose. Complete Form W-4 so that your employer can withhold the correct federal income tax from your pay. Consider completing a new Form W-4 each year and when your personal or financial situation changes.

Exemption from withholding. If you are exempt, complete **only** lines 1, 2, 3, 4, and 7 and sign the form to validate it. Your exemption for 2013 expires February 17, 2014. See Pub. 505, Tax Withholding and Estimated Tax.

Note. If another person can claim you as a dependent on his or her tax return, you cannot claim exemption from withholding if your income exceeds $1,000 and includes more than $350 of unearned income (for example, interest and dividends).

Basic instructions. If you are not exempt, complete the **Personal Allowances Worksheet** below. The worksheets on page 2 further adjust your withholding allowances based on itemized deductions, certain credits, adjustments to income, or two-earners/multiple jobs situations.

Complete all worksheets that apply. However, you may claim fewer (or zero) allowances. For regular wages, withholding must be based on allowances you claimed and may not be a flat amount or percentage of wages.

Head of household. Generally, you can claim head of household filing status on your tax return only if you are unmarried and pay more than 50% of the costs of keeping up a home for yourself and your dependent(s) or other qualifying individuals. See Pub. 501, Exemptions, Standard Deduction, and Filing Information, for information.

Tax credits. You can take projected tax credits into account in figuring your allowable number of withholding allowances. Credits for child or dependent care expenses and the child tax credit may be claimed using the **Personal Allowances Worksheet** below. See Pub. 505 for information on converting your other credits into withholding allowances.

Nonwage income. If you have a large amount of nonwage income, such as interest or dividends, consider making estimated tax payments using Form 1040-ES, Estimated Tax for Individuals. Otherwise, you may owe additional tax. If you have pension or annuity income, see Pub. 505 to find out if you should adjust your withholding on Form W-4 or W-4P.

Two earners or multiple jobs. If you have a working spouse or more than one job, figure the total number of allowances you are entitled to claim on all jobs using worksheets from only one Form W-4. Your withholding usually will be most accurate when all allowances are claimed on the Form W-4 for the highest paying job and zero allowances are claimed on the others. See Pub. 505 for details.

Nonresident alien. If you are a nonresident alien, see Notice 1392, Supplemental Form W-4 Instructions for Nonresident Aliens, before completing this form.

Check your withholding. After your Form W-4 takes effect, use Pub. 505 to see how the amount you are having withheld compares to your projected total tax for 2013. See Pub. 505, especially if your earnings exceed $130,000 (Single) or $180,000 (Married).

Future developments. Information about any future developments affecting Form W-4 (such as legislation enacted after we release it) will be posted at *www.irs.gov/w4*.

Personal Allowances Worksheet (Keep for your records.)

A Enter "1" for **yourself** if no one else can claim you as a dependent . . . . **A** ______

B Enter "1" if:
- You are single and have only one job; or
- You are married, have only one job, and your spouse does not work; or
- Your wages from a second job or your spouse's wages (or the total of both) are $1,500 or less.

. . . **B** ______

C Enter "1" for your **spouse.** But, you may choose to enter "-0-" if you are married and have either a working spouse or more than one job. (Entering "-0-" may help you avoid having too little tax withheld.) . . . . **C** ______

D Enter number of **dependents** (other than your spouse or yourself) you will claim on your tax return . . . . **D** ______

E Enter "1" if you will file as **head of household** on your tax return (see conditions under **Head of household** above) . . **E** ______

F Enter "1" if you have at least $1,900 of **child or dependent care expenses** for which you plan to claim a credit . . . **F** ______
(**Note.** Do **not** include child support payments. See Pub. 503, Child and Dependent Care Expenses, for details.)

G **Child Tax Credit** (including additional child tax credit). See Pub. 972, Child Tax Credit, for more information.
- If your total income will be less than $65,000 ($95,000 if married), enter "2" for each eligible child; then **less** "1" if you have three to six eligible children or **less** "2" if you have seven or more eligible children.
- If your total income will be between $65,000 and $84,000 ($95,000 and $119,000 if married), enter "1" for each eligible child . . . **G** ______

H Add lines A through G and enter total here. (**Note.** This may be different from the number of exemptions you claim on your tax return.) ► **H** ______

For accuracy, **complete all worksheets that apply.**
- If you plan to **itemize** or **claim adjustments to income** and want to reduce your withholding, see the **Deductions and Adjustments Worksheet** on page 2.
- If you are **single and have more than one job** or are **married and you and your spouse both work** and the combined earnings from all jobs exceed $40,000 ($10,000 if married), see the **Two-Earners/Multiple Jobs Worksheet** on page 2 to avoid having too little tax withheld.
- If **neither** of the above situations applies, **stop here** and enter the number from line H on line 5 of Form W-4 below.

---------- **Separate here and give Form W-4 to your employer. Keep the top part for your records.** ----------

Form **W-4**
Department of the Treasury
Internal Revenue Service

Employee's Withholding Allowance Certificate

► **Whether you are entitled to claim a certain number of allowances or exemption from withholding is subject to review by the IRS. Your employer may be required to send a copy of this form to the IRS.**

OMB No. 1545-0074

2013

1 Your first name and middle initial	Last name	2 **Your social security number**
Home address (number and street or rural route)		3 ☐ Single ☐ Married ☐ Married, but withhold at higher Single rate. **Note.** If married, but legally separated, or spouse is a nonresident alien, check the "Single" box.
City or town, state, and ZIP code		4 **If your last name differs from that shown on your social security card, check here. You must call 1-800-772-1213 for a replacement card.** ► ☐

5 Total number of allowances you are claiming (from line **H** above **or** from the applicable worksheet on page 2) **5** ______

6 Additional amount, if any, you want withheld from each paycheck . . . . **6** $ ______

7 I claim exemption from withholding for 2013, and I certify that I meet **both** of the following conditions for exemption.
- Last year I had a right to a refund of **all** federal income tax withheld because I had **no** tax liability, **and**
- This year I expect a refund of **all** federal income tax withheld because I expect to have **no** tax liability.

If you meet both conditions, write "Exempt" here . . . . ► **7** ______

Under penalties of perjury, I declare that I have examined this certificate and, to the best of my knowledge and belief, it is true, correct, and complete.

Employee's signature
(This form is not valid unless you sign it.) ► **Date ►**

8 Employer's name and address (Employer: Complete lines 8 and 10 only if sending to the IRS.)	9 Office code (optional)	10 Employer identification number (EIN)

For Privacy Act and Paperwork Reduction Act Notice, see page 2. Cat. No. 10220Q Form **W-4** (2013)

Form W-4 (Page 2)

Form W-4 (2013) Page **2**

Deductions and Adjustments Worksheet

Note. Use this worksheet *only* if you plan to itemize deductions or claim certain credits or adjustments to income.

1 Enter an estimate of your 2013 itemized deductions. These include qualifying home mortgage interest, charitable contributions, state and local taxes, medical expenses in excess of 10% (7.5% if either you or your spouse was born before January 2, 1949) of your income, and miscellaneous deductions. For 2013, you may have to reduce your itemized deductions if your income is over $300,000 and you are married filing jointly or are a qualifying widow(er); $275,000 if you are head of household; $250,000 if you are single and not head of household or a qualifying widow(er); or $150,000 if you are married filing separately. See Pub. 505 for details . . . **1** $______

2 Enter: { $12,200 if married filing jointly or qualifying widow(er); $8,950 if head of household; $6,100 if single or married filing separately } . . . . **2** $______

3 **Subtract** line 2 from line 1. If zero or less, enter "-0-" . . . . **3** $______

4 Enter an estimate of your 2013 adjustments to income and any additional standard deduction (see Pub. 505) **4** $______

5 **Add** lines 3 and 4 and enter the total. (Include any amount for credits from the *Converting Credits to Withholding Allowances for 2013 Form W-4* worksheet in Pub. 505.) . . . . **5** $______

6 Enter an estimate of your 2013 nonwage income (such as dividends or interest) . . . . **6** $______

7 **Subtract** line 6 from line 5. If zero or less, enter "-0-" . . . . **7** $______

8 **Divide** the amount on line 7 by $3,900 and enter the result here. Drop any fraction . . . . **8** ______

9 Enter the number from the **Personal Allowances Worksheet,** line H, page 1 . . . . **9** ______

10 **Add** lines 8 and 9 and enter the total here. If you plan to use the **Two-Earners/Multiple Jobs Worksheet,** also enter this total on line 1 below. Otherwise, **stop here** and enter this total on Form W-4, line 5, page 1 **10**

Two-Earners/Multiple Jobs Worksheet (See *Two earners or multiple jobs* on page 1.)

Note. Use this worksheet *only* if the instructions under line H on page 1 direct you here.

1 Enter the number from line H, page 1 (or from line 10 above if you used the **Deductions and Adjustments Worksheet**) **1** ______

2 Find the number in **Table 1** below that applies to the **LOWEST** paying job and enter it here. **However,** if you are married filing jointly and wages from the highest paying job are $65,000 or less, do not enter more than "3" . . . . **2** ______

3 If line 1 is **more than or equal to** line 2, subtract line 2 from line 1. Enter the result here (if zero, enter "-0-") and on Form W-4, line 5, page 1. **Do not** use the rest of this worksheet . . . . **3** ______

Note. If line 1 is **less than** line 2, enter "-0-" on Form W-4, line 5, page 1. Complete lines 4 through 9 below to figure the additional withholding amount necessary to avoid a year-end tax bill.

4 Enter the number from line 2 of this worksheet . . . . **4** ______

5 Enter the number from line 1 of this worksheet . . . . **5** ______

6 **Subtract** line 5 from line 4 . . . . **6** ______

7 Find the amount in **Table 2** below that applies to the **HIGHEST** paying job and enter it here . . . . **7** $______

8 **Multiply** line 7 by line 6 and enter the result here. This is the additional annual withholding needed . . **8** $______

9 Divide line 8 by the number of pay periods remaining in 2013. For example, divide by 25 if you are paid every two weeks and you complete this form on a date in January when there are 25 pay periods remaining in 2013. Enter the result here and on Form W-4, line 6, page 1. This is the additional amount to be withheld from each paycheck **9** $

Table 1

Married Filing Jointly: If wages from **LOWEST** paying job are—	Enter on line 2 above	All Others: If wages from **LOWEST** paying job are—	Enter on line 2 above
$0 - $5,000	0	$0 - $8,000	0
5,001 - 13,000	1	8,001 - 16,000	1
13,001 - 24,000	2	16,001 - 25,000	2
24,001 - 26,000	3	25,001 - 30,000	3
26,001 - 30,000	4	30,001 - 40,000	4
30,001 - 42,000	5	40,001 - 50,000	5
42,001 - 48,000	6	50,001 - 70,000	6
48,001 - 55,000	7	70,001 - 80,000	7
55,001 - 65,000	8	80,001 - 95,000	8
65,001 - 75,000	9	95,001 - 120,000	9
75,001 - 85,000	10	120,001 and over	10
85,001 - 97,000	11		
97,001 - 110,000	12		
110,001 - 120,000	13		
120,001 - 135,000	14		
135,001 and over	15		

Table 2

Married Filing Jointly: If wages from **HIGHEST** paying job are—	Enter on line 7 above	All Others: If wages from **HIGHEST** paying job are—	Enter on line 7 above
$0 - $72,000	$590	$0 - $37,000	$590
72,001 - 130,000	980	37,001 - 80,000	980
130,001 - 200,000	1,090	80,001 - 175,000	1,090
200,001 - 345,000	1,290	175,001 - 385,000	1,290
345,001 - 385,000	1,370	385,001 and over	1,540
385,001 and over	1,540		

Privacy Act and Paperwork Reduction Act Notice. We ask for the information on this form to carry out the Internal Revenue laws of the United States. Internal Revenue Code sections 3402(f)(2) and 6109 and their regulations require you to provide this information; your employer uses it to determine your federal income tax withholding. Failure to provide a properly completed form will result in your being treated as a single person who claims no withholding allowances; providing fraudulent information may subject you to penalties. Routine uses of this information include giving it to the Department of Justice for civil and criminal litigation; to cities, states, the District of Columbia, and U.S. commonwealths and possessions for use in administering their tax laws; and to the Department of Health and Human Services for use in the National Directory of New Hires. We may also disclose this information to other countries under a tax treaty, to federal and state agencies to enforce federal nontax criminal laws, or to federal law enforcement and intelligence agencies to combat terrorism.

You are not required to provide the information requested on a form that is subject to the Paperwork Reduction Act unless the form displays a valid OMB control number. Books or records relating to a form or its instructions must be retained as long as their contents may become material in the administration of any Internal Revenue law. Generally, tax returns and return information are confidential, as required by Code section 6103.

The average time and expenses required to complete and file this form will vary depending on individual circumstances. For estimated averages, see the instructions for your income tax return.

If you have suggestions for making this form simpler, we would be happy to hear from you. See the instructions for your income tax return.

Form 8109
(Obsolete effective January 1, 2011)

AMOUNT OF DEPOSIT (Do NOT type, please print.)

DOLLARS	CENTS
☐☐☐,☐☐☐,☐☐☐.	☐☐

MONTH TAX YEAR ENDS → ☐☐

EMPLOYER IDENTIFICATION NUMBER → ☐☐ ☐☐☐☐☐☐☐

Darken only one TYPE OF TAX		Darken only one TAX PERIOD
◄ 941	◄ 945	◄ 1st Quarter
◄ 1120	◄ 1042	◄ 2nd Quarter
◄ 943	◄ 990-T	◄ 3rd Quarter
◄ 720	◄ 990-PF	◄ 4th Quarter
◄ CT-1	◄ 944	
◄ 940		

BANK NAME/ DATE STAMP

Name ______________________

____

Address ______________________

____

City ______________________

State ______________ ZIP ____________

IRS USE ONLY

86

Telephone number ( ) ______________

FOR BANK USE IN MICR ENCODING

Federal Tax Deposit Coupon
Form 8109-B (Rev. 12-2009)

SEPARATE ALONG THIS LINE AND SUBMIT TO DEPOSITARY WITH PAYMENT **OMB NO. 1545-0257**

What's new. For Forms CT-1, 940, 943, 944, 945, and 1042, darken only the 4th quarter space for the proper tax period.

Do not use a federal tax deposit coupon (Form 8109 or Form 8109-B) to make a payment with Forms CT-1X, 941-X, 943-X, 944-X, 945-X, or with Formulario 941-X(PR).

Note. Pen or #2 pencil can be used to complete the form. The name, address, and telephone number may be completed other than by hand. You cannot use photocopies of the coupons to make your deposits. Do not staple, tape, or fold the coupons.

The IRS encourages you to make federal tax deposits using the Electronic Federal Tax Payment System (EFTPS). For more information on EFTPS, go to *www.eftps.gov* or call 1-800-555-4477.

Purpose of form. Use Form 8109-B to make a tax deposit only in the following two situations.

1. You have not yet received your resupply of preprinted deposit coupons (Form 8109).

2. You are a new entity and have already been assigned an employer identification number (EIN), but you have not received your initial supply of preprinted deposit coupons (Form 8109). If you have not received your EIN, see *Exceptions* below.

Note. If you do not receive your resupply of deposit coupons and a deposit is due or you do not receive your initial supply within 5–6 weeks of receipt of your EIN, call 1-800-829-4933.

Caution. Do not use these coupons to deposit delinquent taxes assessed by the IRS. Pay delinquent taxes directly to the IRS using the stub included with the notice or by using EFTPS.

How to complete the form. Enter your name as shown on your return or other IRS correspondence, address, and EIN in the spaces provided. Do not make a name or address change on this form (see Form 8822, Change of Address). If you are required to file a Form 1120, 1120-C, 990-PF (with net investment income), 990-T, or 2438, enter the month in which your tax year ends in the MONTH TAX YEAR ENDS boxes. For example, if your tax year ends in January, enter 01; if it ends in December, enter 12. Make your entries for EIN and MONTH TAX YEAR ENDS (if applicable) as shown in *Amount of deposit* below.

Exceptions. If you have applied for an EIN, have not received it, and a deposit must be made, do not use Form 8109-B. Instead, send your payment to the IRS address where you file your return. Make your check or money order payable to the United States Treasury and show on it your name (as shown on Form SS-4, Application for Employer Identification Number), address, kind of tax, period covered, and date you applied for an EIN.

Amount of deposit. Enter the amount of the deposit in the space provided. Enter the amount legibly, forming the characters as shown below:

1	2	3	4	5	6	7	8	9	0

Hand print money amounts without using dollar signs, commas, a decimal point, or leading zeros. If the deposit is for whole dollars only, enter "00" in the CENTS boxes. For example, a deposit of $7,635.22 would be entered like this:

DOLLARS	CENTS
☐☐☐,☐☐7,635.	22

Caution. Darken only one space for TYPE OF TAX and only one space for TAX PERIOD. Darken the space to the left of the applicable form and tax period. Darkening the wrong space or multiple spaces may delay proper crediting to your account. See below for an explanation of *Types of Tax* and *Marking the Proper Tax Period.*

Types of Tax

Form 941	Employer's QUARTERLY Federal Tax Return (includes Forms 941-M, 941-PR, and 941-SS)
Form 943	Employer's Annual Federal Tax Return for Agricultural Employees
Form 944	Employer's ANNUAL Federal Tax Return (includes Forms 944-PR, 944(SP), and 944-SS)
Form 945	Annual Return of Withheld Federal Income Tax
Form 720	Quarterly Federal Excise Tax Return
Form CT-1	Employer's Annual Railroad Retirement Tax Return
Form 940	Employer's Annual Federal Unemployment (FUTA) Tax Return (includes Form 940-PR)
Form 1120	U.S. Corporation Income Tax Return (includes Form 1120 series of returns and Form 2438)
Form 990-T	Exempt Organization Business Income Tax Return
Form 990-PF	Return of Private Foundation or Section 4947(a)(1) Nonexempt Charitable Trust Treated as a Private Foundation
Form 1042	Annual Withholding Tax Return for U.S. Source Income of Foreign Persons

Marking the Proper Tax Period

Payroll taxes and withholding. For Form 941, if your liability was incurred during:

- January 1 through March 31, darken the 1st quarter space;
- April 1 through June 30, darken the 2nd quarter space;
- July 1 through September 30, darken the 3rd quarter space; and
- October 1 through December 31, darken the 4th quarter space.

For Forms CT-1, 940, 943, 944, 945, and 1042, darken only the 4th quarter space.

Do not use a federal tax deposit coupon (Form 8109 or Form 8109-B) to make a payment with Forms CT-1X, 941-X, 943-X, 944-X, 945-X, or with Formulario 941-X(PR).

Note. If the liability for Form 941 was incurred during one quarter and deposited in another quarter, darken the space for the quarter in which the tax liability was incurred. For example, if the liability was incurred in March and deposited in April, darken the 1st quarter space.

Excise taxes. For Form 720, follow the instructions above for Form 941. For Form 990-PF, with net investment income, follow the instructions on page 2 for Form 1120, 990-T, and 2438.

Department of the Treasury
Internal Revenue Service

Cat. No. 61042S

Form **8109-B** (Rev. 12-2009)

Form 8109—Instructions (Obsolete effective January 1, 2011)

Income Taxes (Forms 1120, 990-T, and 2438). To make estimated income tax deposits before the end of your tax year, darken only the 1st quarter space.

To make deposits after the end of your tax year, darken only the 4th quarter space. This includes:

- Deposits of estimated tax payments made after the end of your tax year.
- Deposits of balance due shown on the return (Forms 1120, 990-T, and 990-PF).
- Deposits of balance due shown on Form 7004, Application for Automatic Extension of Time To File Certain Business Income Tax, Information, and Other Returns (be sure to darken the 1120 or 1042 space as appropriate).
- Deposits of balance due (Forms 990-T and 990-PF filers) shown on Form 8868, Application for Extension of Time To File an Exempt Organization Return (be sure to darken the 990-T or 990-PF space as appropriate).
- Deposits of tax due shown on Form 2438, Undistributed Capital Gains Tax Return (darken the 1120 space).

How to ensure your deposit is credited to the correct account.

- Make sure your name and EIN are correct.
- Prepare only one coupon for each type of tax deposit.
- Darken only one space for the type of tax you are depositing.
- Darken only one space for the tax period for which you are making a deposit.
- Use separate FTD coupons for each return period.

Telephone number. We need your daytime telephone number to call if we have difficulty processing your deposit.

Miscellaneous. We use the "IRS USE ONLY" box to ensure proper crediting to your account. Do not darken this space when making a deposit.

How to make deposits. Mail or deliver the completed coupon with the amount of the deposit to an authorized depositary (financial institution) for federal taxes. Make your check or money order payable to that depositary. To help ensure proper crediting to your account, write your EIN, the type of tax (for example, Form 940), and the tax period to which the payment applies on your check or money order.

Authorized depositaries must accept cash, postal money orders drawn to the order of the depositary, or checks or drafts drawn on and to the order of the depositary. You can deposit taxes with a check drawn on another financial institution only if the depositary is willing to accept that form of payment.

If you prefer, you may mail your coupon and payment to Financial Agent, Federal Tax Deposit Processing, P.O. Box 970030, St. Louis, MO 63197. Make your check or money order payable to "Financial Agent."

The Financial Agent cannot process foreign checks. If you send a check written on a foreign bank to pay a federal tax deposit, you generally will be charged a deposit penalty and will receive a bill in the mail. For more information, see *How to deposit with a FTD coupon* in Pub. 15 (Circular E), Employer's Tax Guide.

Timeliness of deposits. The IRS determines whether deposits are on time by the date they are received by an authorized depositary. However, a deposit received by the authorized depositary after the due date will be considered timely if the taxpayer establishes that it was mailed in the United States in a properly addressed, postage prepaid envelope at least 2 days before the due date.

Note. If you are required to deposit any taxes more than once a month, any deposit of $20,000 or more must be received by its due date to be timely.

When to deposit. See the instructions for the applicable return. See Pub. 15 (Circular E) for deposit rules on employment taxes. Generally, you can get copies of forms and instructions by calling 1-800-TAX-FORM (1-800-829-3676) or by visiting IRS's website at *www.irs.gov.*

Penalties. You may be charged a penalty for not making deposits when due or in sufficient amounts, unless you have reasonable cause. This penalty may also apply if you mail or deliver federal tax deposits to unauthorized institutions or IRS offices, rather than to authorized depositaries. Additionally, a trust fund recovery penalty may be imposed on all persons who are determined by the IRS to be responsible for collecting, accounting for, and paying over employment and excise taxes, and who acted willfully in not doing so. For more information on penalties, see Pub. 15 (Circular E). See the Instructions for Form 720 for when these penalties apply to excise taxes.

Privacy Act and Paperwork Reduction Act Notice. Internal Revenue Code section 6302 requires certain persons to make periodic deposits of taxes. If you do not deposit electronically, you must provide the information requested on this form. IRC section 6109 requires you to provide your EIN. The information on this form is used to ensure that you are complying with the Internal Revenue laws and to ensure proper crediting of your deposit. Routine uses of this information include providing it to the Department of Justice for civil and criminal litigation, and to cities, states, and the District of Columbia for use in administering their tax laws. We may also disclose this information to federal and state agencies to enforce federal nontax criminal laws and to combat terrorism. We may give this information to other countries pursuant to tax treaties. Providing incomplete, incorrect, or fraudulent information may subject you to interest and penalties.

You are not required to provide the information requested on a form that is subject to the Paperwork Reduction Act unless the form displays a valid OMB control number. Books or records relating to a form or its instructions must be retained as long as their contents may become material in the administration of any Internal Revenue law. Generally, tax returns and return information are confidential, as required by IRC section 6103.

The time needed to complete and file this form will vary depending on individual circumstances. The estimated average time is 3 minutes. If you have comments concerning the accuracy of this time estimate or suggestions for making this form simpler, we would be happy to hear from you. You can write to the Internal Revenue Service, Tax Products Coordinating Committee, SE:W:CAR:MP:T:T:SP, IR-6526, 1111 Constitution Ave. NW, Washington, DC 20224. Do not send this form to this address. Instead, see the instructions under *How to make deposits* on this page.

Form 940 (Page 1)

Form **940 for 2012: Employer's Annual Federal Unemployment (FUTA) Tax Return** 850112

Department of the Treasury — Internal Revenue Service

OMB No. 1545-0028

Employer identification number (EIN) ☐☐ – ☐☐☐☐☐☐☐

Name *(not your trade name)*

Trade name *(if any)*

Address

Number Street Suite or room number

City State ZIP code

Type of Return
(Check all that apply.)

☐ **a.** Amended

☐ **b.** Successor employer

☐ **c.** No payments to employees in 2012

☐ **d.** Final: Business closed or stopped paying wages

Instructions and prior-year forms are available at *www.irs.gov/form940.*

Read the separate instructions before you complete this form. Please type or print within the boxes.

Part 1: Tell us about your return. If any line does NOT apply, leave it blank.

1a If you had to pay state unemployment tax in one state only, enter the state abbreviation . 1a ☐☐

1b If you had to pay state unemployment tax in more than one state, you are a multi-state employer . . . . 1b ☐ Check here. Complete Schedule A (Form 940).

2 If you paid wages in a state that is subject to CREDIT REDUCTION . . . . 2 ☐ Check here. Complete Schedule A (Form 940).

Part 2: Determine your FUTA tax before adjustments for 2012. If any line does NOT apply, leave it blank.

3 Total payments to all employees . . . . 3 ______ .

4 Payments exempt from FUTA tax . . . . 4 ______ .

Check all that apply: 4a ☐ Fringe benefits 4c ☐ Retirement/Pension 4e ☐ Other

4b ☐ Group-term life insurance 4d ☐ Dependent care

5 Total of payments made to each employee in excess of $7,000 . . . . 5 ______ .

6 Subtotal (line 4 + line 5 = line 6) . . . . 6 ______ .

7 Total taxable FUTA wages (line 3 – line 6 = line 7) (see instructions) . . . . 7 ______ .

8 FUTA tax before adjustments (line 7 x .006 = line 8) . . . . 8 ______ .

Part 3: Determine your adjustments. If any line does NOT apply, leave it blank.

9 If ALL of the taxable FUTA wages you paid were excluded from state unemployment tax, multiply line 7 by .054 (line 7 × .054 = line 9). Go to line 12 . . . . 9 ______ .

10 If SOME of the taxable FUTA wages you paid were excluded from state unemployment tax, OR you paid ANY state unemployment tax late (after the due date for filing Form 940), complete the worksheet in the instructions. Enter the amount from line 7 of the worksheet . . 10 ______ .

11 If credit reduction applies, enter the total from Schedule A (Form 940) . . . . 11 ______ .

Part 4: Determine your FUTA tax and balance due or overpayment for 2012. If any line does NOT apply, leave it blank.

12 Total FUTA tax after adjustments (lines 8 + 9 + 10 + 11 = line 12) . . . . 12 ______ .

13 FUTA tax deposited for the year, including any overpayment applied from a prior year . 13 ______ .

14 Balance due (If line 12 is more than line 13, enter the excess on line 14.)

- If line 14 is more than $500, you must deposit your tax.
- If line 14 is $500 or less, you may pay with this return. (see instructions) . . . . 14 ______ .

15 Overpayment (If line 13 is more than line 12, enter the excess on line 15 and check a box below.) . . . . 15 ______ .

▶ You **MUST** complete both pages of this form and **SIGN** it. Check one: ☐ Apply to next return. ☐ Send a refund.

Next ▶

For Privacy Act and Paperwork Reduction Act Notice, see the back of Form 940-V, Payment Voucher. Cat. No. 11234O Form **940** (2012)

Form 940 (Page 2)

850212

Name *(not your trade name)* | Employer identification number (EIN)

Part 5: Report your FUTA tax liability by quarter only if line 12 is more than $500. If not, go to Part 6.

16 **Report the amount of your FUTA tax liability for each quarter; do NOT enter the amount you deposited. If you had no liability for a quarter, leave the line blank.**

16a **1st quarter** (January 1 – March 31) . . . . 16a ____ .

16b **2nd quarter** (April 1 – June 30) . . . . 16b ____ .

16c **3rd quarter** (July 1 – September 30) . . . . 16c ____ .

16d **4th quarter** (October 1 – December 31) . . . . 16d ____ .

17 **Total tax liability for the year** (lines 16a + 16b + 16c + 16d = line 17) **17** ____ . **Total must equal line 12.**

Part 6: May we speak with your third-party designee?

Do you want to allow an employee, a paid tax preparer, or another person to discuss this return with the IRS? See the instructions for details.

☐ **Yes.** Designee's name and phone number ____ ____

Select a 5-digit Personal Identification Number (PIN) to use when talking to IRS ☐☐☐☐☐

☐ **No.**

Part 7: Sign here. You MUST complete both pages of this form and SIGN it.

Under penalties of perjury, I declare that I have examined this return, including accompanying schedules and statements, and to the best of my knowledge and belief, it is true, correct, and complete, and that no part of any payment made to a state unemployment fund claimed as a credit was, or is to be, deducted from the payments made to employees. Declaration of preparer (other than taxpayer) is based on all information of which preparer has any knowledge.

X Sign your name here ____

Print your name here ____

Print your title here ____

Date ____ / /

Best daytime phone ____

Paid Preparer Use Only

Check if you are self-employed . . . ☐

Preparer's name ____ PTIN ____

Preparer's signature ____ Date ____ / /

Firm's name (or yours if self-employed) ____ EIN ____

Address ____ Phone ____

City ____ State ____ ZIP code ____

Page **2** Form **940** (2012)

Form 940—Instructions (Page 1)

2012 Instructions for Form 940

Department of the Treasury
Internal Revenue Service

Employer's Annual Federal Unemployment (FUTA) Tax Return

Section references are to the Internal Revenue Code unless otherwise noted.

Future Developments

For the latest information about developments related to Form 940 and its instructions, such as legislation enacted after they were published, go to www.irs.gov/form940.

What's New

FUTA tax rate. The FUTA tax rate remains 6.0%.

Credit reduction state. A state that has not repaid money it borrowed from the federal government to pay unemployment benefits is a "credit reduction state." The Department of Labor determines these states. If an employer pays wages that are subject to the unemployment tax laws of a credit reduction state, that employer must pay additional federal unemployment tax when filing its Form 940.

For 2012, there are credit reduction states. If you paid any wages that are subject to the unemployment compensation laws of any of those states, the regular .054 credit is reduced. Use Schedule A (Form 940), Multi-State Employer and Credit Reduction Information, to figure the tax. For more information, see the Schedule A (Form 940) instructions or visit IRS.gov.

Change of address. Use Form 8822-B, Change of Address—Business, to notify the IRS of an address change.

Reminders

Federal tax deposits must be made by electronic funds transfer. You must use electronic funds transfer to make all federal tax deposits. Generally, electronic funds transfers are made using the Electronic Federal Tax Payment System (EFTPS). If you do not want to use EFTPS, you can arrange for your tax professional, financial institution, payroll service, or other trusted third party to make deposits on your behalf. Also, you may arrange for your financial institution to initiate a same-day wire payment on your behalf. EFTPS is a free service provided by the Department of Treasury. Services provided by your tax professional, financial institution, payroll service, or other third party may have a fee. For more information on making federal tax deposits, see section 11 of Pub. 15 (Circular E), Employer's Tax Guide. To get more information about EFTPS or to enroll in EFTPS, visit www.eftps.gov or call 1-800-555-4477. Additional information about EFTPS is also available in Pub. 966, Electronic Federal Tax Payment System: A Guide to Getting Started.

Aggregate Form 940 filers. Agents must complete Schedule R (Form 940), Allocation Schedule for Aggregate Form 940 Filers, when filing an aggregate Form 940. Aggregate Forms 940 are filed by agents of home care service recipients approved by the IRS under section 3504 of the Internal Revenue Code. To request approval to act as an agent for an employer, the agent must file Form 2678, Employer/Payer Appointment of Agent, with the IRS unless you are a state or local government agency acting as agent under the special procedures provided in Notice 2003-70, 2003-43 I.R.B. 916, available at www.irs.gov/irb/2003-43_IRB/ar09.html.

Disregarded entities and qualified subchapter S subsidiaries (QSubs). Business entities that are disregarded as separate from their owner, including qualified subchapter S subsidiaries, are required to withhold and pay employment taxes and file employment tax returns using the name and employer identification number (EIN) of the disregarded entity. For more information, see *Disregarded entities*, later.

State unemployment information. When you registered as an employer with your state, the state assigned you a state reporting number. If you do not have a state unemployment account and state experience tax rate, or if you have questions about your state account, you must contact your state unemployment agency. For a list of state unemployment agencies, visit the U.S. Department of Labor's website at www.workforcesecurity.doleta.gov/unemploy/agencies.asp.

You can file and pay electronically. Using electronic options available from the IRS can make filing a return and paying your federal tax easier. You can use IRS *e-file* to file a return and EFTPS to make deposits or pay in full whether you rely on a tax professional or prepare your own taxes.

- For IRS *e-file*, visit IRS.gov for additional information.
- For EFTPS, visit www.eftps.gov, or call EFTPS Customer Service at 1-800-555-4477, 1-800-733-4829 (TDD), or 1-800-244-4829 (Spanish).

Electronic funds withdrawal (EFW). If you file Form 940 electronically, you can *e-file* and e-pay (electronic funds withdrawal) the balance due in a single step using tax preparation software or through a tax professional. However, **do not** use EFW to make federal tax deposits. For more information on paying your taxes using EFW, visit the IRS website at www.irs.gov/e-pay. A fee may be charged to file electronically.

You can pay your balance due by credit or debit card. You may pay your FUTA tax shown on line 14 using a major credit card or debit card. However, **do not** use a credit or debit card to pay taxes that are required to be deposited (see *When Must You Deposit Your FUTA Tax*, later). For more information on paying your taxes with a credit or debit card, visit the IRS website at www.irs.gov/e-pay.

Photographs of missing children. The IRS is a proud partner with the National Center for Missing and Exploited Children. Photographs of missing children selected by the Center may appear in instructions on pages that would otherwise be blank. You can help bring these children home by looking at the photographs and calling 1-800-THE-LOST (1-800-843-5678) if you recognize a child.

How Can You Get More Help?

If you want more information about this form, see Pub. 15 (Circular E), visit our website at IRS.gov, or call 1-800-829-4933 (TDD/TTY for persons who are deaf, hard of hearing, or have a speech disability at 1-800-829-4059) Monday through Friday 7 a.m. to 7 p.m. local time (Alaska and Hawaii follow Pacific time).

For a list of related employment tax topics, visit the IRS website at www.irs.gov/businesses and click on the *Employment Taxes* link under *Businesses Topics*. You can order forms,

Nov 20, 2012 Cat. No. 13660I

Form 940—Instructions (Page 2)

instructions, and publications at www.irs.gov/formspubs or by calling 1-800-TAX-FORM (1-800-829-3676).

General Instructions: Understanding Form 940

What's the Purpose of Form 940?

Use Form 940 to report your annual Federal Unemployment Tax Act (FUTA) tax. Together with state unemployment tax systems, the FUTA tax provides funds for paying unemployment compensation to workers who have lost their jobs. Most employers pay both a federal and a state unemployment tax. Only employers pay FUTA tax. Do not collect or deduct FUTA tax from your employees' wages.

The FUTA tax applies to the first $7,000 you pay to each employee during a calendar year after subtracting any payments exempt from FUTA tax.

These instructions give you some background information about Form 940. They tell you who must file the form, how to fill it out line by line, and when and where to file it.

Who Must File Form 940?

Except as noted below, if you answer "Yes" to either one of these questions, you must file Form 940.

- Did you pay wages of $1,500 or more to employees in any calendar quarter during 2011 or 2012?
- Did you have one or more employees for at least some part of a day in any 20 or more different weeks in 2011 or 20 or more different weeks in 2012? Count all full-time, part-time, and temporary employees. However, if your business is a partnership, do not count its partners.

If your business was sold or transferred during the year, each employer who answered "Yes" to at least one question above must file Form 940. However, do not include any wages paid by the predecessor employer on your Form 940 unless you are a successor employer. For details, see *Successor employer* under *Type of Return*.

If you are not liable for FUTA tax for 2012 because you made no payments to employees in 2012, check box *c* in the top right corner of the form. Then go to Part 7, sign the form, and file it with the IRS.

If you will not be liable for filing Form 940 in the future because your business has closed or because you stopped paying wages, check box *d* in the top right corner of the form. See *Final: Business closed or stopped paying wages* under *Type of Return* for more information.

For Employers of Household Employees . . .

If you are a household employer, you must pay FUTA tax on wages that you paid to your household employees only if you paid cash wages of $1,000 or more in any calendar quarter in 2011 or 2012.

A household employee performs household work in a:

- Private home,
- Local college club, or
- Local chapter of a college fraternity or sorority.

Generally, employers of household employees must file Schedule H (Form 1040), Household Employment Taxes, instead of Form 940.

However, if you have other employees in addition to household employees, you can choose to include the FUTA taxes for your household employees on Form 940 instead of filing Schedule H (Form 1040). If you choose to include household employees on your Form 940, you must also file Form 941, Employer's QUARTERLY Federal Tax Return; Form 943, Employer's Annual Federal Tax Return for Agricultural Employees; or Form 944, Employer's ANNUAL Federal Tax Return; to report social security, Medicare, and any withheld federal income taxes for your household employees.

See Pub. 926, Household Employer's Tax Guide, for more information.

For Agricultural Employers . . .

File Form 940 if you answer "Yes" to either of these questions.

- Did you pay cash wages of $20,000 or more to farmworkers during any calendar quarter in 2011 or 2012?
- Did you employ 10 or more farmworkers during some part of the day (whether or not at the same time) during any 20 or more different weeks in 2011 or 20 or more different weeks in 2012?

Count wages you paid to aliens who were admitted to the United States on a temporary basis to perform farmwork (workers with H-2A visas). However, wages paid to "H-2A visa workers" are not subject to FUTA tax.

See Pub. 51 (Circular A), Agricultural Employer's Tax Guide, for more information.

For Indian Tribal Governments . . .

Services rendered by employees of a federally recognized Indian tribal government employer (including any subdivision, subsidiary, or business enterprise wholly owned by the tribe) are exempt from FUTA tax and no Form 940 is required. However, the tribe must have participated in the state unemployment system for the full year and be in compliance with applicable state unemployment law. For more information, see section 3309(d).

For Tax-Exempt Organizations . . .

Religious, educational, scientific, charitable, and other organizations described in section 501(c)(3) and exempt from tax under section 501(a) are not subject to FUTA tax and do not have to file Form 940.

For Employers of State or Local Governments. . .

Services rendered by employees of a state of a political subdivision or instrumentality of the state are exempt from FUTA tax and no Form 940 is required.

When Must You File Form 940?

The due date for filing Form 940 for 2012 is January 31, 2013. However, if you deposited all your FUTA tax when it was due, you may file Form 940 by February 11, 2013.

If we receive your return after the due date, we will treat your return as filed on time if the envelope containing your return is properly addressed, contains sufficient postage, and is postmarked by the U.S. Postal Service on or before the due date or sent by an IRS-designated private delivery service on or before the due date. However, if you do not follow these guidelines, we will consider your return filed when it is actually received. For a list of IRS-designated private delivery services, see Pub. 15 (Circular E).

Where Do You File?

Where you file depends on whether you include a payment (check or money order) with your return. However, mail your amended return to the *Without a payment* address even if a payment is included.

-2-

Form 940—Instructions (Page 3)

If you are in . . .	Without a payment . . .	With a payment . . .
EXCEPTION for tax-exempt organizations, Federal, State and Local Governments, and Indian Tribal Governments, regardless of your location	Department of the Treasury Internal Revenue Service Ogden, UT 84201-0046	Internal Revenue Service P.O. Box 37940 Hartford, CT 06176-7940
Connecticut, Delaware, District of Columbia, Florida, Georgia, Illinois, Indiana, Kentucky, Maine, Maryland, Massachusetts, Michigan, New Hampshire, New Jersey, New York, North Carolina, Ohio, Pennsylvania, Rhode Island, South Carolina, Tennessee, Vermont, Virginia, West Virginia, Wisconsin	Department of the Treasury Internal Revenue Service Cincinnati, OH 45999-0046	Internal Revenue Service P.O. Box 804521 Cincinnati, OH 45280-4521
Alabama, Alaska, Arizona, Arkansas, California, Colorado, Hawaii, Idaho, Iowa, Kansas, Louisiana, Minnesota, Mississippi, Missouri, Montana, Nebraska, Nevada, New Mexico, North Dakota, Oklahoma, Oregon, South Dakota, Texas, Utah, Washington, Wyoming	Department of the Treasury Internal Revenue Service Ogden, UT 84201-0046	Internal Revenue Service P.O. Box 37940 Hartford, CT 06176-7940
Puerto Rico U.S. Virgin Islands	Internal Revenue Service P.O. Box 409101 Ogden, UT 84409	Internal Revenue Service P.O. Box 37940 Hartford, CT 06176-7940
If the location of your legal residence, principal place of business, office, or agency is not listed . . .	Internal Revenue Service P.O. Box 409101 Ogden, UT 84409	Internal Revenue Service P.O. Box 37940 Hartford, CT 06176-7940

CAUTION *Private delivery services cannot deliver to P.O. boxes. You must use the U.S. Postal Service to mail an item to a P.O. box address.*

Credit for State Unemployment Tax Paid to a State Unemployment Fund

You get a credit for amounts you pay to a state (including the District of Columbia, Puerto Rico, and the U.S. Virgin Islands) unemployment fund by January 31, 2013 (or February 11, 2013, if that is your Form 940 due date). Your FUTA tax will be higher if you do not pay the state unemployment tax timely. If you did not pay all state unemployment tax by the due date of Form 940, see the line 10 instructions.

State unemployment taxes are sometimes called "contributions." These contributions are payments that a state requires an employer to make to its unemployment fund for the payment of unemployment benefits. They **do not include:**

- Any payments deducted or deductible from your employees' pay;
- Penalties, interest, or special administrative taxes; and
- Voluntary amounts you paid to get a lower assigned state experience rate.

Additional credit. You may receive an additional credit if you have a state experience rate lower than 5.4% (.054). This applies even if your rate varies during the year. This additional credit is the difference between your actual state unemployment tax payments and the amount you would have been required to pay at 5.4%.

Special credit for successor employers. You may be eligible for a credit based on the state unemployment taxes paid by a predecessor. You may claim this credit if you are a successor employer who acquired a business in 2012 from a predecessor who was not an employer for FUTA purposes and, therefore, was not required to file Form 940 for 2012. See section 3302(e). You can include amounts paid by the predecessor on the *Worksheet* as if you paid them. For details on successor employers, see *Successor employer* under *Type of Return*. If the predecessor was required to file Form 940, see the line 5 instructions.

When Must You Deposit Your FUTA Tax?

Although Form 940 covers a calendar year, you may have to deposit your FUTA tax before you file your return. If your FUTA tax is more than $500 for the calendar year, you must deposit at least one quarterly payment.

You must determine when to deposit your tax based on the amount of your quarterly tax liability. If your FUTA tax is $500 or less in a quarter, carry it over to the next quarter. Continue carrying your tax liability over until your cumulative tax is more than $500. At that point, you must deposit your tax for the quarter. Deposit your FUTA tax by the last day of the month after the end of the quarter. If your tax for the next quarter is $500 or less, you are not required to deposit your tax again until the cumulative amount is more than $500.

Fourth quarter liabilities. If your FUTA tax for the fourth quarter (plus any undeposited amounts from earlier quarters) is more than $500, deposit the entire amount by January 31, 2013. If it is $500 or less, you can either deposit the amount or pay it with your Form 940 by January 31, 2013.

In years when there are credit reduction states, you must include liabilities owed for credit reduction with your fourth quarter deposit.

When To Deposit Your FUTA Tax

If your undeposited FUTA tax is more than $500 on . . .*	Deposit your tax by . . .
March 31	April 30
June 30	July 31
September 30	October 31
December 31	January 31

*Also, see the instructions for line 16.

TIP *If any deposit due date falls on a Saturday, Sunday, or legal holiday, you may deposit on the next business day.*

How Do You Figure Your FUTA Tax Liability for Each Quarter?

You owe FUTA tax on the first $7,000 of wages that you paid to each employee during the calendar year. The FUTA tax is 6.0% (.060) for 2012. Most employers receive a maximum credit of up to 5.4% (.054) against this FUTA tax. Every quarter, you must figure how much of the first $7,000 of each employee's annual wages you paid during that quarter.

-3-

Form 940—Instructions (Page 4)

Figure Your Tax Liability

Before you can figure the amount to deposit, figure your FUTA tax liability for the quarter. To figure your tax liability, add the first $7,000 of each employee's annual wages you paid during the quarter for FUTA wages paid and multiply that amount by .006.

The tax rates are based on your receiving the maximum credit against FUTA taxes. You are entitled to the maximum credit if you paid all state unemployment tax by the due date of your Form 940 or if you were not required to pay state unemployment tax during the calendar year due to your state experience rate.

Example. During first quarter, you had three employees: Employees A, B, and C. You paid $11,000 to Employee A, $2,000 to Employee B, and $4,000 to Employee C.

To figure your liability for the first quarter, add the first $7,000 of each employee's wages:

$7,000	Employee A's wages subject to FUTA tax
2,000	Employee B's wages subject to FUTA tax
+ 4,000	Employee C's wages subject to FUTA tax
$13,000	Total wages subject to FUTA tax for the first quarter
$13,000	Total wages subject to FUTA tax for the first quarter
x .006	Tax rate (based on maximum credit of 5.4%)
$78	Your liability for the first quarter

In this example, you do not have to make a deposit because your liability is $500 or less for the first quarter. However, you must carry this liability over to the second quarter.

If any wages subject to FUTA tax are not subject to state unemployment tax, you may be liable for FUTA tax at a higher rate (up to 6.0%). For instance, in certain states, wages paid to corporate officers, certain payments of sick pay by unions, and certain fringe benefits are excluded from state unemployment tax.

Example. Employee A and Employee B are corporate officers whose wages are excluded from state unemployment tax in your state. Employee C's wages are not excluded from state unemployment tax. During the first quarter, you paid $11,000 to Employee A, $2,000 to Employee B, and $4,000 to Employee C.

$ 9,000	Total FUTA wages for Employees A and B in first quarter
x .060	Tax rate
$540	Your liability for the first quarter for Employees A and B
$4,000	Total FUTA wages subject to state unemployment tax
x .006	Tax rate (based on maximum credit of 5.4%)
$24	Your liability for the first quarter for Employee C
$540	Your liability for the first quarter for Employees A and B
+ 24	Your liability for first quarter for Employee C
$564	Your liability for the first quarter for Employees A, B, and C

In this example, you must deposit $564 by April 30 because your liability for the first quarter is more than $500.

How Must You Deposit Your FUTA Tax?

You Must Deposit Your FUTA Tax Using EFT

You must deposit all depository taxes using electronic funds transfers (EFT). Generally, electronic funds transfers are made using the Electronic Federal Tax Payment System (EFTPS). To get more information or to enroll in EFTPS, visit the EFTPS website at www.eftps.gov, or call 1-800-555-4477. Additional information about EFTPS is also available in Pub. 966.

If your business is new, IRS will automatically pre-enroll you in EFTPS when you apply for an employer identification number (EIN). Follow the instructions on your EIN package to activate your enrollment.

CAUTION *To make your EFTPS deposits on time, you must initiate the transaction by 8 p.m. Eastern time the day before the date the deposit is due.*

Same-day payment option. If you fail to initiate a deposit transaction on EFTPS by 8 p.m. Eastern time the day before the date a deposit is due, you can still make your deposit on time by using the Federal Tax Application (FTA). To use the same-day wire payment method, you will need to make arrangements with your financial institution ahead of time. Please check with your financial institution regarding availability, deadlines, and costs. Your financial institution may charge you a fee for payments made this way. To learn more about the information you will need to provide your financial institution to make a same-day wire payment, visit www.eftps.gov to download the *Same-Day Payment Worksheet.*

Timeliness of federal tax deposits. If a deposit is required to be made on a day that is not a business day, the deposit is considered timely if it is made by the close of the next business day. A business day is any day other than a Saturday, Sunday, or legal holiday. The term "legal holiday" for deposit purposes includes only those legal holidays in the District of Columbia. Legal holidays in the District of Columbia are provided in Pub. 15 (Circular E).

How Can You Avoid Penalties and Interest?

Penalties and interest are assessed at a rate set by law on taxes paid late, returns filed late or incorrectly, insufficient payments made, and failure to make deposits using EFT.

You can avoid paying penalties and interest if you:

- Deposit or pay your tax when it is due,
- File your completed Form 940 accurately and on time, and
- Ensure your checks for tax payments are valid.

If you receive a notice about a penalty after you file this return, reply to the notice with an explanation and we will determine if you meet reasonable-cause criteria. Do not attach an explanation when you file your Form 940.

Can You Amend a Return?

You use the 2012 Form 940 to amend a return that you previously filed for 2012. If you are amending a return for a previous year, use the previous year's Form 940.

Follow the steps below to amend your return.

- Use a paper return to amend a Form 940 filed under an electronic filing program.
- Check the amended return box in the top right corner of Form 940, page 1, box a.
- Fill in all the amounts that should have been on the original form.
- Sign the form.
- Attach an explanation of why you are amending your return. For example, tell us if you are filing to claim credit for tax paid to your state unemployment fund after the due date of Form 940.
- File the amended return using the *Without a payment* address (even if a payment is included) under *Where Do You File.*
- If you file an amended return for an aggregate Form 940, be sure to attach Schedule R (Form 940). Complete Schedule R (Form 940) only for employers who have adjustments on the amended Form 940.

-4-

Form 940—Instructions (Page 5)

Completing Your Form 940

Follow These Guidelines to Correctly Fill Out the Form

To help us accurately scan and process your form, please follow these guidelines.

- Make sure your business name and EIN are on every page of the form and any attachments.
- If you type or use a computer to fill out your form, use a 12-point Courier font, if possible.
- Make sure you enter dollars to the left of the preprinted decimal point and cents to the right.
- Do not enter dollar signs or decimal points. Commas are optional.
- You may choose to round your amounts to the nearest dollar, instead of reporting cents on this form. If you choose to round, you must round all entries. To round, drop the amounts under 50 cents and increase the amounts from 50 to 99 cents to the next dollar. For example, $1.49 becomes $1.00 and $2.50 becomes $3.00. If you use two or more amounts to figure an entry on the form, use cents to figure the answer and round the answer only.
- If you have a line with the value of zero, leave it blank.

Employer Identification Number (EIN), Name, Trade Name, and Address

Enter Your Business Information at the Top of the Form

Enter your EIN, name, and address in the spaces provided. You must enter your name and EIN here and on page 2. Enter the business (legal) name that you used when you applied for your EIN on Form SS-4, Application for Employer Identification Number. For example, if you are a sole proprietor, enter "Ronald Smith" on the *Name* line and "Ron's Cycles" on the *Trade Name* line. Leave the *Trade Name* line blank if it is the same as your *Name*.

If you pay a tax preparer to fill out Form 940, make sure the preparer shows your business name exactly as it appeared when you applied for your EIN.

Employer identification number (EIN). The IRS monitors tax filings and payments by using a numerical system to identify taxpayers and to make sure that businesses comply with federal tax laws. A unique nine-digit EIN is assigned to all corporations, partnerships, and some sole proprietors. Businesses that need an EIN must apply for a number and use it throughout the life of the business on all tax returns, payments, and reports.

Your business should have only one EIN. If you have more than one and are unsure which one to use, call 1-800-829-4933 to verify your correct EIN.

If you do not have an EIN, apply for one by:

- Visiting the IRS website at IRS.gov and clicking on *Apply for an EIN Online* under *Tools*.
- Calling 1-800-829-4933 and applying by telephone, or
- Filling out Form SS-4 and mailing it to the address in the Instructions for Form SS-4 or faxing it to the number in the Instructions for Form SS-4.

If you have not received your EIN by the time a return is due, write *"Applied For"* and the date you applied in the space shown for the EIN on pages 1 and 2 of your return.

CAUTION *If you are filing your tax return electronically, a valid EIN is required at the time the return is filed. If a valid EIN is not provided, the return will not be accepted. This may result in penalties.*

TIP *Always be sure the EIN on the form you file exactly matches the EIN that the IRS assigned to your business. Do not use a social security number or individual taxpayer identification number (ITIN) on forms that ask for an EIN. Filing a Form 940 with an incorrect EIN or using the EIN of another's business may result in penalties and delays in processing your return.*

Tell Us if You Change Your Name or Address

Notify the IRS immediately if you change your business name or address.

- If your business name changes, write to the IRS using the *Without a payment* address under *Where Do You File?* Also see Pub. 1635, Employer Identification Number: Understanding Your EIN, for general information on EINs.
- If your address changes, complete and mail Form 8822-B, Change of Address—Business. Do not attach Form 8822-B to your Form 940. Mail Form 8822-B separately to the address indicated on Form 8822-B.

Type of Return

Review the box at the top of the form. If any line applies to you, check the appropriate box to tell us which type of return you are filing. You may check more than one box.

Amended. If this is an amended return that you are filing to correct a return that you previously filed, check box *a*.

Successor employer. Check box *b* if you are a successor employer and:

- You are reporting wages paid before you acquired the business by a predecessor who was required to file a Form 940 because the predecessor was an employer for FUTA tax purposes, or
- You are claiming a special credit for state unemployment tax paid before you acquired the business by a predecessor who was not required to file a Form 940 because the predecessor was not an employer for FUTA tax purposes.

A successor employer is an employer who:

- Acquires substantially all the property used in a trade or business of another person (predecessor) or used in a separate unit of a trade or business of a predecessor, and
- Immediately after the acquisition, employs one or more people who were employed by the predecessor.

No payments to employees in 2012. If you are not liable for FUTA tax for 2012 because you made no payments to employees in 2012, check box *c*. Then go to Part 7, sign the form, and file it with the IRS.

Final: Business closed or stopped paying wages. If this is a final return because you went out of business or stopped paying wages and you will not be liable for filing Form 940 in the future, check box *d*. Complete all applicable lines on the form, sign it in Part 7, and file it with the IRS. Include a statement showing the address at which your records will be kept and the name of the person keeping the records.

Disregarded entities. A disregarded entity is required to file Form 940 using its name and EIN, not the name and EIN of its owner. An entity that has a single owner and is disregarded as separate from its owner for federal income tax purposes is treated as a separate entity for purposes of payment and reporting federal employment taxes. If the entity does not currently have an EIN, it must apply for one using one of the

-5-

Form 940—Instructions (Page 6)

methods explained earlier. Disregarded entities include single-owner limited liability companies (LLCs) that have not elected to be taxed as a corporation for federal income tax purposes, qualified subchapter S subsidiaries, and certain foreign entities treated as disregarded entities for U.S. income tax purposes. Although a disregarded entity is treated as a separate entity for employment tax purposes, it is not subject to FUTA tax if it is owned by a tax-exempt organization under section 501(c)(3) and is not required to file Form 940. For more information, see *Disregarded entities and qualified subchapter S subsidiaries* in the *Introduction* section of Pub. 15 (Circular E).

Specific Instructions

Part 1: Tell Us About Your Return

1. If You Were Required to Pay Your State Unemployment Tax In . . .

Identify the state(s) where you were required to pay state unemployment taxes.

1a. One state only. Enter the two-letter U.S. Postal Service abbreviation for the state where you were required to pay your tax on line 1a. For a list of state abbreviations, see the Instructions for Schedule A (Form 940) or visit the website for the U.S. Postal Service at www.usps.com.

1b. More than one state (you are a multi-state employer). Check the box on line 1b. Then fill out Schedule A (Form 940), and attach it to your Form 940.

2. If You Paid Wages in a State That is Subject to Credit Reduction

If you paid wages that are subject to the unemployment tax laws of a credit reduction state, you may have to pay more FUTA tax when filing your Form 940.

A state that has not repaid money it borrowed from the federal government to pay unemployment benefits is called a *credit reduction state*. The U.S. Department of Labor determines which states are credit reduction states.

For tax year 2012, there are credit reduction states. If you paid wages subject to the unemployment tax laws of these states, check the box on line 2 and fill out Schedule A (Form 940). See the instructions for line 9 before completing the Schedule A (Form 940).

Part 2: Determine Your FUTA Tax Before Adjustments for 2012

If any line in Part 2 does not apply, leave it blank.

3. Total Payments to All Employees

Report the total payments you made during the calendar year on line 3. Include payments for the services of all employees, even if the payments are not taxable for FUTA. Your method of payment does not determine whether payments are wages. You may have paid wages hourly, daily, weekly, monthly, or yearly. You may have paid wages for piecework or as a percentage of profits. Include:

- **Compensation,** such as:
  —Salaries, wages, commissions, fees, bonuses, vacation allowances, and amounts you paid to full-time, part-time, or temporary employees.
- **Fringe benefits**, such as:
  —Sick pay (including third-party sick pay if liability is transferred to the employer). For details on sick pay, see Pub. 15-A, Employer's Supplemental Tax Guide.
  —The value of goods, lodging, food, clothing, and non-cash fringe benefits.
  —Section 125 (cafeteria) plan benefits.
- **Retirement/Pension**, such as:
  —Employer contributions to a 401(k) plan, payments to an Archer MSA, payments under adoption assistance programs, and contributions to SIMPLE retirement accounts (including elective salary reduction contributions).
  —Amounts deferred under a non-qualified deferred compensation plan.
- **Other payments**, such as:
  —Tips of $20 or more in a month that your employees reported to you.
  —Payments made by a predecessor employer to the employees of a business you acquired.
  —Payments to nonemployees who are treated as your employees by the state unemployment tax agency.

CAUTION *Wages may be subject to FUTA tax even if they are excluded from your state's unemployment tax.*

For details on wages and other compensation, see section 5 of Pub. 15-A.

Example:

You had 3 employees. You paid $44,000 to Employee A, $8,000 to Employee B, and $16,000 to Employee C.

$44,000	Amount paid to Employee A
8,000	Amount paid to Employee B
+ 16,000	Amount paid to Employee C
$68,000	Total payments to employees. You would enter this amount on line 3.

4. Payments Exempt from FUTA Tax

If you enter an amount on line 4, check the appropriate box or boxes on lines 4a through 4e to show the types of payments exempt from FUTA tax. **You only report a payment as exempt from FUTA tax on line 4 if you included the payment on line 3.**

Some payments are exempt from FUTA tax because the payments are not included in the definition of wages or the services are not included in the definition of employment. Payments exempt from FUTA tax may include:

- **Fringe benefits**, such as:
  —The value of certain meals and lodging.
  —Contributions to accident or health plans for employees, including certain employer payments to a Health Savings Account or an Archer MSA.
  —Employer reimbursements (including payments to a third party) for qualified moving expenses, to the extent that these expenses would otherwise be deductible by the employee.
  —Payments for benefits excluded under section 125 (cafeteria) plans.
- **Group term life insurance.**

For information about group term life insurance and other payments for fringe benefits that may be exempt from FUTA tax, see Pub. 15-B, Employer's Tax Guide to Fringe Benefits.

-6-

Form 940—Instructions (Page 7)

• **Retirement/Pension**, such as employer contributions to a qualified plan, including a SIMPLE retirement account (other than elective salary reduction contributions) and a 401(k) plan.
• **Dependent care**, such as payments (up to $5,000 per employee, $2,500 if married filing separately) for a qualifying person's care that allows your employees to work and that would be excludable by the employee under section 129.
• **Other payments**, such as:

—All non-cash payments and certain cash payments for agricultural labor, and all payments to "H-2A" visa workers. See *For agricultural employers*, earlier, or see Pub. 51 (Circular A).
—Payments made under a workers' compensation law because of a work-related injury or sickness. See section 6 of Pub. 15-A.
—Payments for domestic services if you did not pay cash wages of $1,000 or more (for all domestic employees) in any calendar quarter in 2011 or 2012. See Pub. 926.
—Payments for services provided to you by your parent, spouse, or child under the age of 21. See section 3 of Pub. 15 (Circular E).
—Payments for certain fishing activities. See Pub. 334,Tax Guide for Small Business.
—Payments to certain statutory employees. See section 1 of Pub. 15-A.
—Payments to nonemployees who are treated as your employees by the state unemployment tax agency.

See section 3306 and its related regulations for more information about FUTA taxation of retirement plan contributions, dependent care payments, and other payments.

For more information on payments exempt from FUTA tax, see section 14 in Pub. 15 (Circular E) or section 10 in Pub. 51 (Circular A).

Example:

You had 3 employees. You paid $44,000 to Employee A including $2,000 in health insurance benefits. You paid $8,000 to Employee B, including $500 in retirement benefits. You paid $16,000 to Employee C, including $2,000 in health and retirement benefits.

$ 2,000	Health insurance benefits for Employee A
500	Retirement benefits for Employee B
+ 2,000	Health and retirement benefits for Employee C
$4,500	Total payments exempt from FUTA tax. You would enter this amount on line 4 and check boxes 4a and 4c.

5. Total of Payments Made to Each Employee in Excess of $7,000

Only the first $7,000 you paid to each employee in a calendar year is subject to FUTA tax. This $7,000 is called the *FUTA wage base.*

Enter on line 5 the total of the payments over $7,000 you paid to each employee during 2012 **after subtracting any payments exempt from FUTA tax shown on line 4.**

Following our example:

You had three employees. You paid $44,000 to Employee A, $8,000 to Employee B, and $16,000 to Employee C, including a total of $4,500 in payments exempt from FUTA tax for all three employees. To determine the total payments made to each employee in excess of the FUTA wage base, the payments exempt from FUTA tax and the FUTA wage base must be subtracted from total payments. These amounts are shown in parentheses.

Employees	A	B	C
Total payments to employees	$44,000	$8,000	$16,000
Payments exempt from FUTA tax	(2,000)	(500)	(2,000)
FUTA wage base	(7,000)	(7,000)	(7,000)
	$35,000	$ 500	$ 7,000
Total of payments made to each employee in excess of $7,000. You would enter this amount on line 5.			$42,500

If you are a successor employer . . . When you figure the payments made to each employee in excess of $7,000, you may include the payments that the predecessor made to the employees who continue to work for you **only** if the predecessor was an employer for FUTA tax purposes resulting in the predecessor being required to file Form 940.

Example for successor employers:

During the calendar year, the predecessor employer paid $5,000 to Employee A. You acquired the predecessor's business. After the acquisition, you employed Employee A and paid Employee A an additional $3,000 in wages. None of the amounts paid to Employee A were payments exempt from FUTA tax.

$5,000	Wages paid by predecessor employer
+ 3,000	Wages paid by you
$8,000	Total payments to Employee A. You would include this amount on line 3.
$8,000	Total payments to Employee A
− 7,000	FUTA wage base
$1,000	Payments made to Employee A in excess of $7,000.
$1,000	Payments made to Employee A in excess of $7,000.
+ 5,000	Taxable FUTA wages paid by predecessor employer
$6,000	You would include this amount on line 5.

6. Subtotal

To figure your subtotal, add the amounts on lines 4 and 5 and enter the result on line 6.

line 4
+ line 5
line 6

7. Total Taxable FUTA Wages

To figure your total taxable FUTA wages, subtract line 6 from line 3 and enter the result on line 7.

line 3
− line 6
line 7

-7-

Form 940—Instructions (Page 8)

8. FUTA Tax Before Adjustments

To figure your total FUTA tax before adjustments, multiply line 7 by .006 and then enter the result on line 8.

line 7 x .006
line 8

Part 3: Determine Your Adjustments

If any line in Part 3 does not apply, leave it blank.

9. If ALL of the Taxable FUTA Wages You Paid Were Excluded from State Unemployment Tax. . .

If all of the taxable FUTA wages you paid were excluded from state unemployment tax, multiply line 7 by .054 and enter the result on line 9.

line 7
x .054
line 9

If you were not required to pay state unemployment tax because all of the wages you paid were excluded from state unemployment tax, you must pay FUTA tax at the 6.0% (.060) rate. For example, if your state unemployment tax law excludes wages paid to corporate officers or employees in specific occupations, and the only wages you paid were to corporate officers or employees in those specific occupations, you must pay FUTA tax on those wages at the full FUTA rate of 6.0% (.060). When you figured the FUTA tax before adjustments on line 8, it was based on the maximum allowable credit (5.4%) for state unemployment tax payments. Because you did not pay state unemployment tax, you do not have a credit and must figure this adjustment.

If line 9 applies to you, lines 10 and 11 do not apply to you. Therefore, leave lines 10 and 11 blank. Do not fill out the worksheet in these instructions or Schedule A (Form 940).

10. If SOME of the Taxable FUTA Wages You Paid Were Excluded From State Unemployment Tax, or You Paid any State Unemployment Tax Late...

You must fill out the worksheet on the next page if:

- Some of the taxable FUTA wages you paid were excluded from state unemployment, or
- Any of your payments of state unemployment tax were late.

The worksheet takes you step by step through the process of figuring your credit. You'll find an example of how to use it. Do not complete the worksheet if line 9 applied to you (see instructions above).

Before you can properly fill out the worksheet, you will need to gather the following information.

- Taxable FUTA wages (Form 940, line 7).
- Taxable state unemployment wages (state and federal wage bases may differ).
- The experience rates assigned to you by the states where you paid wages.
- The amount of state unemployment taxes you paid on time (*On time* means that you paid the state unemployment taxes by the due date for filing Form 940).
- The amount of state unemployment taxes you paid late. (*Late* means after the due date for filing Form 940.)

CAUTION *Do not include any penalties, interest, or unemployment taxes deducted from your employees' pay in the amount of state unemployment taxes. Also, do not include as state unemployment taxes any special administrative taxes or voluntary contributions you paid to get a lower assigned experience rate or any surcharges, excise taxes, or employment and training taxes. (These items are generally listed as separate items on the state's quarterly wage report.)*

For line 3 of the worksheet:

- If any of the experience rates assigned to you were less than 5.4% for any part of the calendar year, you must list each assigned experience rate separately on the worksheet.
- If you were assigned six or more experience rates that were less than 5.4% for any part of the calendar year, you must use another sheet to figure the additional credits and then include those additional credits in your line 3 total.

After you complete the worksheet, enter the amount from line 7 of the worksheet on Form 940, line 10. **Do not attach the worksheet to your Form 940.** Keep it with your records.

-8-

Form 940—Instructions (Page 9)

Worksheet—Line 10

Keep for Your Records

Before you begin: Read the *Example* before completing this worksheet.

Use this worksheet to figure your credit if:

√ Some of the wages you paid were excluded from state unemployment tax, OR
√ You paid any state unemployment tax late.

For this worksheet, **do not round your figures**.

Before you can properly fill out this worksheet, you must gather this information:

- Taxable FUTA wages (Form 940, line 7)
- Taxable state unemployment wages
- The experience rates assigned to you by the states where you paid wages
- The amount of state unemployment taxes you paid on time. (*On time* means that you paid the state unemployment taxes by the due date for filing Form 940.) Include any state unemployment taxes you paid on nonemployees who were treated as employees by your state unemployment agency.
- The amount of state unemployment taxes you paid late. (*Late* means after the due date for filing Form 940.)

1. **Maximum allowable credit** — Enter Form 940, line 7 ________ . ____ x .054 on line 1 (Form 940, line 7 x .054 = line 1). **1.** ________ . ____

2. **Credit for timely state unemployment tax payments — How much did you pay on time?** **2.** ________ . ____

- If line 2 is **equal to** or **more than** line 1, **STOP here.** STOP You have completed the worksheet. Leave Form 940, line 10 blank.
- If line 2 is **less than** line 1, continue this worksheet.

3. **Additional credit — Were ALL of your assigned experience rates 5.4% or more?**

- **If yes**, enter zero on line 3. Then go to line 4 of this worksheet.
- **If no**, fill out the computations below. List ONLY THOSE STATES for which your assigned experience rate for any part of the calendar year was less than 5.4%.

	State	Computation rate The difference between 5.4% (.054) and your assigned experience rate (.054 – .XXX (assigned experience rate) = computation rate)		Taxable state unemployment wages at assigned experience rate		Additional Credit
1.	______	. ________	x	________ . ____	=	________ . ____
2.	______	. ________	x	________ . ____	=	________ . ____
3.	______	. ________	x	________ . ____	=	________ . ____
4.	______	. ________	x	________ . ____	=	________ . ____
5.	______	. ________	x	________ . ____	=	________ . ____

If you need more lines, use another sheet and include those additional credits in the total. **Total** ________ . ____

Enter the total on line 3. **3.** ________ . ____

4. **Subtotal** (line 2 + line 3 = line 4) **4.** ________ . ____

- If line 4 is equal to or more than line 1, **STOP here.** STOP You have completed the worksheet. Leave Form 940, line 10 blank.
- If line 4 is less than line 1, continue this worksheet.

5. **Credit for paying state unemployment taxes late:**

5a. What is your remaining allowable credit? (line 1 – line 4 = line 5a) **5a.** ________ . ____

5b. How much state unemployment tax did you pay late? **5b.** ________ . ____

5c. Which is smaller, line 5a or line 5b? Enter the smaller number here. **5c.** ________ . ____

5d. Your allowable credit for paying state unemployment taxes late (line 5c x .90 = line 5d) **5d.** ________ . ____

6. **Your FUTA credit** (line 4 + line 5d = line 6) **6.** ________ . ____

- If line 6 is equal to or more than line 1, **STOP here.** STOP You have completed the worksheet. Leave Form 940, line 10 blank.
- If line 6 is less than line 1, continue this worksheet.

7. **Your adjustment** (line 1 – line 6 = line 7) Enter line 7 from this worksheet on Form 940, line 10. **7.** ________ . ____

Do not attach this worksheet to your Form 940. Keep it for your records.

-9-

Form 940—Instructions (Page 10)

Example for using the worksheet:

Employee A and Employee B are corporate officers whose wages are excluded from state unemployment tax in your state. Employee C's wages are not excluded from state unemployment tax. During 2012, you paid $44,000 to Employee A, $22,000 to Employee B, and $16,000 to Employee C. Your state's wage base is $8,000. You paid some state unemployment tax on time, some late, and some remains unpaid.

Here are the records:

Total taxable FUTA wages (Form 940, line 7)	$21,000.00
Taxable state unemployment wages	$ 8,000.00
Experience rate for 2012	.041(4.1%)
State unemployment tax paid on time	$100.00
State unemployment tax paid late	$78.00
State unemployment tax not paid	$150.00

1. Maximum allowable credit

$21,000.00 (Form 940, line 7)
x .054 (maximum credit rate)
$1,134.00

1. $1,134.00

2. Credit for timely state unemployment tax payments 2. $100.00

3. Additional credit 3. $104.00

.054 (maximum credit rate) $8,000
– .041 (your experience rate) x .013
.013 (your computation rate) $104.00

4. Subtotal (line 2 + line 3) 4. $204.00

$100
+ 104
$204

5. Credit for paying state unemployment taxes late

5a. Remaining allowable credit: (line 1 - line 4) 5a. $930.00

$1,134.00
– 204.00
$930.00

5b. State unemployment tax paid late: 5b. $78.00

5c. Which is smaller? Line 5a or line 5b? 5c. $78.00

5d. Allowable credit (for paying late) 5d. $70.20

$78.00
x .90
$70.20

6. Your FUTA credit (line 4 + line 5d) 6. $274.20

$204.00
+ 70.20
$274.20

7. Your adjustment (line 1 - line 6) 7. $859.80

$1,134.00
– 274.20
$859.80 **You would enter this amount on Form 940, line 10.**

11. If Credit Reduction Applies . . .

If you paid FUTA taxable wages that were also subject to state unemployment taxes in any states that are subject to credit reduction, enter the total amount from Schedule A (Form 940) on Form 940, line 11. However, if you entered an amount on line 9 because all the FUTA taxable wages you paid were excluded from state unemployment tax, skip line 11 and go to line 12.

Part 4: Determine Your FUTA Tax for 2012

If any line in Part 4 does not apply, leave it blank.

12. Total FUTA Tax After Adjustments

Add the amounts shown on lines 8, 9, 10, and 11, and enter the result on line 12.

line 8
line 9
line 10
+ line 11
line 12

CAUTION *If line 9 is greater than zero, lines 10 and 11 must be zero because they would not apply.*

13. FUTA Tax Deposited for the Year

Enter the amount of total FUTA tax that you deposited for the year, including any overpayment that you applied from a prior year.

14. Balance Due

If line 13 is less than line 12, enter the difference on line 14.

line 12
– line 13
line 14

If line 14 is:

- More than $500, you must deposit your tax. See *When Must You Deposit Your FUTA Tax.*
- $500 or less, you can deposit your tax, pay your tax with a major credit card, debit card, or pay your tax by check or money order with your return.
- Less than $1, you do not have to pay it.

CAUTION *If you do not deposit as required and pay any balance due with Form 940, you may be subject to a penalty.*

How to deposit or pay the balance due. You may pay the amount shown on line 14 using EFTPS, a credit or debit card, or electronic funds withdrawal (EFW). **Do not** use a credit or debit card or EFW to pay taxes that were required to be deposited. For more information on paying your taxes with a credit or debit card or EFW, go to www.irs.gov/e-pay.

If you pay by EFTPS, credit or debit card, or EFW, file your return using the *Without a payment* address under *Where Do You File?* and **do not** file Form 940-V, Payment Voucher.

15. Overpayment

If line 13 is more than line 12, enter the difference on line 15.

line 13
– line 12
line 15

If you deposited more than the FUTA tax due for the year, you may choose to have us either:

-10-

Form 940—Instructions (Page 11)

- Apply the refund to your next return, or
- Send you a refund.

Check the appropriate box in line 15 to tell us which option you select. If you do not check either box, we will automatically refund your overpayment. Also, we may apply your overpayment to any past due tax account you have.

If line 15 is less than $1, we will send you a refund or apply it to your next return only if you ask for it in writing.

Part 5: Report Your FUTA Tax Liability by Quarter Only if Line 12 is More Than $500

Fill out Part 5 **only** if line 12 is more than $500. If line 12 is $500 or less, leave Part 5 blank and go to Part 6.

16. Report the Amount of Your FUTA Tax Liability for Each Quarter

Enter the amount of your FUTA tax liability for each quarter on lines 16a–d. **Do not** enter the amount you deposited. If you had no liability for a quarter, leave the line blank.

16a. 1st quarter (January 1 to March 31).
16b. 2nd quarter (April 1 to June 30).
16c. 3rd quarter (July 1 to September 30).
16d. 4th quarter (October 1 to December 31).

To figure your FUTA tax liability for the fourth quarter, complete Form 940 through line 12. Then copy the amount from line 12 onto line 17. Lastly, subtract the sum of lines 16a through 16c from line 17 and enter the result on line 16d.

Example:
You paid wages on March 28 and your FUTA tax on those wages was $200. You were not required to make a deposit for the 1st quarter because your accumulated FUTA tax was $500 or less. You paid additional wages on June 28 and your FUTA tax on those wages was $400. Because your accumulated FUTA tax for the 1st and 2nd quarters exceeded $500, you were required to make a deposit of $600 by July 31.

You would enter $200 in line 16a because your liability for the 1st quarter is $200. You would also enter $400 in line 16b to show your 2nd quarter liability.

TIP *In years when there are credit reduction states, you must include liabilities owed for credit reduction with your fourth quarter deposit. You may deposit the anticipated extra liability throughout the year, but it is not due until the due date for the deposit for the fourth quarter, and the associated liability should be recorded as being incurred in the fourth quarter.*

17. Total Tax Liability for the Year

Your total tax liability for the year **must equal** line 12. Copy the amount from line 12 onto line 17.

Part 6: May We Speak With Your Third-Party Designee?

If you want to allow an employee, your paid tax preparer, or another person to discuss your Form 940 with the IRS, check the "Yes" box. Then enter the name and phone number of the person you choose as your designee. Be sure to give us the specific name of a person — not the name of the firm that prepared your tax return.

Have your designee select a five-digit Personal Identification Number (PIN) that he or she must use as identification when talking to the IRS about your form.

By checking "Yes," you authorize us to talk to your designee about any questions that we may have while we process your return. Your authorization applies only to this form, for this year; it does not apply to other forms or other tax years.

You are authorizing your designee to:

- Give us any information that is missing from your return,
- Ask us for information about processing your return, and
- Respond to certain IRS notices that you have shared with your designee about math errors and in preparing your return. We will **not** send notices to your designee.

You are **not** authorizing your designee to:

- Receive any refund check,
- Bind you to anything (including additional tax liability), or
- Otherwise represent you before the IRS.

The authorization will automatically expire 1 year after the due date for filing your Form 940 (regardless of extensions). If you or your designee want to end the authorization before it expires, write to the IRS office for your location using the *Without a payment* address under *Where Do You File?*

If you want to expand your designee's authorization or if you want us to send your designee copies of your notices, see Pub. 947, Practice Before the IRS and Power of Attorney.

Part 7: Sign Here

You MUST Fill Out Both Pages of This Form and SIGN It

Failure to sign will delay the processing of your return.

On page 2 in Part 7, sign and print your name and title. Then enter the date and the best daytime telephone number, including area code, where we can reach you if we have any questions.

Who Must Sign Form 940?

Form 940 must be signed as follows.

- **Sole proprietorship**—The individual who owns the business.
- **Partnership (including a limited liability company (LLC) treated as a partnership) or unincorporated organization**—A responsible and duly authorized partner, member, or officer having knowledge of its affairs.
- **Corporation (including an LLC treated as a corporation)**—The president, vice president, or other principal officer duly authorized to sign.
- **Single member LLC treated as a disregarded entity for federal income tax purposes**—The owner of the LLC or a principal officer duly authorized to sign.
- **Trust or estate**—The fiduciary.

Form 940 may also be signed by a duly authorized agent of the taxpayer if a valid power of attorney or reporting agent authorization (Form 8655, Reporting Agent Authorization) has been filed.

Alternative signature method. Corporate officers or duly authorized agents may sign Form 940 by rubber stamp, mechanical device, or computer software program. For details and required documentation, see Rev. Proc. 2005-39, 2005-28 I.R.B. 82, available at *www.irs.gov/irb/2005-28_IRB/ar16.html*.

Paid preparers. A paid preparer must sign Form 940 and provide the information in the *Paid Preparer Use Only* section of Part 7 if the preparer was paid to prepare Form 940 and is not an employee of the filing entity. Paid preparers must sign paper returns with a manual signature. The preparer must give you a copy of the return in addition to the copy to be filed with IRS.

If you are a paid preparer, enter your Preparer Tax Identification Number (PTIN) in the space provided. Include your complete address. If you work for a firm, write the firm's name and the EIN of the firm. You can apply for a PTIN online or by

-11-

Form 940—Instructions (Page 12)

filing Form W-12, IRS Paid Preparer Tax Identification Number (PTIN) Application and Renewal. For more information about applying for a PTIN online, visit the IRS website at www.irs.gov/ptin. You cannot use your PTIN in place of the EIN of the tax preparation firm.

Generally, do not complete the Paid Preparer Use Only section if you are filing the return as a reporting agent and have a valid Form 8655 on file with the IRS. However, a reporting agent must complete this section if the reporting agent offered legal advice, for example, by advising the client on determining whether its workers are employees or independent contractors for Federal tax purposes.

Privacy Act and Paperwork Reduction Act Notice

We ask for the information on Form 940 to carry out the Internal Revenue laws of the United States. We need it to figure and collect the right amount of tax. Subtitle C, Employment Taxes, of the Internal Revenue Code imposes unemployment tax under the Federal Unemployment Tax Act. Form 940 is used to determine the amount of the taxes that you owe. Section 6011 requires you to provide the requested information if the tax is applicable to you. Section 6109 requires you to provide your identification number. If you fail to provide this information in a timely manner, or provide false or fraudulent information, you may be subject to penalties and interest.

You are not required to provide the information requested on a form that is subject to the Paperwork Reduction Act unless the form displays a valid OMB control number. Books or records relating to a form or instructions must be retained as long as their contents may become material in the administration of any Internal Revenue law.

Generally, tax returns and return information are confidential, as required by section 6103. However, section 6103 allows or requires the IRS to disclose or give the information shown on your tax return to others as described in the Code. For example, we may disclose your tax information to the Department of Justice for civil and criminal litigation, and to cities, states, the District of Columbia, and U.S. commonwealths and possessions to administer their tax laws. We may also disclose this information to other countries under a tax treaty, to federal and state agencies to enforce federal nontax criminal laws, or to federal law enforcement and intelligence agencies to combat terrorism.

If you have comments concerning the accuracy of these time estimates or suggestions for making these forms simpler, we would be happy to hear from you. You can email us at taxforms@irs.gov. Enter "Form 940" on the subject line. Or write to: Internal Revenue Service, Tax Products Coordinating Committee, SE:W:CAR:MP:T:M:S, 1111 Constitution Avenue, NW, IR-6526, Washington, DC 20224. Do not send Form 940 to this address. Instead, see *Where Do You File*, earlier.

Estimated average times

The time needed to complete and file this form will vary depending on individual circumstances. The estimated average time is:

Form	Recordkeeping	Learning about the law or the form	Preparing the form	Copying, assembling, and sending the form to the IRS
Schedule A (Form 940)	16 hrs., 01 min.		15 min.	
Worksheet (Form 940)	1 hr., 41 min.		21 min.	
Voucher (Form 940-V)	21 min.		4 min.	

-12-

Schedule A, Form 940 (Page 1)

Schedule A (Form 940) for 2012:

860312

Multi-State Employer and Credit Reduction Information

Department of the Treasury — Internal Revenue Service

OMB No. 1545-0028

Employer identification number (EIN) ☐☐ – ☐☐☐☐☐☐☐

Name *(not your trade name)* ____________________

See the instructions on page 2. File this schedule with Form 940.

Place an "X" in the box of EVERY state in which you were required to pay state unemployment tax this year. For states with a credit reduction rate greater than zero, enter the FUTA taxable wages, multiply by the reduction rate, and then enter the credit reduction amount for that state. If any states do not apply to you, leave them blank.

Postal Abbreviation	FUTA Taxable Wages	Reduction Rate	Credit Reduction	Postal Abbreviation	FUTA Taxable Wages	Reduction Rate	Credit Reduction
☐ AK	.	× .000	.	☐ NC	.	× .006	.
☐ AL	.	× .000	.	☐ ND	.	× .000	.
☐ AR	.	× .006	.	☐ NE	.	× .000	.
☐ AZ	.	× .003	.	☐ NH	.	× .000	.
☐ CA	.	× .006	.	☐ NJ	.	× .006	.
☐ CO	.	× .000	.	☐ NM	.	× .000	.
☐ CT	.	× .006	.	☐ NV	.	× .006	.
☐ DC	.	× .000	.	☐ NY	.	× .006	.
☐ DE	.	× .003	.	☐ OH	.	× .006	.
☐ FL	.	× .006	.	☐ OK	.	× .000	.
☐ GA	.	× .006	.	☐ OR	.	× .000	.
☐ HI	.	× .000	.	☐ PA	.	× .000	.
☐ IA	.	× .000	.	☐ RI	.	× .006	.
☐ ID	.	× .000	.	☐ SC	.	× .000	.
☐ IL	.	× .000	.	☐ SD	.	× .000	.
☐ IN	.	× .009	.	☐ TN	.	× .000	.
☐ KS	.	× .000	.	☐ TX	.	× .000	.
☐ KY	.	× .006	.	☐ UT	.	× .000	.
☐ LA	.	× .000	.	☐ VA	.	× .000	.
☐ MA	.	× .000	.	☐ VT	.	× .003	.
☐ MD	.	× .000	.	☐ WA	.	× .000	.
☐ ME	.	× .000	.	☐ WI	.	× .006	.
☐ MI	.	× .000	.	☐ WV	.	× .000	.
☐ MN	.	× .000	.	☐ WY	.	× .000	.
☐ MO	.	× .006	.	☐ PR	.	× .000	.
☐ MS	.	× .000	.	☐ VI	.	× .015	.
☐ MT	.	× .000	.				

Total Credit Reduction. Add all amounts shown in the *Credit Reduction* boxes. Enter the total here and on Form 940, line 11 . . . . [.]

For Privacy Act and Paperwork Reduction Act Notice, see the last page of Form 940. Cat. No. 16997C **Schedule A (Form 940) 2012**

Schedule A, Form 940 (Page 2)

Instructions for Schedule A (Form 940) for 2012:

860412

Multi-State Employer and Credit Reduction Information

For more information on completing Schedule A, see the Frequently Asked Questions, available at *www.irs.gov/form940.*

Specific Instructions: Completing Schedule A

Step 1. Check the box for every state (including the District of Columbia, Puerto Rico, and the U.S. Virgin Islands) in which you were required to pay state unemployment taxes this year even if the state's credit reduction rate is zero.

Note. Make sure that you have applied for a state unemployment number for your business. If you do not have an unemployment account number from a state in which you paid wages, contact the state office to receive one. For a list of state unemployment agencies, visit the U.S. Department of Labor's website at *www.workforcesecurity.doleta.gov/unemploy/agencies.asp.*

The table below provides the two-letter postal abbreviations used on Schedule A.

State	Postal Abbreviation	State	Postal Abbreviation
Alabama	AL	Montana	MT
Alaska	AK	Nebraska	NE
Arizona	AZ	Nevada	NV
Arkansas	AR	New Hampshire	NH
California	CA	New Jersey	NJ
Colorado	CO	New Mexico	NM
Connecticut	CT	New York	NY
Delaware	DE	North Carolina	NC
District of Columbia	DC	North Dakota	ND
Florida	FL	Ohio	OH
Georgia	GA	Oklahoma	OK
Hawaii	HI	Oregon	OR
Idaho	ID	Pennsylvania	PA
Illinois	IL	Rhode Island	RI
Indiana	IN	South Carolina	SC
Iowa	IA	South Dakota	SD
Kansas	KS	Tennessee	TN
Kentucky	KY	Texas	TX
Louisiana	LA	Utah	UT
Maine	ME	Vermont	VT
Maryland	MD	Virginia	VA
Massachusetts	MA	Washington	WA
Michigan	MI	West Virginia	WV
Minnesota	MN	Wisconsin	WI
Mississippi	MS	Wyoming	WY
Missouri	MO	Puerto Rico	PR
		U.S. Virgin Islands	VI

Step 2. You are subject to credit reduction if you paid FUTA taxable wages that were also subject to state unemployment taxes in any state listed that has a credit reduction rate greater than zero.

If you paid FUTA taxable wages that were also subject to state unemployment taxes in any states that are subject to credit reduction, find the lines for each state.

In the *FUTA Taxable Wages* box, enter the total FUTA taxable wages that you paid in that state. (The FUTA wage base for all states is $7,000.) However, do not include in the *FUTA Taxable Wages* box wages that were excluded from state unemployment tax.

Note. Do not enter your state unemployment wages in the *FUTA Taxable Wages* box.

Then multiply the total taxable FUTA wages by the reduction rate.

Enter your total in the *Credit Reduction* box at the end of the line.

Step 3. Total credit reduction

To calculate the total credit reduction, add up all of the *Credit Reduction* boxes and enter the amount in the *Total Credit Reduction* box.

Then enter the total credit reduction on Form 940, line 11.

Example 1

You paid $20,000 in wages to each of three employees in State A. State A is subject to credit reduction at a rate of .003 (.3%). Because you paid wages in a state that is subject to credit reduction, you must complete Schedule A and file it with Form 940.

Total payments to all employees in State A	$60,000
Payments exempt from FUTA tax (see the Instructions for Form 940)	$0
Total payments made to each employee in excess of $7,000 (3 x ($20,000 - $7,000))	$39,000
Total taxable FUTA wages you paid in State A entered in the *FUTA Taxable Wages* box ($60,000 - $0 - $39,000)	$21,000
Credit reduction rate for State A	.003
Total credit reduction for State A ($21,000 x .003)	$63

Caution. *Do not include in the* FUTA Taxable Wages *box wages in excess of the $7,000 wage base for each employee subject to unemployment insurance in the credit reduction state. The credit reduction applies only to taxable FUTA wages.*

In this case, you would write $63.00 in the *Total Credit Reduction* box and then enter that amount on Form 940, line 11.

Example 2

You paid $48,000 ($4,000 a month) in wages to Employee A and no payments were exempt from FUTA tax. Employee A worked in State B (not subject to credit reduction) in January and then transferred to State C (subject to credit reduction) on February 1. Because you paid wages in more than one state, you must complete Schedule A and file it with Form 940.

The total payments in State B that are not exempt from FUTA tax are $4,000. Since this payment to Employee A does not exceed the $7,000 FUTA wage base, the total taxable FUTA wages paid in State B are $4,000.

The total payments in State C that are not exempt from FUTA tax are $44,000. However, $4,000 of FUTA taxable wages was paid in State B with respect to Employee A. Therefore, the total taxable FUTA wages with respect to Employee A in State C is $3,000 ($7,000 (FUTA wage base) - $4,000 (total FUTA taxable wages paid in State B)). Enter $3,000 in the *FUTA Taxable Wages* box, multiply it by the *Reduction Rate*, and then enter the result in the *Credit Reduction* box.

Attach Schedule A to Form 940 when you file your return.

Page **2**

Form 941 (Page 1)

Form **941 for 2013: Employer's QUARTERLY Federal Tax Return** 950113
(Rev. January 2013) Department of the Treasury — Internal Revenue Service OMB No. 1545-0029

Employer identification number (EIN) ☐☐ – ☐☐☐☐☐☐☐

Name *(not your trade name)*

Trade name *(if any)*

Address
Number Street Suite or room number
City State ZIP code

Report for this Quarter of 2013
(Check one.)

☐ **1:** January, February, March
☐ **2:** April, May, June
☐ **3:** July, August, September
☐ **4:** October, November, December

Instructions and prior year forms are available at *www.irs.gov/form941.*

Read the separate instructions before you complete Form 941. Type or print within the boxes.

Part 1: Answer these questions for this quarter.

1	**Number of employees who received wages, tips, or other compensation for the pay period including: *Mar. 12* (Quarter 1), *June 12* (Quarter 2), *Sept. 12* (Quarter 3), or *Dec. 12* (Quarter 4)**	1	
2	**Wages, tips, and other compensation**	2	.
3	**Income tax withheld from wages, tips, and other compensation**	3	.
4	**If no wages, tips, and other compensation are subject to social security or Medicare tax**	☐	**Check and go to line 6.**

		Column 1		Column 2
5a	**Taxable social security wages**	.	× .124 =	.
5b	**Taxable social security tips**	.	× .124 =	.
5c	**Taxable Medicare wages & tips**	.	× .029 =	.
5d	**Taxable wages & tips subject to Additional Medicare Tax withholding**	.	× .009 =	.

5e	**Add Column 2 from lines 5a, 5b, 5c, and 5d**	5e	.
5f	**Section 3121(q) Notice and Demand—Tax due on unreported tips** (see instructions)	5f	.
6	**Total taxes before adjustments** (add lines 3, 5e, and 5f)	6	.
7	**Current quarter's adjustment for fractions of cents**	7	.
8	**Current quarter's adjustment for sick pay**	8	.
9	**Current quarter's adjustments for tips and group-term life insurance**	9	.
10	**Total taxes after adjustments.** Combine lines 6 through 9	10	.
11	**Total deposits for this quarter, including overpayment applied from a prior quarter and overpayment applied from Form 941-X or Form 944-X filed in the current quarter**	11	.
12a	**COBRA premium assistance payments** (see instructions)	12a	.
12b	**Number of individuals provided COBRA premium assistance**		
13	**Add lines 11 and 12a**	13	.
14	**Balance due.** If line 10 is more than line 13, enter the difference and see instructions	14	.
15	**Overpayment.** If line 13 is more than line 10, enter the difference .	Check one: ☐ Apply to next return. ☐ Send a refund.	

▶ **You MUST complete both pages of Form 941 and SIGN it.** Next ▶

For Privacy Act and Paperwork Reduction Act Notice, see the back of the Payment Voucher. Cat. No. 17001Z Form **941** (Rev. 1-2013)

Form 941 (Page 2)

950213

Name *(not your trade name)* | Employer identification number (EIN)

Part 2: Tell us about your deposit schedule and tax liability for this quarter.

If you are unsure about whether you are a monthly schedule depositor or a semiweekly schedule depositor, see Pub. 15 (Circular E), section 11.

16 Check one: ☐ **Line 10 on this return is less than $2,500 or line 10 on the return for the prior quarter was less than $2,500, and you did not incur a $100,000 next-day deposit obligation during the current quarter.** If line 10 for the prior quarter was less than $2,500 but line 10 on this return is $100,000 or more, you must provide a record of your federal tax liability. If you are a monthly schedule depositor, complete the deposit schedule below; if you are a semiweekly schedule depositor, attach Schedule B (Form 941). Go to Part 3.

☐ **You were a monthly schedule depositor for the entire quarter.** Enter your tax liability for each month and total liability for the quarter, then go to Part 3.

Tax liability: Month 1 ______ .

Month 2 ______ .

Month 3 ______ .

Total liability for quarter ______ . **Total must equal line 10.**

☐ **You were a semiweekly schedule depositor for any part of this quarter.** Complete Schedule B (Form 941), Report of Tax Liability for Semiweekly Schedule Depositors, and attach it to Form 941.

Part 3: Tell us about your business. If a question does NOT apply to your business, leave it blank.

17 If your business has closed or you stopped paying wages . . . . ☐ Check here, and

enter the final date you paid wages ___ / ___ / ___ .

18 If you are a seasonal employer and you do not have to file a return for every quarter of the year . . ☐ Check here.

Part 4: May we speak with your third-party designee?

Do you want to allow an employee, a paid tax preparer, or another person to discuss this return with the IRS? See the instructions for details.

☐ Yes. Designee's name and phone number ______ ______

Select a 5-digit Personal Identification Number (PIN) to use when talking to the IRS. ☐☐☐☐☐

☐ No.

Part 5: Sign here. You MUST complete both pages of Form 941 and SIGN it.

Under penalties of perjury, I declare that I have examined this return, including accompanying schedules and statements, and to the best of my knowledge and belief, it is true, correct, and complete. Declaration of preparer (other than taxpayer) is based on all information of which preparer has any knowledge.

X Sign your name here ______

Print your name here ______

Print your title here ______

Date ___ / ___ / ___

Best daytime phone ______

Paid Preparer Use Only

Check if you are self-employed . . . ☐

Preparer's name		PTIN	
Preparer's signature		Date	/ /
Firm's name (or yours if self-employed)		EIN	
Address		Phone	
City	State	ZIP code	

Page **2** Form **941** (Rev. 1-2013)

Form 941—Instructions (Page 1)

Instructions for Form 941

Department of the Treasury
Internal Revenue Service

(Rev. January 2012)

Employer's QUARTERLY Federal Tax Return

Section references are to the Internal Revenue Code unless otherwise noted.

What's New

Future developments. The IRS has created a page on IRS.gov for information about Form 941, at *www.irs.gov/form941*. Information about any future developments affecting Form 941 (such as legislation enacted after we release it) will be posted on that page.

Social security and Medicare tax for 2012. The employee tax rate for social security is 4.2% and the employer tax rate for social security is 6.2%, unchanged from 2011. The social security wage base limit is $110,100. The Medicare tax rate is 1.45% each for the employee and employer, unchanged from 2011. There is no wage base limit for Medicare tax.

Social security and Medicare taxes apply to the wages of household workers you pay $1,800 or more in cash or an equivalent form of compensation in 2012. Social security and Medicare taxes apply to election workers who are paid $1,500 or more in cash or an equivalent form of compensation in 2012.

VOW to Hire Heroes Act of 2011. On November 21, 2011, the President signed into law the VOW to Hire Heroes Act of 2011. This new law provides an expanded work opportunity tax credit to businesses that hire eligible unemployed veterans and, for the first time, also makes part of the credit available to certain tax-exempt organizations. Businesses claim the credit as part of the general business credit and tax-exempt organizations claim it against their payroll tax liability using Form 5884-C, Work Opportunity Credit for Qualified Tax-Exempt Organizations Hiring Qualified Veterans. The liability reported on Form 941 is not reduced by the amount of the credit. The credit is available for eligible unemployed veterans who begin work on or after November 22, 2011, and before January 1, 2013. For more information about the credit, visit *www.irs.gov/form5884c*.

Change of address. Beginning in 2012, employers must use new Form 8822-B, Change of Address—Business, for any address change.

Reminders

Section 3121(q) Notice and Demand—Tax due on unreported tips. An employer enters the amount of social security and Medicare taxes on unreported tips shown on the Section 3121(q) Notice and Demand on line 5e of the employer's Form 941 for the calendar quarter corresponding to the "Date of Notice and Demand."

Employers can choose to file Forms 941 instead of Form 944. Employers that would otherwise be required to file Form 944, Employer's ANNUAL Federal Tax Return, can notify the IRS if they want to file quarterly Forms 941 instead of annual Form 944. See Rev. Proc. 2009-51 2009-45 I.R.B. 625, available at *www.irs.gov/irb/2009-45_IRB/ar12.html*.

Correcting a previously filed Form 941. If you discover an error on a previously filed Form 941, make the correction using Form 941-X, Adjusted Employer's QUARTERLY Federal Tax Return or Claim for Refund. Form 941-X is filed separately from Form 941. For more information, see section 13 of Pub. 15 (Circular E), Employer's Tax Guide, or visit IRS.gov and enter the keywords *Correcting Employment Taxes*.

Paid preparers must sign Form 941. Paid preparers must complete and sign the paid preparer's section of Form 941.

Aggregate Form 941 filers. Agents must complete Schedule R (Form 941), Allocation Schedule for Aggregate Form 941 Filers, when filing an aggregate Form 941. Aggregate Forms 941 are filed by agents approved by the IRS under section 3504. To request approval to act as an agent for an employer, the agent files Form 2678, Employer/Payer Appointment of Agent, with the IRS.

COBRA premium assistance credit. The credit for COBRA premium assistance payments applies to premiums paid for employees involuntarily terminated between September 1, 2008, and May 31, 2010, and to premiums paid for up to 15 months. See *COBRA Premium Assistance Payments*, later.

Federal tax deposits must be made by electronic funds transfer. You must use electronic funds transfer to make all federal tax deposits. Generally, electronic funds transfers are made using the Electronic Federal Tax Payment System (EFTPS). If you do not want to use EFTPS, you can arrange for your tax professional, financial institution, payroll service, or other trusted third party to make deposits on your behalf. Also, you may arrange for your financial institution to initiate a same-day wire payment on your behalf. EFTPS is a free service provided by the Department of Treasury. Services provided by your tax professional, financial institution, payroll service, or other third party may have a fee.

For more information on making federal tax deposits, see section 11 of Pub. 15 (Circular E). To get more information about EFTPS or to enroll in EFTPS, visit *www.eftps.gov* or call 1-800-555-4477. Additional information about EFTPS is also available in Pub. 966, The Secure Way to Pay Your Federal Taxes.

CAUTION *For an EFTPS deposit to be on time, you must initiate the deposit by 8 p.m. Eastern time the day before the date the deposit is due.*

Same-day wire payment option. If you fail to initiate a deposit transaction on EFTPS by 8 p.m. Eastern time the day before the date a deposit is due, you can still make your deposit on time by using the Federal Tax Application (FTA). If you ever need the same-day wire payment method, you will need to make arrangements with your financial institution ahead of time. Please check with your financial institution regarding availability, deadlines, and costs. Your financial institution may charge you a fee for payments made this way. To learn more about the information you will need to provide your financial institution to make a same-day wire payment, visit *www.eftps.gov* to download the *Same-Day Payment Worksheet*.

Timeliness of federal tax deposits. If a deposit is required to be made on a day that is not a business day, the deposit is considered timely if it is made by the close of the next business day. A business day is any day other than a Saturday, Sunday, or legal holiday. The term "legal holiday"

Feb 24, 2012 Cat. No. 14625L

Form 941—Instructions (Page 2)

for deposit purposes includes only those legal holidays in the District of Columbia. Legal holidays in the District of Columbia are provided in Pub. 15 (Circular E). Previously, legal holidays for deposits included statewide legal holidays.

Electronic filing and payment. Now, more than ever before, businesses can enjoy the benefits of filing tax returns and paying their federal taxes electronically. Whether you rely on a tax professional or handle your own taxes, the IRS offers you convenient programs to make filing and paying easier. Spend less time and worry on taxes and more time running your business. Use e-file and the Electronic Federal Tax Payment System (EFTPS) to your benefit.

- For e-file, visit the IRS website at *www.irs.gov/efile* for additional information.
- For EFTPS, visit *www.eftps.gov* or call EFTPS Customer Service at 1-800-555-4477, 1-800-733-4829 (TDD), or 1-800-244-4829 (Spanish).

CAUTION *If you are filing your tax return or paying your federal taxes electronically, a valid EIN is required at the time the return is filed. If a valid EIN is not provided, the return or payment will not be processed. This may result in penalties and delays in processing your return or payment.*

Electronic funds withdrawal (EFW). If you file Form 941 electronically, you can e-file and e-pay (electronic funds withdrawal) the balance due in a single step using tax preparation software or through a tax professional. However, **do not** use EFW to make federal tax deposits. For more information on paying your taxes using EFW, visit the IRS website at *www.irs.gov/e-pay*. A fee may be charged to file electronically.

Credit or debit card payments. Employers can pay the balance due shown on Form 941 by credit or debit card. **Do not** use a credit or debit card to make federal tax deposits. For more information on paying your taxes with a credit or debit card, visit the IRS website at *www.irs.gov/e-pay*.

Employer's liability. Employers are responsible to ensure that tax returns are filed and deposits and payments are made, even if the employer contracts with a third party. The employer remains liable if the third party fails to perform a required action.

Where can you get telephone help? You can call the IRS Business and Specialty Tax Line toll-free at 1-800-829-4933 (TTY/TDD for the hearing impaired at 1-800-829-4059), Monday through Friday from 7 a.m. to 7 p.m. local time (Alaska and Hawaii follow Pacific time) for answers to your questions about completing Form 941, tax deposit rules, or obtaining an employer identification number (EIN).

Photographs of missing children. The Internal Revenue Service is a proud partner with the National Center for Missing and Exploited Children. Photographs of missing children selected by the Center may appear in instructions on pages that would otherwise be blank. You can help bring these children home by looking at the photographs and calling 1-800-THE-LOST (1-800-843-5678) if you recognize a child.

General Instructions:

Purpose of Form 941

These instructions give you some background information about Form 941. They tell you who must file Form 941, how to complete it line by line, and when and where to file it.

If you want more in-depth information about payroll tax topics relating to Form 941, see Pub. 15 (Circular E) or visit the IRS website at *www.irs.gov/businesses* and click on the *Employment Taxes* link.

Federal law requires you, as an employer, to withhold taxes from your employees' paychecks. Each time you pay wages, you must withhold – or take out of your employees' paychecks – certain amounts for federal income tax, social security tax, and Medicare tax. Under the withholding system, taxes withheld from your employees are credited to your employees in payment of their tax liabilities.

Federal law also requires you to pay any liability for the employer's portion of social security and Medicare taxes. This portion of social security and Medicare taxes is not withheld from employees.

Who Must File Form 941?

Use Form 941 to report the following amounts.

- Wages you have paid.
- Tips your employees have received.
- Federal income tax you withheld.
- Both the employer's and the employee's share of social security and Medicare taxes.
- Current quarter's adjustments to social security and Medicare taxes for fractions of cents, sick pay, tips, and group-term life insurance.
- Credit for COBRA premium assistance payments.

Do not use the Form 941 to report backup withholding or income tax withholding on **nonpayroll** payments such as pensions, annuities, and gambling winnings. Report these types of withholding on Form 945, Annual Return of Withheld Federal Income Tax.

After you file your first Form 941, you must file a return for each quarter, even if you have no taxes to report, unless you filed a **final return** or one of the exceptions listed below applies.

Exceptions

Special rules apply to some employers.

- **Seasonal employers** do not have to file a Form 941 for quarters in which they have no tax liability because they have paid no wages. To tell the IRS that you will not file a return for one or more quarters during the year, check the box on line 18 **every quarter** you file Form 941. See section 12 of Pub. 15 (Circular E) for more information.
- Employers of **household employees** do not usually file Form 941. See Pub. 926, Household Employer's Tax Guide, and Schedule H (Form 1040), Household Employment Taxes, for more information.
- Employers of **farm employees** do not usually file Form 941. See Form 943, Employer's Annual Federal Tax Return for Agricultural Employees, and Pub. 51 (Circular A), Agricultural Employer's Tax Guide.

TIP *If none of the above exceptions applies and you have not filed a final return, you **must** file Form 941 each quarter even if you did not pay wages during the quarter. Use IRS e-file, if possible.*

What if You Reorganize or Close Your Business?

If You Sell or Transfer Your Business . . .

If you sell or transfer your business, you and the new owner must each file a Form 941 for the quarter in which the transfer occurred. Report only the wages you paid.

When two businesses merge, the continuing firm must file a return for the quarter in which the change took place and the other firm should file a **final return**.

Form 941—Instructions (Page 3)

Changing from one form of business to another—such as from a sole proprietorship to a partnership or corporation—is considered a transfer. If a transfer occurs, you may need a new EIN. See section 1 of Pub. 15 (Circular E). Attach a statement to your return with:

- The new owner's name (or the new name of the business);
- Whether the business is now a sole proprietorship, partnership, or corporation;
- The kind of change that occurred (a sale or transfer);
- The date of the change; and
- The name of the person keeping the payroll records and the address where those records will be kept.

If Your Business Has Closed . . .

If you go out of business or stop paying wages to your employees, you must file a **final return.** To tell the IRS that Form 941 for a particular quarter is your final return, check the box on line 17 and enter the date you last paid wages. Also attach a statement to your return showing the name of the person keeping the payroll records and the address where those records will be kept.

See the General Instructions for Forms W-2 and W-3 for information about earlier dates for the expedited furnishing and filing of Forms W-2, Wage and Tax Statement, when a final Form 941 is filed.

If you participated in a statutory merger or consolidation, or qualify for predecessor-successor status due to an acquisition, you should generally file Schedule D (Form 941), Report of Discrepancies Caused by Acquisitions, Statutory Mergers, or Consolidations. See the Instructions for Schedule D (Form 941) to determine whether you should file Schedule D (Form 941) and when you should file it.

When Must You File?

File your initial Form 941 for the quarter in which you first paid wages that are subject to social security and Medicare taxes or subject to federal income tax withholding. See the table below titled, *When To File Form 941.*

Then you must file for every quarter after that—every 3 months—even if you have no taxes to report, unless you are a seasonal employer or are filing your final return. See *Seasonal employers* and *If Your Business Has Closed*, earlier.

File Form 941 only once for each quarter. If you filed electronically, do not file a paper Form 941. For more information about filing Form 941 electronically, see *Electronic filing and payment*, earlier.

When To File Form 941

Your Form 941 is due by the last day of the month that follows the end of the quarter.

The Quarter Includes . . .	Quarter Ends	Form 941 Is Due
1. January, February, March	March 31	April 30
2. April, May, June	June 30	July 31
3. July, August, September	September 30	October 31
4. October, November, December	December 31	January 31

For example, you generally must report wages you pay during the first quarter—which is January through March—by April 30. If you made timely deposits in full payment of your taxes for a quarter, you have 10 more days after the due dates shown above to file your Form 941.

If we receive Form 941 after the due date, we will treat Form 941 as filed on time if the envelope containing Form 941 is properly addressed, contains sufficient postage, and is postmarked by the U.S. Postal Service on or before the due date, or sent by an IRS-designated private delivery service on or before the due date. If you do not follow these guidelines, we will consider Form 941 filed when it is actually received. See Pub. 15 (Circular E) for more information on IRS-designated private delivery services.

If any due date for filing shown above falls on a Saturday, Sunday, or legal holiday, you may file your return on the next business day.

How Should You Complete Form 941?

Type or print your EIN, name, and address in the spaces provided. Also enter your name and EIN on the top of page 2. **Do not** use your social security number (SSN) or individual taxpayer identification number (ITIN). Generally, enter the business (legal) name you used when you applied for your EIN on Form SS-4, Application for Employer Identification Number. For example, if you are a sole proprietor, enter "Haleigh Smith" on the "Name" line and "Haleigh's Cycles" on the "Trade name" line. Leave the "Trade name" line blank if it is the same as your "Name."

Employer identification number (EIN). To make sure businesses comply with federal tax laws, the IRS monitors tax filings and payments by using a numerical system to identify taxpayers. A unique nine-digit employer identification number (EIN) is assigned to all corporations, partnerships, and some sole proprietors. Businesses needing an EIN must apply for a number and use it throughout the life of the business on all tax returns, payments, and reports.

Your business should have only one EIN. If you have more than one and are not sure which one to use, write to the IRS office where you file your returns (using the *Without a payment* address under *Where Should You File*, later) or call the IRS at 1-800-829-4933.

If you do not have an EIN, you may apply for one online. Go to IRS.gov and click on the *Apply for an EIN Online* link. You may also apply for an EIN by calling 1-800-829-4933, or you can fax or mail Form SS-4 to the IRS. If you have not received your EIN by the due date of Form 941, write "Applied For" and the date you applied in this entry space.

CAUTION *If you are filing your tax return electronically, a valid EIN is required at the time the return is filed. If a valid EIN is not provided, the return will not be accepted. This may result in penalties and delays in processing your return.*

TIP *Always be sure the EIN on the form you file exactly matches the EIN the IRS assigned to your business. Do not use your social security number on forms that ask for an EIN. Filing a Form 941 with an incorrect EIN or using another business's EIN may result in penalties and delays in processing your return.*

If you change your name or address... Notify the IRS immediately if you change your business name or address.

- Write to the IRS office where you file your returns (using the *Without a payment* address under *Where Should You File*, later) to notify the IRS of any name change. See Pub. 1635, Understanding Your Employer Identification Number (EIN), to see if you need to apply for a new EIN.
- Complete and mail Form 8822-B, Change of Address—Business, for any address change.

Check the Box for the Quarter

Under "Report for this Quarter of 2012" at the top of Form 941, check the appropriate box of the quarter for which you are filing. Make sure the quarter checked is the same as

Form 941—Instructions (Page 4)

shown on any attached Schedule B (Form 941), Report of Tax Liability for Semiweekly Schedule Depositors.

Completing and Filing Form 941

Make entries on Form 941 as follows to enable accurate scanning and processing.
- Use 10-point Courier font (if possible) for all entries if you are typing or using a computer to complete your form.
- Omit dollar signs and decimal points. Commas are optional. Enter dollars to the left of the preprinted decimal point and cents to the right of it.
- Leave blank any data field (except lines 1, 2, and 10) with a value of zero.
- Enter negative amounts using a minus sign (if possible). Otherwise, use parentheses.
- Enter your name and EIN on all pages and attachments.
- Staple multiple sheets in the upper left corner when filing.

Other Forms You Must Use

To notify employees about the earned income credit (EIC), you must give the employees one of the following items.
- The IRS Form W-2, which has the required information about the EIC on the back of Copy B.
- A substitute Form W-2 with the same EIC information on the back of the employee's copy that is on Copy B of the IRS Form W-2.
- Notice 797, Possible Federal Tax Refund Due to the Earned Income Credit (EIC).
- Your written statement with the same wording as Notice 797.

For more information, see section 10 of Pub. 15 (Circular E) and Pub. 596, Earned Income Credit (EIC).

Reconciling Forms 941 and Form W-3

The IRS matches amounts reported on your four quarterly Forms 941 with Form W-2 amounts totaled on your yearly Form W-3, Transmittal of Wage and Tax Statements. If the amounts do not agree, you may be contacted by the IRS or the Social Security Administration (SSA). The following amounts are reconciled.
- Federal income tax withholding.
- Social security wages.
- Social security tips.
- Medicare wages and tips.

For more information, see section 12 of Pub. 15 (Circular E) and the Instructions for Schedule D (Form 941).

Where Should You File?

Where you file depends on whether you include a payment with Form 941.

If you are in . . .		Without a payment . . .	With a payment . . .
Special filing addresses for exempt organizations; federal, state, and local governmental entities; and Indian tribal governmental entities; regardless of location		Department of the Treasury Internal Revenue Service Ogden, UT 84201-0005	Internal Revenue Service P.O. Box 105083 Atlanta, GA 30348-5083
Connecticut Delaware District of Columbia Georgia Illinois Indiana Kentucky Maine Maryland Massachusetts Michigan New Hampshire	New Jersey New York North Carolina Ohio Pennsylvania Rhode Island South Carolina Tennessee Vermont Virginia West Virginia Wisconsin	Department of the Treasury Internal Revenue Service Cincinnati, OH 45999-0005	Internal Revenue Service P.O. Box 804522 Cincinnati, OH 45280-4522
Alabama Alaska Arizona Arkansas California Colorado Florida Hawaii Idaho Iowa Kansas Louisiana Minnesota Mississippi	Missouri Montana Nebraska Nevada New Mexico North Dakota Oklahoma Oregon South Dakota Texas Utah Washington Wyoming	Department of the Treasury Internal Revenue Service Ogden, UT 84201-0005	Internal Revenue Service P.O. Box 105083 Atlanta, GA 30348-5083
No legal residence or principal place of business in any state		Internal Revenue Service P.O. Box 409101 Ogden, UT 84409	Internal Revenue Service P.O. Box 105273 Atlanta, GA 30348-5273

Depositing Your Taxes: When Must You Deposit Your Taxes?

Determine if You Are a Monthly or Semiweekly Schedule Depositor for the Quarter

The IRS uses two different sets of deposit rules to determine when businesses must deposit their social security, Medicare, and withheld federal income taxes. These schedules tell you when a deposit is due after you have a payday.

Your deposit schedule is not determined by how often you pay your employees. Your deposit schedule depends on the total tax liability you reported on Form 941 during the previous four-quarter **lookback period** (July 1 of the second preceding calendar year through June 30 of last year). See section 11 of Pub. 15 (Circular E) for details. If you filed Form 944 in either 2010 or 2011, your lookback period is the 2010 calendar year.

Before the beginning of each calendar year, determine which type of deposit schedule you must use.
- If you reported $50,000 or less in taxes during the lookback period, you are a **monthly schedule depositor**.
- If you reported more than $50,000 of taxes during the lookback period, you are a **semiweekly schedule depositor**.

CAUTION *See section 11 of Pub. 15 (Circular E) for the Next Day Deposit Rule on taxes of $100,000 or more accumulated on any day during the deposit period.*

How Must You Deposit Your Taxes?

You may have to deposit the federal income taxes you withheld and both the employer and employee social security taxes and Medicare taxes.
- **If your total taxes (line 10) are less than $2,500 for the current quarter or the preceding quarter, and you did not incur a $100,000 next-day deposit obligation during the current quarter.** You do not have to make a deposit. To avoid a penalty, you must pay the amount in full with a timely filed return or you must deposit the amount timely. If you are not sure your total tax liability for the current quarter will be less than $2,500 (and your liability for the preceding quarter was not less than $2,500), make deposits using the semi-weekly or monthly rules so you won't be subject to failure to deposit penalties.

Form 941—Instructions (Page 5)

• **If your total taxes (line 10) are $2,500 or more for the current quarter and the preceding quarter.** You must make deposits according to your deposit schedule. See section 11 of Pub. 15 (Circular E) for information and rules about federal tax deposits.

CAUTION *The IRS has issued regulations under section 6302 which provide that you must deposit all depository taxes electronically by electronic funds transfers. For more information about electronic funds transfers, visit the IRS website at www.irs.gov/e-pay.*

You may reduce your deposits during the quarter by the amount of COBRA premium assistance payments on line 12a.

What About Penalties and Interest?

Avoiding Penalties and Interest

You can avoid paying penalties and interest if you do all of the following.

- Deposit or pay your taxes when they are due.
- File your fully completed Form 941 on time.
- Report your tax liability accurately.
- Submit valid checks for tax payments.
- Furnish accurate Forms W-2 to employees.
- File Form W-3 and Copies A of Form W-2 with the Social Security Administration (SSA) on time and accurately.

Penalties and interest are charged on taxes paid late and returns filed late at a rate set by law. See sections 11 and 12 of Pub. 15 (Circular E) for details.

Use Form 843, Claim for Refund and Request for Abatement, to request abatement of assessed penalties or interest. **Do not** request abatement of assessed penalties or interest on Form 941 or Form 941-X.

CAUTION ***A trust fund recovery penalty** may apply if federal income, social security, and Medicare taxes that must be withheld are not withheld or paid. The penalty is the full amount of the unpaid trust fund tax. This penalty may apply when these unpaid taxes cannot be collected from the employer. The trust fund recovery penalty may be imposed on all people the IRS determines to be responsible for collecting, accounting for, and paying these taxes, and who acted willfully in not doing so. For details, see section 11 of Pub. 15 (Circular E).*

Specific Instructions:

Part 1: Answer These Questions for This Quarter

1. Number of Employees Who Received Wages, Tips, or Other Compensation This Quarter

Enter the number of employees on your payroll for the pay period including March 12, June 12, September 12, or December 12, **for the quarter indicated** at the top of Form 941. Do not include:

- Household employees,
- Employees in nonpay status for the pay period,
- Farm employees,
- Pensioners, or
- Active members of the Armed Forces.

TIP *If you enter "250" or more on line 1, you must file Forms W-2 electronically. For details, call the SSA at 1-800-772-6270 or visit SSA's Employer W-2 Filing Instructions & Information website at www.socialsecurity.gov/employer.*

2. Wages, Tips, and Other Compensation

Enter amounts on line 2 that would also be included in box 1 of your employees' Forms W-2. Include sick pay paid by a third party if you were given timely notice of the payments and transferred liability for the employees' taxes. See the General Instructions for Forms W-2 and W-3 for details.

If you are a third-party payer of sick pay, do not include sick pay that you paid to policyholders' employees here if you gave the policyholders timely notice of the payments.

3. Income Tax Withheld From Wages, Tips, and Other Compensation

Enter the federal income tax you withheld (or were required to withhold) from your employees on this quarter's wages, tips, taxable fringe benefits, and supplemental unemployment compensation benefits. Do not include any income tax withheld by a third-party payer of sick pay even if you reported it on Form W-2. You will reconcile this difference on Form W-3. Also include here any excise taxes you were required to withhold on golden parachute payments (section 4999).

If you are a third-party payer of sick pay, enter the federal income tax you withheld (or were required to withhold) on third-party sick pay here.

4. If No Wages, Tips, and Other Compensation are Subject to Social Security or Medicare Tax . . .

If no wages, tips, and other compensation on line 2 are subject to social security or Medicare tax, check the box on line 4. If this question does not apply to you, leave the box blank. For more information about exempt wages, see section 15 of Pub. 15 (Circular E) and section 4 of Pub. 15-A, Employer's Supplemental Tax Guide.

CAUTION *If you are a government employer, wages you pay are not automatically exempt from social security and Medicare taxes. Your employees may be covered by law or by a voluntary Section 218 Agreement with the SSA. For more information, see Pub. 963, Federal-State Reference Guide.*

5a–5d. Taxable Social Security and Medicare Wages and Tips

5a. Taxable social security wages. Enter the total wages, sick pay, and fringe benefits subject to social security taxes you paid to your employees during the quarter. For this purpose, sick pay includes payments made by an insurance company to your employees for which you received timely notice from the insurance company. See Section 6 in Pub. 15-A for more information about sick pay reporting.

Enter the amount before deductions. **Do not** include tips on this line. For information on types of wages subject to social security taxes, see section 5 of Pub. 15 (Circular E).

For 2012, the rate of social security tax on taxable wages is 6.2% (.062) for the employer and 4.2% (.042) for the employee or 10.4% (.104) for both. Stop paying social security tax on and entering an employee's wages on line 5a when the employee's taxable wages (including tips) reach $110,100 for the year. However, continue to withhold income and Medicare taxes for the whole year on wages

Form 941—Instructions (Page 6)

and tips even when the social security wage base of $110,100 has been reached.

line 5a (column 1)
x .104
line 5a (column 2)

5b. Taxable social security tips. Enter all tips your employees reported to you during the quarter until the total of the tips and wages for an employee reach $110,100 for the year. Include all tips your employee reported to you even if you were unable to withhold the employee tax of 4.2%.

An employee must report cash tips to you, including tips you paid the employee for charge customers, totaling $20 or more in a month by the 10th of the next month. Employees may use Form 4070, Employee's Report of Tips to Employer (available only in Pub. 1244, Employee's Daily Record of Tips and Report to Employer), or submit a written statement or electronic tip record.

Do not include allocated tips on this line. Instead, report them on Form 8027, Employer's Annual Information Return of Tip Income and Allocated Tips. Allocated tips are not reportable on Form 941 and are not subject to withholding of federal income, social security, or Medicare taxes.

line 5b (column 1)
x .104
line 5b (column 2)

5c. Taxable Medicare wages & tips. Enter all wages, tips, sick pay, and taxable fringe benefits that are subject to Medicare tax. Unlike social security wages, there is no limit on the amount of wages subject to Medicare tax.

Include all tips your employees reported during the quarter, even if you were unable to withhold the employee tax of 1.45%.

line 5c (column 1)
x .029
line 5c (column 2)

For more information on tips, see section 6 of Pub. 15 (Circular E).

5d. Total social security and Medicare taxes. Add the social security wages tax (line 5a), social security tips tax (line 5b), and Medicare wages and tips tax (line 5c) and enter the result on line 5d.

5e. Section 3121(q) Notice and Demand—Tax on Unreported Tips

Enter the tax due from your Section 3121(q) Notice and Demand on line 5e. The IRS issues a Section 3121(q) Notice and Demand to advise an employer of the amount of tips received by employees who failed to report or underreported tips to the employer. An employer is not liable for the employer share of the social security and Medicare taxes on unreported tips until notice and demand for the taxes is made to the employer by the IRS in a Section 3121(q) Notice and Demand. The tax due may have been determined from tips reported to the IRS on employees' Forms 4137, Social Security and Medicare Tax on Unreported Tip Income, or other tips that were not reported to their employer as determined by the IRS during an examination.

Deposit the tax within the time period required under your deposit schedule to avoid any possible deposit penalty. The tax is treated as accumulated by the employer on the "Date of Notice and Demand" as printed on the Section 3121(q) Notice and Demand. The employer must include this amount on the appropriate line of the record of federal tax liability (Part 2 of Form 941 for a monthly schedule depositor or Schedule B (Form 941) for a semiweekly schedule depositor).

6. Total Taxes Before Adjustments

Add the total federal income tax withheld from wages, tips, and other compensation (line 3), the total social security and Medicare taxes before adjustments (line 5d), and any tax due under section 3121(q) as entered on line 5e. Enter the result on line 6.

7–9. Tax Adjustments

Enter **tax amounts** on lines 7–9 that result from current quarter adjustments. Use a minus sign (if possible) to show an adjustment that decreases the total taxes shown on line 6 instead of parentheses. Doing so enhances the accuracy of our scanning software. For example, enter "-10.59" instead of "(10.59)." However, if your software only allows for parentheses in entering negative amounts, you may use them.

Current quarter's adjustments. In certain cases, you must adjust the amounts you entered as social security and Medicare taxes in column 2 of lines 5a, 5b, and 5c to figure your correct tax liability for this quarter's Form 941. See section 13 of Pub. 15 (Circular E).

7. Current quarter's adjustment for fractions of cents. Enter adjustments for fractions of cents (due to rounding) relating to the employee share of social security and Medicare taxes withheld. The employee share of amounts shown in column 2 of lines 5a, 5b, and 5c may differ slightly from amounts actually withheld from employees' paychecks due to the rounding of social security and Medicare taxes based on statutory rates.

8. Current quarter's adjustment for sick pay. Enter the adjustment for the employee share of social security and Medicare taxes that were withheld and deposited by your third-party sick pay payer with regard to sick pay paid by the third-party. These wages should be included on lines 5a and 5c. If you are the third-party sick pay payer, enter the adjustment for any employer share of these taxes required to be paid by the employer.

9. Current quarter's adjustments for tips and group-term life insurance. Enter adjustments for:

- Any uncollected employee share of social security and Medicare taxes on tips, and
- The uncollected employee share of social security and Medicare taxes on group-term life insurance premiums paid for former employees.

Prior quarter's adjustments. If you need to correct any adjustment reported on a previously filed Form 941, complete and file Form 941-X. Form 941-X is filed separately from Form 941. See section 13 of Pub. 15 (Circular E).

10. Total Taxes After Adjustments

Combine lines 6–9 and enter the result on line 10.

- **If line 10 is less than $2,500 or line 10 on the preceding quarterly return was less than $2,500, and you did not incur a $100,000 next-day deposit obligation during the current quarter.** You may pay the amount with Form 941 or you may deposit the amount. To avoid a penalty, you must pay the amount in full with a timely filed return or you must deposit the amount timely.
- **If line 10 is $2,500 or more and line 10 on the preceding quarterly return was $2,500 or more, or if you incurred a $100,000 next-day deposit obligation during the current quarter.** You must make deposits according to your deposit schedule. See section 11 of Pub. 15 (Circular E) for information and rules about federal tax deposits. The amount shown on line 10 **must** equal the "Total liability for

Form 941—Instructions (Page 7)

the quarter" shown on line 16 or the "Total liability for the quarter" shown on Schedule B (Form 941).

For more information on federal tax deposits, see *Depositing Your Taxes*, earlier, and section 11 of Pub. 15 (Circular E).

CAUTION *If you are a **semiweekly depositor,** you **must** complete Schedule B (Form 941). If you fail to complete and submit Schedule B (Form 941), the IRS will assert deposit penalties based on available information.*

11. Total Deposits for This Quarter

Enter your deposits for this quarter, including any overpayment from a prior quarter. Also include in the amount shown any overpayment from filing Form 941-X or Form 944-X, Adjusted Employer's ANNUAL Federal Tax Return or Claim for Refund, in the current quarter.

12a. COBRA Premium Assistance Payments

Enter 65% of the COBRA premiums for assistance eligible individuals. Take the COBRA premium assistance credit on this line only after the assistance eligible individual's 35% share of the premium has been paid. For COBRA coverage provided under a self-insured plan, COBRA premium assistance is treated as having been made for each assistance eligible individual who pays 35% of the COBRA premium. Do not include the assistance eligible individual's 35% of the premium in the amount entered on this line. For more information on the COBRA premium assistance credit, visit IRS.gov and enter the keyword *COBRA.*

CAUTION *The amount entered on line 12a is treated as a deposit of taxes on the first day of your return period and must not be used to adjust line 16 or Schedule B (Form 941).*

If you provided premium assistance in a prior quarter of the current year and did not report the amount of that premium assistance on Form 941 for that quarter, you may include the amount of that premium assistance in the amount entered on this line, or file form 941-X to report the amount for the prior quarter of the current year.

12b. Number of Individuals Provided COBRA Premium Assistance on Line 12a

Enter the total number of assistance eligible individuals provided COBRA premium assistance for the amount entered on line 12a. Count each assistance eligible individual who paid a reduced COBRA premium in the quarter as one individual, whether or not the reduced premium was for insurance that covered more than one assistance eligible individual. For example, if the reduced COBRA premium was for coverage for a former employee, spouse, and two children, you would include one individual in the number entered on line 12b for the premium assistance. Further, each individual is entered only once per quarter. For example, an assistance eligible individual who made monthly premium payments during the quarter would only be entered as one individual.

13. Total Deposits and Credits

Add lines 11 and 12a.

14. Balance Due

If line 10 is more than line 13, enter the difference on line 14. Otherwise, see *Overpayment* below. **You do not have to pay if line 14 is under $1.** Generally, you should have a balance due only if your total taxes (line 10) for the current quarter or preceding quarter are less than $2,500, and you did not incur a $100,000 next-day deposit obligation during the current quarter. However, see section 11 of Pub. 15 (Circular E) for information about payments made under the accuracy of deposit rule.

You may pay the amount shown on line 14 using EFTPS, a credit or debit card, a check or money order, or electronic funds withdrawal (EFW). **Do not** use a credit or debit card or EFW to pay taxes that were required to be deposited. For more information on electronic payment options, visit the IRS website at *www.irs.gov/e-pay.*

If you pay by EFTPS, credit or debit card, or EFW, file your return using the *Without a payment* address under *Where Should You File*, earlier, and **do not** file Form 941-V, Payment Voucher.

If you pay by check or money order, make it payable to the "United States Treasury." Enter your EIN, Form 941, and the tax period on your check or money order. Complete Form 941-V and enclose with Form 941.

If line 10 is $2,500 or more and you have deposited all taxes when due, the balance due on line 14 should be zero.

CAUTION *If you do not deposit as required and, instead, pay the taxes with Form 941, you may be subject to a penalty.*

15. Overpayment

If line 13 is more than line 10, enter the difference on line 15. **Never make an entry on both lines 14 and 15.**

If you deposited more than the correct amount for the quarter, you can choose to have the IRS either refund the overpayment or apply it to your next return. Check only one box on line 15. If you do not check either box or if you check both boxes, generally we will apply the overpayment to your account. We may apply your overpayment to any past due tax account that is shown in our records under your EIN.

If line 15 is under $1, we will send a refund or apply it to your next return only if you ask us in writing to do so.

Complete Both Pages

You must complete both pages of Form 941 and sign on page 2. An incomplete return may delay processing.

Part 2: Tell Us About Your Deposit Schedule and Tax Liability for This Quarter

16. Tax Liability for the Quarter

- If line 10 is less than $2,500 or line 10 on the preceding quarterly return was less than $2,500, and you did not incur a $100,000 next-day deposit obligation during the current quarter, check the appropriate box on line 16 and go to Part 3.
- If you reported $50,000 or less in taxes during the lookback period, you are a **monthly schedule depositor** unless the *$100,000 Next-Day Deposit Rule* discussed in section 11 of Pub. 15 (Circular E) applies. Check the appropriate box on line 16 and enter your tax liability for each month in the quarter. Add the amounts for each month. Enter the result in the *Total liability for quarter* box.

Note that your total tax liability for the quarter must equal your total taxes shown on line 10. If it does not, your tax deposits and payments may not be counted as timely. **Do not** change your tax liability on line 16 by adjustments reported on any Forms 941-X.

You are a **monthly schedule depositor** for the calendar year if the amount of your Form 941 taxes reported for the lookback period is $50,000 or less. The **lookback period** is the four consecutive quarters ending on June 30 of the prior year. For 2012, the lookback period begins July 1, 2010,

Instructions for Form 941 (Rev. 1-2012) -7-

Form 941—Instructions (Page 8)

and ends June 30, 2011. For details on the deposit rules, see section 11 of Pub. 15 (Circular E). If you filed Form 944 in either 2010 or 2011, your lookback period is the 2010 calendar year.

CAUTION *The amounts entered on line 16 are a summary of your monthly* ***tax liability,*** *not a summary of deposits you made. If you do not properly report your liabilities when required or if you are a semiweekly schedule depositor and enter your liabilities on line 16 instead of on Schedule B (Form 941), you may be assessed an "averaged" failure-to-deposit (FTD) penalty. See* Deposit Penalties *in section 11 of Pub. 15 (Circular E) for more information.*

- If you reported more than $50,000 of taxes for the lookback period, you are a **semiweekly schedule depositor.** Check the appropriate box on line 16.

You **must** complete Schedule B (Form 941) and submit it with your Form 941. **Do not** use Schedule B (Form 941) if you are a monthly schedule depositor.

Do not change your tax liability on Schedule B (Form 941) by adjustments reported on any Forms 941-X.

Part 3: Tell Us About Your Business

In Part 3, answer only those questions that apply to your business. If the questions do not apply, leave them blank and go to Part 4.

17. If Your Business Has Closed . . .

If you go out of business or stop paying wages, you must file a **final return**. To tell the IRS that a particular Form 941 is your final return, check the box on line 17 and enter the date you last paid wages in the space provided. For additional filing requirements, see *If Your Business Has Closed,* earlier.

18. If You are a Seasonal Employer . . .

If you hire employees seasonally—such as for summer or winter only—check the box on line 18. Checking the box tells the IRS not to expect four Forms 941 from you throughout the year because you have not paid wages regularly.

Generally, we will not ask about unfiled returns if you file at least one return showing tax due each year. However, you must check the box **every time** you file a Form 941.

Also, when you complete Form 941, be sure to check the box on the top of the form that corresponds to the quarter reported.

Part 4: May We Speak With Your Third-party Designee?

If you want to allow an employee, a paid tax preparer, or another person to discuss your Form 941 with the IRS, check the "Yes" box in Part 4. Then tell us the name, phone number, and the five-digit personal identification number (PIN) of the specific person to speak with—not the name of the firm who prepared your tax return. The designee may choose any five numbers as his or her PIN.

By checking "Yes," you authorize the IRS to talk to the person you named (your designee) about any questions we may have while we process your return. You also authorize your designee to:
- Give us any information that is missing from your return,
- Call us for information about processing your return, and
- Respond to certain IRS notices that you have shared with your designee about math errors and return preparation. The IRS will not send notices to your designee.

You are not authorizing your designee to bind you to anything (including additional tax liability) or to otherwise represent you before the IRS. If you want to expand your designee's authorization, see Pub. 947, Practice Before the IRS and Power of Attorney.

The authorization will automatically expire 1 year from the due date (without regard to extensions) for filing your Form 941. If you or your designee want to terminate the authorization, write to the IRS office for your location using the *Without a payment* address under *Where Should You File*, earlier.

Part 5: Sign Here

Complete all information in Part 5 and sign Form 941 as follows.

- **Sole proprietorship—** The individual who owns the business.
- **Corporation (including a limited liability company (LLC) treated as a corporation)—** The president, vice president, or other principal officer duly authorized to sign.
- **Partnership (including an LLC treated as a partnership) or unincorporated organization—** A responsible and duly authorized member, partner, or officer having knowledge of its affairs.
- **Single member LLC treated as a disregarded entity for federal income tax purposes—** The owner of the LLC or a principal officer duly authorized to sign.
- **Trust or estate—** The fiduciary.

Form 941 may also be signed by a duly authorized agent of the taxpayer if a valid power of attorney has been filed.

Alternative signature method. Corporate officers or duly authorized agents may sign Form 941 by rubber stamp, mechanical device, or computer software program. For details and required documentation, see Rev. Proc. 2005-39, 2005-28 I.R.B. 82, at *www.irs.gov/irb/2005-28_IRB/ar16.html.*

Paid Preparer Use Only

A paid preparer must sign Form 941 and provide the information in the *Paid Preparer Use Only* section of Part 5 if the preparer was paid to prepare Form 941 and is not an employee of the filing entity. Paid preparers must sign paper returns with a manual signature. The preparer must give you a copy of the return in addition to the copy to be filed with the IRS.

If you are a paid preparer, enter your Preparer Tax Identification Number (PTIN) in the space provided. Include your complete address. If you work for a firm, enter the firm's name and the EIN of the firm. You can apply for a PTIN online or by filing Form W-12, IRS Paid Preparer Tax Identification Number (PTIN) Application and Renewal. For more information about applying for a PTIN online, visit the IRS website at *www.irs.gov/ptin*. You cannot use your PTIN in place of the EIN of the tax preparation firm.

Generally, do not complete this section if you are filing the return as a reporting agent and have a valid Form 8655, Reporting Agent Authorization, on file with the IRS. However, a reporting agent must complete this section if the reporting agent offered legal advice, for example, advising the client on determining whether its workers are employees or independent contractors for federal tax purposes.

Form 941—Instructions (Page 9)

How to Order Forms and Publications from the IRS

Call 1-800-829-3676.

Visit *www.irs.gov/formspubs*.

Other IRS Products You May Need

- Form SS-4, Application for Employer Identification Number
- Form W-2, Wage and Tax Statement
- Form W-2c, Corrected Wage and Tax Statement
- Form W-3, Transmittal of Wage and Tax Statements
- Form W-3c, Transmittal of Corrected Wage and Tax Statements
- Form W-4, Employee's Withholding Allowance Certificate
- Form 940, Employer's Annual Federal Unemployment (FUTA) Tax Return
- Form 941-X, Adjusted Employer's QUARTERLY Federal Tax Return or Claim for Refund
- Form 943, Employer's Annual Federal Tax Return for Agricultural Employees
- Form 944, Employer's ANNUAL Federal Tax Return
- Form 944-X, Adjusted Employer's ANNUAL Federal Tax Return or Claim for Refund
- Form 4070, Employee's Report of Tips to Employer
- Form 8027, Employer's Annual Information Return of Tip Income and Allocated Tips
- Form 8655, Reporting Agent Authorization
- Notice 797, Possible Federal Tax Refund Due to the Earned Income Credit (EIC)
- Pub. 15 (Circular E), Employer's Tax Guide
- Pub. 15-A, Employer's Supplemental Tax Guide
- Pub. 15-B, Employer's Tax Guide to Fringe Benefits
- Pub. 596, Earned Income Credit
- Pub. 926, Household Employer's Tax Guide
- Schedule B (Form 941), Report of Tax Liability for Semiweekly Schedule Depositors
- Schedule D (Form 941), Report of Discrepancies Caused by Acquisitions, Statutory Mergers, or Consolidations
- Schedule H (Form 1040), Household Employment Taxes
- Schedule R (Form 941), Allocation Schedule for Aggregate Form 941 Filers

Instructions for Form 941 (Rev. 1-2012) **-9-**

Schedule B, Form 941

960311

Schedule B (Form 941):

Report of Tax Liability for Semiweekly Schedule Depositors

(Rev. June 2011) Department of the Treasury — Internal Revenue Service

OMB No. 1545-0029

(EIN)
Employer identification number ☐☐ – ☐☐☐☐☐☐☐

Name *(not your trade name)* ______________________

Calendar year ☐☐☐☐ (Also check quarter)

Report for this Quarter...
(Check one.)

☐ **1:** January, February, March
☐ **2:** April, May, June
☐ **3:** July, August, September
☐ **4:** October, November, December

Use this schedule to show your TAX LIABILITY for the quarter; DO NOT use it to show your deposits. When you file this form with Form 941 or Form 941-SS, DO NOT change your tax liability by adjustments reported on any Forms 941-X. You must fill out this form and attach it to Form 941 or Form 941-SS if you are a semiweekly schedule depositor or became one because your accumulated tax liability on any day was $100,000 or more. Write your daily tax liability on the numbered space that corresponds to the date wages were paid. See Section 11 in Pub. 15 (Circular E), Employer's Tax Guide, for details.

Month 1

1	.	9	.	17	.	25	.	Tax liability for Month 1 .
2	.	10	.	18	.	26	.	
3	.	11	.	19	.	27	.	
4	.	12	.	20	.	28	.	
5	.	13	.	21	.	29	.	
6	.	14	.	22	.	30	.	
7	.	15	.	23	.	31	.	
8	.	16	.	24	.			

Month 2

1	.	9	.	17	.	25	.	Tax liability for Month 2 .
2	.	10	.	18	.	26	.	
3	.	11	.	19	.	27	.	
4	.	12	.	20	.	28	.	
5	.	13	.	21	.	29	.	
6	.	14	.	22	.	30	.	
7	.	15	.	23	.	31	.	
8	.	16	.	24	.			

Month 3

1	.	9	.	17	.	25	.	Tax liability for Month 3 .
2	.	10	.	18	.	26	.	
3	.	11	.	19	.	27	.	
4	.	12	.	20	.	28	.	
5	.	13	.	21	.	29	.	
6	.	14	.	22	.	30	.	
7	.	15	.	23	.	31	.	
8	.	16	.	24	.			

Fill in your total liability for the quarter (Month 1 + Month 2 + Month 3) ▶
Total must equal line 10 on Form 941 or Form 941-SS.

Total liability for the quarter .

For Paperwork Reduction Act Notice, see separate instructions. Cat. No. 11967Q **Schedule B (Form 941)** (Rev. 6-2011)

Schedule B, Form 941—Instructions (Page 1)

Instructions for Schedule B (Form 941)

Department of the Treasury
Internal Revenue Service

(Rev. June 2011)

Report of Tax Liability for Semiweekly Schedule Depositors

Section references are to the Internal Revenue Code unless otherwise noted.

Reminders

Reporting prior period adjustments. Prior period adjustments are reported on Form 941-X, Amended Employer's QUARTERLY Federal Tax Return or Claim for Refund, and are not taken into account when figuring the tax liability for the current quarter.

When you file Schedule B (Form 941) with your Form 941 (or Form 941-SS), do not change your tax liability by adjustments reported on any Form 941-X.

Amended Schedule B. If you have been assessed a failure-to-deposit (FTD) penalty, you may be able to file an amended Schedule B (Form 941). See *Amending a Previously Filed Schedule B (Form 941)* on page 2.

General Instructions

Purpose of Schedule B (Form 941)

These instructions tell you about Schedule B (Form 941), Report of Tax Liability for Semiweekly Schedule Depositors. To determine if you are a semiweekly depositor, visit IRS.gov and type "semiweekly depositor" in the search box. Also see Pub. 15 (Circular E), Employer's Tax Guide, or Pub. 80 (Circular SS), Federal Tax Guide for Employers in the U.S. Virgin Islands, Guam, American Samoa, and the Commonwealth of the Northern Mariana Islands.

Federal law requires you, as an employer, to withhold taxes from your employees' paychecks. Each time you pay wages, you must withhold – or take out of your employees' paychecks – certain amounts for federal income tax, social security tax, and Medicare tax (payroll taxes). Under the withholding system, taxes withheld from your employees are credited to your employees in payment of their tax liabilities.

Federal law also requires employers to pay any liability for the employer's portion of social security and Medicare taxes. This portion of social security and Medicare taxes is not withheld from employees.

On Schedule B (Form 941), list your **tax liability** for each day. Your liability includes:
- The federal income tax you withheld from your employees' paychecks, and
- Both employee and employer social security and Medicare taxes.

Do not use the Schedule B (Form 941) to show federal tax deposits. The IRS gets deposit data from electronic funds transfers.

CAUTION *The IRS uses Schedule B (Form 941) to determine if you have deposited your federal employment tax liabilities on time. If you do not properly complete and file your Schedule B (Form 941) with Form 941 or Form 941-SS, the IRS may propose an "averaged" failure-to-deposit penalty. See* Deposit Penalties *in section 11 of Pub. 15 (Circular E) for more information.*

Who Must File?

File Schedule B (Form 941) if you are a semiweekly schedule depositor. You are a semiweekly depositor if you reported more than $50,000 of employment taxes in the lookback period or accumulated a tax liability of $100,000 or more on any given day in the current or prior calendar year. See section 11 of Pub. 15 (Circular E) for more information.

CAUTION *Do not complete Schedule B (Form 941) if you have a tax liability that is less than $2,500 during the quarter.*

When Must You File?

Schedule B (Form 941) is filed with Form 941, Employer's QUARTERLY Federal Tax Return, or Form 941-SS, Employer's QUARTERLY Federal Tax Return (American Samoa, Guam, the Commonwealth of the Northern Mariana Islands, and the U.S. Virgin Islands). File Schedule B (Form 941) with your Form 941 or Form 941-SS every quarter when Form 941 or Form 941-SS is due.

Do not file Schedule B (Form 941) as an attachment to Form 944, Employer's ANNUAL Federal Tax Return, or Form 944-SS, Employer's ANNUAL Federal Tax Return (American Samoa, Guam, the Commonwealth of the Northern Mariana Islands, and the U.S. Virgin Islands). Instead, if required to file a report of tax liability with either of these forms, use Form 945-A, Annual Record of Federal Tax Liability.

Specific Instructions

Completing Schedule B (Form 941)

Enter Your Business Information

Carefully enter your employer identification number (EIN) and name at the top of the schedule. Make sure that they exactly match the name of your business and the EIN that the IRS assigned to your business and also agree with the name and EIN shown on the attached Form 941 or Form 941-SS.

Calendar Year

Enter the calendar year that applies to the quarter checked.

Check the Box for the Quarter

Under *Report for this Quarter* at the top of Schedule B (Form 941), check the appropriate box of the quarter for which you are filing this schedule. Make sure the quarter checked on the top of the Schedule B (Form 941) matches the quarter checked on your Form 941 or Form 941-SS.

Enter Your Tax Liability by Month

Schedule B (Form 941) is divided into the 3 months that make up a quarter of a year. Each month has 31 numbered spaces that correspond to the dates of a typical month. Enter your tax liabilities in the spaces that correspond to the dates you **paid** wages to your employees, not the date payroll deposits were made.

For example, if your payroll period ended on December 31, 2010, and you **paid** the wages for that period on January 6, 2011, you would:
- Go to Month 1 (because January is the first month of the quarter), and

Schedule B, Form 941—Instructions (Page 2)

- Enter your tax liability on line 6 (because line 6 represents the sixth day of the month).

TIP *Make sure you have checked the appropriate box in Part 2 of Form 941 or Form 941-SS to show that you are a semiweekly schedule depositor.*

Total Liability for the Quarter

To find your total liability for the quarter, add your monthly tax liabilities.

Tax Liability for Month 1
+Tax Liability for Month 2
+Tax Liability for Month 3
Total Liability for the Quarter

Your total liability for the quarter must equal line 10 on Form 941 or Form 941-SS.

Example 1. Employer A is a **semiweekly** schedule depositor who pays wages for each month on the last day of the month. On December 22, 2010, Employer A also paid its employees year-end bonuses (subject to employment taxes). Employer A must report employment tax liabilities on Schedule B (Form 941) for the 4th quarter (October, November, December), as follows.

Month	Lines for dates wages were paid
1 (October)	line 31 (pay day, last day of the month)
2 (November)	line 30 (pay day, last day of the month)
3 (December)	line 22 (bonus paid December 22, 2010)
3 (December)	line 31 (pay day, last day of the month)

Example 2. Employer B is a **semiweekly** schedule depositor who pays employees every other Friday. Employer B accumulated a $20,000 employment tax liability on each of these pay dates: 1/14/11, 1/28/11, 2/11/11, 2/25/11, 3/11/11, and 3/25/11. Employer B must report employment tax liabilities on Schedule B (Form 941) as follows.

Month	Lines for dates wages were paid
1 (January)	lines 14 and 28
2 (February)	lines 11 and 25
3 (March)	lines 11 and 25

Example 3. Employer C is a new business and **monthly** schedule depositor for 2011. Employer C pays wages every Friday and has accumulated a $2,000 employment tax liability on 1/14/11 and a $110,000 employment tax liability on 1/21/11 and on every subsequent Friday during 2011. Under the deposit rules, employers **become semiweekly schedule depositors** on the day after any day they accumulate $100,000 or more of employment tax liability in a deposit period. Employer C became a semiweekly schedule depositor on 1/22/11, because Employer C had a total accumulated employment tax liability of $112,000 on 1/21/11. For more information, see section 11 of Pub. 15 (Circular E) or section 8 of Pub. 80 (Circular SS).

Employer C must complete Schedule B (Form 941) as shown below and file it with Form 941 or 941-SS.

Month	Lines for dates wages were paid	Amount to report
1 (January)	line 14	$2,000
1 (January)	lines 21, 28	$110,000
2 (February)	lines 4, 11, 18, 25	$110,000
3 (March)	lines 4, 11, 18, 25	$110,000

Amending a Previously Filed Schedule B (Form 941)

Semiweekly schedule depositors. If you have been assessed a failure-to-deposit (FTD) penalty for a quarter and you made an error on Schedule B (Form 941) and the correction will not change the total liability for the quarter you reported on Schedule B (Form 941), you may be able to reduce your penalty by filing a corrected Schedule B (Form 941).

Example. You reported a liability of $3,000 on day 1 of month 1. However, the liability was actually for month 3. Prepare an amended Schedule B (Form 941) showing the $3,000 liability on day 1 of month 3. Also, you must enter the liabilities previously reported for the quarter that did not change. Write "Amended" at the top of Schedule B (Form 941). The IRS will refigure the penalty and notify you of any change in the penalty.

Monthly schedule depositors. You can also file an amended Schedule B (Form 941) if you have been assessed an FTD penalty for a quarter and you made an error on the monthly tax liability section of Form 941. When completing Schedule B (Form 941), only enter the monthly totals. The daily entries are not required.

Where to file. File your amended Schedule B at the address provided in the penalty notice you received. You do not have to submit your original Schedule B (Form 941).

Form 941-X

Tax decrease. If you are filing Form 941-X for a quarter, you can file an amended Schedule B (Form 941) with Form 941-X if both of the following apply.

1. You have a tax decrease.
2. You were assessed an FTD penalty.

File your amended Schedule B (Form 941) with Form 941-X. The total liability for the quarter reported on your corrected Schedule B (Form 941) must equal the corrected amount of tax reported on Form 941-X. If your penalty is decreased, the IRS will include the penalty decrease with your tax decrease.

Tax increase — Form 941-X filed timely. If you are filing a timely Form 941-X, do not file an amended Schedule B (Form 941), unless you were assessed an FTD penalty caused by an incorrect, incomplete, or missing Schedule B (Form 941). If you are filing an amended Schedule B (Form 941), do not include the tax increase reported on Form 941-X.

Tax increase — Form 941-X filed late. If you owe tax and are filing a late Form 941-X, that is, after the due date of the return for the filing period of the Form 941 in which you discovered the error, you must file an amended Schedule B (Form 941) with Form 941-X. Otherwise, the IRS may assess an "averaged" FTD penalty.

The total tax reported on the "Total liability for the quarter" line of the amended Schedule B (Form 941) must match the corrected tax (line 10 of Form 941 combined with any correction reported on line 21 of Form 941-X for the quarter), less any previous abatements and interest-free adjustments.

Paperwork Reduction Act Notice. We ask for the information on Schedule B (Form 941) to carry out the Internal Revenue laws of the United States. You are required to give us the information. We need it to ensure that you are complying with these laws and to allow us to figure and collect the right amount of tax.

You are not required to provide the information requested on a form that is subject to the Paperwork Reduction Act unless the form displays a valid OMB control number. Books or records relating to a form or its instructions must be retained as long as their contents may become material in the administration of any Internal Revenue law. Generally, tax returns and return information are confidential, as required by Code section 6103.

The time needed to complete and file Schedule B (Form 941) will vary depending on individual circumstances. The estimated average time is 2 hours, 53 minutes.

If you have comments concerning the accuracy of this time estimate or suggestions for making Schedule B (Form 941) simpler, we would be happy to hear from you. You can email us at: *taxforms@irs.gov*. Enter "Schedule B (Form 941)" on the subject line. Or write to: Internal Revenue Service, Tax Products Coordinating Committee, SE:W:CAR:MP:T:T:SP, 1111 Constitution Ave. NW, IR-6526, Washington, DC 20224. **Do not** send Schedule B (Form 941) to this address. Instead, see *Where Should You File?* in the Form 941 or Form 941-SS instructions.

-2-

Form 941-X (Page 1)

Form **941-X:** **Adjusted Employer's QUARTERLY Federal Tax Return or Claim for Refund**
(Rev. April 2012) Department of the Treasury — Internal Revenue Service OMB No. 1545-0029

Employer identification number (EIN) ☐☐ – ☐☐☐☐☐☐☐

Name *(not your trade name)*

Trade name *(if any)*

Address
Number Street Suite or room number
City State ZIP code

Return You Are Correcting ...
Check the type of return you are correcting:
☐ **941**
☐ **941-SS**

Check the ONE quarter you are correcting:
☐ **1:** January, February, March
☐ **2:** April, May, June
☐ **3:** July, August, September
☐ **4:** October, November, December

Enter the calendar year of the quarter you are correcting:
(YYYY)

Enter the date you discovered errors:
/ /
(MM / DD / YYYY)

Read the instructions before completing this form. Use this form to correct errors you made on Form 941 or Form 941-SS. Use a separate Form 941-X for each quarter that needs correction. Type or print within the boxes. You MUST complete all three pages. Do not attach this form to Form 941 or Form 941-SS.

Part 1: Select ONLY one process.

☐ **1. Adjusted employment tax return.** Check this box if you underreported amounts. Also check this box if you overreported amounts and you would like to use the adjustment process to correct the errors. You must check this box if you are correcting both underreported and overreported amounts on this form. The amount shown on line 21, if less than zero, may only be applied as a credit to your Form 941, Form 941-SS, or Form 944 for the tax period in which you are filing this form.

☐ **2. Claim.** Check this box if you overreported amounts only and you would like to use the claim process to ask for a refund or abatement of the amount shown on line 21. Do not check this box if you are correcting ANY underreported amounts on this form.

Part 2: Complete the certifications.

☐ **3. I certify that I have filed or will file Forms W-2, Wage and Tax Statement, or Forms W-2c, Corrected Wage and Tax Statement, as required.**

Note. If you are correcting underreported amounts only, go to Part 3 on page 2 and skip lines 4 and 5.

4. If you checked line 1 because you are adjusting overreported amounts, check all that apply. You must check at least one box.
I certify that:

☐ **a.** I repaid or reimbursed each affected employee for the overcollected federal income tax for the current year and the overcollected social security and Medicare taxes for current and prior years. For adjustments of employee social security and Medicare taxes overcollected in prior years, I have a written statement from each employee stating that he or she has not claimed (or the claim was rejected) and will not claim a refund or credit for the overcollection.

☐ **b.** The adjustments of social security tax and Medicare tax are for the employer's share only. I could not find the affected employees or each employee did not give me a written statement that he or she has not claimed (or the claim was rejected) and will not claim a refund or credit for the overcollection.

☐ **c.** The adjustment is for federal income tax, social security tax, and Medicare tax that I did not withhold from employee wages.

5. If you checked line 2 because you are claiming a refund or abatement of overreported employment taxes, check all that apply. You must check at least one box.
I certify that:

☐ **a.** I repaid or reimbursed each affected employee for the overcollected social security and Medicare tax. For claims of employee social security and Medicare tax overcollected in prior years, I have a written statement from each employee stating that he or she has not claimed (or the claim was rejected) and will not claim a refund or credit for the overcollection.

☐ **b.** I have a written consent from each affected employee stating that I may file this claim for the employee's share of social security and Medicare tax. For refunds of employee social security and Medicare tax overcollected in prior years, I also have a written statement from each employee stating that he or she has not claimed (or the claim was rejected) and will not claim a refund or credit for the overcollection.

☐ **c.** The claim for social security tax and Medicare taxes is for the employer's share only. I could not find the affected employees; or each employee did not give me a written consent to file a claim for the employee's share of social security and Medicare taxes; or each employee did not give me a written statement that he or she has not claimed (or the claim was rejected) and will not claim a refund or credit for the overcollection.

☐ **d.** The claim is for federal income tax, social security tax, and Medicare tax that I did not withhold from employee wages.

Next ▶

For Paperwork Reduction Act Notice, see the separate instructions. IRS.gov/form941x Cat. No. 17025J Form **941-X** (Rev. 4-2012)

Form 941-X (Page 2)

Name *(not your trade name)*	Employer identification number *(EIN)*	Correcting quarter (1, 2, 3, 4) **Correcting calendar year** (YYYY)

Part 3: Enter the corrections for this quarter. If any line does not apply, leave it blank.

	Column 1 **Total corrected amount (for ALL employees)**		*Column 2* **Amount originally reported or as previously corrected (for ALL employees)**		*Column 3* **Difference (If this amount is a negative number, use a minus sign.)**		*Column 4* **Tax correction**
6. Wages, tips, and other compensation (Form 941, line 2)	.	–	.	=	.	Use the amount in Column 1 when you prepare your Forms W-2 or Forms W-2c.	
7. Income tax withheld from wages, tips, and other compensation (Form 941, line 3)	.	–	.	=	.	Copy Column 3 here ▶	.
8. Taxable social security wages (Form 941 or Form 941-SS, line 5a, Column 1)	.	–	.	=	.	× .124* =	.
	*If you are correcting a 2011 or 2012 return, use .104. If you are correcting your employer share only, use .062. See instructions.						
9. Taxable social security tips (Form 941 or Form 941-SS, line 5b, Column 1)	.	–	.	=	.	× .124* =	.
	*If you are correcting a 2011 or 2012 return, use .104. If you are correcting your employer share only, use .062. See instructions.						
10. Taxable Medicare wages and tips (Form 941 or Form 941-SS, line 5c, Column 1)	.	–	.	=	.	× .029* =	.
					*If you are correcting your employer share only, use .0145. See instructions.		
11. Section 3121(q) Notice and Demand—Tax due on unreported tips (Form 941 or Form 941-SS, line 5e)	.	–	.	=	.	Copy Column 3 here ▶	.
12a. Number of qualified employees *first* paid exempt wages/tips this quarter (Form 941 or Form 941-SS, line 6a)*		–		=			*Complete lines 12a, 12b, and 12c only for corrections to quarters ending after March 31, 2010, and before January 1, 2011.
12b. Number of qualified employees paid exempt wages/tips this quarter (Form 941 or Form 941-SS, line 6b)*		–		=			
12c. Exempt wages/tips paid to qualified employees this quarter (Form 941 or Form 941-SS, line 6c)*	.	–	.	=	.	× .062 =	.
13. Tax adjustments (Form 941 or Form 941-SS, lines 7–9 (lines 7a–7c for quarters ending before January 1, 2011))	.	–	.	=	.	Copy Column 3 here ▶	.
14. Special addition to wages for federal income tax	.	–	.	=	.	See instructions	.
15. Special addition to wages for social security taxes	.	–	.	=	.	See instructions	.
16. Special addition to wages for Medicare taxes	.	–	.	=	.	See instructions	.
17. Combine the amounts on lines 7–16 of Column 4							.
18. Advance earned income credit (EIC) payments made to employees (Form 941, line 9; only for quarters ending before January 1, 2011)	.	–	.	=	.	See instructions	.
19a. COBRA premium assistance payments (Form 941 or Form 941-SS, line 12a)	.	–	.	=	.	See instructions	.
19b. Number of individuals provided COBRA premium assistance (Form 941 or Form 941-SS, line 12b)		–		=			*Complete lines 19c and 19d only for corrections to the second quarter of 2010.
19c. Number of qualified employees paid exempt wages/tips March 19–31, 2010 (Form 941 or Form 941-SS, line 12c)*		–		=			
19d. Exempt wages/tips paid to qualified employees March 19–31, 2010 (Form 941 or Form 941-SS, line 12d)*	.	–	.	=	.	× .062 =	.
20. Total. Combine the amounts on lines 17–19d of Column 4. Continue on next page							.

Next ▶

Page **2** | Form **941-X** (Rev. 4-2012)

Form 941-X (Page 3)

Name *(not your trade name)*	Employer identification number *(EIN)*	Correcting quarter (1, 2, 3, 4) **Correcting calendar year** (YYYY)

Part 3: Continued

21. Amount from line 20 on page 2 . . . . [.]

If line 21 is less than zero:

- If you checked line 1, this is the amount you want applied as a credit to your Form 941 or Form 941-SS for the tax period in which you are filing this form. If you are currently filing Form 944, Employer's ANNUAL Federal Tax Return, see the instructions.
- If you checked line 2, this is the amount you want refunded or abated.

If line 21 is more than zero, this is the amount you owe. Pay this amount by the time you file this return. For information on how to pay, see *Amount you owe* in the instructions.

Part 4: Explain your corrections for this quarter.

☐ **22. Check here if any corrections you entered on a line include both underreported and overreported amounts.** Explain both your underreported and overreported amounts on line 24.

☐ **23. Check here if any corrections involve reclassified workers.** Explain on line 24.

24. You must give us a detailed explanation of how you determined your corrections. See the instructions.

Part 5: Sign here. You must complete all three pages of this form and sign it.

Under penalties of perjury, I declare that I have filed an original Form 941 or Form 941-SS and that I have examined this adjusted return or claim, including accompanying schedules and statements, and to the best of my knowledge and belief, they are true, correct, and complete. Declaration of preparer (other than taxpayer) is based on all information of which preparer has any knowledge.

X Sign your name here

Print your name here

Print your title here

Date / /

Best daytime phone

Paid Preparer Use Only

Check if you are self-employed . . . ☐

Preparer's name		PTIN	
Preparer's signature		Date	/ /
Firm's name (or yours if self-employed)		EIN	
Address		Phone	
City	State	ZIP code	

Page **3** Form **941-X** (Rev. 4-2012)

Form 941-X (Page 4)

Form 941-X: Which process should you use?

Type of errors you are correcting			
Underreported amounts ONLY	**Use the adjustment process** to correct underreported amounts. • Check the box on line 1. • Pay the amount you owe from line 21 by the time you file Form 941-X.		
Overreported amounts ONLY	The process you use depends on **when** you file Form 941-X.	**If you are filing Form 941-X MORE THAN 90 days before the period of limitations on credit or refund for Form 941 or Form 941-SS expires ...**	Choose either process to correct the overreported amounts. **Choose the adjustment process** if you want the amount shown on line 21 credited to your Form 941, Form 941-SS, or Form 944 for the period in which you file Form 941-X. Check the box on line 1. OR **Choose the claim process** if you want the amount shown on line 21 refunded to you or abated. Check the box on line 2.
		If you are filing Form 941-X WITHIN 90 days of the expiration of the period of limitations on credit or refund for Form 941 or Form 941-SS ...	You must use the **claim process** to correct the overreported amounts. Check the box on line 2.
BOTH underreported and overreported amounts	The process you use depends on **when** you file Form 941-X.	**If you are filing Form 941-X MORE THAN 90 days before the period of limitations on credit or refund for Form 941 or Form 941-SS expires ...**	Choose either the adjustment process or both the adjustment process and the claim process when you correct both underreported and overreported amounts. **Choose the adjustment process** if combining your underreported amounts and overreported amounts results in a balance due or creates a credit that you want applied to Form 941, Form 941-SS, or Form 944. • File one Form 941-X, and • Check the box on line 1 and follow the instructions on line 21. OR **Choose both the adjustment process and the claim process** if you want the overreported amount refunded to you or abated. File two separate forms. **1. For the adjustment process,** file one Form 941-X to correct the underreported amounts. Check the box on line 1. Pay the amount you owe from line 21 by the time you file Form 941-X. **2. For the claim process,** file a second Form 941-X to correct the overreported amounts. Check the box on line 2.
		If you are filing Form 941-X WITHIN 90 days of the expiration of the period of limitations on credit or refund for Form 941 or Form 941-SS ...	You must use both the adjustment process and claim process. File two separate forms. **1. For the adjustment process,** file one Form 941-X to correct the underreported amounts. Check the box on line 1. Pay the amount you owe from line 21 by the time you file Form 941-X. **2. For the claim process,** file a second Form 941-X to correct the overreported amounts. Check the box on line 2.

Form **941-X** (Rev. 4-2012)

Form 941-X—Instructions (Page 1)

Instructions for Form 941-X

Department of the Treasury
Internal Revenue Service

(April 2012)

Adjusted Employer's QUARTERLY Federal Tax Return or Claim for Refund

Section references are to the Internal Revenue Code unless otherwise noted.

Future Developments

For the latest information about developments related to Form 941-X and its instructions, such as legislation enacted after they were published, go to *www.irs.gov/form941x*.

What's New

Social security tax rate for 2012. The employee social security tax rate is 4.2% and the employer social security tax rate is 6.2% (10.4% total). Be sure to use the correct rate when correcting amounts reported on lines 8 and 9.

Reminders

Section 3121(q) Notice and Demand—Tax due on unreported tips. An employer enters the amount of social security and Medicare taxes on unreported tips shown on the Section 3121(q) Notice and Demand on line 5e of the employer's Form 941 for the calendar quarter corresponding to the "Date of Notice and Demand." Any errors discovered on previously filed Forms 941 for these taxes are corrected on Form 941-X, line 11. In addition, any errors relating to Section 3121(q) Notice and Demand amounts reported on Form 941, line 7c (for quarters ending before January 1, 2011) should be corrected on Form 941-X, line 11.

Qualified employer's social security tax exemption expired. The qualified employer's exemption for their share (6.2%) of social security tax on wages/tips paid to qualified employees expired on December 31, 2010. Any errors discovered on previously filed Forms 941 (for quarters ending after March 31, 2010, and before January 1, 2011) for this exemption are corrected on Form 941-X, lines 12a–12c.

Advance payment of earned income credit (EIC). The option of receiving advance payroll payments of EIC expired on December 31, 2010. Any errors discovered on a previously filed Form 941 for this credit are corrected on Form 941-X, line 18.

Adjusting COBRA premium assistance payments. Employers who make COBRA premium assistance payments for assistance eligible individuals are allowed a credit for the payments on Form 941. Any errors discovered on previously filed Forms 941 for this credit are corrected on Form 941-X. See *COBRA Premium Assistance Payments*, later.

Adjusting an aggregate Form 941. Agents must complete Schedule R (Form 941), Allocation Schedule for Aggregate Form 941 Filers, when adjusting an aggregate Form 941. Schedule R (Form 941) is completed only for those clients who have adjustments reported on Form 941-X. Schedule R (Form 941) is filed as an attachment to Form 941-X. Aggregate Forms 941 are filed by agents approved by the IRS under section 3504. To request approval to act as an agent for an employer, the agent files Form 2678, Employer/Payer Appointment of Agent, with the IRS.

General Instructions: Understanding Form 941-X

What Is the Purpose of Form 941-X?

Use Form 941-X to correct errors on a Form 941 that you previously filed. Use Form 941-X to correct:
- Wages, tips, and other compensation;
- Income tax withheld from wages, tips, and other compensation;
- Taxable social security wages;
- Taxable social security tips;
- Taxable Medicare wages and tips;
- Advance earned income credit (EIC) payments made to employees (for quarters ending before January 1, 2011);
- Credits for COBRA premium assistance payments;
- Credits for qualified employer's share of social security tax on wages/tips paid to qualified employees March 19–31, 2010 (second quarter 2010 only); and
- Exemptions for qualified employer's share of social security tax on wages/tips paid to qualified employees (for quarters ending after March 31, 2010, and before January 1, 2011).

Use Form 843, Claim for Refund and Request for Abatement, to request a refund or abatement of assessed interest or penalties. **Do not** request abatement of assessed interest or penalties on Form 941 or Form 941-X.

TIP *References to Form 941 on Form 941-X and in these instructions also apply to Form 941-SS, Employer's QUARTERLY Federal Tax Return, unless otherwise noted. We use the terms "correct" and "corrections" on Form 941-X and in these instructions to include interest-free adjustments under sections 6205 and 6413 and claims for refund and abatement under sections 6402, 6414, and 6404. See Rev. Rul. 2009-39 for examples of how the interest-free adjustment and claim for refund rules apply in 10 different situations. You can find Rev. Rul. 2009-39, 2009-52, I.R.B. 951 at* www.irs.gov/irb/2009-52_IRB/ar14.html.

When you discover an error on a previously filed Form 941, you must:
- Correct that error using Form 941-X,
- File a separate Form 941-X for each Form 941 that you are correcting, and
- File Form 941-X separately. Do not file Form 941-X with Form 941.

If you did not file a Form 941 for one or more quarters, **do not** use Form 941-X. Instead, file Form 941 for each of those quarters. See also *When Should You File Form 941-X*, later. However, if you did not file Forms 941 because you improperly treated workers as independent contractors or nonemployees and are now reclassifying them as employees, see the instructions for line 23, later.

Report the correction of underreported and overreported amounts for the same tax period on a single Form 941-X, unless you are requesting a refund or abatement. If you are requesting a refund or abatement and are correcting both underreported and overreported amounts, file one Form 941-X correcting the underreported amounts only and a second Form 941-X correcting the overreported amounts.

You will use the adjustment process if you underreported employment taxes and are making a payment, or if you

Apr 30, 2012

Cat. No. 20331U

Form 941-X—Instructions (Page 2)

overreported employment taxes and will be applying the credit to Form 941 for the period during which you file Form 941-X. However, see the *Caution* under *Is There a Deadline for Filing Form 941-X*, later, if you are correcting overreported amounts during the last 90 days of a period of limitations. You will use the claim process if you overreported employment taxes and are requesting a refund or abatement of the overreported amount. Follow the chart on the back of Form 941-X for help in choosing whether to use the adjustment process or the claim process. Be sure to give us a detailed explanation on line 24 for each correction that you show on Form 941-X.

Continue to report current quarter fractions of cents, third-party sick pay, tips, and group-term life insurance on Form 941, lines 7–9.

You have additional requirements to complete when filing Form 941-X, such as certifying that you filed (or will file) all applicable Forms W-2, Wage and Tax Statements, and Forms W-2c, Corrected Wage and Tax Statements, with the Social Security Administration (SSA). For corrections of overreported federal income tax, social security tax, or Medicare tax, you must make any certifications that apply to your situation.

CAUTION *Do not use Form 941-X to correct Form CT-1, 943, 944, 944-SS, or 945. Instead, use the "X" form that corresponds to those forms (Form CT-1 X, 943-X, 944-X, or 945-X).*

Where Can You Get Help?

For help filing Form 941-X or for questions about federal employment taxes and tax corrections, you can:

- Call the IRS Business and Specialty Tax Line toll-free at 1-800-829-4933 (TTY/TDD for hearing and speech-impaired individuals at 1-800-829-4059), Monday through Friday from 7 a.m. to 7 p.m. local time (Alaska and Hawaii follow Pacific time),
- Visit the IRS website at www.irs.gov/businesses and click on "Employment Taxes," or
- See Pub. 15 (Circular E), Employer's Tax Guide, for correcting Form 941, or Pub. 80 (Circular SS), Federal Tax Guide for Employers in the U.S. Virgin Islands, Guam, American Samoa, and the Commonwealth of the Northern Mariana Islands, for correcting Form 941-SS.

See also *How Can You Order Forms and Publications from the IRS*, later.

When Should You File Form 941-X?

File Form 941-X when you discover an error on a previously filed Form 941.

However, if your only errors on Form 941 relate to the number of employees who received wages or to federal tax liabilities reported on Form 941, Part 2, or on Schedule B (Form 941), do not file Form 941-X. For more information about correcting federal tax liabilities reported on Form 941, Part 2, or on Schedule B (Form 941), Report of Tax Liability for Semiweekly Schedule Depositors, see the Instructions for Schedule B (Form 941).

Due dates. The due date for filing Form 941-X depends on when you discover an error and if you underreported or overreported tax. If you underreported tax, see *Underreported tax* below. For overreported amounts, you may choose to either make an interest-free adjustment or file a claim for refund or abatement. If you are correcting overreported amounts, see *Overreported tax—credit* or *Overreported tax—claim* below.

If any due date falls on a Saturday, Sunday, or legal holiday, you may file Form 941-X on the next business day. If we receive Form 941-X after the due date, we will treat Form 941-X as filed on time if the envelope containing Form 941-X is properly addressed, contains sufficient postage, and is postmarked by the U.S. Postal Service on or before the due date, or sent by an IRS-designated private delivery service on or before the due date. If you do not follow these guidelines, we will consider Form 941-X filed when it is actually received. See Pub. 15 (Circular E) or Pub. 80 (Circular SS) for more information on IRS-designated private delivery services.

Underreported tax. If you are correcting underreported tax, you must file Form 941-X by the due date of the return for the return period in which you discovered the error and **pay** the amount you owe by the time you file. Doing so will generally ensure that your correction is interest free and not subject to failure-to-pay or failure-to-deposit penalties. See *What About Penalties and Interest*, later. For details on how to make a payment, see the instructions for lines 20–21, later.

If Form 941-X is filed late (after the due date of the return for the return period in which you discovered the error), you must attach an amended Schedule B (Form 941) to Form 941-X. Otherwise, the IRS may assess an "averaged" failure-to-deposit penalty. The total tax reported on the "Total liability for the quarter" line of Schedule B (Form 941) must match the corrected tax (Form 941, line 10, combined with any correction entered on Form 941-X, line 17, minus any advance EIC reported on Form 941-X, line 18) for the quarter, less any previous abatements and interest-free tax assessments.

If you discover an error in	Form 941-X is due . . .
1. January, February, March	April 30
2. April, May, June	July 31
3. July, August, September	October 31
4. October, November, December	January 31

The dates shown in the table above apply only to corrections of underreported amounts. If any due date falls on a Saturday, Sunday, or legal holiday, you may file Form 941-X on the next business day.

Example—You owe tax. On February 10, 2012, you discover that you underreported $10,000 of social security and Medicare wages on your 2011 fourth quarter Form 941. File Form 941-X and pay the amount you owe by April 30, 2012, because you discovered the error in the first quarter of 2012, and April 30, 2012, is the due date for that quarter. If you file Form 941-X before April 30, pay the amount you owe when you file.

Overreported tax—credit. If you overreported tax on Form 941 and choose to apply the credit to Form 941 or Form 944, file Form 941-X soon after you discovered the error but more than 90 days before the period of limitations on the credit or refund for Form 941 expires. See *Is There a Deadline for Filing Form 941-X?* below.

Overreported tax—claim. If you overreported tax on Form 941, you may choose to file a claim for refund or abatement on Form 941-X any time before the period of limitations on credit or refund expires on Form 941. If you need to correct **any** underreported amounts, you must file another Form 941-X reporting only corrections to the underreported amounts. See *Is There a Deadline for Filing Form 941-X?* next.

Is There a Deadline for Filing Form 941-X?

Generally, you may correct overreported taxes on a previously filed Form 941 if you file Form 941-X within 3 years of the date Form 941 was filed or 2 years from the date you paid the tax reported on Form 941, whichever is later. You may correct underreported taxes on a previously filed Form 941 if you file Form 941-X within 3 years of the date the Form 941 was filed. We call each of these time frames a "period of limitations." For purposes of the period of limitations, Forms 941 for a calendar year are considered filed on April 15 of the succeeding year if filed before that date.

Example. You filed your 2009 fourth quarter Form 941 on January 27, 2010, and payments were timely made. The IRS treats the return as if it were filed on April 15, 2010. On January

-2- Instructions for Form 941-X (Rev. 4-2012)

Form 941-X—Instructions (Page 3)

20, 2013, you discover that you overreported social security and Medicare wages on that form by $350. To correct the error you must file Form 941-X by April 15, 2013, which is the end of the period of limitations for Form 941, and use the claim process.

CAUTION *If you file Form 941-X to correct overreported amounts in the last 90 days of a period of limitations (after January 15, 2013, in the example above), you must use the claim process. You cannot use the adjustment process. If you are also correcting underreported amounts, you must file another Form 941-X to correct the underreported amounts using the adjustment process and pay any tax due.*

Where Should You File Form 941-X?

Send your completed Form 941-X to the Internal Revenue Service Center shown below.

IF you are in	THEN use this address . . .
Special filing addresses for exempt organizations; federal, state, and local governmental entities; and Indian tribal governmental entities; regardless of location	Department of the Treasury Internal Revenue Service Ogden, UT 84201-0005
Connecticut, Delaware, District of Columbia, Georgia, Illinois, Indiana, Kentucky, Maine, Maryland, Massachusetts, Michigan, New Hampshire, New Jersey, New York, North Carolina, Ohio, Pennsylvania, Rhode Island, South Carolina, Tennessee, Vermont, Virginia, West Virginia, Wisconsin	Department of the Treasury Internal Revenue Service Cincinnati, OH 45999-0005
Alabama, Alaska, Arizona, Arkansas, California, Colorado, Florida, Hawaii, Idaho, Iowa, Kansas, Louisiana, Minnesota, Mississippi, Missouri, Montana, Nebraska, Nevada, New Mexico, North Dakota, Oklahoma, Oregon, South Dakota, Texas, Utah, Washington, Wyoming	Department of the Treasury Internal Revenue Service Ogden, UT 84201-0005
No legal residence or principal place of business in any state	Internal Revenue Service P.O. Box 409101 Ogden, UT 84409

How Should You Complete Form 941-X?

Use a Separate Form 941-X for Each Quarter You Are Correcting

Use a separate Form 941-X for each Form 941 that you are correcting. For example, if you found errors on your Forms 941 for the third and fourth quarters of 2010, file one Form 941-X to correct the 2010 third quarter Form 941. File a second Form 941-X to correct the 2010 fourth quarter Form 941.

EIN, Name, and Address

Enter your EIN, name, and address in the spaces provided. Also enter your name and EIN on the top of pages 2 and 3, and on any attachments. If your address has changed since you filed your Form 941, enter the corrected information and the IRS will update your address of record.

Return You Are Correcting

In the box at the top of page 1, check the type of return (Form 941 or Form 941-SS) you are correcting. Check the appropriate box for the **one** quarter you are correcting. Enter the calendar year of the Form 941 you are correcting. Enter the quarter and calendar year on pages 2 and 3. Be sure to write your name, EIN, Form 941-X, the quarter, and calendar year on the top of any attachments.

Enter the Date You Discovered Errors

You **must** enter the date you discovered errors. If you are reporting several errors that you discovered at different times, enter the earliest date you discovered them here. You discover an error when you have enough information to be able to correct it. Report any subsequent dates and related errors on line 24.

Must You Make an Entry on Each Line?

You must provide all of the information requested at the top of page 1. You must check one box (but not both) in Part 1. You must check the box on line 3 and any applicable boxes on lines 4 and 5. In Part 3, if any line does not apply, leave it blank. Complete Parts 4 and 5 as instructed.

How Should You Report Negative Amounts?

Form 941-X uses negative numbers to show reductions in tax (credits) and positive numbers to show additional tax (amounts you owe).

When reporting a negative amount in columns 3 and 4, use a minus sign instead of parentheses. For example, enter "-10.59" instead of "(10.59)." However, if you are completing the return on your computer and your software only allows you to use parentheses to report negative amounts, you may use them.

How Should You Make Entries on Form 941-X?

You can help the IRS process Form 941-X timely and accurately if you follow these guidelines.

- Type or print your entries.
- Use Courier font (if possible) for all typed or computer-generated entries.
- Omit dollar signs. You may use commas and decimal points, if desired. Enter dollar amounts to the left of any preprinted decimal point and cents to the right of it.
- Always show an amount for cents. Do not round entries to whole dollars.
- Complete all three pages and sign Form 941-X on page 3.
- Staple multiple sheets in the upper-left corner.

What About Penalties and Interest?

Generally, your correction of an underreported amount will not be subject to a failure-to-pay penalty, failure-to-deposit penalty, or interest if you:

- File on time (by the due date of the quarter in which you discover the error),
- Pay the amount shown on line 21 **by the time you file** Form 941-X,
- Enter the date you discovered the error, and
- Explain in detail the grounds and facts relied on to support the correction.

No correction will be eligible for interest-free treatment if any of the following apply.

- The amounts underreported relate to an issue that was raised in an examination of a prior period.
- You knowingly underreported your employment tax liability.
- You received a notice and demand for payment.
- You received a Notice of Determination of Worker Classification.

Overview of the Process

The process to correct a previously filed Form 941 or file a claim is outlined below.

If you underreported the tax. If you underreported the tax on a previously filed Form 941, check the box on line 1 and **pay** any additional amount you owe by the time you file Form 941-X. For details on how to make a payment, see the instructions for lines 20–21, later.

Example—You underreported employment taxes. On June 20, 2012, you discover an error that results in additional tax on your 2011 fourth quarter Form 941. File Form 941-X by

Instructions for Form 941-X (Rev. 4-2012) -3-

Form 94-X—Instructions (Page 4)

July 31, 2012, and pay the amount you owe by the time you file. See *When Should You File Form 941-X,* earlier. **Do not** attach Form 941-X to your 2012 second quarter Form 941.

If you overreported the tax. If you overreported the tax on a previously filed Form 941, you may **choose** one of the following options.

- *Use the adjustment process.* Check the box on line 1 to apply any credit (negative amount) from line 21 to Form 941 for the quarter during which you file Form 941-X.
- *Use the claim process.* Check the box on line 2 to file a claim on Form 941-X requesting a refund or abatement of the amount shown on line 21.

TIP *To ensure that the IRS has enough time to process a credit for an **overreporting adjustment** in the quarter during which you file Form 941-X, you are encouraged to file Form 941-X correcting the overreported amount in the first two months of a quarter. For example, if you discover an overreported amount in March, June, September, or December, you may want to file Form 941-X in the first two months of the next quarter. However, there must be 90 days remaining on the period of limitations when you file Form 941-X. See the* Caution *under* Is There a Deadline for Filing Form 941-X, *earlier. This should ensure that the IRS will have enough time to process Form 941-X so the credit will be posted before you file Form 941, thus avoiding an erroneous balance due notice from the IRS. See the example below.*

If you currently file Form 944 instead of Form 941 and will claim a credit on Form 944, file Form 941-X before December in any year before the expiration of the period of limitations on Form 941. In the year of the expiration of the period of limitations on Form 941, file Form 941-X at least 90 days before the expiration date.

Example—You want your overreported tax applied as a credit to Form 941. On June 22, 2012, you discover you overreported your tax on your 2011 fourth quarter Form 941 and want to choose the adjustment process. To allow the IRS enough time to process the credit, you file Form 941-X on July 1, 2012, and take the credit on your third quarter 2012 Form 941.

Specific Instructions:

Part 1: Select ONLY one process

Because Form 941-X may be used to file either an adjusted employment tax return or a claim for refund or abatement, you **must** check one box on either line 1 or line 2. Do not check both boxes.

1. Adjusted Employment Tax Return

Check the box on line 1 if you are correcting underreported amounts or overreported amounts and you would like to use the adjustment process to correct the errors.

If you are correcting both underreported amounts and overreported amounts on this form, you **must** check this box. If you check this box, any negative amount shown on line 21 will be applied as a credit (tax deposit) to your Form 941 or Form 944 for the period in which you are filing this form. See *Example—You want your overreported tax applied as a credit to Form 941* above.

If you owe tax. Pay the amount shown on line 21 by the time you file Form 941-X. Generally, you will not be charged interest if you file on time, pay on time, enter the date you discovered the error, and explain the correction on line 24.

If you have a credit. You overreported employment taxes (you have a negative amount on line 21) and want the IRS to apply the credit to Form 941 or Form 944 for the period during which you filed Form 941-X. The IRS will apply your credit on the first day of the Form 941 or Form 944 period during which you filed Form 941-X. However, the credit you show on line 21 of Form 941-X may not be fully available on your Form 941 or Form 944 if the IRS corrects it during processing or you owe other taxes, penalties, or interest. The IRS will notify you if your claimed credit changes or if the amount available as a credit on Form 941 or Form 944 was reduced because of unpaid taxes, penalties, or interest.

CAUTION *Do not check the box on line 1 if you are correcting overreported amounts and the period of limitations on credit or refund for Form 941 will expire within 90 days of the date you file Form 941-X. Instead, check the box on line 2. See* Is There a Deadline for Filing Form 941-X, *earlier.*

2. Claim

Check the box on line 2 to use the claim process if you are correcting **overreported amounts only** and you are claiming a refund or abatement for the negative amount (credit) shown on line 21. Do not check this box if you are correcting any underreported amounts on this form.

You must check the box on line 2 if you have a credit and the period of limitations on credit or refund for Form 941 will expire within 90 days of the date you file Form 941-X. See *Is There a Deadline for Filing Form 941-X,* earlier.

The IRS usually processes claims shortly after they are filed. The IRS will notify you if your claim is denied, accepted as filed, or selected to be examined. See Pub. 556, Examination of Returns, Appeal Rights, and Claims for Refund, for more information.

Unless the IRS corrects Form 941-X during processing or you owe other taxes, penalties, or interest, the IRS will refund the amount shown on line 21, plus any interest that applies.

Part 2: Complete the Certifications

You must complete all certifications that apply by checking the appropriate boxes. If all of your corrections relate to underreported amounts, complete line 3 only; skip lines 4 and 5 and go to Part 3. If your corrections relate to overreported amounts, you have a duty to ensure that your employees' rights to recover overpaid employee social security and Medicare taxes that you withheld are protected. The certifications on lines 4 and 5 address the requirement to:

- Repay or reimburse your employees for the overcollection of employee social security and Medicare taxes, or
- Obtain consents from your employees to file a claim on their behalf.

3. Filing Forms W-2 or Forms W-2c

Check the box on line 3 to certify that you filed or will file Forms W-2 or Forms W-2c with the SSA, as required, showing your employees' correct wage and tax amounts. See the Instructions for Forms W-2 and W-3 and the Instructions for Forms W-2c and W-3c for detailed information about filing requirements. References to Form W-2 on Form 941-X and in these instructions also apply to Forms W-2AS, W-2CM, W-2GU, and W-2VI unless otherwise noted.

You must check the box on line 3 to certify that you filed Forms W-2 or Forms W-2c even if your corrections on Form 941-X do not change amounts shown on those forms. For example, if your only correction to Form 941 involves misstated tax adjustments (see the instructions for line 13, later), check the box on line 3 to certify that you already filed all required Forms W-2 and W-2c with the SSA.

4. Certifying Overreporting Adjustments

If you overreported federal income tax, social security tax, or Medicare tax and checked the box on line 1, check the appropriate box on line 4. You may need to check more than one box. If you obtained written statements from some employees but you could not locate or secure the cooperation of the remaining employees, check all applicable boxes. Provide a summary on line 24 of the amount of the corrections both for the employees who provided written statements and for those who did not.

4a. Check the box on line 4a if your overreported amount includes each affected employee's share of overcollected taxes.

-4- Instructions for Form 941-X (Rev. 4-2012)

Form 941-X—Instructions (Page 5)

You are certifying that you repaid or reimbursed the employee's share of current and prior year taxes and you received written statements from the employees stating that they did not and will not receive a refund or credit for the prior year taxes. You are certifying that you adjusted federal income tax withheld from employees for the current calendar year only.

Example. The following is an example of the written statement that is required from employees.

Employee name ________________
Employer name ________________
I have received a repayment of $________ as overcollected social security and Medicare taxes for 20___. I have not claimed a refund of or credit for the overcollected taxes from the IRS, or if I did, that claim has been rejected; and I will not claim a refund or a credit of the amount.
Employee signature ________________
Date ________

Do not send these statements to the IRS. Keep them for your records. Generally, all employment tax records must be kept for at least 4 years.

4b. Check the box on line 4b to certify that your overreported amount is only for the employer share of taxes on those employees who you were unable to find or those who would not (or could not) give you a statement described on line 4a.

4c. Check the box on line 4c to certify that your overreported amount is only for federal income tax, social security tax, and Medicare tax that you did not withhold from your employees.

5. Certifying Claims

If you are filing a claim for refund or abatement of overreported federal income tax, social security tax, or Medicare tax and checked the box on line 2, check the appropriate box on line 5. You may need to check more than one box. If you obtained written statements or consents from some employees but you could not locate or secure the cooperation of the remaining employees, check all applicable boxes. Provide a summary on line 24 of the amount of the corrections for both the employees who provided statements or consents and for those who did not. You may not file a refund claim to correct federal income tax actually withheld from employees.

5a. Check the box on line 5a if your overreported tax includes each affected employee's share of social security and Medicare taxes. You are certifying that you repaid or reimbursed to the employees their share of social security and Medicare taxes. For refunds of employee social security and Medicare taxes overcollected in prior years, you are certifying that you received written statements from those employees stating that they did not and will not receive a refund or credit for the prior year taxes.

5b. Check the box on line 5b if your overreported tax includes each affected employee's share of social security and Medicare taxes and you have not yet repaid or reimbursed the employee share of taxes. You are certifying that you received consent from each affected employee to file a claim on the employee share of those taxes and you received written statements from those employees stating that they did not and will not receive a refund or credit for the prior year taxes.

Example. The following is an example of the consent and written statement that is required from employees when you are filing a claim for refund and have not yet paid or reimbursed the employee share of taxes.

Employee name ________________
Employer name ________________
I give my consent to have my employer (named above) file a claim on my behalf with the IRS requesting $________ in overcollected social security and Medicare taxes for 20___. I have not claimed a refund of or credit for the overcollected taxes from the IRS, or if I did, that claim has been rejected; and I will not claim a refund or a credit of the amount.
Employee signature ________________
Date ________

Do not send these statements to the IRS. Keep them for your records. Generally, all employment tax records must be kept for at least 4 years.

In certain situations, you may not have repaid or reimbursed your employees or obtained their consents prior to filing a claim, such as in cases where the period of limitations on credit or refund is about to expire. In those situations, file Form 941-X, but do not check a box on line 5. Tell us on line 24 that you have not repaid or reimbursed employees or obtained consents. However, you must certify that you have repaid or reimbursed your employees or obtained consents before the IRS can grant the claim.

5c. Check the box on line 5c to certify that your overreported tax is only for the employer share of social security and Medicare taxes. Affected employees did not give you consent to file a claim for refund for the employee share of social security and Medicare taxes, they could not be found, or would not (or could not) give you a statement described on line 5b.

5d. Check the box on line 5d to certify that your overreported amount is only for federal income tax, social security tax, and Medicare tax that you did not withhold from your employees.

Part 3: Enter the Corrections for This Quarter

What Amounts Should You Report in Part 3?

On lines 6–10, columns 1 and 2, show amounts for **all** of your employees, not just for those employees whose amounts you are correcting.

If a correction that you report in column 4 includes both underreported and overreported amounts (see the instructions for lines 20–21, later), give us details for each error on line 24.

Because special circumstances apply for lines 11–16 and 18–19d, read the instructions for each line carefully before entering amounts in the columns.

CAUTION *If you previously adjusted or amended Form 941 by using Form 941c, Form 941-X, Form 843, an "amended" Form 941, a "supplemental" Form 941, or because of an IRS examination change, show amounts in column 2 that include those previously reported corrections.*

6. Wages, Tips, and Other Compensation

If you are correcting the wages, tips, and other compensation you reported on Form 941, line 2, enter the total corrected amount for ALL employees in column 1. In column 2, enter the amount you originally reported. In column 3, enter the difference between columns 1 and 2. This line does not apply to Form 941-SS.

If you or the IRS previously corrected the amount reported on Form 941, line 2, enter in column 2 the amount after any previous corrections.

line 6 (column 1)
\- line 6 (column 2)
line 6 (column 3) — If the amount in column 2 is larger than the amount in column 1, use a minus sign in column 3.

Example — Wages, tips, and other compensation increased. You reported $9,000 as total wages, tips, and other compensation on line 2 of your 2009 third quarter Form 941. In July of 2010, you discovered that you had overlooked $1,000 in tips for one of your part-time employees. To correct the error, figure the difference on Form 941-X as shown.

Column 1 (corrected amount)	10,000.00
Column 2 (Form 941, line 2)	- 9,000.00
Column 3 (difference)	-1,000.00

Instructions for Form 941-X (Rev. 4-2012) -5-

Form 941-X—Instructions (Page 6)

Example —Wages, tips, and other compensation decreased. You reported $9,000 as wages, tips, and other compensation on line 2 of your 2009 fourth quarter Form 941. In December of 2010, you discovered that you included $2,000 in wages for one of your employees twice. To correct the error, figure the difference on Form 941-X as shown.

Column 1 (corrected amount)	7,000.00
Column 2 (Form 941, line 2)	- 9,000.00
Column 3 (difference)	-2,000.00

Example—Auto allowance; wages, tips, and other compensation increased. You paid one of your employees a $500 monthly auto allowance from October through December 2010, and did not treat the payments as taxable wages. In February 2011, you realized that the payments were wages because they were not reimbursements of deductible business expenses that were substantiated and paid under an accountable plan. You correct the error by treating the auto allowance as wages subject to income, social security, and Medicare taxes. Report the additional $1,500 of wages on lines 6, 8, and 10.

TIP *Use the amount on line 6, column 1, when you prepare your Forms W-2 or Forms W-2c.*

7. Income Tax Withheld from Wages, Tips, and Other Compensation

If you are correcting the federal income tax withheld from wages, tips, and other compensation you reported on Form 941, line 3, enter the total corrected amount in column 1. In column 2, enter the amount you originally reported or as previously corrected. In column 3, enter the difference between columns 1 and 2. This line does not apply to Form 941-SS.

line 7 (column 1)	
- line 7 (column 2)	
line 7 (column 3)	If the amount in column 2 is larger than the amount in column 1, use a minus sign in column 3.

Copy the amount in column 3 to column 4. Include any minus sign shown in column 3.

CAUTION *Generally, you may correct federal income tax withholding errors **only** if you discovered the errors in the same calendar year you paid the wages. However, you may correct federal income tax withholding errors for prior years if the amounts shown on Form 941 do not agree with the amounts you actually withheld, that is, an administrative error or if section 3509 rates apply. See section 13 of Pub. 15 (Circular E) for more information about corrections during the calendar year and about administrative errors. See section 2 of Pub. 15 (Circular E) for more information about section 3509.*

Example—Failure to withhold income tax when required. You were required to withhold $400 of federal income tax from an employee's bonus that was paid in December of 2011 but you withheld nothing. You discovered the error on March 15, 2012. You cannot file Form 941-X to correct your 2011 fourth quarter Form 941 because the error involves a previous year and the amount previously reported for the employee represents the actual amount withheld from the employee during 2011.

Example—Administrative error reporting income tax. You had three employees. In the fourth quarter of 2011, you withheld $1,000 of federal income tax from employee A, $2,000 from employee B, and $6,000 from employee C. The total amount of federal income tax you withheld was $9,000. You mistakenly reported $6,000 on line 3 of your 2011 fourth quarter Form 941. You discovered the error on March 16, 2012. This is an example of an administrative error that may be corrected in a later calendar year because the amount actually withheld from employees' wages differs from the amount reported on Form 941. Use Form 941-X to correct the error. Enter $9,000 in column 1 and $6,000 in column 2. Subtract the amount in column 2 from the amount in column 1.

Column 1 (corrected amount)	9,000.00
Column 2 (Form 941, line 3)	- 6,000.00
Column 3 (difference)	3,000.00

Report the 3,000.00 as a tax correction in column 4.

Be sure to explain the reasons for this correction on line 24.

8. Taxable Social Security Wages

CAUTION *The 2011 and 2012 employee tax rate for social security is 4.2%. The employer tax rate for social security is 6.2%.*

If you are correcting the taxable social security wages you reported on Form 941, line 5a, column 1, enter the total corrected amount in column 1. In column 2, enter the amount you originally reported or as previously corrected. In column 3, enter the difference between columns 1 and 2.

line 8 (column 1)	
- line 8 (column 2)	
line 8 (column 3)	If the amount in column 2 is larger than the amount in column 1, use a minus sign in column 3.

Multiply the amount in column 3 by .124 (.104 for corrections to a 2011 or 2012 return) and enter that result in column 4.

line 8 (column 3)	
x .124	(Use .104 for corrections to a 2011 or 2012 return.)
line 8 (column 4)	If the amount in column 3 used a minus sign, also use a minus sign in column 4.

Note. If you are correcting only the employer share of tax on a decrease to social security wages, use .062 (6.2%) when multiplying the amount shown in column 3. If you are correcting both shares of tax for some employees and only the employer share for other employees, enter the properly calculated amount in column 4. Be sure to show your calculations on line 24.

Example—Social security wages decreased. Following *Example—Wages, tips and other compensation decreased* in the instructions for line 6, the wages that you counted twice were also taxable social security wages. To correct the error, figure the difference on Form 941-X as shown.

Column 1 (corrected amount)	7,000.00
Column 2 (Form 941, line 5a, column 1)	- 9,000.00
Column 3 (difference)	-2,000.00

Use the difference in column 3 to determine your tax correction.

Column 3 (difference)	-2,000.00
Tax rate (12.4%)	x .124
Column 4 (tax correction)	-248.00

Be sure to explain the reasons for this correction on line 24.

Note. If the example above was for a correction to a 2011 or 2012 return, the amount in column 3 would be multiplied by .104.

Form 941-X—Instructions (Page 7)

9. Taxable Social Security Tips

CAUTION *The 2011 and 2012 employee tax rate for social security is 4.2%. The employer tax rate for social security is 6.2%.*

If you are correcting the taxable social security tips you reported on Form 941, line 5b, column 1, enter the total corrected amount in column 1. In column 2, enter the amount you originally reported or as previously corrected. In column 3, enter the difference between columns 1 and 2.

line 9 (column 1)	
- line 9 (column 2)	
line 9 (column 3)	If the amount in column 2 is larger than the amount in column 1, use a minus sign in column 3.

Multiply the amount in column 3 by .124 (.104 for corrections to a 2011 or 2012 return) and report that result in column 4.

line 9 (column 3)	
x .124	(Use .104 for corrections to a 2011 or 2012 return.)
line 9 (column 4)	If the amount in column 3 used a minus sign, also use a minus sign in column 4.

Note. If you are correcting only the employer share of tax on a decrease to social security tips, use .062 (6.2%) when multiplying the amount shown in column 3. If you are correcting both shares of tax for some employees and only the employer share for other employees, report the properly calculated amount in column 4. Be sure to show your calculations on line 24.

Following the *Example—Wages, tips, and other compensation increased* in the instructions for line 6, the tips that you overlooked were also taxable social security tips. To correct the error, figure the difference on Form 941-X as shown.

Column 1 (corrected amount)	10,000.00
Column 2 (Form 941, line 5b, column 1)	- 9,000.00
Column 3 (difference)	1,000.00

Use the difference in column 3 to determine your tax correction.

Column 3 (difference)	1,000.00
Tax rate (12.4%)	x .124
Column 4 (tax correction)	124.00

Be sure to explain the reasons for this correction on line 24.

Note. If the example above was for a correction to a 2011 or 2012 return, the amount in column 3 would be multiplied by .104.

10. Taxable Medicare Wages and Tips

If you are correcting the taxable Medicare wages and tips you reported on Form 941, line 5c, column 1, enter the total corrected amount in column 1. In column 2, enter the amount you originally reported or as previously corrected. In column 3, enter the difference between columns 1 and 2.

line 10 (column 1)	
- line 10 (column 2)	
line 10 (column 3)	If the amount in column 2 is larger than the amount in column 1, use a minus sign in column 3.

Multiply the amount in column 3 by .029 (2.9% tax rate) and enter that result in column 4.

line 10 (column 3)	
x .029	
line 10 (column 4)	If the amount in column 3 used a minus sign, also use a minus sign in column 4.

Note. If you are correcting only the employer share of tax on a decrease to Medicare wages and tips, use .0145 (1.45%) when multiplying the amount in column 3. If you are correcting both shares of tax for some employees and only the employer share for other employees, enter the properly calculated amount in column 4. Be sure to explain your calculations on line 24.

Example—Medicare wages and tips decreased. Following *Example—Wages, tips and other compensation decreased* in the instructions for line 6, the wages that you counted twice were also taxable Medicare wages and tips. To correct the error, figure the difference on Form 941-X as shown.

Column 1 (corrected amount)	7,000.00
Column 2 (Form 941, line 5c, column 1)	- 9,000.00
Column 3 (difference)	-2,000.00

Use the difference in column 3 to determine your tax correction.

Column 3 (difference)	-2,000.00
Tax rate (2.9%)	x .029
Column 4 (tax correction)	-58.00

Be sure to explain the reasons for this correction on line 24.

11. Section 3121(q) Notice and Demand—Tax on Unreported Tips

Enter any corrections, including amounts reported on line 7c (for quarters ending before 2011) and amounts reported on line 5e (for quarters ending after 2010), to the tax due from a Section 3121(q) Notice and Demand on line 11. The IRS issues a Section 3121(q) Notice and Demand to advise an employer of the amount of tips received by employees who failed to report or underreported tips to the employer. An employer is not liable for the employer share of the social security and Medicare taxes on unreported tips until a Section 3121(q) Notice and Demand for the taxes is made to the employer by the IRS.

CAUTION *Lines 12a–12c apply only for corrections to quarters ending after March 31, 2010, and before January 1, 2011.*

12. Employer's Social Security Tax Exemption

Complete lines 12a–12c to correct the payroll tax exemption for the employer's share (6.2%) of social security tax on exempt wages/tips paid to one or more qualified employees from April 1–December 31, 2010.

An employer must be a qualified employer to qualify for the employer's social security tax exemption. A **qualified employer** is any employer other than Federal, State, and any related government entities. All public institutions of higher education and Indian tribal governments are also qualified employers.

For more information regarding the employer's social security tax exemption visit IRS.gov and enter the keywords *HIRE Act* in the search box.

12a. Number of qualified employees first paid exempt wages/tips this quarter. Enter on line 12a (column 2) the number of qualified employees originally reported on Form 941, line 6a. If you are not correcting Form 941, line 6a, and are making a correction on line 12b, enter the amount from Form 941, line 6a, on line 12a.

A **qualified employee** is an employee who:

- Began employment with you after February 3, 2010, and before January 1, 2011;
- Certifies by signed affidavit (Form W-11, Hiring Incentives to Restore Employment (HIRE) Act Employee Affidavit, or similar statement) under penalties of perjury that he or she has not been employed for more than 40 hours during the 60-day period (including 2009) ending on the date the employee begins employment with you;
- Is not employed by you to replace another employee unless the other employee separated from employment voluntarily or for cause (including downsizing); and
- Is not related to you. An employee is related to you if he or she is your child or a descendant of your child, your sibling or stepsibling, your parent or ancestor of your parent, your stepparent, your niece or nephew, your aunt or uncle, or your

Instructions for Form 941-X (Rev. 4-2012) -7-

Form 941-X—Instructions (Page 8)

in-law. An employee is also related to you if he or she is related to anyone who owns more than 50% of your outstanding stock or capital and profits interest or is your dependent or a dependent of anyone who owns more than 50% of your outstanding stock or capital and profits interest. If you are an estate or trust, see section 51(i)(1) and section 152(d)(2) for more details.

Exempt wages/tips are the wages/tips paid to qualified employees for which the employer is exempt from paying the employer's 6.2% share of social security tax.

CAUTION *If you make a correction on line 12a, then you must complete line 12b.*

12b. Number of qualified employees paid exempt wages/tips this quarter. Enter on line 12b (column 1) the total corrected number of qualified employees paid exempt wages/tips to which you applied the social security tax exemption in the quarter you are correcting. Enter on line 12b (column 2) the total number of qualified employees originally reported on Form 941, line 6b. If you are not correcting Form 941, line 6b, and are making a correction on line 12a, enter on line 12b the amount from Form 941, line 6b. See the instructions for line 12a for definitions of qualified employee and exempt wages/tips.

CAUTION *If you make a correction on line 12b, then you must complete line 12a.*

12c. Exempt wages/tips paid to qualified employees this quarter. Enter the amount of exempt wages/tips paid in the quarter you are correcting to all qualified employees. Enter the corrected amount from Form 941, line 6c. Enter the corrected amount in column 1. In column 2, enter the amount you originally reported or as previously corrected. In column 3, enter the difference between columns 1 and 2. If the amount in column 2 is larger than the amount in column 1, use a minus sign in column 3. Multiply the amount in column 3 by .062 and enter the result in column 4. However, to properly show the correction as a credit or balance due item, enter a positive number in column 3 as a negative number in column 4 or a negative number in column 3 as a positive number in column 4. See the instructions for line 12a for definitions of qualified and exempt wages/tips.

13. Tax Adjustments

Use line 13 to correct any adjustments reported on Form 941, lines 7–9 (lines 7a–7c for quarters ending before 2011). Enter in column 1 the total **corrected** amount for Form 941, lines 7–9 (lines 7a–7c for quarters ending before 2011).

Enter in column 2 the total originally reported or previously corrected amounts from Form 941, lines 7–9 (lines 7a–7c for quarters ending before 2011). In column 3, enter the difference between columns 1 and 2.

line 13 (column 1)
-line 13 (column 2)
line 13 (column 3)

TIP *You may need to report negative numbers in any column. Make sure that the difference you enter in column 3 accurately represents the change to adjustments originally reported or previously corrected on Form 941, lines 7–9 (lines 7a–7c for quarters ending before 2011).*

Copy the amount in column 3 to column 4. Include any minus sign shown in column 3.

On line 24, describe what you misreported on Form 941. Tell us if your adjustment is for fractions of cents, third-party sick pay, tips, or group-term life insurance.

Example—Current quarter's third-party sick pay underreported. You reported $6,900 (shown as "-6,900.00") as a third-party sick pay adjustment (reduction to tax) on line 7b of your 2010 second quarter Form 941. You did not report any amounts on lines 7a and 7c. Your third-party sick pay adjustment should have been $9,600 (shown as "-9,600.00") because your third-party sick pay payer withheld that amount of social security and Medicare taxes from your employees. You discovered the error in April of 2011. To correct the error, figure the difference on Form 941-X as shown.

Column 1 (corrected amount)	-9,600.00
Column 2 (Form 941, line 7b)	- (6,900.00)
Column 3 (difference)	-2,700.00

Here is how you would enter the numbers on Form 941-X.

Column 1 (corrected amount)	Column 2 (Form 941, line 7b)	Column 3 (difference)
-9,600.00	-6,900.00	-2,700.00

Report "-2,700.00" as your correction in column 4.

In this example, you are claiming a credit for $2,700 in overreported tax for your 2010 second quarter Form 941. Always enter the same amount in column 4 (including any minus sign) that you enter in column 3.

Be sure to explain the reasons for this correction on line 24.

Note. If the example above was for a correction to a 2011 or 2012 return, the references to line 7b change to line 8.

CAUTION *Do not use line 13 to report corrections to amounts reported on lines 7d–7g of pre-2009 Forms 941.*

14–16. Special Additions to Wages for Federal Income Tax, Social Security Tax, and Medicare Tax

Section 3509 provides special rates for the employee share of social security and Medicare taxes and income tax withholding when workers are reclassified as employees in certain circumstances. The applicable rate depends on whether you filed required information returns. An employer cannot recover any tax paid under this provision from the employees. The full employer share of social security and Medicare taxes is due for all reclassifications.

Note. Section 3509 rates are not available if you intentionally disregarded the requirements to withhold taxes from the employee, or if you withheld income tax but did not withhold social security and Medicare taxes. Section 3509 rates are also not available for certain statutory employees.

On lines 14–16 enter **only** corrections to wages resulting from reclassifying certain workers as employees when section 3509 rates are used to calculate the taxes.

If the employer issued the required information returns, use the section 3509 rates as follows.

- For social security taxes, use the employer rate of 6.2% plus 20% of the employee rate of 6.2% (4.2% for 2011 and 2012), for a total rate of 7.44% (7.04% for 2011 and 2012) of wages.
- For Medicare taxes, use the employer rate of 1.45% plus 20% of the employee rate of 1.45%, for a total rate of 1.74% of wages.
- For income tax withholding, the rate is 1.5% of wages.

If the employer did not issue the required information returns, use the section 3509 rates as follows.

- For social security taxes, use the employer rate of 6.2% plus 40% of the employee rate of 6.2% (4.2% for 2011 and 2012), for a total rate of 8.68% (7.88% for 2011 and 2012) of wages.
- For Medicare taxes, use the employer rate of 1.45% plus 40% of the employee rate of 1.45%, for a total rate of 2.03% of wages.
- For income tax withholding, the rate is 3.0% of wages.

Unlike other lines on Form 941-X, enter in column 1 only the corrected wages for workers being reclassified, **not** the amount paid to ALL employees. Enter previously reported wages to reclassified employees (if any) in column 2. To get the amount for column 4, use the applicable section 3509 rates. The tax correction in column 4 will be a positive number if you increased the amount of wages you previously reported. See the instructions for line 23 for more information.

Form 941-X—Instructions (Page 9)

TIP *If you misreported the taxes from worker reclassification on line 7f or line 7g on a pre-2009 Form 941, you may correct the amount using lines 14–16 of Form 941-X. Be sure to complete all of the columns and provide a detailed explanation on line 24.*

17. Subtotal

Combine the amounts from column 4 on lines 7–16.

Example. You entered "1,400.00" in column 4 on line 7, "-500.00" in column 4 on line 8, and "-100.00" in column 4 on line 10. Combine these amounts and enter "800.00" in column 4 on line 17.

Line 7	1,400.00
Line 8	-500.00
Line 10	-100.00
Line 17	800.00

18. Advance EIC Payments Made to Employees

CAUTION *The option of receiving advance payroll payments of EIC expired on December 31, 2010. Corrections to advance EIC can be made only for quarters ending before January 1, 2011.*

If you are correcting the advance EIC payments made to your employees that you reported on Form 941, line 9 (only for quarters ending before January 1, 2011), enter the total corrected amount for ALL employees in column 1. In column 2, enter the amount you originally reported or as previously corrected. In column 3, enter the difference between columns 1 and 2. This line does not apply to Form 941-SS.

line 18 (column 1)
- line 18 (column 2)
line 18 (column 3) — If the amount in column 2 is larger than the amount in column 1, use a minus sign in column 3.

CAUTION *Copy the amount in column 3 to column 4. However, to properly show the correction as a credit or balance due item, enter a positive number in column 3 as a negative number in column 4 or a negative number in column 3 as a positive number in column 4. Remember, negative amounts in column 4 represent credits and positive amounts in column 4 represent additional tax.*

Examples. If line 18, column 3 shows "560.00," enter "-560.00" in column 4.

If line 18, column 3 shows "-990.00," enter "990.00" in column 4.

Example—Advance EIC payments increased. You filed your 2010 fourth quarter Form 941 reporting zero (line left blank) on line 9. On February 17, 2011, you discovered that you forgot to report the $1,000 in advance EIC payments you made on behalf of John Smith, one of your employees. You made no other EIC payments for your other employees. This is an example of an administrative error. To correct the error, file Form 941-X showing the following.

Column 1 (corrected amount)	1,000.00
Column 2 (Form 941, line 9)	- 0.00
Column 3 (difference)	1,000.00

Reverse the mathematical sign of the amount in column 3 and enter your correction in column 4.

Column 4 (tax correction) -1,000.00

Be sure to explain the reasons for this correction on line 24.

CAUTION *See section 13 of Pub. 15 (Circular E) for more information about administrative errors and corrections during the calendar year. The same rules that apply to withheld federal income taxes also apply to advance EIC payments made to employees.*

19a. COBRA Premium Assistance Payments

If you are correcting the total COBRA premium assistance payments reported on Form 941, line 12a, report on this line 65% of the COBRA premiums for assistance eligible individuals. Report the premium assistance credit on this line only after the assistance eligible individual's 35% share of the premium has been paid. For COBRA coverage provided under a self-insured plan, COBRA premium assistance is treated as having been made for each assistance eligible individual who pays 35% of the COBRA premium.

Do not include the assistance eligible individual's 35% of the premium in the amount entered on this line. For more information on the COBRA premium subsidy, visit IRS.gov and enter the keyword *COBRA*.

Copy the amount in column 3 to column 4. However, to properly show the correction as a credit or balance due item, enter a positive number in column 3 as a negative number in column 4 or a negative number in column 3 as a positive number in column 4. This is the same procedure as the advance EIC on line 18.

19b. Number of Individuals Provided COBRA Premium Assistance on line 19a

Complete this line only if you are correcting Form 941, line 12b. Enter in column 1 on line 19b the corrected number of assistance eligible individuals provided COBRA premium assistance. Count each assistance eligible individual who paid a reduced COBRA premium in the quarter as one individual, whether or not the reduced premium was for insurance that covered more than one assistance eligible individual. For example, if the reduced COBRA premium was for coverage for a former employee, spouse, and two children, you would include one individual in the number entered on line 19b for the premium assistance entered on line 19a. Further, each individual is reported only once per quarter. For example, an assistance eligible individual who made monthly premium payments during the quarter would only be reported as one individual on line 19b for that quarter.

Enter in column 2 on line 19b the number of assistance eligible individuals provided COBRA premium assistance originally reported on Form 941, line 12b.

CAUTION *Lines 19c and 19d apply only to the second quarter of 2010. These lines are used to report the number of qualified employees, amount of exempt wages/tips, and amount of employer social security tax exemption as if the exemption were allowed for the first quarter of 2010.*

19c. Number of Qualified Employees Paid Exempt Wages/Tips March 19–31

Complete this line when correcting Form 941 for the second quarter of 2010 only. Enter on line 19c (column 1) the corrected number of qualified employees paid exempt wages/tips from March 19, 2010, through March 31, 2010. Include only qualified employees for whom you are claiming the exemption. Enter on line 19c (column 2) the number of qualified employees originally reported on line 12c of the second quarter 2010 Form 941. If you are not correcting line 12c of the second quarter 2010 Form 941 but you are making a correction on line 19d, enter the amount from line 12c of the second quarter 2010 Form 941 on line 19c. For the definition of qualified employee, see the instructions for line 12a.

19d. Exempt Wages/Tips Paid to Qualified Employees March 19-31

Complete this line when correcting Form 941 for the second quarter of 2010 only. Enter on line 19d the amount of exempt wages/tips paid to qualified employees from March 19, 2010, through March 31, 2010. For the definition of exempt wages/tips, see the instructions for line 12a. Enter the corrected amount in column 1. In column 2, enter the amount you originally reported or as previously corrected. In column 3, enter the difference between columns 1 and 2. If the amount in column 2 is larger than the amount in column 1, use a minus

Instructions for Form 941-X (Rev. 4-2012) -9-

Form 941-X—Instructions (Page 10)

sign in column 3. Multiply the amount in column 3 by .062 and enter the result in column 4. However, to properly show the correction as a credit or balance due item, enter a positive number in column 3 as a negative number in column 4 or a negative number in column 3 as a positive number in column 4.

20–21. Total

Combine lines 17–19d of column 4 and enter the result on line 20. Copy the amount from line 20 on page 2 to line 21 on page 3.

Your credit. If the amount entered on line 21 is less than zero, for example, "-115.00," you have a credit because you overreported your federal employment taxes.

- If you checked the box on line 1, include this amount on Form 941, line 11 ("Total deposits" line), for the quarter during which you filed Form 941-X or Form 944, line 8 ("Total deposits" line), for the year during which you filed Form 941-X. Do not make any changes to your record of federal tax liability reported on Form 941, line 17, or Schedule B (Form 941), if your Form 941-X is filed timely. The amounts reported on the record should reflect your actual tax liability for the period.
- If you checked the box on line 2, you are filing a claim for refund or abatement of the amount shown.

If your credit is less than $1, we will send a refund or apply it only if you ask us in writing to do so.

Amount you owe. If the amount on line 21 is a positive number, you must pay the amount you owe by the time you file Form 941-X. You may not use any credit that you show on another Form 941-X to pay the amount you owe, even if you filed for the amount you owe and the credit at the same time.

If you owe tax and are filing a timely Form 941-X, do not file an amended Schedule B (Form 941) unless you were assessed an FTD penalty caused by an incorrect, incomplete, or missing Schedule B (Form 941). Do not include the tax increase reported on Form 941-X on any amended Schedule B (Form 941) you file.

If you owe tax and are filing a late Form 941-X, that is, after the due date for Form 941 for the quarter in which you discovered the error, you must file an amended Schedule B (Form 941) with the Form 941-X. Otherwise, the IRS may assess an "averaged" FTD penalty. The total tax reported on the "Total liability for the quarter" line of Schedule B (Form 941), must match the corrected tax (Form 941, line 10, combined with any correction reported on Form 941-X, line 17, minus any advance EIC reported on Form 941-X, line 18), less any previous abatements and interest-free tax assessments.

Payment methods. You may pay the amount you owe on line 21 electronically using the Electronic Federal Tax Payment System (EFTPS), by credit or debit card, or by a check or money order.

- The preferred method of payment is EFTPS. For more information, visit *www.eftps.gov*, call EFTPS Customer Service at 1-800-555-4477 toll free, or see Pub. 966, Electronic Federal Tax Payment System: A Guide to Getting Started.
- To pay by credit or debit card, visit the IRS website at *www.irs.gov/e-pay*.
- If you pay by check or money order, make it payable to "United States Treasury." On your check or money order, be sure to write your EIN, "Form 941-X," and the quarter and year corrected.

You do not have to pay if the amount you owe is less than $1.

Previously assessed FTD penalty. If line 21 reflects overreported tax and the IRS previously assessed a failure-to-deposit (FTD) penalty, you may be able to reduce the penalty. For more information, see the Instructions for Schedule B (Form 941).

Part 4: Explain Your Corrections for This Quarter

22. Correction of Both Underreported and Overreported Amounts

Check the box on line 22 if any corrections you entered on lines 6–19d, column 3, reflect both underreported and overreported amounts.

Example. If you had an increase to social security wages of $15,000 for employee A and a decrease to social security wages of $5,000 for employee B, you would enter $10,000 on line 8, column 3. That $10,000 represents the net change from corrections.

On line 24, you must explain the reason for both the $15,000 increase and the $5,000 decrease.

23. Did You Reclassify Any Workers?

Check the box on line 23 if you reclassified any workers to be independent contractors or nonemployees. Also check this box if the IRS (or you) determined that workers you treated as independent contractors or nonemployees should be classified as employees. On line 24, give us a detailed reason why any worker was reclassified and, if you used section 3509 rates on lines 14–16, for any worker reclassified as an employee, explain why section 3509 rates apply and what rates you used.

Return not filed because you did not treat any workers as employees. If you did not previously file Form 941 because you mistakenly treated all workers as independent contractors or as nonemployees, file a Form 941 for each delinquent quarter.

On each Form 941 for which you are entitled to use section 3509 rates, complete the following steps.

- Write "Misclassified Employees" in dark, bold letters across the top margin of page 1.
- Enter a zero on line 10 ("Total taxes after adjustments").
- Complete the signature area.
- Attach a completed Form 941-X (see instructions below).

On each Form 941-X complete the following steps.

- Complete the top of Form 941-X, including the date you discovered the error.
- Enter the wage amounts on lines 14–16, column 1.
- Enter zeros on lines 14–16, column 2.
- Complete columns 3 and 4 as instructed in Part 3.
- Provide a detailed statement on line 24.
- Complete the signature area.

CAUTION *If you cannot use section 3509 rates (for example, because the workers you treated as nonemployees were certain statutory employees), file a Form 941 for each delinquent quarter. Write "Misclassified Employees" in dark, bold letters across the top margin of page 1 of each Form 941. Complete Form 941 using the Instructions for Form 941. Attach a Form 941-X to each Form 941. Complete the top of Form 941-X, including the date you discovered the error, and provide a detailed explanation on line 24.*

24. Explain Your Corrections

Treasury regulations require you to explain in detail the grounds and facts relied upon to support each correction. On line 24, describe in detail each correction you entered on lines 6–19d, column 3. If you need more space, attach additional sheets, but be sure to write your name, EIN, Form 941-X, quarter, and calendar year on the top of each sheet.

You must describe the events that caused the underreported or overreported amounts. Explanations such as "social security and Medicare wages were overstated" or "administrative/payroll errors were discovered" are insufficient and may delay processing your Form 941-X because the IRS may need to ask for a more complete explanation.

-10- **Instructions for Form 941-X (Rev. 4-2012)**

Form 941-X—Instructions (Page 11)

Provide the following information in your explanation for each correction.
- Form 941-X line number(s) affected.
- Date you discovered the error.
- Difference (amount of the error).
- Cause of the error.

You may report the information in paragraph form. The following paragraph is an example.

"The $1,000 difference shown in column 3 on lines 6, 8, and 10 was discovered on May 16, 2011, during an internal payroll audit. We discovered that we included $1,000 of wages for one of our employees twice. This correction removes the reported wages that were never paid."

For corrections shown on lines 14–16, column 3, explain why the correction was necessary and attach any notice you received from the IRS.

Part 5. Sign Here

You must complete all three pages of Form 941-X and sign it on page 3. If you do not sign, processing of Form 941-X will be delayed.

Who must sign the Form 941-X? Form 941-X must be signed by one of the following.
- **Sole proprietorship**—The individual who owns the business.
- **Corporation (including a limited liability company (LLC) treated as a corporation)**—The president, vice president, or other principal officer duly authorized to sign.
- **Partnership (including an LLC treated as a partnership) or unincorporated organization**—A responsible and duly authorized member, partner, or officer having knowledge of its affairs.
- **Single member LLC treated as a disregarded entity for federal income tax purposes**—The owner of the LLC or a principal officer duly authorized to sign.
- **Trust or estate**—The fiduciary.

Form 941-X may also be signed by a duly authorized agent of the taxpayer if a valid power of attorney has been filed.

Alternative signature method. Corporate officers or duly authorized agents may sign Form 941-X by rubber stamp, mechanical device, or computer software program. For details and required documentation, see Rev. Proc. 2005-39. You can find Rev. Proc. 2005-39, 2005-28 I.R.B. 82, at *www.irs.gov/irb/2005-28_IRB/ar16.html.*

Paid Preparer Use Only

A paid preparer must sign Form 941-X and provide the information in the *Paid Preparer Use Only* section of Part 5 if the preparer was paid to prepare Form 941-X and is not an employee of the filing entity. Paid preparers must sign paper returns with a manual signature. The preparer must give you a copy of the return in addition to the copy to be filed with the IRS.

If you are a paid preparer, enter your Preparer Tax Identification Number (PTIN) in the space provided. Include your complete address. If you work for a firm, enter the firm's name and the EIN of the firm. You can apply for a PTIN online or by filing Form W-12, IRS Paid Preparer Tax Identification Number (PTIN) Application and Renewal. For more information about applying for a PTIN online, visit the IRS website at *www.irs.gov/ptin*. You cannot use your PTIN in place of the EIN of the tax preparation firm.

Generally, you are not required to complete this section if you are filing the return as a reporting agent and have a valid Form 8655, Reporting Agent Authorization, on file with the IRS. However, a reporting agent must complete this section if the reporting agent offered legal advice, for example, advising the client on determining whether its workers are employees or independent contractors for federal tax purposes.

How Can You Order Forms and Publications from the IRS?

Call 1-800-829-3676.

Visit the IRS website at *www.irs.gov/formspubs.*

Additional Information

You may find the following products helpful when using Form 941-X.
- Form W-2, Wage and Tax Statement
- Form W-3, Transmittal of Wage and Tax Statements
- Instructions for Forms W-2 and W-3
- Form W-2AS, American Samoa Wage and Tax Statement
- Form W-2CM, Wage and Tax Statement (Northern Mariana Islands)
- Form W-2GU, Guam Wage and Tax Statement
- Form W-2VI, U.S. Virgin Islands Wage and Tax Statement
- Form W-3SS, Transmittal of Wage and Tax Statements
- Instructions for Forms W-2AS, W-2GU, W-2VI, and W-3SS
- Form W-2c, Corrected Wage and Tax Statement
- Form W-3c, Transmittal of Corrected Wage and Tax Statements
- Instructions for Forms W-2c and W-3c
- Form W-11, Hiring Incentives to Restore Employment (HIRE) Act Employee Affidavit
- Instructions for Form 843
- Instructions for Form 941
- Instructions for Schedule B (Form 941)
- Instructions for Form 941-SS
- Pub. 15 (Circular E), Employer's Tax Guide
- Pub. 80 (Circular SS), Federal Tax Guide for Employers in the U.S. Virgin Islands, Guam, American Samoa, and the Commonwealth of the Northern Mariana Islands
- Pub. 966, Electronic Federal Tax Payment System: A Guide to Getting Started

Instructions for Form 941-X (Rev. 4-2012) **-11-**

Form 941-X—Instructions (Page 12)

Paperwork Reduction Act Notice We ask for the information on Form 941-X to carry out the Internal Revenue laws of the United States. We need it to figure and collect the right amount of tax. Subtitle C, Employment Taxes, of the Internal Revenue Code imposes employment taxes on wages, including income tax withholding. This form is used to determine the amount of taxes that you owe. Section 6011 requires you to provide the requested information if the tax is applicable to you.

You are not required to provide the information requested on a form that is subject to the Paperwork Reduction Act unless the form displays a valid OMB control number. Books and records relating to a form or instructions must be retained as long as their contents may become material in the administration of any Internal Revenue law.

The time needed to complete and file Form 941-X will vary depending on individual circumstances. The estimated average time is:

Recordkeeping	16 hr., 15 min.
Learning about the law or the form	30 min.
Preparing and sending the form to the IRS	47 min.

If you have comments concerning the accuracy of these time estimates or suggestions for making Form 941-X simpler, we would be happy to hear from you. You can email us at: *taxforms@irs.gov*. Enter "Form 941-X" on the subject line. Or write to: Internal Revenue Service, Tax Products Coordinating Committee, SE:W:CAR:MP:T:MS, 1111 Constitution Ave. NW, IR-6526, Washington, DC 20224. **Do not** send Form 941-X to this address. Instead, see *Where Should You File Form 941-X*, earlier.

-12- **Instructions for Form 941-X (Rev. 4-2012)**

Form 944 (Page 1)

Form **944 for 2012: Employer's ANNUAL Federal Tax Return**

Department of the Treasury — Internal Revenue Service

OMB No. 1545-2007

Employer identification number (EIN) ☐☐ – ☐☐☐☐☐☐☐

Name *(not your trade name)*

Trade name *(if any)*

Address

Number | Street | Suite or room number

City | State | ZIP code

Who Must File Form 944

You must file annual Form 944 instead of filing quarterly Forms 941 **only if the IRS notified you in writing.** You also must file Form 944 (or Form 944 (SP)) for 2012 if you filed Form 944-SS or Form 944-PR in 2011 and you did not request to file Forms 941-SS or Forms 941-PR for 2012.

Instructions and prior-year forms are available at *www.irs.gov/form944.*

Read the separate instructions before you complete Form 944. Type or print within the boxes.

Part 1: Answer these questions for this year. Employers in American Samoa, Guam, the Commonwealth of the Northern Mariana Islands, the U.S. Virgin Islands, and Puerto Rico can skip lines 1 and 2.

1 **Wages, tips, and other compensation** . . . . 1 [.]

2 **FEDERAL income tax withheld from wages, tips, and other compensation** . . . . . . 2 [.]

3 **If no wages, tips, and other compensation are subject to social security or Medicare tax** 3 ☐ **Check and go to line 5.**

4 **Taxable social security and Medicare wages and tips:**

	Column 1		*Column 2*
4a Taxable social security wages	.	× .104 =	.
4b Taxable social security tips	.	× .104 =	.
4c Taxable Medicare wages & tips	.	× .029 =	.

For 2012, the employee social security tax rate is 4.2% and the Medicare tax rate is 1.45%. The employer social security tax rate is 6.2% and the Medicare tax rate is 1.45%.

4d Add *Column 2* line 4a, *Column 2* line 4b, and *Column 2* line 4c . . . . 4d [.]

5 **Total taxes before adjustments** (add lines 2 and 4d) . . . . 5 [.]

6 **Current year's adjustments** (see instructions) . . . . 6 [.]

7 **Total taxes after adjustments.** Combine lines 5 and 6 . . . . 7 [.]

8 **Total deposits for this year, including overpayment applied from a prior year and overpayment applied from Form 944-X, 944-X (PR), 944-X (SP), 941-X, or 941-X (PR)** . . 8 [.]

9a **COBRA premium assistance payments** (see instructions) . . . . 9a [.]

9b **Number of individuals provided COBRA premium assistance** [ ]

10 **Add lines 8 and 9a** . . . . 10 [.]

11 **Balance due.** If line 7 is more than line 10, enter the difference and see instructions . . . . 11 [.]

12 **Overpayment.** If line 10 is more than line 7, enter the difference [.] Check one: ☐ Apply to next return. ☐ Send a refund.

► **You MUST complete both pages of Form 944 and SIGN it.**

Next ■▶

For Privacy Act and Paperwork Reduction Act Notice, see the back of the Payment Voucher. Cat. No. 39316N Form **944** (2012)

Form 944 (Page 2)

Name *(not your trade name)* | **Employer identification number (EIN)**

Part 2: Tell us about your deposit schedule and tax liability for this year.

13 Check one: ☐ **Line 7 is less than $2,500. Go to Part 3.**

☐ **Line 7 is $2,500 or more. Enter your tax liability for each month. If you are a semiweekly depositor or you accumulate $100,000 or more of liability on any day during a deposit period, you must complete Form 945-A instead of the boxes below.**

	Jan.		Apr.		Jul.		Oct.
13a	.	13d	.	13g	.	13j	.
	Feb.		May		Aug.		Nov.
13b	.	13e	.	13h	.	13k	.
	Mar.		Jun.		Sep.		Dec.
13c	.	13f	.	13i	.	13l	.

Total liability for year. Add lines 13a through 13l. Total must equal line 7. **13m** .

Part 3: Tell us about your business. If question 14 does NOT apply to your business, leave it blank.

14 If your business has closed or you stopped paying wages...

☐ Check here and enter the final date you paid wages.

Part 4: May we speak with your third-party designee?

Do you want to allow an employee, a paid tax preparer, or another person to discuss this return with the IRS? See the instructions for details.

☐ Yes. Designee's name and phone number

Select a 5-digit Personal Identification Number (PIN) to use when talking to IRS. ☐☐☐☐☐

☐ No.

Part 5: Sign Here. You MUST complete both pages of Form 944 and SIGN it.

Under penalties of perjury, I declare that I have examined this return, including accompanying schedules and statements, and to the best of my knowledge and belief, it is true, correct, and complete. Declaration of preparer (other than taxpayer) is based on all information of which preparer has any knowledge.

X **Sign your name here**

Print your name here

Print your title here

Date

Best daytime phone

Paid Preparer Use Only Check if you are self-employed ☐

Preparer's name | PTIN

Preparer's signature | Date

Firm's name (or yours if self-employed) | EIN

Address | Phone

City | State | ZIP code

Page **2** Form **944** (2012)

Form 944 (Page 3)

Form 944-V, Payment Voucher

Purpose of Form

Complete Form 944-V, Payment Voucher, if you are making a payment with Form 944, Employer's ANNUAL Federal Tax Return. We will use the completed voucher to credit your payment more promptly and accurately, and to improve our service to you.

Making Payments With Form 944

To avoid a penalty, make your payment with your 2012 Form 944 **only if** one of the following applies.

- Your net taxes for the year (Form 944, line 7) are less than $2,500 and you are paying in full with a timely filed return.
- You already deposited the taxes you owed for the first, second, and third quarters of 2012, and the tax you owe for the fourth quarter of 2012 is less than $2,500, and you are paying, in full, the tax you owe for the fourth quarter of 2012 with a timely filed return.
- Your net taxes for the third quarter are $2,500 or more, net taxes for the fourth quarter are less than $2,500, and you did not incur a $100,000 next-day deposit obligation during the fourth quarter.
- You are a monthly schedule depositor making a payment in accordance with the Accuracy of Deposits Rule. See section 11 of Pub. 15 (Circular E), Employer's Tax Guide, for details. In this case, the amount of your payment may be $2,500 or more.

Otherwise, you must make deposits by electronic funds transfer. See section 11 of Pub. 15 (Circular E) for deposit instructions. Do not use Form 944-V to make federal tax deposits.

Caution. *Use Form 944-V when making any payment with Form 944. However, if you pay an amount with Form 944 that should have been deposited, you may be subject to a penalty. See* Deposit Penalties *in section 11 of Pub. 15 (Circular E).*

Specific Instructions

Box 1—Employer identification number (EIN). If you do not have an EIN, you may apply for one online. Go to IRS.gov and click on the *Apply for an EIN Online* link under *Tools.* You may also apply for an EIN by calling 1-800-829-4933, or you can fax or mail Form SS-4, Application for Employer Identification Number. If you have not received your EIN by the due date of Form 944, write "Applied For" and the date you applied in this entry space.

Box 2—Amount paid. Enter the amount paid with Form 944.

Box 3—Name and address. Enter your name and address as shown on Form 944.

- Enclose your check or money order made payable to the "United States Treasury" and write your EIN, "Form 944," and "2012" on your check or money order. Do not send cash. Do not staple Form 944-V or your payment to Form 944 (or to each other).
- Detach Form 944-V and send it with your payment and Form 944 to the address provided in the Instructions for Form 944. Do not send a photocopy of Form 944-V because your payment may be misapplied or delayed.

Note. You must also complete the entity information above Part 1 on Form 944.

Detach Here and Mail With Your Payment and Form 944.

Form **944-V** Department of the Treasury Internal Revenue Service	**Payment Voucher** ► **Do not staple this voucher or your payment to Form 944.**		OMB No. 1545-2007 **2012**
1 Enter your employer identification number (EIN).	2 **Enter the amount of your payment.** ► Make your check or money order payable to **"United States Treasury"**	Dollars	Cents
	3 Enter your business name (individual name if sole proprietor).		
	Enter your address.		
	Enter your city, state, and ZIP code.		

Form 944—Instructions (Page 1)

2012 Instructions for Form 944

Employer's ANNUAL Federal Tax Return

Department of the Treasury
Internal Revenue Service

Section references are to the Internal Revenue Code unless otherwise noted.

Future Developments

For the latest information about developments related to Form 944 and its instructions, such as legislation enacted after they were published, go to www.irs.gov/form944.

What's New

Forms 944-SS and 944-PR discontinued. Form 944-SS, Employer's ANNUAL Federal Tax Return—American Samoa, Guam, the Commonwealth of the Northern Mariana Islands, and the U.S. Virgin Islands, and Form 944-PR, Planilla para la Declaración Federal ANUAL del Patrono, will no longer be issued by the IRS after 2011.

Beginning with tax year 2012, employers who previously filed Form 944-SS or 944-PR will continue to file annually using Form 944 (or Form 944 (SP), Declaración Federal ANUAL de Impuestos del Patrono o Empleador, the Spanish language equivalent of Form 944). Alternatively, employers in American Samoa, Guam, the Commonwealth of the Northern Mariana Islands, and the U.S. Virgin Islands may request to file Forms 941-SS, Employer's QUARTERLY Federal Tax Return—American Samoa, Guam, the Commonwealth of the Northern Mariana Islands, and the U.S. Virgin Islands, instead of Form 944 or Form 944 (SP). Employers in Puerto Rico may request to file Forms 941-PR, Planilla para la Declaración Federal TRIMESTRAL del Patrono, instead of Form 944 or Form 944 (SP).

Social security and Medicare taxes for 2012. The employee tax rate for social security is 4.2%. The employer tax rate for social security remains unchanged at 6.2%. The Medicare tax rate is 1.45% each for the employee and employer, unchanged from 2011. The social security wage base limit is $110,100. There is no wage base limit for Medicare tax.

Social security and Medicare taxes apply to the wages of household workers you pay $1,800 or more in cash or an equivalent form of compensation. Social security and Medicare taxes apply to election workers who are paid $1,500 or more in cash or an equivalent form of compensation.

VOW to Hire Heroes Act of 2011. On November 21, 2011, the President signed into law the VOW to Hire Heroes Act of 2011. This new law provides an expanded work opportunity tax credit to businesses that hire eligible unemployed veterans and, for the first time, also makes part of the credit available to certain tax-exempt organizations. Businesses claim the credit as part of the general business credit and tax-exempt organizations claim it against their payroll tax liability using Form 5884-C, Work Opportunity Credit for Qualified Tax-Exempt Organizations Hiring Qualified Veterans. The liability reported on Form 944 is not reduced by the amount of the credit. The credit is available for eligible unemployed veterans who begin work on or after November 22, 2011, and before January 1, 2013. For more information about the credit, visit www.irs.gov/form5884c.

Change of address. Use Form 8822-B, Change of Address—Business, to notify the IRS of an address change.

Reminders

Employers can choose to file Forms 941, 941-SS, or 941-PR instead of Form 944. Employers required to file Form 944, who want to file Forms 941, 941-SS, or 941-PR instead, must notify the IRS they are electing to file quarterly Forms 941, 941-SS, or 941-PR and opting out of filing Form 944. See *What if you want to file Forms 941, 941-SS, or 941-PR instead of Form 944*, later.

Correcting a previously filed Form 944 or 944-SS. If you discover an error on a previously filed Form 944 or 944-SS, make the correction using Form 944-X, Adjusted Employer's ANNUAL Federal Tax Return or Claim for Refund. Form 944-X is filed separately from Form 944. For more information, see section 13 of Pub. 15 (Circular E), Employer's Tax Guide, or section 9 of Pub. 80 (Circular SS), Federal Tax Guide for Employers in the U.S. Virgin Islands, Guam, American Samoa, and the Commonwealth of the Northern Mariana Islands. You may also visit IRS.gov and enter the keywords *Correcting Employment Taxes*.

Correcting a previously filed Form 944-PR. If you discover an error on a previously filed Form 944-PR, make the correction using Form 944-X (PR), Ajuste a la Declaración Federal ANNUAL del Patrono o Reclamación de Reembolso. Form 944-X (PR) is filed separately from Form 944. For more information, see section 12 of Pub. 179 (Circular PR), Guía Contributiva Federal para Paronos Puertorriqueños. You may also visit IRS.gov and enter the keywords *Correcting Employment Taxes*.

Paid preparers must sign Form 944. Paid preparers must complete and sign the paid preparer's section of Form 944.

COBRA premium assistance credit. The credit for COBRA premium assistance payments applies to premiums paid for employees involuntarily terminated between September 1, 2008, and May 31, 2010, and to premiums paid for up to 15 months. See the instructions for line 9a, later.

Federal tax deposits must be made by electronic funds transfer. You must use electronic funds transfer to make all federal tax deposits. Generally, electronic funds transfers are made using the Electronic Federal Tax Payment System (EFTPS). If you do not want to use EFTPS, you can arrange for your tax professional, financial institution, payroll service, or other trusted third party to make deposits on your behalf. Also, you may arrange for your financial institution to initiate a same-day wire payment on your behalf. EFTPS is a free service provided by the Department of Treasury. Services provided by your tax professional, financial institution, payroll service, or other third party may have a fee.

For more information on making federal tax deposits, see section 11 of Pub. 15 (Circular E), section 8 of Pub. 80

Oct 22, 2012 Cat. No. 39820A

Form 944—Instructions (Page 2)

(Circular SS), or section 11 of Pub. 179 (Circular PR). To get more information about EFTPS or to enroll in EFTPS, visit www.eftps.gov or call one of the following numbers.

- 1-800-555-4477
- 1-800-733-4829 (TDD)
- 1-800-244-4829 (Spanish)
- 303-967-5916 (toll call)

Additional information about EFTPS is also available in Pub. 966, Electronic Federal Tax Payment System: A Guide to Getting Started, or Pub. 966 (SP), Sistema de Pago Electrónico del Impuesto Federal: La Manera Segura de Pagar los Impuestos Federales.

CAUTION *For an EFTPS deposit to be on time, you must initiate the deposit by 8 p.m. Eastern time the day before the date the deposit is due.*

Same-day wire payment option. If you fail to initiate a deposit transaction on EFTPS by 8 p.m. Eastern time the day before the date a deposit is due, you can still make your deposit on time by using the Federal Tax Application (FTA). To use the same-day wire payment method, you will need to make arrangements with your financial institution ahead of time. Please check with your financial institution regarding availability, deadlines, and costs. Your financial institution may charge you a fee for payments made this way. To learn more about the information you will need to provide to your financial institution to make a same-day wire payment, visit www.eftps.gov to download the *Same-Day Payment Worksheet.*

Timeliness of federal tax deposits. If a deposit is required to be made on a day that is not a business day, the deposit is considered timely if it is made by the close of the next business day. A business day is any day other than a Saturday, Sunday, or legal holiday. The term *legal holiday* for deposit purposes includes only those legal holidays in the District of Columbia. Legal holidays in the District of Columbia are provided in Pub. 15 (Circular E).

Electronic filing and payment. Now, more than ever before, businesses can enjoy the benefits of filing tax returns and paying their federal taxes electronically. Whether you rely on a tax professional or handle your own taxes, the IRS offers you convenient programs to make filing and paying easier. Spend less time and worry on taxes and more time running your business. Use e-file and Electronic Federal Tax Payment System (EFTPS) to your benefit.

- For e-file, visit www.irs.gov/efile.
- For EFTPS, visit www.eftps.gov or call EFTPS at one of the numbers provided under *Federal tax deposits must be made by electronic funds transfer*, earlier.

CAUTION *If you are filing your tax return or paying your federal taxes electronically, a valid EIN is required at the time the return is filed. If a valid EIN is not provided, the return or payment will not be processed. This may result in penalties.*

CAUTION *If you were a semiweekly schedule depositor at any time during 2012, you must file a paper Form 944 and Form 945-A, Annual Record of Federal Tax Liability.*

Electronic funds withdrawal (EFW). If you file Form 944 electronically, you can e-file and e-pay (electronic funds withdrawal) the balance due in a single step using tax preparation software or through a tax professional. However, **do not** use EFW to make federal tax deposits. For more information on paying your taxes using EFW, visit the IRS website at www.irs.gov/e-pay. A fee may be charged to file electronically.

Credit or debit card payments. Employers can pay the balance due shown on Form 944 by credit or debit card. **Do not** use a credit or debit card to make federal tax deposits. For more information on paying your taxes with a credit or debit card, visit the IRS website at www.irs.gov/e-pay. A convenience fee will be charged for this service.

Employer's liability. Employers are responsible to ensure that tax returns are filed and deposits and payments are made, even if the employer contracts with a third party. The employer remains liable if the third party fails to perform a required action.

Where can you get telephone help? For answers to your questions about completing Form 944, tax deposit rules, or obtaining an employer identification number (EIN) call the IRS at one of the numbers listed below.

- 1-800-829-4933 (Business and Specialty Tax Line) or 1-800-829-4059 (TDD/TTY for persons who are deaf, hard of hearing, or have a speech disability); Monday–Friday 7:00 a.m.–7:00 p.m. local time (Alaska and Hawaii follow Pacific time; employers in Puerto Rico receive service from 8:00 a.m.–8:00 p.m. local time).
- 267-941-1000 (toll call); Monday–Friday 6:00 a.m.–11:00 p.m. Eastern time.

Photographs of missing children. The IRS is a proud partner with the National Center for Missing and Exploited Children. Photographs of missing children selected by the Center may appear in instructions on pages that would otherwise be blank. You can help bring these children home by looking at the photographs and calling 1-800-THE-LOST (1-800-843-5678) if you recognize a child.

General Instructions

Federal law requires employers to withhold taxes from employees' paychecks. Each time wages are paid, employers must withhold — or take out of employees' paychecks — certain amounts for federal income tax, social security tax, and Medicare tax. Under the withholding system, taxes withheld from employees are credited to employees in payment of their tax liabilities.

CAUTION *References to federal income tax withholding do not apply to employers in American Samoa, Guam, the Commonwealth of the Northern Mariana Islands, the U.S. Virgin Islands, and Puerto Rico.*

Federal law also requires employers to pay any liability for the employer's portion of social security and Medicare taxes. This portion of social security and Medicare taxes is not withheld from employees.

What Is the Purpose of Form 944?

Form 944 is designed so the smallest employers (those whose annual liability for social security, Medicare, and withheld federal income taxes is $1,000 or less) will file and pay these taxes only once a year instead of every quarter. These instructions give you some background information about Form 944, who must file Form 944, how to complete it line by line, and when and where to file it.

Form 944—Instructions (Page 3)

For more information about annual employment tax filing and tax deposit rules, see Treasury Decision 9566, 2012-8 I.R.B. 389, at www.irs.gov/irb/2012-08_IRB/ar09.html.

If you want more in-depth information about payroll tax topics, see Pub. 15 (Circular E), Pub. 80 (Circular SS), Pub. 179 (Circular PR), or visit the IRS website at www.irs.gov/businesses and click on the *Employment Taxes* link under *Businesses Topics*.

Who Must File Form 944?

In general, if the IRS has notified you to file Form 944, you must file Form 944 instead of Forms 941, 941-SS, or 941-PR to report the following amounts.

- Wages you have paid.
- Tips your employees have received.
- Federal income tax you withheld.
- Both the employer's and the employee's share of social security and Medicare taxes.
- Current year's adjustments to social security and Medicare taxes for fractions of cents, sick pay, tips, and group-term life insurance.
- Credit for COBRA premium assistance payments.

If you received notification to file Form 944, you must file Form 944 to report your social security, Medicare, and withheld federal income taxes for the 2012 calendar year unless you contacted the IRS by April 2, 2012, to request to file Forms 941, 941-SS, or 941-PR quarterly instead and received written confirmation that your filing requirement was changed. You must file Form 944 even if you have no taxes to report (or you have taxes in excess of $1,000 to report) unless you filed a final return. See *If your business has closed...*, later. Also see *What if you want to file Forms 941, 941-SS, or 941-PR instead of Form 944*, later.

TIP *If you have not received notification to file Form 944 but estimate your employment tax liability for calendar year 2013 will be $1,000 or less and would like to file Form 944 instead of Forms 941, 941-SS, or 941-PR, you can contact the IRS to request to file Form 944. To file Form 944 for calendar year 2013, you must call the IRS at 1-800-829-4933 or 267-941-1000 (toll call) by April 1, 2013, or send a written request postmarked by March 15, 2013. The mailing addresses for written requests are provided below under* What if you want to file Forms 941, 941-SS, or 941-PR instead of Form 944. *The IRS will send you a written notice that your filing requirement has been changed to Form 944. If you do not receive this notice, you must file Forms 941, 941-SS, or 941-PR for calendar year 2013.*

New employers are also eligible to file Form 944 if they will meet the eligibility requirements. New employers filing Form SS-4, Application for Employer Identification Number, or Form SS-4PR, Solicitud de Número de Identificación Patronal (*EIN*), must complete line 13 of Form SS-4 or SS-4PR indicating the highest number of employees expected in the next 12 months and must check the box on line 14 to indicate whether they expect to have $1,000 or less in employment tax liability for the calendar year and would like to file Form 944. Generally, if you pay $4,000 or less in wages subject to social security and Medicare taxes and federal income tax withholding, you are likely to pay $1,000 or less in employment taxes. Generally, if you are an employer in Puerto Rico, American Samoa, Guam, the Commonwealth of the Northern Mariana Islands, or the U.S. Virgin Islands and you pay $6,536 or less in wages subject to social security and Medicare taxes, you are likely to pay $1,000 or less in employment taxes. New employers are advised of their employment tax filing requirement when they are issued their EIN.

TIP *If the IRS notified you to file Form 944 for 2012, file Form 944 (and not Forms 941, 941-SS, or 941-PR) even if your tax liability for 2012 exceeds $1,000.*

What if you want to file Forms 941, 941-SS, or 941-PR instead of Form 944?

You must file Form 944 if the IRS has notified you to do so, unless you contact the IRS to request to file quarterly Forms 941, 941-SS, or 941-PR instead. To request to file quarterly Forms 941, 941-SS, or 941-PR to report your social security, Medicare, and withheld federal income taxes for the 2013 calendar year, call the IRS at 1-800-829-4933 or 267-941-1000 (toll call) by April 1, 2013, or send a written request postmarked by March 15, 2013. Written requests should be sent to:

Department of Treasury Internal Revenue Service Ogden, UT 84201-0038	or	Department of Treasury Internal Revenue Service Cincinnati, OH 45999-0038

Select one of the addresses above based on the state filing alignment for returns filed *Without a payment* under *Where Should You File*, later. After you contact the IRS, the IRS will send you a written notice that your filing requirement has been changed. If you do not receive this notice, you must file Form 944 for calendar year 2013. See Rev. Proc. 2009-51, 2009-45 I.R.B. 625, available at www.irs.gov/irb/2009-45_IRB/ar12.html.

Who cannot file Form 944?

The following employers **cannot** file Form 944.

- **Employers who are not notified.** If the IRS does not notify you to file Form 944, do not file Form 944. If you would like to file Form 944 instead of Forms 941, 941-SS, or 941-PR, see the *TIP* under *Who Must File Form 944*, earlier.
- **Household employers.** If you employ only household employees, do not file Form 944. For more information, see Pub. 926, Household Employer's Tax Guide, and Schedule H (Form 1040), Household Employment Taxes, or Pub. 179 (Circular PR) and Schedule H-PR (Form 1040-PR), Contribuciones sobre el Empleo de Empleados Domésticos.
- **Agricultural employers.** If you employ only agricultural employees, do not file Form 944. For more information, see Pub. 51 (Circular A), Agricultural Employer's Tax Guide, and Form 943, Employer's Annual Federal Tax Return for Agricultural Employees, or Pub. 179 (Circular PR) and Form 943-PR, Planilla para la Declaración Anual de la Contribución Federal del Patrono de Empleados Agrícolas.

What if you reorganize or close your business?

If you sell or transfer your business...

If you sell or transfer your business, you and the new owner must each file a Form 944, 941, 941-SS, or 941-PR, whichever is required, for the year in which the transfer occurred. Report only the wages you paid.

When two businesses merge, the continuing firm must file a return for the year in which the change took place and the other firm should file a **final return**.

Form 944—Instructions (Page 4)

Changing from one form of business to another—such as from a sole proprietorship to a partnership or corporation—is considered a transfer. If a transfer occurs, you may need a new EIN. See section 1 of Pub. 15 (Circular E). Attach a statement to your return with all the following information.

- The new owner's name (or the new name of the business).
- Whether the business is now a sole proprietorship, partnership, or corporation.
- The kind of change that occurred (a sale or transfer).
- The date of the change.
- The name of the person keeping the payroll records and the address where those records will be kept.

If your business has closed...

If you go out of business or stop paying wages to your employees, you must file a **final return.** To tell the IRS that Form 944 for a particular year is your final return, check the box in Part 3 on page 2 of Form 944 and enter the final date you paid wages. Also attach a statement to your return showing the name of the person keeping the payroll records and the address where those records will be kept.

If you participated in a statutory merger or consolidation, or qualify for predecessor-successor status due to an acquisition, you should generally file Schedule D (Form 941), Report of Discrepancies Caused by Acquisitions, Statutory Mergers, or Consolidations. See the Instructions for Schedule D (Form 941) to determine whether you should file Schedule D (Form 941) and when you should file it.

When Must You File?

File Form 944 by January 31, after the end of the calendar year. If you made timely deposits in full payment of your taxes by January 31, you have 10 more calendar days after that date to file your Form 944.

File Form 944 only once for each calendar year. If you filed Form 944 electronically, do not file a paper Form 944. For more information about filing Form 944 electronically, see *Electronic filing and payment*, earlier.

If we receive Form 944 after the due date, we will treat Form 944 as filed on time if the envelope containing Form 944 is properly addressed, contains sufficient postage, and is postmarked by the U.S. Postal Service on or before the due date, or sent by an IRS-designated private delivery service on or before the due date. If you do not follow these guidelines, we will consider Form 944 filed when it is actually received. See Pub. 15 (Circular E), Pub. 80 (Circular SS), or Pub. 179 (Circular PR) for more information on IRS-designated private delivery services.

If any due date for filing falls on a Saturday, Sunday, or legal holiday, you may file your return on the next business day.

How Should You Complete Form 944?

Enter your EIN, name, and address in the spaces provided. Also enter your name and EIN at the top of page 2. Do not use your social security number (SSN) or individual taxpayer identification number (ITIN). Generally, enter the business (legal) name that you used when you applied for your EIN. For example, if you are a sole proprietor, enter "Tyler Smith" on the *Name* line and "Tyler's Cycles" on the *Trade name* line. Leave the *Trade name* line blank if it is the same as your *Name* line.

If you use a tax preparer to complete Form 944, make sure the preparer uses your correct business name and EIN.

Employer identification number (EIN). To make sure that businesses comply with federal tax laws, the IRS monitors tax filings and payments by using a numerical system to identify taxpayers. A unique nine-digit EIN is assigned to all corporations, partnerships, and some sole proprietors. Businesses needing an EIN must apply for a number and use it throughout the life of the business on all tax returns, payments, and reports.

Your business should have only one EIN. If you have more than one and are not sure which one to use, write to the IRS office where you file your returns (using the *Without a payment* address under *Where Should You File*, later) or call the IRS at 1-800-829-4933 or 267-941-1000 (toll call).

If you do not have an EIN, you may apply for one online. Visit IRS.gov and click on the *Apply for an EIN Online* link under *Tools*. You may also apply for an EIN by calling 1-800-829-4933 or 267-941-1000 (toll call), or you can fax or mail Form SS-4 or SS-4PR to the IRS. If you have applied for an EIN but do not have your EIN by the time a return is due, write "Applied For" and the date you applied in the space shown for the number.

TIP *Always be sure the EIN on the form you file exactly matches the EIN the IRS assigned to your business. Do not use your SSN or ITIN on forms that ask for an EIN. Filing a Form 944 with an incorrect EIN or using another business's EIN may result in penalties and delays in processing your return.*

If you change your name or address... Notify the IRS **immediately** if you change your business name or address.

- **Name change.** Write to the IRS office where you filed your return (using the *Without a payment* address under *Where Should You File*, later) to notify the IRS of any name change. See Pub. 1635, Employer Identification Number: Understanding Your EIN, to see if you need to also apply for a new EIN.
- **Address change.** Complete and mail Form 8822-B, Change of Address—Business, to notify the IRS of an address change.

Completing and Filing Form 944

Make entries on Form 944 as follows to enable accurate processing.

- Use 12-point Courier font (if possible) for all entries if you are using a typewriter or computer to complete Form 944.
- Do not enter dollar signs and decimal points. Commas are optional. Report dollars to the left of the preprinted decimal point and cents to the right of it.
- Leave blank any data field with a value of zero (except line 7).
- Enter negative amounts using a minus sign (if possible). Otherwise, use parentheses.
- Enter your name and EIN on **all** pages and attachments.

Other Forms You Must Use

To notify employees about the earned income credit (EIC), employers in the United States must give the employees one of the following:

- The IRS Form W-2, Wage and Tax Statement, which has the required information about the EIC on the back of Copy B.

-4- Instructions for Form 944 (2012)

Form 944—Instructions (Page 5)

• A substitute Form W-2 with the same EIC information on the back of the employee's copy that is on the back of Copy B of the IRS Form W-2.
• Notice 797, Possible Federal Tax Refund Due to the Earned Income Credit (EIC).
• Your written statement with the same wording as Notice 797.

For more information, see section 10 of Pub. 15 (Circular E) and Pub. 596, Earned Income Credit (EIC).

Reconciling Form 944 and Form W-3, W-3SS, or W-3PR

The IRS matches amounts reported on your Form 944 with Form W-2, W-2AS, W-2GU, W-2CM, W-2VI, or Form 499R-2/W-2PR amounts totaled on your Form W-3 or W-3SS, Transmittal of Wage and Tax Statements, or Form W-3PR. Informe de Comprobantes de Retención. If the amounts do not agree, the IRS may contact you. The following amounts are reconciled.

• Federal income tax withholding, if applicable.
• Social security wages.
• Social security tips.
• Medicare wages and tips.

For more information, see section 12 of Pub. 15 (Circular E).

Must You Deposit Your Taxes?

If your liability for social security, Medicare, and withheld federal income taxes is less than $2,500 for the year, you can pay the taxes with your return. To avoid a penalty, you should pay in full and file on time. You do not have to deposit the taxes. However, you may choose to make deposits of these taxes even if your liability is less than $2,500. If your liability for these taxes is $2,500 or more, you are generally required to deposit the taxes instead of paying them when you file Form 944. See the *Federal Tax Deposit Requirements for Form 944 Filers* chart below. If you do not deposit the taxes when required, you may be subject to penalties and interest.

The $2,500 threshold at which federal tax deposits must be made is different from the amount of annual tax liability ($1,000 or less) that makes an employer eligible to file Form 944. Form 944 filers whose businesses grow during the year may be required to make federal tax deposits (see chart below), but they will still file Form 944 for the year.

Federal Tax Deposit Requirements for Form 944 Filers

If Your Tax Liability is:	Your Deposit Requirement is:
Less than $2,500 for the year	No deposit required. You may pay the tax with your return. If you are unsure that your tax liability for the year will be less than $2,500, deposit under the rules below.
$2,500 or more for the year, but less than $2,500 for the quarter	You can deposit by the last day of the month after the end of a quarter. However, if your fourth quarter tax liability is less than $2,500, you may pay the fourth quarter's tax liability with Form 944.
$2,500 or more for the quarter	You must deposit monthly or semiweekly depending on your deposit schedule. But, if you accumulate $100,000 or more of taxes on any day, you must deposit the tax by the next business day. See section 11 of Pub. 15 (Circular E), section 8 of Pub. 80 (Circular SS), or section 11 of Pub. 179 (Circular PR).

Note. When you make deposits depends on your deposit schedule, which is either monthly or semiweekly, depending on the amount of your tax liability during the lookback period. The lookback period for Form 944 filers is different than the lookback period for Form 941, 941-SS, and 941-PR filers, so your deposit schedule may have changed. For more information, see section 11 of Pub. 15 (Circular E), section 8 of Pub. 80 (Circular SS), or section 11 of Pub. 179 (Circular PR).

What About Penalties and Interest?

Avoiding penalties and interest

You can avoid paying penalties and interest if you do all of the following.

• Deposit or pay your taxes when they are due.
• File your fully completed Form 944 on time.
• Report your tax liability accurately in Part 2 of Form 944.
• Submit valid checks for tax payments.
• Give accurate Forms W-2, W-2AS, W-2GU, W-2CM, W-2VI, or Form 499R-2/W-2PR to employees.
• File Form W-3, W-3SS, or W-3PR and Copies A of Forms W-2, W-2AS, W-2GU, W-2CM, W-2VI, or Form 499R-2/W-2PR with the Social Security Administration (SSA) on time and accurately.

Penalties and interest are charged on taxes paid late and returns filed late at a rate set by law. See sections 11 and 12 of Pub. 15 (Circular E), section 8 of Pub. 80 (Circular SS), or section 11 of Pub. 179 (Circular PR) for details. Use Form 843, Claim for Refund and Request for Abatement, to request abatement of assessed penalties or interest. Do not request abatement of assessed penalties or interest on Form 944, Form 944-X, 944-X (PR), 944-X (SP), 941-X, or 941-X (PR).

If you receive a notice about a penalty after you file your return, reply to the notice with an explanation and we will determine if you meet reasonable-cause criteria. **Do not** include an explanation when you file your return.

Instructions for Form 944 (2012) **-5-**

Form 944—Instructions (Page 6)

A trust fund recovery penalty may apply if federal income, social security, or Medicare taxes that must be withheld are not withheld or paid. The penalty is the full amount of the unpaid trust fund tax. This penalty may apply when these unpaid taxes cannot be collected from the employer. The trust fund recovery penalty may be imposed on all people the IRS determines to be responsible for collecting, accounting for, and paying over these taxes, and who acted willfully in not doing so. For details, see section 11 of Pub. 15 (Circular E), section 8 of Pub. 80 (Circular SS), or section 11 of Pub. 179 (Circular PR).

Where Should You File?

Where you file depends on whether you include a payment with your form.

If you are in . . .		Without a payment . . .	With a payment . . .
Special filing address for exempt organizations; federal, state and local governmental entities; and Indian tribal governmental entities; regardless of location		Department of the Treasury Internal Revenue Service Ogden, UT 84201-0044	Internal Revenue Service P.O. Box 37944 Hartford, CT 06176-7944
Connecticut Delaware District of Columbia Florida Georgia Illinois Indiana Kentucky Maine Maryland Massachusetts Michigan New Hampshire	New Jersey New York North Carolina Ohio Pennsylvania Rhode Island South Carolina Tennessee Vermont Virginia West Virginia Wisconsin	Department of the Treasury Internal Revenue Service Cincinnati, OH 45999-0044	Internal Revenue Service P.O. Box 804522 Cincinnati, OH 45280-4522
Alabama Alaska Arizona Arkansas California Colorado Hawaii Idaho Iowa Kansas Louisiana Minnesota Mississippi	Missouri Montana Nebraska Nevada New Mexico North Dakota Oklahoma Oregon South Dakota Texas Utah Washington Wyoming	Department of the Treasury Internal Revenue Service Ogden, UT 84201-0044	Internal Revenue Service P. O Box 37944 Hartford, CT 06176-7944
No legal residence or principal place of business in any state		Internal Revenue Service P.O. Box 409101 Ogden, UT 84409	Internal Revenue Service P. O Box 37944 Hartford, CT 06176-7944

Your filing address may have changed from that used to file your employment tax return in prior years. Do not send Form 944 or any payments to the Social Security Administration (SSA). Private delivery services cannot deliver to P.O. boxes.

Specific Instructions

Part 1: Answer These Questions for This Year

Employers in American Samoa, Guam, the Commonwealth of the Northern Mariana Islands, the U.S. Virgin Islands, and Puerto Rico may skip lines 1 and 2.

1. Wages, Tips, and Other Compensation

Enter amounts on line 1 that would also be included in box 1 of your employees' Forms W-2. See the General Instructions for Forms W-2 and W-3 for details.

2. Federal Income Tax Withheld From Wages, Tips, and Other Compensation

Enter the federal income tax that you withheld (or were required to withhold) from your employees on this year's wages, tips, taxable fringe benefits, and supplemental unemployment compensation benefits.

References to federal income tax withholding do not apply to employers in American Samoa, Guam, the Commonwealth of the Northern Mariana Islands, the U.S. Virgin Islands, and Puerto Rico.

3. If No Wages, Tips, and Other Compensation are Subject to Social Security or Medicare Tax

If no wages, tips, and other compensation are subject to social security or Medicare taxes, check the box on line 3 and go to line 5. If this question does not apply to you, leave the box blank. For more information about exempt wages, see section 15 of Pub. 15 (Circular E), section 12 of Pub. 80 (Circular SS), or section 15 of Pub. 179 (Circular PR). For religious exemptions, see section 4 of Pub. 15-A, Employer's Supplemental Tax Guide.

4. Taxable Social Security and Medicare Wages and Tips

4a. Taxable social security wages. Report the total wages, sick pay, and fringe benefits subject to social security taxes that you paid to your employees during the year.

Enter the amount before deductions. **Do not** include tips on this line. For information on types of wages subject to social security taxes, see section 5 of Pub. 15 (Circular E), section 4 of Pub. 80 (Circular SS), or section 5 of Pub. 179 (Circular PR).

For 2012, the rate of social security tax on taxable wages is 6.2% (.062) for the employer and 4.2% (.042) for the employee, or 10.4% (.104) for both. Stop paying social security tax on and reporting an employee's wages on line 4a when the employee's taxable wages (including tips) reach $110,100 for the year. However, continue to withhold income and Medicare taxes for the whole year on wages and tips even when the social security wage base of $110,100 has been reached.

line 4a (column 1)
x .104
line 4a (column 2)

Form 944—Instructions (Page 7)

4b. Taxable social security tips. Enter all tips your employees reported to you during the year until the total of the tips and wages for an employee reach $110,100 for the year. Include all tips your employees reported to you even if you were unable to withhold the 4.2% employee's share of social security tax.

Your employee must report cash tips to you by the 10th day of the month after the month the tips are received. The report should include charged tips you paid over to the employee for charge customers, tips the employee received directly from customers, and tips received from other employees under any tip-sharing arrangement. Both directly and indirectly tipped employees must report tips to you. No report is required for months when tips are less than $20. Employees may use Form 4070, Employee's Report of Tips to Employer (available only in Pub. 1244, Employee's Daily Record of Tips and Report of Tips to Employer), or Form 4070-PR, Informe al Patrono de Propinas Recibidas por el(la) Empleado(a) (available only in Pub. 1244-PR, Registro Diario de Propinas Recibidas por el(la) Empleado(a) e Informe al Patrono), or submit a written statement or electronic tip record.

line 4b (column 1)
x .104
line 4b (column 2)

4c. Taxable Medicare wages and tips. Report all wages, tips, sick pay, and taxable fringe benefits that are subject to Medicare tax. Unlike social security wages, there is no limit on the amount of wages subject to Medicare tax.

The rate of Medicare tax is 1.45% (.0145) each for the employer and employee, or 2.9% (.029) for both. Include all tips your employees reported during the year, even if you were unable to withhold the employee tax of 1.45%.

line 4c (column 1)
x .029
line 4c (column 2)

For more information on tips, see section 6 of Pub. 15 (Circular E), section 5 of Pub. 80 (Circular SS), or section 6 of Pub. 179 (Circular PR).

4d. Total social security and Medicare taxes. Add the social security tax, social security tips tax, and Medicare tax.

line 4a (column 2)
line 4b (column 2)
\+ line 4c (column 2)
line 4d

5. Total Taxes Before Adjustments

Add the income tax withheld from wages, tips, and other compensation from line 2 and the total social security and Medicare taxes before adjustments from line 4d. Enter the result on line 5.

6. Current Year's Adjustments

Enter **tax amounts** that result from current period adjustments. Use a minus sign (if possible) to show an adjustment that decreases the total taxes shown on line 5. Otherwise, use parentheses.

In certain cases, you must adjust the amounts you reported as social security and Medicare taxes in column 2 of lines 4a, 4b, and 4c to figure your correct tax liability for this year's Form 944. See section 13 of Pub. 15 (Circular E), section 9 of Pub. 80 (Circular SS), or section 12 of Pub. 179 (Circular PR).

If you need to adjust any amount reported on line 6 or 6a from a previously filed Form 944 or 944-SS, complete and file Form 944-X. Form 944-X is an adjusted returns and is filed separately from Form 944. See section 13 of Pub. 15 (Circular E) or section 9 of Pub. 80 (Circular SS).

If you need to adjust any amount reported on line 6 or 6a from a previously filed Form 944-PR, complete and file Form 944-X (PR). Form 944-X (PR) is an adjusted return and is filed separately from Form 944. See section 12 of Pub. 179 (Circular PR).

Fractions of cents. Enter adjustments for fractions of cents (due to rounding) relating to the employee share of social security and Medicare taxes withheld. The employee share of amounts shown in column 2 of lines 4a, 4b, and 4c may differ slightly from amounts actually withheld from employees' paychecks due to rounding social security and Medicare taxes based on statutory rates.

Sick pay. Enter the adjustment for the employee share of social security and Medicare taxes that were withheld and deposited by your third-party sick pay payer with regard to sick pay paid by the third party. These wages should be included on lines 4a and 4c. If you are the third-party sick pay payer, enter the adjustment for any employer share of these taxes required to be paid by the employer.

Adjustments for tips and group-term life insurance. Enter adjustments for both of the following items.

- Any uncollected employee share of social security and Medicare taxes on tips.
- The uncollected employee share of social security and Medicare taxes on group-term life insurance premiums paid for former employees.

7. Total Taxes After Adjustments

Combine the amounts shown on lines 5 and 6 and enter the result on line 7.

- **If line 7 is less than $2,500,** you may pay the amount with Form 944 or you may deposit the amount. See section 11 of Pub. 15 (Circular E), section 8 of Pub. 80 (Circular SS), or section 11 of Pub. 179 (Circular PR) for information about federal tax deposits.
- **If line 7 is $2,500 or more,** you generally must deposit your tax liabilities by electronic funds transfer. However, if you deposited all taxes accumulated in the first three quarters of the year and your fourth quarter liability is less than $2,500, you may pay taxes accumulated during the fourth quarter with Form 944. The amount shown on line 7 **must** equal the amount shown on line 13m.

8. Total Deposits for This Year

Enter your deposits for this year, including any overpayment that you applied from filing Form 944-X, 944-X (PR), 944-X (SP), 941-X, or 941-X (PR) in the current year. Also include in the amount shown any overpayment from a previous period that you applied to this return.

9a. COBRA Premium Assistance Payments

Report 65% of the COBRA premiums for assistance eligible individuals. Take the COBRA premium assistance credit on this line only after the assistance eligible individual's 35% share of the premium has been paid. For COBRA coverage provided under a self-insured plan, COBRA premium

Form 944—Instructions (Page 8)

assistance is treated as having been made for each assistance eligible individual who pays 35% of the COBRA premium. Do not include the assistance eligible individual's 35% of the premium in the amount entered on this line. For more information on the COBRA premium assistance credit, visit IRS.gov and enter the keyword *COBRA*.

CAUTION *The amount reported on line 9a is treated as a deposit of taxes on the first day of the return period and must not be used to adjust line 13 or Form 945-A.*

9b. Number of Individuals Provided COBRA Premium Assistance on Line 9a

Enter the total number of assistance eligible individuals provided COBRA premium assistance reported on line 9a. Count each assistance eligible individual who paid a reduced COBRA premium in the year as one individual, whether or not the reduced premium was for insurance that covered more than one assistance eligible individual. For example, if the reduced COBRA premium was for coverage for a former employee, spouse, and two children, you would include one individual in the number entered on line 9b for the premium assistance. Further, each individual is reported only once per year. For example, an assistance eligible individual who made monthly premium payments during the year would only be reported as one individual.

10. Total Deposits and Credits

Add lines 8 and 9a.

11. Balance Due

If line 7 is more than line 10, enter the difference on line 11. Otherwise, see *Overpayment*, later.

You do not have to pay if line 11 is less than $1. Generally, you should have a balance due only if your total taxes after adjustments (line 7) are less than $2,500. See *If line 7 is $2,500 or more*, earlier, for an exception.

If line 11 is:

- Less than $1, you do not have to pay it.
- $1 or more, but less than $2,500, you can pay the amount owed with your return. Make your check or money order payable to the "United States Treasury" and write your EIN, "Form 944," and "2012" on the check or money order. Complete Form 944-V, Payment Voucher, and enclose it with your return.
- $2,500 or more, you must deposit your tax. See *Must You Deposit Your Taxes*, earlier.

You may pay the amount shown on line 11 using EFTPS, a credit or debit card, or electronic funds withdrawal (EFW). **Do not** use a credit or debit card or EFW to pay taxes that were required to be deposited. For more information on electronic payment options, visit the IRS website at *www.irs.gov/e-pay*.

If you pay by EFTPS or credit or debit card, file your return using the *Without a payment* address under *Where Should You File*, earlier. **Do not** file Form 944-V.

CAUTION *If you are required to make deposits and, instead, pay the taxes with Form 944, you may be subject to a penalty.*

12. Overpayment

If line 10 is more than line 7, enter the amount on line 12. **Never** make an entry on both lines 11 and 12.

If you deposited more than the correct amount for the year, you can choose to have the IRS either refund the overpayment or apply it to your next return. Check only one box on line 12. If you do not check either box or if you check both boxes, generally we will apply the overpayment to your account. We may apply your overpayment to any past due tax account that is shown in our records under your EIN.

If line 12 is less than $1, we will send a refund or apply it to your next return only if you ask us in writing to do so.

Complete both pages.

You must complete both pages of Form 944 and sign it on page 2. Failure to do so may delay processing of your return.

Part 2: Tell Us About Your Deposit Schedule and Tax Liability for This Year

13. Check One

If line 7 is less than $2,500, check the first box on line 13 and go to line 14.

If line 7 is $2,500 or more, check the second box on line 13. If you are a monthly schedule depositor, enter your tax liability for each month and figure the total liability for the year. If you do not enter your tax liability for each month, the IRS will not know when you should have made deposits and may assess an "averaged" failure-to-deposit penalty. See section 11 of Pub. 15 (Circular E), section 8 of Pub. 80 (Circular SS), or section 11 of Pub. 179 (Circular PR). If your tax liability for any month is negative (for example, if you are adjusting an overreported liability in a prior month), do not enter a negative amount for the month. Instead, enter zero for the month and subtract that negative amount from your tax liability for the next month.

Note. The amount shown on line 13m must equal the amount shown on line 7.

If you are a semiweekly schedule depositor or if you accumulate $100,000 or more in tax liability on any day in a deposit period, you must complete Form 945-A and file it with Form 944. See the *$100,000 Next Day Deposit Rule* in section 11 of Pub. 15 (Circular E), section 8 of Pub. 80 (Circular SS), or section 11 of Pub. 179 (Circular PR). Do not complete lines 13a–13m if you file Form 945-A.

Part 3: Tell Us About Your Business

In Part 3, answer question 14 only if it applies to your business. If it does not apply, leave it blank and go to Part 4.

14. If Your Business Has Closed...

If you go out of business or stop paying wages, you must file a **final return.** To notify the IRS that a particular Form 944 is your final return, check the box on line 14 and enter the date you last paid wages in the space provided.

-8- **Instructions for Form 944 (2012)**

Form 944—Instructions (Page 9)

Part 4: May We Speak With Your Third-party Designee?

If you want to allow an employee, a paid tax preparer, or another person to discuss your Form 944 with the IRS, check the "Yes" box in Part 4. Enter the name, phone number, and the 5-digit personal identification number (PIN) of the specific person to contact—not the name of the firm that prepared your tax return. The designee may choose any numbers as his or her PIN.

By checking "Yes," you authorize the IRS to talk to the person you named (your designee) about any questions we may have while we process your return. You also authorize your designee to do all of the following.

- Give us any information that is missing from your return.
- Call us for information about processing your return.
- Respond to certain IRS notices that you have shared with your designee about math errors and return preparation. The IRS will not send notices to your designee.

You are not authorizing your designee to bind you to anything (including additional tax liability) or to otherwise represent you before the IRS. If you want to expand your designee's authorization, see Pub. 947, Practice Before the IRS and Power of Attorney.

The authorization will automatically expire 1 year after the due date (without regard to extensions) for filing Form 944. If you or your designee want to terminate the authorization, write to the IRS office for your locality using the *Without a payment* address under *Where Should You File*, earlier.

Part 5: Sign Here

Complete all information in Part 5 and sign Form 944 as follows.

- **Sole proprietorship—** The individual who owns the business.
- **Corporation (including a limited liability company (LLC) treated as a corporation)—** The president, vice president, or other principal officer duly authorized to sign.
- **Partnership (including an LLC treated as a partnership) or unincorporated organization—** A responsible and duly authorized member, partner, or officer having knowledge of its affairs.
- **Single member LLC treated as a disregarded entity for federal income tax purposes—** The owner of the LLC or a principal officer duly authorized to sign.
- **Trust or estate—** The fiduciary.

If you have filed a valid power of attorney, your duly authorized agent may also sign Form 944.

Alternative signature method. Corporate officers or duly authorized agents may sign Form 944 by rubber stamp, mechanical device, or computer software program. For details and required documentation, see Rev. Proc. 2005-39, 2005-28 I.R.B. 82, available at *www.irs.gov/irb/2005-28_IRB/ar16.html*.

Paid Preparer Use Only

A paid preparer must sign Form 944 and provide the information in the *Paid Preparer Use Only* section of Part 5 if the preparer was paid to prepare Form 944 and is not an employee of the filing entity. Paid preparers must sign paper returns with a manual signature. The preparer must give you a copy of the return in addition to the copy to be filed with the IRS.

If you are a paid preparer, enter your Preparer Tax Identification Number (PTIN) in the space provided. Include your complete address. If you work for a firm, enter the firm's name and the EIN of the firm. You can apply for a PTIN online or by filing Form W-12, IRS Paid Preparer Tax Identification Number (PTIN) Application and Renewal. For more information about applying for a PTIN online, visit the IRS website at *www.irs.gov/ptin*. You cannot use your PTIN in place of the EIN of the tax preparation firm.

Generally, do not complete this section if you are filing the return as a reporting agent and have a valid Form 8655, Reporting Agent Authorization, on file with the IRS. However, a reporting agent must complete this section if the reporting agent offered legal advice, for example, advising the client on determining whether its workers are employees or independent contractors for federal tax purposes.

How to Order Forms, Instructions, and Publications From the IRS

Call 1-800-TAX-FORM (1-800-829-3676).

Visit *www.irs.gov/formspubs*.

Instructions for Form 944 (2012) -9-

Form 945 (Page 1)

Form **945** Department of the Treasury Internal Revenue Service

Annual Return of Withheld Federal Income Tax

▶ For withholding reported on Forms 1099 and W-2G.
▶ See separate instructions. For more information on income tax withholding, see Pub. 15 (Circ. E) and Pub. 15-A.
Information about Form 945 and its separate instructions is at *www.irs.gov/form945*.

OMB No. 1545-1430

2012

Type or Print			
	Name (as distinguished from trade name)	Calendar year	If address is different from prior return, check here. ▶ ☐
	Trade name, if any	Employer identification number (EIN)	
	Address (number and street)	City, state, and ZIP code	

A If you **do not have to file** returns in the future, check here ▶ ☐ and enter date final payments made. ▶ ------------------------

1	Federal income tax withheld from pensions, annuities, IRAs, gambling winnings, etc.	1		
2	Backup withholding	2		
3	**Total taxes.** If $2,500 or more, this must equal line 7M below or line M of Form 945-A	3		
4	Total deposits for 2012, including overpayment applied from a prior year and overpayment applied from Form 945-X	4		
5	**Balance due.** If line 3 is more than line 4, enter the difference and see the separate instructions .	5		

6 **Overpayment.** If line 4 is more than line 3, enter the difference ▶ $ ____________

Check one: ☐ Apply to next return. ☐ Send a refund.

- **All filers:** If line 3 is less than $2,500, **do not** complete line 7 **or** Form 945-A.
- **Semiweekly schedule depositors:** Complete **Form 945-A** and check here . . . . ▶ ☐
- **Monthly schedule depositors:** Complete **line 7, entries A through M,** and check here . . . . ▶ ☐

7 Monthly Summary of Federal Tax Liability. (**Do not** complete if you were a semiweekly schedule depositor.)

	Tax liability for month		Tax liability for month		Tax liability for month
A January . . .		**F** June		**K** November . .	
B February . .		**G** July		**L** December . .	
C March . . .		**H** August		**M** Total liability for year (add lines **A** through **L**) . .	
D April		**I** September . . .			
E May		**J** October			

Third-Party Designee

Do you want to allow another person to discuss this return with the IRS (see the instructions)? ☐ Yes. Complete the following. ☐ No.

Designee's name ▶ **Phone no.** ▶ **Personal identification number (PIN)** ▶

Sign Here

Under penalties of perjury, I declare that I have examined this return, including accompanying schedules and statements, and to the best of my knowledge and belief, it is true, correct, and complete. Declaration of preparer (other than taxpayer) is based on all information of which preparer has any knowledge.

Signature ▶ **Print Your Name and Title** ▶ **Date** ▶

Paid Preparer Use Only

Print/Type preparer's name	Preparer's signature	Date	Check ☐ if self-employed	PTIN
Firm's name ▶			Firm's EIN ▶	
Firm's address ▶			Phone no.	

For Privacy Act and Paperwork Reduction Act Notice, see the separate instructions. Cat. No. 14584B Form **945** (2012)

Form 945 (Page 2)

Form 945-V, Payment Voucher

Purpose of Form

Complete Form 945-V, Payment Voucher, if you are making a payment with Form 945, Annual Return of Withheld Federal Income Tax. We will use the completed voucher to credit your payment more promptly and accurately, and to improve our service to you.

Making Payments With Form 945

To avoid a penalty, make your payment with your 2012 Form 945 **only if**:

• Your total taxes for the year (Form 945, line 3) are less than $2,500 and you are paying in full with a timely filed return, or

• You are a monthly schedule depositor making a payment in accordance with the Accuracy of Deposits Rule. See section 11 of Pub. 15 (Circular E), Employer's Tax Guide, for details. In this case, the amount of your payment may be $2,500 or more.

Otherwise, you must make deposits by electronic funds transfer. See section 11 of Pub. 15 (Circular E) for deposit instructions. Do not use Form 945-V to make federal tax deposits.

Caution. *Use Form 945-V when making any payment with Form 945. However, if you pay an amount with Form 945 that should have been deposited, you may be subject to a penalty. See* Deposit Penalties *in section 11 of Pub. 15 (Circular E).*

Specific Instructions

Box 1—Employer identification number (EIN). If you do not have an EIN, you may apply for one online. Go to IRS.gov and click on the *Apply for an EIN Online* link under "Tools." You may also apply for an EIN by calling 1-800-829-4933, or you can fax or mail Form SS-4, Application for Employer Identification Number. If you have not received your EIN by the due date of Form 945, write "Applied For" and the date you applied in this entry space.

Box 2—Amount paid. Enter the amount paid with Form 945.

Box 3—Name and address. Enter your name and address as shown on Form 945.

• Enclose your check or money order made payable to the "United States Treasury." Be sure to enter your EIN, "Form 945," and "2012" on your check or money order. Do not send cash. Do not staple Form 945-V or your payment to the return (or to each other).

• Detach Form 945-V and send it with your payment and Form 945 to the address provided in the Instructions for Form 945.

Note. You must also complete the entity information above line A on Form 945.

▼ **Detach Here and Mail With Your Payment and Form 945.** ▼

Form **945-V** Department of the Treasury Internal Revenue Service	**Payment Voucher** ► **Do not attach this voucher or your payment to Form 945.**	OMB No. 1545-1430 **2012**
1 Enter your employer identification number (EIN).	2 **Enter the amount of your payment** . . ► Make your check or money order payable to "**United States Treasury**"	Dollars / Cents
	3 Enter your business name (individual name if sole proprietor). Enter your address. Enter your city, state, and ZIP code.	

Form 945—Instructions (Page 1)

2012 Instructions for Form 945

Annual Return of Withheld Federal Income Tax

Department of the Treasury
Internal Revenue Service

Section references are to the Internal Revenue Code unless otherwise noted.

Future Developments

For the latest information about developments related to Form 945 and its instructions, such as legislation enacted after they were published, go to www.irs.gov/form945.

What's New

Voluntary income tax withholding rates for 2013. The voluntary income tax withholding rates will be available in January 2013 at www.irs.gov/form945.

Reminders

Correcting a previously filed Form 945. If you discover an error on a previously filed Form 945, make the correction using Form 945-X, Adjusted Annual Return of Withheld Federal Income Tax or Claim for Refund. Form 945-X is a stand-alone form, meaning taxpayers can file Form 945-X when an error is discovered. For more information, get the Instructions for Form 945-X or visit IRS.gov and type *Correcting Employment Taxes* in the search box.

Federal tax deposits must be made by electronic funds transfer. You must use electronic funds transfer to make all federal tax deposits. Generally, electronic funds transfers are made using the Electronic Federal Tax Payment System (EFTPS). If you do not want to use EFTPS, you can arrange for your tax professional, financial institution, payroll service, or other trusted third party to make deposits on your behalf. Also, you may arrange for your financial institution to initiate a same-day wire payment on your behalf. EFTPS is a free service provided by the Department of Treasury. Services provided by your tax professional, financial institution, payroll service, or other third party may have a fee.

For more information on making federal tax deposits, see section 11 of Pub. 15 (Circular E), Employer's Tax Guide. To get more information about EFTPS or to enroll in EFTPS, visit the EFTPS website at www.eftps.gov, or call 1-800-555-4477. Additional information about EFTPS is also available in Pub. 966, Electronic Federal Tax Payment System: A Guide to Getting Started.

Paid preparers must sign Form 945. Paid preparers must complete and sign the paid preparer's section of Form 945.

Credit or debit card payments. Payors can pay the balance due shown on Form 945 by credit or debit card. Do not use a credit or debit card to make federal tax deposits. For more information on paying your taxes with a credit or debit card, visit the IRS website at www.irs.gov/e-pay.

How to get forms and publications. You can get most IRS forms and publications by accessing the IRS website at IRS.gov or by calling the IRS at 1-800-TAX-FORM (1-800-829-3676).

Telephone help. You can call the IRS Business and Specialty Tax Line toll free at 1-800-829-4933 or 1-800-829-4059 (TTY/TDD for persons who are deaf, hard of hearing, or have a speech disability) Monday–Friday 7 a.m.–7 p.m. local time (Alaska and Hawaii follow Pacific time) for answers to your questions about completing Form 945, tax deposit rules, or obtaining an employer identification number (EIN).

Additional information. Pub. 15 (Circular E) explains the rules for withholding, depositing, and reporting federal income tax. Pub. 15-A, Employer's Supplemental Tax Guide, includes information on federal income tax withholding from pensions, annuities, and Indian gaming profits. For information on withholding from gambling winnings, see the Instructions for Forms W-2G and 5754.

For a list of employment tax products, visit the IRS website at www.irs.gov/businesses and select click on the *Employment Taxes* link under "Businesses Topics."

Photographs of Missing Children

The Internal Revenue Service is a proud partner with the National Center for Missing and Exploited Children. Photographs of missing children selected by the Center may appear in instructions on pages that would otherwise be blank. You can help bring these children home by looking at the photographs and calling 1-800-THE-LOST (1-800-843-5678) if you recognize a child.

General Instructions

Purpose of Form 945

Use Form 945 to report withheld federal income tax from nonpayroll payments. Nonpayroll payments include:

- Pensions (including distributions from tax-favored retirement plans, for example, section 401(k), section 403(b), and governmental section 457(b) plans) and annuities;
- Military retirement;
- Gambling winnings;
- Indian gaming profits;
- Voluntary withholding on certain government payments; and
- Backup withholding.

Report all federal income tax withholding from nonpayroll payments or distributions annually on one Form 945. **Do not** file more than one Form 945 for any calendar year.

All federal income tax withholding reported on

Sep 06, 2012 Cat. No. 20534D

Form 945—Instructions (Page 2)

Forms 1099 (for example, Form 1099-R or 1099-MISC) or Form W-2G must be reported on Form 945. **Do not** report federal income tax withholding from wages on Form 945.

All employment taxes and federal income tax withholding reported on Form W-2, Wage and Tax Statement, must be reported on Form 941 or Form 944, Form 943 for agricultural employees, Schedule H (Form 1040) for household employees, or Form CT-1 for railroad employees.

Do not report on Form 945 federal income tax withheld on distributions to participants from nonqualified pension plans (including **nongovernmental** section 457(b) plans) and some other deferred compensation arrangements that are treated as wages and are reported on Form W-2. Report such withholding on Form 941 or Form 944. See Pub. 15 (Circular E) for more information.

Compensation paid to H-2A visa holders. Generally, report compensation of $600 or more paid to foreign agricultural workers who entered the country on H-2A visas on Form W-2 and Form 943, Employer's Annual Tax Return for Agricultural Employees. However, if an H-2A visa worker did not provide the employer with a taxpayer identification number, the employee is subject to backup withholding. The employer must report the wages and backup withholding on Form 1099-MISC, Miscellaneous Income. The employer must also report the backup withholding on Form 945, line 2.

Who Must File

If you withhold federal income tax (including backup withholding) from nonpayroll payments, you must file Form 945. See *Purpose of Form 945,* earlier. You do not have to file Form 945 for those years in which you do not have a nonpayroll tax liability. **Do not** report on Form 945 withholding that is required to be reported on Form 1042, Annual Withholding Tax Return for U.S. Source Income of Foreign Persons.

When To File

For 2012, file Form 945 by January 31, 2013. However, if you made deposits on time in full payment of the taxes for the year, you may file the return by February 11, 2013. Your return will be considered timely filed if it is properly addressed and mailed First-Class or sent by an IRS-designated private delivery service on or before the due date. See Pub. 15 (Circular E) for more information on IRS-designated private delivery services.

Where To File

In the list below, find the location of your legal residence, principal place of business, office, or agency. Send Form 945 to the address listed for your location.

TIP *Where you file depends on whether or not you are including a payment with the return.*

If you are in . . .		Without a payment . . .	With a payment . . .
Connecticut Delaware District of Columbia Florida Georgia Illinois Indiana Kentucky Maine Maryland Massachusetts Michigan New Hampshire	New Jersey New York North Carolina Ohio Pennsylvania Rhode Island South Carolina Tennessee Vermont Virginia West Virginia Wisconsin	Department of the Treasury Internal Revenue Service Cincinnati, OH 45999-0042	Internal Revenue Service P. O. Box 804524 Cincinnati, OH 45280-4524
Alabama Alaska Arizona Arkansas California Colorado Hawaii Idaho Iowa Kansas Louisiana Minnesota Mississippi	Missouri Montana Nebraska Nevada New Mexico North Dakota Oklahoma Oregon South Dakota Texas Utah Washington Wyoming	Department of the Treasury Internal Revenue Service Ogden, UT 84201-0042	Internal Revenue Service P. O. Box 37945 Hartford, CT 06176-7945
No legal residence or principal place of business in any state:		Internal Revenue Service P.O. Box 409101 Ogden, UT 84409	Internal Revenue Service P. O. Box 37945 Hartford, CT 06176-7945
If you are filing Form 945 for an exempt organization or government entity (federal, state, local, or Indian tribal government), use the following addresses, regardless of your location:		Department of the Treasury Internal Revenue Service Ogden, UT 84201-0042	Internal Revenue Service P. O. Box 37945 Hartford, CT 06176-7945

Employer Identification Number (EIN)

If you do not have an EIN, you may apply for one online. Go to IRS.gov and click on the *Apply for an EIN Online* link under "Tools." You may also apply for an EIN by calling 1-800-829-4933, or you can fax or mail Form SS-4, Application for Employer Identification Number, to the IRS. If you have not received your EIN by the due date of Form 945, write "Applied For" and the date you applied in this entry space.

Penalties and Interest

There are penalties for filing Form 945 late and for paying or depositing taxes late, unless there is reasonable cause. See section 11 of Pub. 15 (Circular E) for more information on deposit penalties. There are also penalties for failure to furnish information returns (for example, Forms 1099-MISC, 1099-R, or W-2G) to payees and failure to file copies with the IRS. Interest is charged on taxes paid late at a rate set by law.

If you receive a notice about a penalty after you file this return, reply to the notice with an explanation and we will determine if you meet reasonable-cause criteria. Do **not** attach an explanation when you file your return.

Use Form 843, Claim for Refund and Request for Abatement, to request abatement of assessed penalties or interest. Do not request abatement of assessed penalties or interest on Form 945 or Form 945-X.

-2- **Instructions for Form 945 (2012)**

Form 945—Instructions (Page 3)

If amounts that must be withheld are not withheld or are not deposited or paid to the United States Treasury, the ***trust fund recovery penalty*** *may apply. The penalty is the full amount of any unpaid trust fund tax. This penalty may apply when these unpaid taxes cannot be immediately collected from the employer or business. The trust fund recovery penalty may be imposed on all persons who are determined by the IRS to have been responsible for collecting, accounting for, and paying over these taxes, and who acted willfully in not doing so. "Willfully" in this case means voluntarily, consciously, and intentionally. A responsible person acts willfully if the person knows that the required actions are not taking place.*

Voluntary Income Tax Withholding

States must allow unemployment compensation recipients to elect to have federal income tax withheld. Recipients paid under the Railroad Unemployment Insurance Act may also elect withholding.

Recipients of any of the following federal payments may request federal income tax withholding.

- Social security and Tier 1 railroad retirement benefits.
- Certain crop disaster payments.
- Commodity Credit Corporation loans.

The voluntary income tax withholding rates will be available in January 2013 at www.irs.gov/form945.

The payee may request withholding on Form W-4V, Voluntary Withholding Request, or you may develop your own substitute form. Any voluntary withholding on these payments must be reported on Form 945 (and on the required information return—Form 1099-G, Form SSA-1099, or Form RRB-1099) and is subject to the deposit rules.

Depositing Withheld Taxes

Deposit all nonpayroll (Form 945) withheld federal income tax, including backup withholding, by electronic funds transfer. Combine all Form 945 taxes for deposit purposes. **Do not** combine deposits for Forms 941, 943, 944, or Form CT-1 with deposits for Form 945.

Generally, the deposit rules that apply to Form 941 also apply to Form 945. However, because Form 945 is an annual return, the rules for determining your deposit schedule (discussed below) are different from those for Form 941. See section 11 of Pub. 15 (Circular E) for a detailed discussion of the deposit rules.

Determining Your Deposit Schedule

There are two deposit schedules—**monthly** or **semiweekly**— for determining when you must deposit withheld federal income tax. These schedules tell you when a deposit is due after a tax liability arises (that is, you make a payment subject to federal income tax withholding, including backup withholding). Before the beginning of each calendar year, you must determine which of the two deposit schedules you must use.

For 2013, you are a monthly schedule depositor for Form 945 if the total tax reported on your 2011 Form 945 (line 3) was $50,000 or less. If the total tax reported for 2011 exceeded $50,000, you are a semiweekly schedule depositor.

If you are a monthly schedule depositor and accumulate a $100,000 liability or more on any day during a calendar month, your deposit schedule changes on the next day to semiweekly for the remainder of the year and for the following year. For more information, see the $100,000 Next-Day Deposit Rule *in section 11 of Pub. 15 (Circular E).*

Specific Instructions

Line A. Final Return

If you go out of business or end operations and you will not have to file Form 945 in the future, file a final return. Be sure to check the box on line A and enter the date that final nonpayroll payments were made.

Line 1. Federal Income Tax Withheld

Enter the federal income tax that you withheld (or were required to withhold) from pensions (including distributions from tax-favored retirement plans, for example, section 401(k), section 403(b), and governmental section 457(b) plans), annuities, IRA distributions, military retirement, Indian gaming profits, and gambling winnings (regular gambling withholding only). Also enter any voluntary amount that you withheld on certain government payments. If you are required to report federal income tax withholding on Forms 1099 (for example, Form 1099-R or 1099-MISC) or Form W-2G, you must report the federal income tax withheld on Form 945.

Federal income tax withholding reported on Form W-2 ***must*** *be reported on Form 941, Form 943, Form 944, or Schedule H (Form 1040), as appropriate.*

Line 2. Backup Withholding

Enter any backup withholding, including backup withholding on gambling winnings.

Regulated investment companies (RICs) and real estate investment trusts (REITs) must report any backup withholding on Form 945 in the year that the dividends are actually paid. This includes January payments of dividends declared during October, November, and December of the prior year. See the Instructions for Form 1099-DIV for special reporting requirements.

Line 3. Total Taxes

Add lines 1 and 2. If total taxes are $2,500 or more, the amount reported on line 3 must equal the total liability for the year reported on line 7M of the Monthly Summary of Federal Tax Liability, or line M of Form 945-A, Annual Return of Federal Tax Liability.

Line 4. Total Deposits

Enter your total Form 945 deposits for the year, including any overpayment that you applied from filing Form 945-X and any overpayment that you applied from your 2011 return.

Form 945—Instructions (Page 4)

Line 5. Balance Due

If line 3 is more than line 4, enter the difference on line 5. Otherwise, see *Overpayment* below. You do not have to pay if line 5 is under $1. Generally, you should have a balance due only if your total taxes for the year (line 3) are less than $2,500. If you made payments under the accuracy of deposits rule, see section 11 of Pub. 15 (Circular E).

You may pay the amount shown on line 5 using EFTPS, a credit or debit card, or a check or money order. Do not use a credit or debit card to pay taxes that were required to be deposited. For more information on electronic payment options, visit the IRS website at *www.irs.gov/e-pay*.

If you pay by EFTPS or credit or debit card, file your return using the *Without a payment* address under *Where To File*, earlier. Do not file Form 945-V, Payment Voucher. If you pay by check or money order, make it payable to the "United States Treasury." Enter your EIN, Form 945, and the tax period on your check or money order. Complete Form 945-V and enclose with Form 945.

If line 3 is $2,500 or more and you deposited all taxes when due, the amount on line 5 should be zero.

CAUTION *If you did not make deposits as required and instead pay the taxes with Form 945, you may be subject to a penalty.*

Line 6. Overpayment

If line 4 is more than line 3, enter the difference on line 6. **Never make an entry on both lines 5 and 6.**

If you deposited more than the correct amount for the year, you can have the overpayment refunded or applied to your next return by checking the appropriate box. Check only one box below line 6. If you do not check either box or if you check both boxes, generally we will apply the overpayment to your account. We may apply your overpayment to any past due tax account that is shown in our records under your EIN. If line 6 is under $1, we will send a refund or apply it to your next return only on written request.

Line 7. Monthly Summary of Federal Tax Liability

CAUTION *This is a summary of your monthly tax liability, not a summary of deposits made. If line 3 is less than $2,500,* ***do not*** *complete line 7 or Form 945-A.*

Complete line 7 only if you were a **monthly schedule depositor** for the entire year and line 3 is $2,500 or more. See *Determining Your Deposit Schedule,* earlier.

CAUTION *The amount entered on line 7M must equal the amount reported on line 3.*

Report your liabilities on Form 945-A instead of on line 7 if either of the following apply.

- You were a **semiweekly schedule depositor** during 2012. **Do not** complete entries A through M of line 7. Instead, complete and file Form 945-A with Form 945.
- You were a **monthly schedule depositor** for 2012 and during any month you accumulated nonpayroll taxes of $100,000 or more. Because this converted you to a semiweekly schedule depositor for the remainder of 2012 (and for 2013), you must report your liabilities on Form 945-A for the entire year. **Do not** complete entries A through M of line 7. For more information, see the *$100,000 Next-Day Deposit Rule* in section 11 of Pub. 15 (Circular E).

Third-Party Designee

If you want to allow any individual, corporation, firm, organization, or partnership to discuss your 2012 Form 945 with the IRS, check the "Yes" box in the "Third-Party Designee" section of Form 945. Also, enter the name, phone number, and any five-digit personal identification number (PIN) for the specific person to speak with — not the name of the firm who prepared your return.

By checking the "Yes" box, you are authorizing the IRS to speak with the designee to answer any questions relating to the information reported on your tax return. You are also authorizing the designee to:

- Give the IRS any information that is missing from your return,
- Call the IRS for information about the processing of your return or the status of your refund or payments,
- Receive copies of notices or transcripts related to your return upon request, and
- Respond to certain IRS notices about math errors, offsets, and return preparation.

You are not authorizing the designee to receive any refund check, bind you to anything (including additional tax liability), or otherwise represent you before the IRS. If you want to expand the designee's authorization, see Pub. 947, Practice Before the IRS and Power of Attorney.

The authorization will automatically expire 1 year from the due date (without regard to extensions) for filing your 2012 Form 945. If you or your designee wants to terminate the authorization, write to the IRS office for your locality using *Without a payment* address under *Where To File*, earlier.

Who Must Sign

Form 945 must be signed as follows:

- **Sole proprietorship** — The individual who owns the business.
- **Corporation (including a limited liability company (LLC) treated as a corporation)** — The president, vice president, or other principal officer duly authorized to sign.
- **Partnership (including an LLC treated as a partnership) or unincorporated organization** — A responsible and duly authorized partner, member, or officer having knowledge of its affairs.
- **Single member LLC treated as a disregarded entity** — The owner of the limited liability company (LLC).
- **Trust or estate** — The fiduciary.

Form 945 may also be signed by a duly authorized agent of the taxpayer if a valid power of attorney has been filed.

Alternative signature method. Corporate officers or duly authorized agents may sign Form 945 by rubber

-4- **Instructions for Form 945 (2012)**

Form 945—Instructions (Page 5)

stamp, mechanical device, or computer software program. For details and required documentation, see Rev. Proc. 2005-39, 2005-28 I.R.B. 82, available at *www.irs.gov/irb/2005-28_IRB/ar16.html.*

Paid Preparer Use Only

A paid preparer must sign Form 945 and provide the information in the *Paid Preparer Use Only* section if the preparer was paid to prepare Form 945 and is not an employee of the filing entity. Paid preparers must sign paper returns with a manual signature. The preparer must give you a copy of the return in addition to the copy to be filed with the IRS.

If you are a paid preparer, enter your Preparer Tax Identification Number (PTIN) in the space provided. Include your complete address. If you work for a firm, enter the firm's name and the EIN of the firm. You can apply for a PTIN online or by filing Form W-12, IRS Paid Preparer Tax Identification Number (PTIN) Application and Renewal. For more information about applying for a PTIN online, visit the IRS website at *www.irs.gov/ptin*. You cannot use your PTIN in place of the EIN of the tax preparation firm.

Generally, do not complete this section if you are filing the return as a reporting agent and have a valid Form 8655, Reporting Agent Authorization, on file with the IRS. However, a reporting agent must complete this section if the reporting agent offered legal advice, for example, advising the client on determining whether federal income tax withholding is required on certain payments.

Privacy Act and Paperwork Reduction Act Notice. We ask for the information on Form 945 to carry out the Internal Revenue laws of the United States. We need it to figure and collect the right amount of tax. Sections 3402, 3405, and 3406 of the Internal Revenue Code require taxpayers to pay over to the IRS federal income tax withheld from certain nonpayroll payments and distributions, including backup withholding. Form 945 is used to report these withholdings. Section 6011 requires you to provide the requested information if the tax applies to you. Section 6109 requires you to provide your identification number. If you fail to provide this information in a timely manner, or provide false or fraudulent information, you may be subject to penalties and interest.

You do not have to provide the information requested on a form that is subject to the Paperwork Reduction Act unless the form displays a valid OMB control number. Books or records relating to a form or its instructions must be retained as long as their contents may become material in the administration of any Internal Revenue law.

Generally, tax returns and return information are confidential, as required by section 6103. However, section 6103 allows or requires the Internal Revenue Service to disclose or give the information shown on your tax return to others described in the Code. For example, we may disclose your tax information to the Department of Justice for civil and criminal litigation, and to cities, states, the District of Columbia, and U.S. commonwealths and possessions to administer their tax laws. We may also disclose this information to other countries under a tax treaty, to federal and state agencies to enforce federal nontax criminal laws, or to federal law enforcement and intelligence agencies to combat terrorism.

The time needed to complete and file Form 945 will vary depending on individual circumstances. The estimated average time is: **Recordkeeping,** 7 hr., 9 min.; **Learning about the law or the form,** 47 min.; and **Preparing and sending the form to the IRS,** 56 min. If you have comments concerning the accuracy of these time estimates or suggestions for making Form 945 simpler, we would be happy to hear from you. You can email us at *taxforms@irs.gov*. Enter "Form 945" on the subject line. Or write to the Internal Revenue Service, Tax Products Coordinating Committee, SE:W:CAR:MP:T:M:S, 1111 Constitution Ave. NW, IR-6526, Washington, DC 20224. **Do not** send Form 945 to this address. Instead, see *Where To File,* earlier.

Form 945-A (Page 1)

Form **945-A** (Rev. October 2012) Department of the Treasury Internal Revenue Service	**Annual Record of Federal Tax Liability** ▶ **Information about Form 945-A and its instructions is at *www.irs.gov/form945*.** ▶ **File with Form 945, 945-X, CT-1, CT-1 X, 944, or 944-X.**	OMB No. 1545-1430 ___ ___ ___ ___ Calendar Year
Name (as shown on Form 945, 945-X, CT-1, CT-1 X, 944, or 944-X)		**Employer identification number (EIN)**

You must complete this form if you are required to deposit on a semiweekly schedule or if your tax liability during any month was $100,000 or more. Show tax liability here, not deposits. (The IRS gets deposit data from electronic funds transfers.) **DO NOT change your tax liability by adjustments reported on any Form 945-X, 944-X, or CT-1 X.**

January Tax Liability

Day	Amount	Day	Amount
1		17	
2		18	
3		19	
4		20	
5		21	
6		22	
7		23	
8		24	
9		25	
10		26	
11		27	
12		28	
13		29	
14		30	
15		31	
16			

A Total for month ▶

February Tax Liability

Day	Amount	Day	Amount
1		17	
2		18	
3		19	
4		20	
5		21	
6		22	
7		23	
8		24	
9		25	
10		26	
11		27	
12		28	
13		29	
14			
15			
16			

B Total for month ▶

March Tax Liability

Day	Amount	Day	Amount
1		17	
2		18	
3		19	
4		20	
5		21	
6		22	
7		23	
8		24	
9		25	
10		26	
11		27	
12		28	
13		29	
14		30	
15		31	
16			

C Total for month ▶

April Tax Liability

Day	Amount	Day	Amount
1		17	
2		18	
3		19	
4		20	
5		21	
6		22	
7		23	
8		24	
9		25	
10		26	
11		27	
12		28	
13		29	
14		30	
15			
16			

D Total for month ▶

May Tax Liability

Day	Amount	Day	Amount
1		17	
2		18	
3		19	
4		20	
5		21	
6		22	
7		23	
8		24	
9		25	
10		26	
11		27	
12		28	
13		29	
14		30	
15		31	
16			

E Total for month ▶

June Tax Liability

Day	Amount	Day	Amount
1		17	
2		18	
3		19	
4		20	
5		21	
6		22	
7		23	
8		24	
9		25	
10		26	
11		27	
12		28	
13		29	
14		30	
15			
16			

F Total for month ▶

For Paperwork Reduction Act Notice, see page 4. Cat. No. 14733M Form **945-A** (Rev. 10-2012)

Form 945-A and Instructions (Page 2)

Form 945-A (Rev. 10-2012) Page **2**

July Tax Liability

1		17	
2		18	
3		19	
4		20	
5		21	
6		22	
7		23	
8		24	
9		25	
10		26	
11		27	
12		28	
13		29	
14		30	
15		31	
16			

G **Total for month ▶**

August Tax Liability

1		17	
2		18	
3		19	
4		20	
5		21	
6		22	
7		23	
8		24	
9		25	
10		26	
11		27	
12		28	
13		29	
14		30	
15		31	
16			

H **Total for month ▶**

September Tax Liability

1		17	
2		18	
3		19	
4		20	
5		21	
6		22	
7		23	
8		24	
9		25	
10		26	
11		27	
12		28	
13		29	
14		30	
15			
16			

I **Total for month ▶**

October Tax Liability

1		17	
2		18	
3		19	
4		20	
5		21	
6		22	
7		23	
8		24	
9		25	
10		26	
11		27	
12		28	
13		29	
14		30	
15		31	
16			

J **Total for month ▶**

November Tax Liability

1		17	
2		18	
3		19	
4		20	
5		21	
6		22	
7		23	
8		24	
9		25	
10		26	
11		27	
12		28	
13		29	
14		30	
15			
16			

K **Total for month ▶**

December Tax Liability

1		17	
2		18	
3		19	
4		20	
5		21	
6		22	
7		23	
8		24	
9		25	
10		26	
11		27	
12		28	
13		29	
14		30	
15		31	
16			

L **Total for month ▶**

M Total tax liability for the year (add lines **A** through **L**). This should equal line 3 on Form 945 (line 13 on Form CT-1, line 7 on Form 944.) . . . . ▶

Form **945-A** (Rev. 10-2012)

Form 945-A and Instructions (Page 3)

Form 945-A (Rev. 10-2012) Page **3**

Future Developments

For the latest information about developments related to Form 945-A and its instructions, such as legislation enacted after they were published, go to *www.irs.gov/form945*.

Reminders

Reporting prior period adjustments. Prior period adjustments are reported on Form 945-X, Adjusted Annual Return of Federal Income Tax or Claim for Refund; Form CT-1 X, Adjusted Employer's Annual Railroad Retirement Tax Return or Claim for Refund; and Form 944-X, Adjusted Employer's ANNUAL Federal Tax Return or Claim for Refund; respectively, and are not taken into account when figuring the tax liability for the current year.

When you file Form 945-A with your Form 945, CT-1, or 944, **do not** change your tax liability by adjustments reported on any Form 945-X, CT-1 X, or 944-X.

Amended Form 945-A. If you have been assessed a failure-to-deposit (FTD) penalty, you may be able to file an amended Form 945-A. For more information, see *Amending a Previously Filed Form 945-A,* later.

General Instructions

Purpose of form. Use Form 945-A to report your federal tax liability (based on the dates payments were made or wages were paid) for the following tax returns.

• Forms 945 and 945-X for federal income tax withholding on nonpayroll payments. Nonpayroll withholding includes backup withholding and federal income tax withholding on pensions, annuities, IRAs, Indian gaming profits, gambling winnings, and military retirement.

• Forms CT-1 and CT-1 X for both employee and employer Tier I taxes and employer Tier II taxes.

• Forms 944 and 944-X for federal income tax withheld plus both employee and employer social security and Medicare taxes.

Forms 944(SP), 944-X (SP), and 944-X (PR). If you are a semiweekly schedule depositor who files Formulario 944(SP), Declaración Federal ANUAL de Impuestos del Patrono o Empleador, you should use Formulario 943A-PR, Registro de la Obligación Contributiva Federal del Patrono Agrícola, to report your tax liability. You should also file Form 943A-PR if you file Form 944-X(SP) or Form 944-X(PR) and you need to amend a previously filed Form 943A-PR.

Who must file. Semiweekly schedule depositors must complete and file Form 945-A with their tax return. **Do not** file Form 945-A if your tax liability for the return period is less than $2,500. **Do not** file this form if you are a monthly schedule depositor unless you accumulated a tax liability of $100,000 during any month of the year. Monthly schedule depositors who accumulate $100,000 become semiweekly schedule depositors for the remainder of the year (and the next year) and must complete Form 945-A for the entire year.

The deposit rules, including the $100,000 Next-Day Deposit Rule, are explained in section 11 of Pub. 15 (Circular E), Employer's Tax Guide, and in the instructions for your tax return.

Caution. IRS uses Form 945-A to match the tax liability you reported on the returns indicated above with your deposits. The IRS also uses Form 945-A to determine if you have deposited your tax liabilities on time. Unless Form 945-A is properly completed and filed (if applicable) with your tax return, the IRS may propose an "averaged" failure-to-deposit penalty. See *Deposit Penalties* in section 11 of Pub. 15 (Circular E) for more information.

Specific Instructions

If you must report your tax liabilities on Form 945-A as discussed above, file it with your tax return. Each numbered space on Form 945-A corresponds to a date during the year. Report your tax liabilities in the spaces that correspond to the dates you made payments, not the date tax deposits were made. For example, if you became liable for a pension distribution on December 31, 2011, but did not make the distribution until January 3, 2012, the federal income tax withholding liability for the distribution must be reported on Form 945-A for 2012, on line 3 under January Tax Liability.

Enter your business information. Carefully enter your employer identification number (EIN) and name at the top of the form. Make sure that they exactly match the name of your business and the EIN that the IRS assigned to your business and also agree with the name and EIN shown on the attached Form 945, 945-X, CT-1, CT-1 X, 944, or 944-X.

Calendar year. Enter the calendar year of the Form 945, 945-X, CT-1, CT-1 X, 944, or 944-X to which Form 945-A is attached.

Form 945 filers. Do not complete entries A through M of the Monthly Summary of Federal Tax Liability (Form 945, line 7). Be sure to mark the semiweekly schedule depositor checkbox above line 7 on Form 945.

Form CT-1 filers. Do not complete the Monthly Summary of Railroad Retirement Tax Liability (Form CT-1).

Form 944 filers. On Form 944, check the box for "Line 7 is $2,500 or more" at line 13, and leave blank lines 13a–13m.

Enter your tax liability by month. Enter your tax liabilities in the spaces that correspond to the dates you **paid** wages to your employees or made nonpayroll payments, not the date deposits were made. The total tax liability for the year (line M) must equal net taxes on Form 945 (line 3), Form 944 (line 7) or Form CT-1 (line 13). Report your tax liabilities on this form corresponding to the dates of each wage payment or nonpayroll payment, **not** to when the liabilities are accrued. Enter the monthly totals on lines A, B, C, D, E, F, G, H, I, J, K, and L. Enter the total for the year on line M.

For example, if you are a Form 945 filer, your payroll period ended on December 31, 2011, and you **paid** the nonpayroll payments for that period on January 6, 2012, you would:

• Go to January (on Form 945-A filed with your 2012 return), and

• Enter your tax liability on line 6 (because line 6 represents the sixth day of the month).

TIP *Make sure you have checked the appropriate box below line 6 of Form 945 to show that you are a semiweekly schedule depositor.*

Example 1. Cedar Co., which has a semiweekly deposit schedule, makes periodic payments on gambling winnings on the 15th day of each month. On December 24, 2012, in addition to its periodic payments, it withheld from a payment on gambling winnings under the backup withholding rules. Since Cedar Co. is a semiweekly schedule depositor, it **must** record these nonpayroll withholding liabilities on Form 945-A. It must report tax liabilities on line 15 for each month and line 24 for December.

Cedar Co. enters the monthly totals on lines **A** through **L**. It adds these monthly subtotals and enters the total tax liability for the year on line **M**. The amount on line **M** should equal Form 945, line 3.

Example 2. Fir Co. is a semiweekly schedule depositor. During January, it withheld federal income tax on pension distributions as follows: $52,000 on January 10; $35,000 on January 24. Since Fir Co. is a semiweekly schedule depositor, it **must** record its federal income tax withholding liabilities on Form 945-A. It must record $52,000 on line 10 and $35,000 on line 24 for January.

Form 945-A and Instructions (Page 4)

Form 945-A (Rev. 10-2012) Page **4**

Example 3. Because Elm Co. is a new business, it is a monthly schedule depositor at the beginning of 2012. During January, it withheld federal income tax on nonpayroll payments as follows: $2,000 on January 10; $99,000 on January 24. The deposit rules require that a monthly schedule depositor begin depositing on a semiweekly deposit schedule when a $100,000 or more tax liability is accumulated on any day within a month (see section 11 of Pub. 15 (Circular E) for details). Since Elm Co. accumulated $101,000 ($2,000 + $99,000) on January 24, 2012, it became a semiweekly schedule depositor on January 25, 2012. Elm Co. must complete Form 945-A and file it with Form 945. It must record $2,000 on line 10 and $99,000 on line 24 for January. **No entries** should be made on Form 945, line 7, although Elm Co. was a monthly schedule depositor until January 25.

Amending a Previously Filed Form 945-A

Semiweekly schedule depositors. If you have been assessed a failure-to-deposit (FTD) penalty and you made an error on Form 945-A and the correction will not change the total liability you reported on Form 945-A, you may be able to reduce your penalty by filing an amended Form 945-A.

Example. You reported a liability of $3,000 on January 1. However, the liability was actually for March. Prepare an amended Form 945-A showing the $3,000 liability on March 1. Also, you must enter the liabilities previously reported for the year that did not change. Write "Amended" at the top of Form 945-A. The IRS will refigure the penalty and notify you of any change in the penalty.

Monthly schedule depositors. You can also file an amended Form 945-A if you have been assessed an FTD penalty and you made an error on the monthly tax liability section of Form 945. When completing Form 945-A, only enter the monthly totals. The daily entries are not required.

Where to file. File your amended Form 945-A at the address provided in the penalty notice you received. You do not have to submit your original Form 945-A.

Forms 945-X, CT-1 X, and 944-X

Tax decrease. If you are filing Form 945-X, CT-1 X, or 944-X, you can file an amended Form 945-A with the form if **both** of the following apply.

1. You have a tax decrease.
2. You were assessed an FTD penalty.

File your amended Form 945-A with Form 945-X, CT-1 X, or 944-X. The total liability reported on your amended Form 945-A must equal the corrected amount of tax reported on Form 945-X, CT-1 X, or 944-X. If your penalty is decreased, the IRS will include the penalty decrease with your tax decrease.

Tax increase—Form 945-X, CT-1 X, or 944-X filed timely. If you are filing a timely Form 945-X, CT-1 X, or 944-X showing a tax increase, do not file an amended Form 945-A, unless you were assessed an FTD penalty caused by an incorrect, incomplete, or missing Form 945-A. Do not include the tax increase reported on Form 945-X, CT-1 X, or 944-X on an amended Form 945-A you file.

Tax increase—Form 945-X, CT-1 X, or 944-X filed late. If you owe tax and are filing late, that is, after the due date of the return for the filing period in which you discovered the error, you must file the form with an amended Form 945-A. Otherwise, IRS may assess an "averaged" FTD penalty.

The total tax reported on line M of Form 945-A must match the corrected tax (Form 945, line 3; Form 944, line 7 (line 9 for years before 2011); Form CT-1, line 13) combined with any correction reported on Form 945-X, line 5 (Form 944-X, line 16 minus any advance EIC reported on Form 944-X, line 17; Form CT-1X, line 18) for the year, less any previous abatements and interest-free tax assessments.

Paperwork Reduction Act Notice. We ask for the information on this form to carry out the Internal Revenue laws of the United States. You are required to give us the information. We need it to ensure that you are complying with these laws and to allow us to figure and collect the right amount of tax.

You are not required to provide the information requested on a form that is subject to the Paperwork Reduction Act unless the form displays a valid OMB control number. Books or records relating to a form or its instructions must be retained as long as their contents may become material in the administration of any Internal Revenue law. Generally, tax returns and return information are confidential, as required by Code section 6103.

The time needed to complete and file this form will vary depending on individual circumstances. The estimated average time is:

Recordkeeping . . . . 6 hr., 27 min.
Learning . . . . 6 min.
Preparing and sending the form to the IRS . . . . 12 min.

If you have comments concerning the accuracy of these time estimates or suggestions for making this form simpler, we would be happy to hear from you. You can write to the IRS at the address listed in the Privacy Act Notice for your tax return.

Form W-2-Copy A

22222 | Void ☐ | a Employee's social security number | For Official Use Only ▶ OMB No. 1545-0008

b Employer identification number (EIN)	1 Wages, tips, other compensation	2 Federal income tax withheld
c Employer's name, address, and ZIP code	3 Social security wages	4 Social security tax withheld
	5 Medicare wages and tips	6 Medicare tax withheld
	7 Social security tips	8 Allocated tips
d Control number	9	10 Dependent care benefits
e Employee's first name and initial / Last name / Suff.	11 Nonqualified plans	12a See instructions for box 12 (Code)
	13 Statutory employee ☐ Retirement plan ☐ Third-party sick pay ☐	12b (Code)
	14 Other	12c (Code)
f Employee's address and ZIP code		12d (Code)

15 State / Employer's state ID number	16 State wages, tips, etc.	17 State income tax	18 Local wages, tips, etc.	19 Local income tax	20 Locality name

Form **W-2** **Wage and Tax Statement** **2012**

Department of the Treasury—Internal Revenue Service

For Privacy Act and Paperwork Reduction Act Notice, see the separate instructions.

Cat. No. 10134D

Copy A For Social Security Administration — Send this entire page with Form W-3 to the Social Security Administration; photocopies are **not** acceptable.

Do Not Cut, Fold, or Staple Forms on This Page

Form W-2 (Page 2)

Notice to Employee

Refund. Even if you do not have to file a tax return, you should file to get a refund if box 2 shows federal income tax withheld or if you can take the earned income credit.

Earned income credit (EIC). You may be able to take the EIC for 2012 if (a) you do not have a qualifying child and you earned less than $13,980 ($19,190 if married filing jointly), (b) you have one qualifying child and you earned less than $36,920 ($42,130 if married filing jointly), (c) you have two qualifying children and you earned less than $41,952 ($47,162 if married filing jointly), or (d) you have three or more qualifying children and you earned less than $45,060 ($50,270 if married filing jointly). You and any qualifying children must have valid social security numbers (SSNs). You cannot take the EIC if your investment income is more than $3,200. **Any EIC that is more than your tax liability is refunded to you, but only if you file a tax return.**

Clergy and religious workers. If you are not subject to social security and Medicare taxes, see Pub. 517, Social Security and Other Information for Members of the Clergy and Religious Workers.

Corrections. If your name, SSN, or address is incorrect, correct Copies B, C, and 2 and ask your employer to correct your employment record. Be sure to ask the employer to file Form W-2c, Corrected Wage and Tax Statement, with the Social Security Administration (SSA) to correct any name, SSN, or money amount error reported to the SSA on Form W-2. If your name and SSN are correct but are not the same as shown on your social security card, you should ask for a new card that displays your correct name at any SSA office or by calling 1-800-772-1213. You also may visit the SSA at *www.socialsecurity.gov.*

Cost of employer-sponsored health coverage (if such cost is provided by the employer). The reporting in Box 12, using Code DD, of the cost of employer-sponsored health coverage is for your information only. **The amount reported with Code DD is not taxable.**

Credit for excess taxes. If you had more than one employer in 2012 and more than $6,826.20 in social security and/or Tier I railroad retirement (RRTA) taxes were withheld, you may be able to claim a credit for the excess against your federal income tax. If you had more than one railroad employer and more than $3,192.90 in Tier II RRTA tax was withheld, you also may be able to claim a credit. See your Form 1040 or Form 1040A instructions and Pub. 505, Tax Withholding and Estimated Tax.

(Also see *Instructions for Employee* on the back of Copy C.)

Form W-2 (Page 3)

Instructions for Employee (Also see *Notice to Employee,* on the back of Copy B.)

Box 1. Enter this amount on the wages line of your tax return.

Box 2. Enter this amount on the federal income tax withheld line of your tax return.

Box 8. This amount is **not** included in boxes 1, 3, 5, or 7. For information on how to report tips on your tax return, see your Form 1040 instructions.

Unless you have records that show you did not receive the amount reported in box 8 as allocated tips, you must file Form 4137, Social Security and Medicare Tax on Unreported Tip Income, with your income tax return to report the allocated tip amount. On Form 4137 you will figure the social security and Medicare tax owed on the allocated tips shown on your Form(s) W-2 that you must report as income and on other tips you did not report to your employer. By filing Form 4137, your social security tips will be credited to your social security record (used to figure your benefits).

Box 10. This amount is the total dependent care benefits that your employer paid to you or incurred on your behalf (including amounts from a section 125 (cafeteria) plan). Any amount over $5,000 is also included in box 1. Complete Form 2441, Child and Dependent Care Expenses, to compute any taxable and nontaxable amounts.

Box 11. This amount is (a) reported in box 1 if it is a distribution made to you from a nonqualified deferred compensation or nongovernmental section 457(b) plan or (b) included in box 3 and/or 5 if it is a prior year deferral under a nonqualified or section 457(b) plan that became taxable for social security and Medicare taxes this year because there is no longer a substantial risk of forfeiture of your right to the deferred amount.

Box 12. The following list explains the codes shown in box 12. You may need this information to complete your tax return. Elective deferrals (codes D, E, F, and S) and designated Roth contributions (codes AA, BB, and EE) under all plans are generally limited to a total of $17,000 ($11,500 if you only have SIMPLE plans; $20,000 for section 403(b) plans if you qualify for the 15-year rule explained in Pub. 571). Deferrals under code G are limited to $17,000. Deferrals under code H are limited to $7,000.

However, if you were at least age 50 in 2012, your employer may have allowed an additional deferral of up to $5,500 ($2,500 for section 401(k)(11) and 408(p) SIMPLE plans). This additional deferral amount is not subject to the overall limit on elective deferrals. For code G, the limit on elective deferrals may be higher for the last 3 years before you reach retirement age. Contact your plan administrator for more information. Amounts in excess of the overall elective deferral limit must be included in income. See the "Wages, Salaries, Tips, etc." line instructions for Form 1040.

Note. If a year follows code D through H, S, Y, AA, BB, or EE, you made a make-up pension contribution for a prior year(s) when you were in military service. To figure whether you made excess deferrals, consider these amounts for the year shown, not the current year. If no year is shown, the contributions are for the current year.

A—Uncollected social security or RRTA tax on tips. Include this tax on Form 1040. See "Other Taxes" in the Form 1040 instructions.

B—Uncollected Medicare tax on tips. Include this tax on Form 1040. See "Other Taxes" in the Form 1040 instructions.

C—Taxable cost of group-term life insurance over $50,000 (included in boxes 1, 3 (up to social security wage base), and 5)

D—Elective deferrals to a section 401(k) cash or deferred arrangement. Also includes deferrals under a SIMPLE retirement account that is part of a section 401(k) arrangement.

E—Elective deferrals under a section 403(b) salary reduction agreement

(continued on back of Copy 2)

Instructions for Employee (*continued from back of Copy C*)

F—Elective deferrals under a section 408(k)(6) salary reduction SEP

G—Elective deferrals and employer contributions (including nonelective deferrals) to a section 457(b) deferred compensation plan

H—Elective deferrals to a section 501(c)(18)(D) tax-exempt organization plan. See "Adjusted Gross Income" in the Form 1040 instructions for how to deduct.

J—Nontaxable sick pay (information only, not included in boxes 1, 3, or 5)

K—20% excise tax on excess golden parachute payments. See "Other Taxes" in the Form 1040 instructions.

L—Substantiated employee business expense reimbursements (nontaxable)

M—Uncollected social security or RRTA tax on taxable cost of group-term life insurance over $50,000 (former employees only). See "Other Taxes" in the Form 1040 instructions.

N—Uncollected Medicare tax on taxable cost of group-term life insurance over $50,000 (former employees only). See "Other Taxes" in the Form 1040 instructions.

P—Excludable moving expense reimbursements paid directly to employee (not included in boxes 1, 3, or 5)

Q—Nontaxable combat pay. See the instructions for Form 1040 or Form 1040A for details on reporting this amount.

R—Employer contributions to your Archer MSA. Report on Form 8853, Archer MSAs and Long-Term Care Insurance Contracts.

S—Employee salary reduction contributions under a section 408(p) SIMPLE plan (not included in box 1)

T—Adoption benefits (not included in box 1). Complete Form 8839, Qualified Adoption Expenses, to compute any taxable and nontaxable amounts.

V—Income from exercise of nonstatutory stock option(s) (included in boxes 1, 3 (up to social security wage base), and 5). See Pub. 525 and instructions for Schedule D (Form 1040) for reporting requirements.

W—Employer contributions (including amounts the employee elected to contribute using a section 125 (cafeteria) plan) to your health savings account. Report on Form 8889, Health Savings Accounts (HSAs).

Y—Deferrals under a section 409A nonqualified deferred compensation plan

Z—Income under section 409A on a nonqualified deferred compensation plan. This amount is also included in box 1. It is subject to an additional 20% tax plus interest. See "Other Taxes" in the Form 1040 instructions.

AA—Designated Roth contributions under a section 401(k) plan

BB—Designated Roth contributions under a section 403(b) plan

DD—Cost of employer-sponsored health coverage. **The amount reported with Code DD is not taxable.**

EE—Designated Roth contributions under a governmental section 457(b) plan. This amount does not apply to contributions under a tax-exempt organization section 457(b) plan.

Box 13. If the "Retirement plan" box is checked, special limits may apply to the amount of traditional IRA contributions you may deduct.

Note. Keep **Copy C** of Form W-2 for at least 3 years after the due date for filing your income tax return. However, to help **protect your social security benefits,** keep Copy C until you begin receiving social security benefits, just in case there is a question about your work record and/or earnings in a particular year.

Form W-2 (Page 4)

Employers, Please Note—

Specific information needed to complete Form W-2 is available in a separate booklet titled the 2012 General Instructions for Forms W-2 and W-3. You can order those instructions and additional forms by calling 1-800-TAX-FORM (1-800-829-3676). You also can get forms and instructions at IRS.gov.

Caution. *Do not send the SSA Forms W-2 and W-3 that you have printed from IRS.gov. The SSA is unable to process these forms. Instead, you can create and submit them online. See* E-filing, *later.*

Due dates. By January 31, 2013, furnish Copies B, C, and 2 to each person who was your employee during 2012. By February 28, 2013, send Copy A of Form(s) W-2 and W-3 to the SSA. However, if you file electronically, the due date is April 1, 2013. See the separate instructions.

Need help? If you have questions about reporting on Form W-2, call the information reporting customer service site toll free at 1-866-455-7438 or 304-263-8700 (not toll free). For TTY/TDD equipment, call 304-579-4827 (not toll free). The hours of operation are 8:30 a.m. to 4:30 p.m. Eastern time.

E-filing. If you file 250 or more Form(s) W-2, you must file electronically. E-filing can save you time and effort, even if you are not required to do so. Employers may now use the SSA's W-2 Online service to create, save, print, and submit up to 50 Form(s) W-2 at a time over the internet. For information, visit the SSA's Employer W-2 Filing Instructions & Information website at *www.socialsecurity.gov/employer*.

Future developments. The IRS has created a page on IRS.gov for information about Form W-2 and its instructions at *www.irs.gov/w2.* Information about any future developments affecting Form W-2 (such as legislation enacted after we release it) will be posted on that page.

Form W-2 & W-3 Instructions (Page 1)

2012 General Instructions for Forms W-2 and W-3

Department of the Treasury
Internal Revenue Service

(Including Forms W-2AS, W-2GU, W-2VI, W-3SS, W-2c, and W-3c)

Contents **Page**

Section references are to the Internal Revenue Code unless otherwise noted.

What's New

Future developments. The IRS has created a page on IRS.gov for information about Forms W-2 and W-3 and their instructions, at *www.irs.gov/w2*. Information about any future developments affecting Forms W-2 and W-3 and their instructions (such as legislation enacted after we release them) will be posted on that page.

New title for instructions. The title of the Instructions for Forms W-2 and W-3 has been changed to the General Instructions for Forms W-2 and W-3. These instructions now include instructions for U.S. possessions and corrected wage and tax statements. The separate Instructions for Forms W-2AS, W-2GU, W-2VI, and W-3SS, and the Instructions for Forms W-2c and W-3c will not be updated. In these instructions, references to Forms W-2 and W-3 include Forms W-2AS, W-2GU, W-2VI, and W-3SS, respectively, unless otherwise noted.

Form W-3, Kind of Employer. The specific instructions for the checkboxes in box b, Kind of Employer, of Form W-3 (box c for Form W-3c) include examples for various types of section 501(c) organizations. For more information, see *Box b—Kind of Employer* on page 18.

Form W-3c, Box b. Box b of Form W-3c has been expanded to include an additional line for name, address, and ZIP code.

Form W-3c, Kind of Employer. Box c of Form W-3c has been expanded to include a new section, Kind of Employer, which contains five new checkboxes. All filers are required to check one of these new checkboxes. For more information, see *Box c—Kind of Employer* on page 23.

Foreign agricultural workers. You must report on Form W-2 compensation of $600 or more that you pay to H-2A visa agricultural workers. See *Foreign agricultural workers* on page 7 for details.

Employee social security tax withholding. The rate of social security tax withholding (for employees only) is restored to 6.2% for wage payments made in 2012. See *Box 4—Social security tax withheld* on page 13.

Reporting the cost of group health insurance coverage. You must report the cost of employer-sponsored health coverage in box 12 using code DD. However, transitional relief applies to certain employers and certain types of plans. For more information, see *Code DD* on page 17.

Reminders

TIP ***Get it done faster... E-file your Forms W-2 with the SSA. See page 2.***

Automatic extension for e-filers. Receive an automatic filing extension by e-filing your Forms W-2 with the Social Security Administration (SSA). The due date for e-filing 2012 Form W-2 Copy A with the SSA is extended to April 1, 2013. See *E-filing* on page 2.

Business Services Online (BSO). The SSA has enhanced its secure BSO website to make it easier to register and navigate. Use BSO's online fill-in forms to create, save, and submit Forms W-2 and W-2c to the SSA electronically. BSO lets you print copies of these forms to file with state or local governments, distribute to your employees, and keep for your records. BSO generates Form W-3 automatically based on your Forms W-2. You also can use BSO to upload wage files to the SSA, check on the status of previously submitted wage reports, and take advantage of other convenient services for employers and businesses. Visit the SSA's Employer W-2 Filing Instructions & Information website at *www.socialsecurity.gov/employer* for more information about using BSO to save time for your organization. Here you also will find forms and publications used for wage reporting, information about verifying employee social security numbers online, how to reach an SSA employer services representative for your region, and more.

TIP *Preview BSO by viewing a brief online tutorial. Go to www.socialsecurity.gov/bso/bsowelcome.html and click on "Tutorial."*

Correcting wage reports. You can use BSO to create, save, print, and submit Forms W-2c, Corrected Wage and Tax Statement, online for the current year as well as

Nov 04, 2011 Cat. No. 25979S

Form W-2 & W-3 Instructions (Page 2)

for prior years. After logging in to BSO, navigate to the Electronic Wage Reporting home page and click on the "Forms W-2c/W-3c Online" tab. See *E-filing* below and *E-filing Forms W-2c and W-3c* on page 20.

Distributions from governmental section 457(b) plans of state and local agencies. Generally, report distributions from section 457(b) plans of state and local agencies on Form 1099-R, Distributions From Pensions, Annuities, Retirement or Profit-Sharing Plans, IRAs, Insurance Contracts, etc. See Notice 2003-20 for details. You can find Notice 2003-20 on page 894 of Internal Revenue Bulletin 2003-19 at *www.irs.gov/pub/irs-irbs/irb03-19.pdf.*

Earned income credit (EIC) notice (not applicable to Forms W-2AS, W-2GU, and W-2VI). You must notify employees who have no income tax withheld that they may be able to claim an income tax refund because of the EIC. You can do this by using the official IRS Form W-2 with the EIC notice on the back of Copy B or a substitute Form W-2 with the same statement. You must give your employee Notice 797, Possible Federal Tax Refund Due to the Earned Income Credit (EIC), or your own statement that contains the same wording if (a) you use a substitute Form W-2 that does not contain the EIC notice, (b) you are not required to furnish Form W-2, or (c) you do not furnish a timely Form W-2 to your employee. For more information, see section 10 in Pub. 15 (Circular E), Employer's Tax Guide.

Electronic statements for employees. Furnishing Copies B, C, and 2 of Forms W-2 to your employees electronically may save you time and effort. See Pub. 15-A, Employer's Supplemental Tax Guide, for additional information.

E-filing. The SSA encourages all employers to *e-file.* E-filing can save you time and effort and helps ensure accuracy. You must *e-file* if you are required to file 250 or more Forms W-2 or W-2c. If you are required to *e-file* but fail to do so, you may incur a penalty.

Waiver from e-filing. You can request a waiver from this requirement by filing Form 8508, Request for Waiver From Filing Information Returns Electronically. Submit Form 8508 to the IRS at least 45 days before the due date of Form W-2, or 45 days before you file your first Form W-2c. See Form 8508 for information about filing this form.

The SSA's BSO website makes e-filing easy by providing two ways to submit your Forms W-2 or W-2c Copy A and Forms W-3 or W-3c information.

- If you need to file 50 or fewer Forms W-2 or W-2c at a time, you can use BSO to create them online. BSO guides you through the process of creating Forms W-2 or W-2c, saving and printing them, and submitting them to the SSA when you are ready. You do not have to wait until you have submitted Forms W-2 or W-2c to the SSA before printing copies for your employees. BSO generates Form W-3 or W-3c automatically based on your Forms W-2 or W-2c.
- If you need to file more than 50 Forms W-2 or W-2c, BSO's "file upload" feature might be the best e-filing method for your business or organization. To obtain file format specifications, visit the SSA's Employer W-2 Filing Instructions & Information website at *www.socialsecurity.gov/employer* and click on "E-Filing Format." This information is also available by calling the SSA's Employer Reporting Branch at 1-800-772-6270 (toll free).

CAUTION: *If you* e-file, *do not file the same returns using paper forms.*

For more information about e-filing Forms W-2 or W-2c and a link to the BSO website, visit the SSA's Employer W-2 Filing Instructions & Information website at *www.socialsecurity.gov/employer.*

In a few situations, reporting instructions vary depending on the filing method you choose. For example, you can include every type of box 12 amount in one employee wage record if you upload an electronic file. If you file on paper or create Forms W-2 online, you can include only four box 12 amounts per Form W-2. See the *TIP* for Copy A on page 14.

Forms 944 or 944-SS. Use the "944" or "944-SS" checkbox in box b of Form W-3 or Form W-3SS if you filed Form 944, Employer's ANNUAL Federal Tax Return, or Form 944-SS, Employer's ANNUAL Federal Tax Return – American Samoa, Guam, the Commonwealth of the Northern Mariana Islands, and the U.S. Virgin Islands. Also use the "944" checkbox if you filed Formulario 944(SP), the Spanish-language version of Form 944.

Forms W-2 for U.S. possessions. In these instructions, reference to Forms W-2 and W-3 includes Forms W-2AS, W-2GU, W-2VI, and W-3SS, unless otherwise noted. These instructions are not applicable to wage and tax statements for Puerto Rico or the Commonwealth of the Northern Mariana Islands. Form W-2AS is used to report American Samoa wages paid by American Samoa employers, Form W-2CM is used to report the Commonwealth of the Northern Mariana Islands (CNMI) wages paid by CNMI employers, Form W-2GU is used to report Guam wages paid by Guam employers, and Form W-2VI is used to report U.S. Virgin Islands (USVI) wages paid by USVI employers. Do not use these forms to report wages subject to U.S. income tax withholding. Instead, use Form W-2 to show U.S. income tax withheld.

Military differential pay. Employers paying their employees while they are on active duty in the United States uniformed services should treat these payments as wages subject to income tax withholding. See *Military differential pay* on page 9.

Military Spouses Residency Relief Act (MSRRA). You may be required to report wages and taxes on a form different from the form you generally use if an employee claims residence or domicile under MSRRA in a different jurisdiction in one of the 50 states, the District of Columbia, American Samoa, the Commonwealth of the Northern Mariana Islands, Puerto Rico, or the U.S. Virgin Islands.

Under MSRRA, the spouse of an active duty servicemember (civilian spouse) may keep his or her prior residence or domicile for tax purposes (tax residence) when accompanying the servicemember spouse, who is relocating under military orders, to a new military duty station in one of the 50 states, the District of Columbia, or a U.S. possession. Before relocating, both spouses must have had the same tax residence.

For example, if a civilian spouse is working in Guam but properly claims tax residence in one of the 50 states under MSRRA, his or her income from services would not be taxable income for Guam tax purposes. Federal income taxes should be withheld and remitted to the IRS. State and local income taxes may need to be withheld

-2- General Instructions for Forms W-2 and W-3 (2012)

Form W-2 & W-3 Instructions (Page 3)

and remitted to state and local tax authorities. You should consult with state, local, or U.S. possession tax authorities regarding your withholding obligations under MSRRA.

Nonqualified deferred compensation plans. You are not required to complete box 12 with code Y (deferrals under a section 409A nonqualified deferred compensation plan). Section 409A provides that all amounts deferred under a nonqualified deferred compensation (NQDC) plan for all tax years are includible in gross income unless certain requirements are satisfied. See *Nonqualified deferred compensation plans* on page 9.

Substitute forms. You may use an acceptable substitute form instead of an official IRS form.

Form W-2. If you are not using the official IRS form to furnish Form W-2 to employees or to file with the SSA, you may use an acceptable substitute form that complies with the rules in Pub. 1141, General Rules and Specifications for Substitute Forms W-2 and W-3. Pub. 1141 is a revenue procedure that explains the requirements for format and content of substitute Forms W-2 and W-3. Your substitute forms must comply with the requirements in Pub. 1141.

Form W-2c. If you are not using the official IRS form to furnish Form W-2c to employees or to file with the SSA, you may use an acceptable substitute form that complies with the rules in Pub. 1223, General Rules and Specifications for Substitute Forms W-2c and W-3c. Pub. 1223 is a revenue procedure that explains the requirements for format and content of substitute Forms W-2c and W-3c. Your substitute forms must comply with the requirements in Pub. 1223.

Need Help?

Help with e-filing. If you have questions about how to register or use BSO, call 1-800-772-6270 (toll free) to speak with an employer reporting specialist at the SSA. The hours of operation are Monday through Friday from 7:00 a.m. to 7:00 p.m. Eastern time. If you experience problems using any of the services within BSO, call 1-888-772-2970 (toll free). To speak with the SSA's employer services liaison officer (ESLO) for the U.S. Virgin Islands, call 1-212-264-1117 (not a toll-free number). For Guam or American Samoa, call 1-510-970-8247 (not a toll-free number). For all other employers, contact the ESLO that services your region. For a complete telephone listing, visit the SSA's Employer W-2 Filing Instructions & Information website at *www.socialsecurity.gov/employer*.

Information reporting customer service site. The IRS operates a centralized customer service site to answer questions about reporting on Forms W-2, W-3, 1099, and other information returns. If you have questions about reporting on these forms, call 1-866-455-7438 (toll free). The hours of operation are Monday through Friday from 8:30 a.m. to 4:30 p.m. Eastern time.

Hearing impaired TTY/TDD equipment. Telephone help is available using TTY/TDD equipment. If you have questions about reporting on information returns (Forms 1096, 1097, 1098, 1099, 3921, 3922, 5498, W-2, W-2G, and W-3), call 1-304-579-4827. For any other tax information, call 1-800-829-4059.

Employment tax information. Detailed employment tax information is given in:

- Pub. 15 (Circular E), Employer's Tax Guide,
- Pub. 15-A, Employer's Supplemental Tax Guide,
- Pub. 15-B, Employer's Tax Guide to Fringe Benefits, and
- Pub. 51 (Circular A), Agricultural Employer's Tax Guide.

You also can call the IRS with your employment tax questions at 1-800-829-4933 or visit IRS.gov and type "Employment Taxes" in the search box.

How To Get Forms and Publications

Internet. You can access IRS.gov 24 hours a day, 7 days a week to:

- Download, view, and order tax forms, instructions, and publications.
- Access commercial tax preparation and *e-file* services.
- Research your tax questions online.
- See answers to frequently asked tax questions.
- Search publications online by topic or keyword.
- View Internal Revenue Bulletins published in the last few years.
- Sign up to receive local and national tax news by email.

CAUTION *Do not download Copy A of Forms W-2, W-3, W-2c, or W-3c from IRS.gov and then file them with the SSA. The SSA accepts only e-filed reports and the official red-ink versions (or approved substitute versions) of these forms. For information about e-filing, see* E-filing *on page 2.*

Free tax services. To find out what services are available, get Pub. 910, IRS Guide to Free Tax Services. It contains lists of free tax information sources, including publications, services, and free tax education and assistance programs. It also has an index of over 100 TeleTax topics (recorded tax information) you can listen to on your telephone. Accessible versions of IRS published products are available on request in a variety of alternative formats.

DVD of tax products. You can order Publication 1796, IRS Tax Products DVD, and obtain:

- Current-year forms, instructions, and publications.
- Prior-year forms, instructions, and publications.
- Tax Map: an electronic research tool and finding aid.
- Tax law frequently asked questions.
- Tax Topics from the IRS telephone response system.
- Internal Revenue Code—Title 26 of the U.S. Code.
- Fill-in, print, and save features for most tax forms.
- Internal Revenue Bulletins.
- Toll free and email technical support.
- Two releases during the year.

-The first release will ship the beginning of January 2012.

-The final release will ship the beginning of March 2012.

Purchase the DVD from National Technical Information Service (NTIS) at *www.irs.gov/cdorders* for $30 (no handling fee) or call 1-877-233-6767 toll free to purchase the DVD for $30 (plus a $6 handling fee).

Mail. You can send your order for forms, instructions, and publications to the following address. You should receive a response within 10 days after your request is received.

General Instructions for Forms W-2 and W-3 (2012) **-3-**

Form W-2 & W-3 Instructions (Page 4)

Internal Revenue Service
1201 N. Mitsubishi Parkway
Bloomington, IL 61705-6613

Phone. Many services are available by phone.

- *Ordering forms, instructions, and publications.* Call 1-800-829-3676 to order current-year forms, instructions, and publications, and prior-year forms and instructions. You should receive your order within 10 days.
- *TTY/TDD equipment.* If you have access to TTY/TDD equipment, call 1-800-829-4059 to order forms and publications.

Common Errors on Forms W-2

Forms W-2 provide information to your employees, the SSA, the IRS, and state and local governments. Avoid making the following errors, which cause processing delays.

Do not:

- Omit the decimal point and cents from entries.
- Make entries using ink that is too light. Use only black ink.
- Make entries that are too small or too large. Use 12-point Courier font, if possible.
- Add dollar signs to the money-amount boxes. They have been removed from Copy A and are not required.
- Inappropriately check the "Retirement plan" checkbox in box 13. See *Retirement plan* on page 17.
- Misformat the employee's name in box e. Enter the employee's first name and middle initial in the first box, his or her surname in the second box, and his or her suffix (such as "Jr.") in the third box (optional).

General Instructions for Forms W-2 and W-3

Who must file Form W-2. Every employer engaged in a trade or business who pays remuneration, including noncash payments, of $600 or more for the year for services performed by an employee must file a Form W-2 for each employee (even if the employee is related to the employer) from whom:

- Income, social security, or Medicare tax was withheld.
- Income tax would have been withheld if the employee had claimed no more than one withholding allowance or had not claimed exemption from withholding on Form W-4, Employee's Withholding Allowance Certificate.

If you are required to file 250 or more Forms W-2 or want to take advantage of the benefits of e-filing, see *E-filing* on page 2.

Who must file Form W-3. Anyone required to file Form W-2 must file Form W-3 to transmit Copy A of Forms W-2. Make a copy of Form W-3; keep it and Copy D (For Employer) of Forms W-2 with your records for 4 years. Be sure to use Form W-3 for the correct year. If you are filing Forms W-2 electronically, see *E-filing* on page 2.

Household employers. Even employers with only one household employee must file Form W-3 to transmit Copy A of Form W-2. On Form W-3 check the "Hshld. emp." checkbox in box b. For more information, see Schedule H (Form 1040), Household Employment Taxes, and its separate instructions. You must have an employer identification number (EIN). See *Box b—Employer identification number (EIN)* on page 12.

Who may sign Form W-3. A transmitter or sender (including a service bureau, reporting agent, paying agent, or disbursing agent) may sign Form W-3 (or use its PIN to *e-file*) for the employer or payer only if the sender satisfies both of the following.

- It is authorized to sign by an agency agreement (whether oral, written, or implied) that is valid under state law; and
- It writes "For (name of payer)" next to the signature (paper Form W-3 only).

CAUTION *Use of a reporting agent or other third-party payroll service provider does not relieve an employer of the responsibility to ensure that Forms W-2 are furnished to employees and that Forms W-2 and W-3 are filed with the SSA, correctly and on time.*

Be sure that the payer's name and EIN on Forms W-2 and W-3 are the same as those used on the Form 941, Employer's QUARTERLY Federal Tax Return; Form 943, Employer's Annual Federal Tax Return for Agricultural Employees; Form 944; Form 944-SS; Form CT-1, Employer's Annual Railroad Retirement Tax Return; or Schedule H (Form 1040) filed by or for the payer.

When to file. If you file using paper forms, you must file Copy A of Form W-2 with Form W-3 by February 28, 2013. However, if you *e-file*, the due date is automatically extended to April 1, 2013. You may owe a penalty for each Form W-2 that you file late. See *Penalties* on page 10. If you terminate your business, see *Terminating a business* on page 10.

Extension to file. You may request an automatic extension of time to file Form W-2 with the SSA by sending Form 8809, Application for Extension of Time To File Information Returns, to the address shown on Form 8809. You must request the extension before the due date of Forms W-2. You will have an additional 30 days to file. See Form 8809 for details.

CAUTION *Even if you request an extension of time to file Form W-2, you still must furnish Form W-2 to your employees by January 31, 2013. But see* Extension of time to furnish Forms W-2 to employees *on page 5.*

Where to file paper Forms W-2 and W-3. File Copy A of Form W-2 with Form W-3 at the following address.

Social Security Administration
Data Operations Center
Wilkes-Barre, PA 18769-0001

TIP *If you use "Certified Mail" to file, change the ZIP code to "18769-0002." If you use an IRS-approved private delivery service, add "Attn: W-2 Process, 1150 E. Mountain Dr." to the address and change the ZIP code to "18702-7997." See Pub. 15 (Circular E) for a list of IRS-approved private delivery services.*

CAUTION *Do not send cash, checks, money orders, or other forms of payment with the Forms W-2 and W-3 that you submit to the SSA. Employment tax forms (for example, Form 941 or Form 943), remittances, and Forms 1099 must be sent to the IRS.*

Copy 1. Send Copy 1 of Form W-2, if required, to your state, city, or local tax department. For more information concerning Copy 1 (including how to complete boxes 15 through 20), contact your state, city, or local tax department.

-4- **General Instructions for Forms W-2 and W-3 (2012)**

Form W-2 & W-3 Instructions (Page 5)

American Samoa. File Copy 1 of Form W-3SS and Forms W-2AS at the following address.

American Samoa Tax Office
Executive Office Building
First Floor
Pago Pago, AS 96799

For additional information about Form W-2AS, see *www.americansamoa.gov*.

Guam. File Copy 1 of Form W-3SS and Forms W-2GU at the following address.

Guam Department of Revenue and Taxation
P.O. Box 23607
GMF, GU 96921

For additional information about Form W-2GU, see *www.guamtax.com*.

United States Virgin Islands. File Copy 1 of Form W-3SS and Forms W-2VI at the following address.

Virgin Islands Bureau of Internal Revenue
6115 Estate Smith Bay
Suite 225
St. Thomas, VI 00802

For additional information about Form W-2VI, see *www.viirb.com*.

Commonwealth of the Northern Mariana Islands. File Form OS-3710 and Copy 1 of Forms W-2CM at the following address.

Division of Revenue and Taxation
Commonwealth of the Northern Mariana Islands
P.O. Box 5234 CHRB
Saipan, MP 96950

Forms OS-3710 and W-2CM are not IRS forms. For additional information about Form W-2CM, see *www.cnmidof.net*.

Shipping and mailing. If you file more than one type of employment tax form, group Forms W-2 of the same type with a separate Form W-3 for each type, and send them in separate groups. See the specific instructions for box b of Form W-3 on page 18.

Prepare and file Forms W-2 either alphabetically by employees' last names or numerically by employees' social security numbers. Do not staple or tape Form W-3 to the related Forms W-2 or Forms W-2 to each other. These forms are machine read. Staple holes or tears interfere with machine reading. Also, do not fold Forms W-2 and W-3. Send the forms to the SSA in a flat mailing.

Furnishing Copies B, C, and 2 to employees. Generally, you must furnish Copies B, C, and 2 of Form W-2 to your employees by January 31, 2013. You will meet the "furnish" requirement if the form is properly addressed and mailed on or before the due date.

If employment ends before December 31, 2012, you may furnish copies to the employee at any time after employment ends, but no later than January 31, 2013. If an employee asks for Form W-2, give him or her the completed copies within 30 days of the request or within 30 days of the final wage payment, whichever is later. However, if you terminate your business, see *Terminating a business* on page 10.

You may furnish Forms W-2 to employees on IRS official forms or on acceptable substitute forms. See *Substitute forms* on page 3. Be sure the Forms W-2 you provide to employees are clear and legible and comply with the requirements in Pub. 1141.

Extension of time to furnish Forms W-2 to employees. You may request an extension of time to furnish Forms W-2 to employees by sending a letter to:

Internal Revenue Service
Information Returns Branch, Mail Stop 4360
Attn: Extension of Time Coordinator
240 Murall Drive
Kearneysville, WV 25430

Mail your letter on or before the due date for furnishing Forms W-2 to employees. It must include:

- Your name and address,
- Your EIN,
- A statement that you are requesting an extension to furnish "Forms W-2" to employees,
- The reason for delay, and
- Your signature or that of your authorized agent.

CAUTION *Requests for an extension of time to furnish recipient statements for more than 10 payers must be submitted electronically. See Publication 1220, Part D, Sec. 4.*

Undeliverable Forms W-2. Keep for 4 years any employee copies of Forms W-2 that you tried to but could not deliver. However, if the undelivered Form W-2 can be produced electronically through April 15th of the fourth year after the year at issue, you do not need to keep undeliverable employee copies. Do not send undeliverable Forms W-2 to the SSA.

Taxpayer identification numbers (TINs). Employers use an employer identification number (EIN) (00-0000000). Employees use a social security number (SSN) (000-00-0000). When you list a number, separate the nine digits properly to show the kind of number. Do not accept an individual taxpayer identification number (ITIN) for employment purposes. For more information, see section 4 of Pub. 15 (Circular E).

The IRS uses SSNs to check the payments that you report against the amounts shown on employees' tax returns. The SSA uses SSNs to record employees' earnings for future social security and Medicare benefits. When you prepare Form W-2, be sure to show the correct SSN for each employee. For information about verifying SSNs, see section 4 of Pub. 15 (Circular E) or visit the SSA's Employer W-2 Filing Instructions & Information website at *www.socialsecurity.gov/employer*.

Special Reporting Situations for Form W-2

Adoption benefits. Amounts paid or expenses incurred by an employer for qualified adoption expenses under an adoption assistance program are not subject to federal income tax withholding and are not reportable in box 1. However, these amounts (including adoption benefits paid from a section 125 (cafeteria) plan, but not including adoption benefits forfeited from a cafeteria plan) are subject to social security, Medicare, and railroad retirement taxes and must be reported in boxes 3 and 5. (Use box 14 if railroad retirement taxes apply.) Also, the total amount must be reported in box 12 with code T.

For more information on adoption benefits, see Notice 97-9, 1997-1 C.B. 365, which is on page 35 of Internal Revenue Bulletin 1997-2 at *www.irs.gov/pub/irs-irbs/*

General Instructions for Forms W-2 and W-3 (2012) -5-

Form W-2 & W-3 Instructions (Page 6)

irb97-02.pdf. Advise your employees to see the Instructions for Form 8839, Qualified Adoption Expenses.

Agent reporting. Generally, an agent who has an approved Form 2678, Employer/Payer Appointment of Agent, should enter the agent's name as the employer in box c of Form W-2 and file only one Form W-2 for each employee. However, if the agent (a) is acting as an agent for two or more employers or is an employer and is acting as an agent for another employer, and (b) pays social security wages to an individual on behalf of more than one employer, and (c) the total of the individual's social security wages from these employers is greater than the social security wage base, the agent must file separate Forms W-2 for the affected employee reflecting the wages paid by each employer.

On the Form W-2 the agent should enter the following in box c of Form W-2.

(Name of agent)
Agent for (name of employer)
Address of agent

Each Form W-2 should reflect the EIN of the agent in box b. An agent files one Form W-3 for all of the Forms W-2 and enters its own information in boxes e, f, and g of Form W-3 as it appears on the agent's related employment tax returns (for example, Form 941). Enter the client-employer's EIN in box h of Form W-3 if the Forms W-2 relate to only one employer (other than the agent); if not, leave box h blank. See Rev. Proc. 70-6, 1970-1 C.B. 420; Notice 2003-70, 2003-43 I.R.B. 916, available at *www.irs.gov/irb/2003-43_IRB/ar09.html*; and the Instructions for Form 2678 for procedures to be followed in applying to be an agent. For state and local health and welfare agencies wishing to act as agents under section 3504, see Rev. Proc. 80-4, 1980-1 C.B. 581.

TIP *Generally, an agent is not responsible for refunding excess social security or railroad retirement (RRTA) tax withheld from employees. If an employee worked for more than one employer during 2012 and had more than $6,826.20 in social security and Tier I RRTA tax withheld, he or she should claim the excess on the appropriate line of Form 1040, Form 1040A, or Form 1040NR. If an employee had more than $3,192.90 in Tier II RRTA tax withheld from more than one employer, the employee should claim a refund on Form 843, Claim for Refund and Request for Abatement.*

Archer MSA. An employer's contribution to an employee's Archer MSA is not subject to federal income tax withholding or social security, Medicare, or railroad retirement taxes if it is reasonable to believe at the time of the payment that the contribution will be excludable from the employee's income. However, if it is not reasonable to believe at the time of payment that the contribution will be excludable from the employee's income, employer contributions are subject to income tax withholding and social security and Medicare taxes (or railroad retirement taxes, if applicable) and must be reported in boxes 1, 3, and 5. (Use box 14 if railroad retirement taxes apply.)

You must report all employer contributions to an Archer MSA in box 12 of Form W-2 with code R. Employer contributions to an Archer MSA that are not excludable from the income of the employee also must be reported in box 1.

An employee's contributions to an Archer MSA are includible in income as wages and are subject to federal income tax withholding and social security and Medicare taxes (or railroad retirement taxes, if applicable). Employee contributions are deductible, within limits, on the employee's Form 1040.

For more information, see Pub. 969, Health Savings Accounts and Other Tax-Favored Health Plans, and Notice 96-53, which is found on page 5 of Internal Revenue Bulletin 1996-51 at *www.irs.gov/pub/irs-irbs/irb96-51.pdf*.

Clergy and religious workers. For certain members of the clergy and religious workers who are not subject to social security and Medicare taxes as employees, boxes 3 and 5 of Form W-2 should be left blank. You may include a minister's parsonage and/or utilities allowance in box 14. For information on the rules that apply to ministers and certain other religious workers, see Pub. 517, Social Security and Other Information for Members of the Clergy and Religious Workers, and *Section 4–Religious Exemptions and Special Rules for Ministers* in Pub. 15-A.

Deceased employee's wages. If an employee dies during the year, you must report the accrued wages, vacation pay, and other compensation paid after the date of death. Also report wages that were available to the employee while he or she was alive, regardless of whether they actually were in the possession of the employee, as well as any other regular wage payment, even if you may have to reissue the payment in the name of the estate or beneficiary.

If you made the payment after the employee's death but in the same year the employee died, you must withhold social security and Medicare taxes on the payment and report the payment on the employee's Form W-2 only as social security and Medicare wages to ensure proper social security and Medicare credit is received. On the employee's Form W-2, show the payment as social security wages (box 3) and Medicare wages and tips (box 5) and the social security and Medicare taxes withheld in boxes 4 and 6. Do not show the payment in box 1.

If you made the payment after the year of death, do not report it on Form W-2, and do not withhold social security and Medicare taxes.

Whether the payment is made in the year of death or after the year of death, you also must report it in box 3 of Form 1099-MISC, Miscellaneous Income, for the payment to the estate or beneficiary. Use the name and taxpayer identification number (TIN) of the payment recipient on Form 1099-MISC. However, if the payment is a reissuance of wages that were constructively received by the deceased individual while he or she was still alive, do not report it on Form 1099-MISC.

Example. Before Employee A's death on June 15, 2012, A was employed by Employer X and received $10,000 in wages on which federal income tax of $1,500 was withheld. When A died, X owed A $2,000 in wages and $1,000 in accrued vacation pay. The total of $3,000 (less the social security and Medicare taxes withheld) was paid to A's estate on July 20, 2012. Because X made the payment during the year of death, X must withhold social security and Medicare taxes on the $3,000 payment and must complete Form W-2 as follows.

- Box a – Employee A's SSN

Form W-2 & W-3 Instructions (Page 7)

- Box e – Employee A's name
- Box f – Employee A's address
- Box 1 – 10000.00 (does not include the $3,000 accrued wages and vacation pay)
- Box 2 – 1500.00
- Box 3 – 13000.00 (includes the $3,000 accrued wages and vacation pay)
- Box 4 – 806.00 (6.2% of the amount in box 3)
- Box 5 – 13000.00 (includes the $3,000 accrued wages and vacation pay)
- Box 6 – 188.50 (1.45% of the amount in box 5)

CAUTION *Employer X also must complete Form 1099-MISC as follows.*

- *Boxes for recipient's name, address, and TIN—the estate's name, address, and TIN.*
- *Box 3: 3000.00 (Even though amounts were withheld for social security and Medicare taxes, the gross amount is reported here.)*

If Employer X made the payment after the year of death, the $3,000 would not be subject to social security and Medicare taxes and would not be shown on Form W-2. However, the employer would still file Form 1099-MISC.

Designated Roth contributions. Under section 402A, a participant in a section 401(k) plan, under a 403(b) salary reduction agreement, or in a governmental 457(b) plan that includes a qualified Roth contribution program, may elect to make designated Roth contributions to the plan or program in lieu of elective deferrals. Designated Roth contributions are subject to federal income tax withholding and social security and Medicare taxes (and railroad retirement taxes, if applicable) and must be reported in boxes 1, 3, and 5. (Use box 14 if railroad retirement taxes apply.)

Section 402A requires separate reporting of the yearly designated Roth contributions. Designated Roth contributions to 401(k) plans will be reported using code AA in box 12; designated Roth contributions under 403(b) salary reduction agreements will be reported using code BB in box 12; and designated Roth contributions under a governmental section 457(b) plan will be reported using Code EE in box 12. For reporting instructions, see *Code AA* and *Code BB* on page 16 and *Code EE* on page 17.

Educational assistance programs. Employer-provided educational assistance that qualifies as a working condition benefit is excludable from an employee's wages. For employer-provided educational assistance that does not qualify as a working condition benefit, a $5,250 exclusion may apply if the assistance is provided under an educational assistance program under section 127. See Pub. 970, Tax Benefits for Education, and section 2 of Pub. 15-B for more information. Also see *Box 1—Wages, tips, other compensation* on page 12.

Election workers. Report on Form W-2 payments of $600 or more to election workers for services performed in state, county, and municipal elections. File Form W-2 for payments of less than $600 paid to election workers if social security and Medicare taxes were withheld under a section 218 (Social Security Act) agreement. Do not report election worker payments on Form 1099-MISC.

If the election worker is employed in another capacity with the same government entity, see Rev. Rul. 2000-6, which is on page 512 of Internal Revenue Bulletin 2000-6 at www.irs.gov/pub/irs-irbs/irb00-06.pdf.

Employee business expense reimbursements. Reimbursements to employees for business expenses must be reported as follows.

- Generally, payments made under an accountable plan are excluded from the employee's gross income and are not reported on Form W-2. However, if you pay a per diem or mileage allowance and the amount paid for substantiated miles or days traveled exceeds the amount treated as substantiated under IRS rules, you must report as wages on Form W-2 the amount in excess of the amount treated as substantiated. The excess amount is subject to income tax withholding and social security and Medicare taxes. Report the amount treated as substantiated (that is, the nontaxable portion) in box 12 using code L. See *Code L— Substantiated employee business expense reimbursements* on page 16.
- Payments made under a nonaccountable plan are reported as wages on Form W-2 and are subject to federal income tax withholding and social security and Medicare taxes.

For more information on accountable plans, nonaccountable plans, amounts treated as substantiated under a per diem or mileage allowance, the standard mileage rate, the per diem substantiation method, and the high-low substantiation method, see Pub. 463, Travel, Entertainment, Gift, and Car Expenses; Pub. 1542, Per Diem Rates; and section 5 of Pub. 15 (Circular E).

Employee's social security and Medicare taxes paid by employer. If you paid your employee's share of social security and Medicare taxes rather than deducting them from the employee's wages, you must include these payments as wages subject to federal (or American Samoa, Guam, or U.S. Virgin Islands) income tax withholding and social security, Medicare, and federal unemployment (FUTA) taxes. The amount to include as wages is determined by using the formula contained in the discussion of *Employee's Portion of Taxes Paid by Employer* in section 7 of Pub. 15-A.

CAUTION *This does not apply to household and agricultural employers. If you pay a household or agricultural employee's social security and Medicare taxes, you must include these payments in the employee's wages for income tax withholding purposes. However, the wage increase due to the tax payments is not subject to social security, Medicare, or FUTA taxes. For information on completing Forms W-2 and W-3 in this situation, see the Instructions for Schedule H (Form 1040) and section 4 of Pub. 51 (Circular A).*

Foreign agricultural workers. You must report compensation of $600 or more paid in a calendar year to an H-2A visa agricultural worker for agricultural labor. If the H-2A visa agricultural worker furnishes a valid taxpayer identification number, report these payments in box 1 of Form W-2. If the worker does not furnish a valid taxpayer identification number, report the payments on Form 1099-MISC. See *Form 1099-MISC* on page 8.

On Form W-2, no amount should be reported in boxes 3 or 5. In most cases, you do not need to withhold federal income tax from compensation paid to H-2A visa agricultural workers. Employers should withhold federal income tax only if the H-2A visa agricultural worker and the employer agree to withhold. The H-2A visa agricultural worker must provide a completed Form W-4. If the employer withholds income tax, the employer must

Form W-2 & W-3 Instructions (Page 8)

report the tax withheld in box 2 of Form W-2 and on line 6 of Form 943. See Publication 51 (Circular A).

Form 1099-MISC. If the H-2A visa agricultural worker fails to furnish a taxpayer identification number to the employer, and the total annual payments made to the H-2A visa agricultural worker are $600 or more, the employer must begin backup withholding on the payments made until the H-2A visa agricultural worker furnishes a valid taxpayer identification number. Employers must report the compensation paid and any backup withholding on Forms 1099-MISC and Form 945. See the 2012 Instructions for Form 1099-MISC and the 2012 Instructions for Form 945.

For more information, visit the Foreign Agricultural Workers page on IRS.gov.

Fringe benefits. Include all taxable fringe benefits in box 1 of Form W-2 as wages, tips, and other compensation and, if applicable, in boxes 3 and 5 as social security and Medicare wages. Although not required, you may include the total value of fringe benefits in box 14 (or on a separate statement). However, if you provided your employee a vehicle and included 100% of its annual lease value in the employee's income, you must separately report this value to the employee in box 14 (or on a separate statement). The employee can then figure the value of any business use of the vehicle and report it on Form 2106, Employee Business Expenses. Also see Pub. 15-B for more information.

CAUTION *If you used the commuting rule or the vehicle cents-per-mile rule to value the personal use of the vehicle, you cannot include 100% of the value of the use of the vehicle in the employee's income. See Pub. 15-B.*

Golden parachute payments (not applicable to Forms W-2AS, W-2GU, or W-2VI). Include any golden parachute payments in boxes 1, 3, and 5 of Form W-2. Withhold federal income, social security, and Medicare taxes as usual and report them in boxes 2, 4, and 6, respectively. Excess parachute payments are also subject to a 20% excise tax. If the excess payments are considered wages, withhold the 20% excise tax and include it in box 2 as income tax withheld. Also report the excise tax in box 12 with code K. For definitions and additional information, see Regulations section 1.280G-1 and Rev. Proc. 2003-68, 2003-34 I.R.B. 398, available at *www.irs.gov/irb/2003-34_IRB/ar16.html*.

Government employers. Federal, state, and local governmental agencies have two options for reporting their employees' wages that are subject to only Medicare tax for part of the year and both social security and Medicare taxes for part of the year.

The first option (which the SSA prefers) is to file a single set of Forms W-2 per employee for the entire year, even if only part of the year's wages are subject to both social security and Medicare taxes. Check "941" (or "944") or "941-SS" (or "944-SS") in box b of Form W-3. The wages in box 5 of Form W-2 must be equal to or greater than the wages in box 3 of Form W-2.

The second option is to file one set of Forms W-2 for wages subject only to Medicare tax and another set for wages subject to both social security and Medicare taxes. Use a separate Form W-3 to transmit each set of Forms W-2. For the Medicare-only Forms W-2, check "Medicare govt. emp." in box b of Form W-3. For the Forms W-2 showing wages subject to both social security and Medicare taxes, check "941" (or "944") or "941-SS" (or "944-SS") in box b of Form W-3. The wages in box 5 of Form W-2 must be equal to or greater than the wages in box 3 of Form W-2.

Group-term life insurance. You must include in boxes 1, 3, and 5 the cost of group-term life insurance that is more than the cost of $50,000 of coverage, reduced by the amount the employee paid toward the insurance. Use the table in section 2 of Pub. 15-B to determine the cost of the insurance. Also, show the amount in box 12 with code C. For employees, you must withhold social security and Medicare taxes, but not federal income tax. For coverage provided to former employees, the former employees must pay the employee part of social security and Medicare taxes on the taxable cost of group-term life insurance over $50,000 on Form 1040. You are not required to collect those taxes. However, you must report the uncollected social security tax with code M and the uncollected Medicare tax with code N in box 12 of Form W-2.

Health savings account (HSA). An employer's contribution (including an employee's contributions through a cafeteria plan) to an employee's HSA is not subject to federal income tax withholding or social security, Medicare, or railroad retirement taxes (or FUTA tax) if it is reasonable to believe at the time of the payment that the contribution will be excludable from the employee's income. However, if it is not reasonable to believe at the time of payment that the contribution will be excludable from the employee's income, employer contributions are subject to federal income tax withholding, social security and Medicare taxes (or railroad retirement taxes, if applicable), and FUTA tax and must be reported in boxes 1, 3, and 5 (use box 14 if railroad retirement taxes apply), and on Form 940, Employer's Annual Federal Unemployment (FUTA) Tax Return.

You must report all employer contributions (including an employee's contributions through a cafeteria plan) to an HSA in box 12 of Form W-2 with code W. Employer contributions to an HSA that are not excludable from the income of the employee also must be reported in boxes 1, 3, and 5. (Use box 14 if railroad retirement taxes apply.)

An employee's contributions to an HSA (unless made through a cafeteria plan) are includible in income as wages and are subject to federal income tax withholding and social security and Medicare taxes (or railroad retirement taxes, if applicable). Employee contributions are deductible, within limits, on the employee's Form 1040. For more information about HSAs, see Notice 2004-2, Notice 2004-50, and Notice 2008-52. Notice 2004-2, 2004-2 I.R.B. 269, is available at *www.irs.gov/irb/2004-02_IRB/ar09.html*. Notice 2004-50, 2004-33 I.R.B. 196, is available at *www.irs.gov/irb/2004-33_IRB/ar08.html*. Notice 2008-52, 2008-25 I.R.B. 1166, is available at *www.irs.gov/irb/2008-25_IRB/ar10.html*. Also see Form 8889, Health Savings Accounts (HSAs), and Pub. 969.

Lost Form W-2—reissued statement. If an employee loses a Form W-2, write "REISSUED STATEMENT" on the new copy and furnish it to the employee. You do not have to add "REISSUED STATEMENT" on Forms W-2 provided to employees electronically. Do not send Copy A of the reissued Form W-2 to the SSA. Employers are

Form W-2 & W-3 Instructions (Page 9)

not prohibited (by the Internal Revenue Code) from charging a fee for the issuance of a duplicate Form W-2.

Military differential pay. Employers paying their employees while they are on active duty in the United States uniformed services should treat these payments as wages. Differential wage payments made to an individual while on active duty for periods scheduled to exceed 30 days are subject to income tax withholding, but are not subject to social security, Medicare, and unemployment taxes. Report differential wage payments in box 1 and any federal income tax withholding in box 2. Differential wage payments made to an individual while on active duty for 30 days or less are subject to income tax withholding, social security, Medicare, and unemployment taxes, and are reported in boxes 1, 3, and 5. See Rev. Rul. 2009-11, 2009-18 I.R.B. 896, available at *www.irs.gov/irb/2009-18_IRB/ar07.html.*

Moving expenses. Report moving expenses as follows.

- Qualified moving expenses that an employer paid to a third party on behalf of the employee (for example, to a moving company) and services that an employer furnished in kind to an employee are not reported on Form W-2.
- Qualified moving expense reimbursements paid directly to an employee by an employer are reported only in box 12 of Form W-2 with code P.
- Nonqualified moving expense reimbursements are reported in boxes 1, 3, and 5 (use box 14 if railroad retirement taxes apply) of Form W-2. These amounts are subject to federal income tax withholding and social security and Medicare taxes (or railroad retirement taxes, if applicable).

For more information on qualified and nonqualified moving expenses, see Pub. 521, Moving Expenses.

Nonqualified deferred compensation plans. Section 409A provides that all amounts deferred under a nonqualified deferred compensation (NQDC) plan for all tax years are currently includible in gross income unless certain requirements are met. Generally, section 409A is effective with respect to amounts deferred in tax years beginning after December 31, 2004, but deferrals made prior to that year may be subject to section 409A under some circumstances.

It is not necessary to show amounts deferred during the year under an NQDC plan subject to section 409A. If you report section 409A deferrals, show the amount in box 12 using code Y. For more information, see Notice 2008-115, 2008-52 I.R.B. 1367, available at *www.irs.gov/irb/2008-52_IRB/ar10.html.*

Income included under section 409A from an NQDC plan will be reported in box 1 and in box 12 using code Z. This income is also subject to an additional tax of 20% that is reported on Form 1040. For more information on amounts includible in gross income and reporting requirements, see proposed Regulations section 1.409A-4, 2008-51 I.R.B 1325, and Notice 2008-115. For information on correcting failures to comply with section 409A and related reporting, see Notice 2008-113, 2008-51 I.R.B. 1305, available at *www.irs.gov/irb/2008-51_IRB/ar12.html*; Notice 2010-6, 2010-3 I.R.B 275, available at *www.irs.gov/irb/2010-3_IRB/ar08.html*; and Notice 2010-80, 2010-51 I.R.B. 853, available at *www.irs.gov/irb/2010-51_IRB/ar08.html.*

Railroad employers (not applicable to Forms W-2AS, W-2GU, or W-2VI). Railroad employers must file Form W-2 to report their employees' wages and income tax withholding in boxes 1 and 2. Electronic reporting may be required; see *E-filing* on page 2. If you have employees covered under the Federal Insurance Contributions Act (FICA) (social security and Medicare) and the Railroad Retirement Tax Act (RRTA), you must file a separate Form W-3 to transmit the Forms W-2 for each group of employees.

For employees covered by social security and Medicare, complete boxes 3, 4, 5, 6, and 7 of Form W-2 to show the social security and Medicare wages and the amounts withheld for social security and Medicare taxes. On the Form W-3 used to transmit these Forms W-2, check the "941" checkbox in box b.

For employees covered by RRTA tax, report the Tier I and Tier II taxes withheld in box 14 of Form W-2. Label them "Tier I tax" and "Tier II tax." Boxes 3, 4, 5, 6, and 7 apply only to covered social security and Medicare wages and taxes and are not to be used to report railroad retirement wages and taxes. On the Form W-3 used to transmit these Forms W-2, check the "CT-1" checkbox in box b.

Repayments. If an employee repays you for wages received in error, do not offset the repayments against current year wages unless the repayments are for amounts received in error in the current year. Repayments made in the current year, but related to a prior year or years, must be repaid in gross, not net, and require special tax treatment by employees in some cases. You may advise the employee of the total repayments made during the current year and the amount (if any) related to prior years. This information will help the employee account for such repayments on his or her federal income tax return.

If the repayment was for a prior year, you must file Form W-2c with the SSA to correct only social security and Medicare wages and taxes. Do not correct "Wages, tips, other compensation" in box 1, or "Federal income tax withheld" in box 2, on Form W-2c. File the "X" return that is appropriate for the return on which the wages were originally reported (Form 941-X, 943-X, 944-X, or CT-1X). Correct the social security and Medicare wages and taxes for the period during which the wages were originally paid. For information on reporting adjustments to Form 941, Form 941-SS, Form 943, Form 944, or Form CT-1, see section 13 of Pub. 15 (Circular E) or section 9 of Pub. 51 (Circular A).

TIP *Tell your employee that the wages paid in error in a prior year remain taxable to him or her for that year. This is because the employee received and had use of those funds during that year. The employee is not entitled to file an amended return (Form 1040X) to recover the income tax on these wages. Instead, the employee is entitled to a deduction (or a credit, in some cases) for the repaid wages on his or her Form 1040 for the year of repayment. Refer your employee to* Repayments *in Pub. 525.*

Scholarship and fellowship grants. Give a Form W-2 to each recipient of a scholarship or fellowship grant only if you are reporting amounts includible in income under section 117(c) (relating to payments for teaching, research, or other services required as a condition for receiving the qualified scholarship). Also see Pub. 15-A and Pub. 970. These payments are subject to federal income tax withholding. However, their taxability for social security and Medicare taxes depends on the nature of the employment and the status of the

Form W-2 & W-3 Instructions (Page 10)

organization. See *Students, scholars, trainees, teachers, etc.,* in section 15 of Pub. 15 (Circular E).

Sick pay. If you had employees who received sick pay in 2012 from an insurance company or other third-party payer and the third party notified you of the amount of sick pay involved, you may be required to report the information on the employees' Forms W-2. If the insurance company or other third-party payer did not notify you in a timely manner about the sick pay payments, it must prepare Forms W-2 and W-3 for your employees showing the sick pay. For specific reporting instructions, see *Sick Pay Reporting* in section 6 of Pub. 15-A.

SIMPLE retirement account. An employee's salary reduction contributions to a SIMPLE (savings incentive match plan for employees) retirement account are not subject to federal income tax withholding but are subject to social security, Medicare, and railroad retirement taxes. Do not include an employee's contribution in box 1, but do include it in boxes 3 and 5. (Use box 14 if railroad retirement taxes apply.) An employee's total contribution also must be included in box 12 with code D or S.

An employer's matching or nonelective contribution to an employee's SIMPLE retirement account is not subject to federal income tax withholding or social security, Medicare, or railroad retirement taxes, and is not to be shown on Form W-2.

For more information on SIMPLE retirement accounts, see Notice 98-4, 1998-1 C.B. 269. You can find Notice 98-4 on page 25 of Internal Revenue Bulletin 1998-2 at *www.irs.gov/pub/irs-irbs/irb98-02.pdf.*

Successor/predecessor employers. If you buy or sell a business during the year, see Rev. Proc. 2004-53 for information on who must file Forms W-2 and employment tax returns. Rev. Proc. 2004-53, 2004-34 I.R.B 320, is available at *www.irs.gov/irb/2004-34_IRB/ar13.html.*

Terminating a business. If you terminate your business, you must provide Forms W-2 to your employees for the calendar year of termination by the due date of your final Form 941, 944, 941-SS, or 944-SS. You also must file Forms W-2 with the SSA by the last day of the month that follows the due date of your final Form 941, 944, 941-SS, or 944-SS. If filing on paper, make sure you obtain Forms W-2 and W-3 preprinted with the correct year. If e-filing, make sure your software has been updated for the current tax year.

However, if any of your employees are immediately employed by a successor employer, see *Successor/ predecessor employers,* earlier. Also, for information on automatic extensions for furnishing Forms W-2 to employees and filing Forms W-2, see Rev. Proc. 96-57, which is on page 14 of Internal Revenue Bulletin 1996-53 at *www.irs.gov/pub/irs-irbs/irb96-53.pdf.*

TIP *Get Schedule D (Form 941), Report of Discrepancies Caused by Acquisitions, Statutory Mergers, or Consolidations, for information on reconciling wages and taxes reported on Forms W-2 with amounts reported on Form 941, Form 941-SS, Form 943, Form 944, or Form 944-SS.*

Uniformed Services Employment and Reemployment Rights Act of 1994 (USERRA) makeup amounts to a pension plan. If an employee returned to your employment after military service and certain makeup amounts were contributed to a pension plan for a prior year(s) under the USERRA, report the prior year contributions separately in box 12. See the *TIP* on page 15. You also may report certain makeup amounts in box 14. See *Box 14—Other* on page 17.

Instead of reporting in box 12 (or box 14), you may choose to provide a separate statement to your employee showing USERRA makeup contributions. The statement must identify the type of plan, the year(s) to which the contributions relate, and the amount contributed for each year.

Penalties

The following penalties apply to the person or employer required to file Form W-2. The penalties apply to both paper filers and e-filers.

CAUTION *Use of a reporting agent or other third-party payroll service provider does not relieve an employer of the responsibility to ensure that Forms W-2 are furnished to employees and that Forms W-2 and W-3 are filed with the SSA, correctly and on time.*

Failure to file correct information returns by the due date. If you fail to file a correct Form W-2 by the due date and cannot show reasonable cause, you may be subject to a penalty as provided under section 6721. The penalty applies if you:

- Fail to file timely,
- Fail to include all information required to be shown on Form W-2,
- Include incorrect information on Form W-2,
- File on paper forms when you are required to *e-file,*
- Report an incorrect TIN,
- Fail to report a TIN, or
- Fail to file paper Forms W-2 that are machine readable.

The amount of the penalty is based on when you file the correct Form W-2. The penalty is:

- $30 per Form W-2 if you correctly file within 30 days (by March 30 if the due date is February 28); the maximum penalty is $250,000 per year ($75,000 for small businesses, defined on page 11).
- $60 per Form W-2 if you correctly file more than 30 days after the due date but by August 1, 2013; the maximum penalty is $500,000 per year ($200,000 for small businesses).
- $100 per Form W-2 if you file after August 1, 2013, or you do not file required Forms W-2; the maximum penalty is $1,500,000 per year ($500,000 for small businesses).

CAUTION *If you do not file corrections and you do not meet any of the exceptions to the penalty, the penalty is $100 per information return. The maximum penalty is $1,500,000 per year.*

Exceptions to the penalty. The following are exceptions to the failure to file correct information returns penalty.

1. The penalty will not apply to any failure that you can show was due to reasonable cause and not to willful neglect. In general, you must be able to show that your failure was due to an event beyond your control or due to significant mitigating factors. You also must be able to show that you acted in a responsible manner and took steps to avoid the failure.

2. An inconsequential error or omission is not considered a failure to include correct information. An inconsequential error or omission does not prevent or

Form W-2 & W-3 Instructions (Page 11)

hinder the SSA/IRS from processing the Form W-2, from correlating the information required to be shown on the form with the information shown on the payee's tax return, or from otherwise putting the form to its intended use. Errors and omissions that are never inconsequential are those relating to:

- A TIN,
- A payee's surname, and
- Any money amounts.

3. De minimis rule for corrections. Even though you cannot show reasonable cause, the penalty for failure to file correct Forms W-2 will not apply to a certain number of returns if you:

- Filed those Forms W-2 on or before the required filing date,
- Either failed to include all of the information required on the form or included incorrect information, and
- Filed corrections of these forms by August 1, 2013.

If you meet all of the de minimis rule conditions, the penalty for filing incorrect information returns (including Form W-2) will not apply to the greater of 10 information returns (including Form W-2) or one-half of 1% of the total number of information returns (including Form W-2) that you are required to file for the calendar year.

Small businesses. For purposes of the lower maximum penalties shown in parentheses on page 10, you are a small business if your average annual gross receipts for the 3 most recent tax years (or for the period that you were in existence, if shorter) ending before the calendar year in which the Forms W-2 were due are $5 million or less.

Intentional disregard of filing requirements. If any failure to file a correct Form W-2 is due to intentional disregard of the filing or correct information requirements, the penalty is at least $250 per Form W-2 with no maximum penalty.

Failure to furnish correct payee statements. If you fail to provide correct payee statements (Forms W-2) to your employees and cannot show reasonable cause, you may be subject to a penalty as provided under section 6722. The penalty applies if you fail to provide the statement by January 31, 2013, if you fail to include all information required to be shown on the statement, or if you include incorrect information on the statement.

The amount of the penalty is based on when you furnish the correct payee statement. This penalty is an additional penalty and is applied in the same manner, and with the same amounts, as the penalty for failure to file correct information returns by the due date (section 6721), described on page 10.

Exceptions to the penalty. An inconsequential error or omission is not considered a failure to include correct information. An inconsequential error or omission cannot reasonably be expected to prevent or hinder the payee from timely receiving correct information and reporting it on his or her income tax return or from otherwise putting the statement to its intended use. Errors and omissions that are never inconsequential are those relating to:

- A dollar amount,
- A significant item in a payee's address, and
- The appropriate form for the information provided, such as whether the form is an acceptable substitute for the official IRS form.

See *Exceptions to the penalty* in *Failure to file correct information returns by the due date,* earlier, for additional exceptions to the penalty for failure to file correct payee statements.

Intentional disregard of payee statement requirements. If any failure to provide a correct payee statement (Form W-2) to an employee is due to intentional disregard of the requirements to furnish a correct payee statement, the penalty is $250 per Form W-2 with no maximum penalty.

Civil damages for fraudulent filing of Forms W-2. If you willfully file a fraudulent Form W-2 for payments that you claim you made to another person, that person may be able to sue you for damages. You may have to pay $5,000 or more.

Specific Instructions for Form W-2

How to complete Form W-2. Form W-2 is a multi-part form. Ensure all copies are legible. Send Copy A to the SSA; Copy 1, if required, to your state, city, or local tax department; and Copies B, C, and 2 to your employee. Keep Copy D, and a copy of Form W-3, with your records for 4 years.

Enter the information on Form W-2 using black ink in 12-point Courier font. Copy A is read by machine and must be typed clearly with no corrections made to the entries and with no entries exceeding the size of the boxes. Entries completed by hand, in script or italic fonts, or in colors other than black cannot be read by the machines. Make all dollar entries on Copy A without the dollar sign and comma but with the decimal point (00000.00). Show the cents portion of the money amounts. If a box does not apply, leave it blank.

Send the whole Copy A page of Form W-2 with Form W-3 to the SSA even if one of the Forms W-2 on the page is blank or void. Do not staple Forms W-2 together or to Form W-3. File Forms W-2 either alphabetically by employees' last names or numerically by employees' SSNs.

Calendar year basis. The entries on Form W-2 must be based on wages paid during the calendar year. Use Form W-2 for the correct tax year. For example, if the employee worked from December 21, 2012, through January 4, 2013, and the wages for that period were paid on January 5, 2013, include those wages on the 2013 Form W-2.

Multiple forms. If necessary, you can issue more than one Form W-2 to an employee. For example, you may need to report more than four coded items in box 12 or you may want to report other compensation on a second form. If you issue a second Form W-2, complete boxes a, b, c, d, e, and f with the same information as on the first Form W-2. Show any items that were not included on the first Form W-2 in the appropriate boxes. Also, see the *TIP* for Copy A (Form W-2) on page 14.

Do not report the same federal, American Samoa, Guam, or U.S. Virgin Islands tax data to the SSA on more than one Copy A.

TIP *For each Form W-2 showing an amount in box 3 or box 7, make certain that box 5 equals or exceeds the sum of boxes 3 and 7.*

Void. Check this box when an error is made on Form W-2 and you are voiding it because you are going to complete a new Form W-2. Do not include any amounts shown on "Void" forms in the totals you enter on Form W-3. See *Corrections* on page 20.

Form W-2 & W-3 Instructions (Page 12)

Box a—Employee's social security number. Enter the number shown on the employee's social security card.

If the employee does not have a card, he or she should apply for one by completing Form SS-5, Application for a Social Security Card. The SSA lets you verify employee names and SSNs online or by telephone. For information about these free services, visit the Employer W-2 Filing Instructions & Information website at *www.socialsecurity.gov/employer*. If you have questions about using these services, call 1-888-772-6270 (toll free) to speak with an employer reporting specialist at the SSA.

If the employee has applied for a card but the number is not received in time for filing, enter "Applied For" in box a on paper Forms W-2 filed with the SSA. If e-filing, enter zeros (000-00-0000 if creating forms online or 000000000 if uploading a file).

Ask the employee to inform you of the number and name as they are shown on the social security card when it is received. Then correct your previous report by filing Form W-2c showing the employee's SSN. If the employee needs to change his or her name from that shown on the card, the employee should call the SSA at 1-800-772-1213.

If you do not provide the correct employee name and SSN on Form W-2, you may owe a penalty unless you have reasonable cause. For more information, see Publication 1586, Reasonable Cause Regulations & Requirements for Missing and Incorrect Name/TINs.

ITINs for aliens. Do not accept an ITIN in place of an SSN for employee identification or for work. An ITIN is only available to resident and nonresident aliens who are not eligible for U.S. employment and need identification for other tax purposes. You can identify an ITIN because it is a 9-digit number, beginning with the number "9" with either a "7"or "8" as the fourth digit, and is formatted like an SSN (for example, 9NN-7N-NNNN). An individual with an ITIN who later becomes eligible to work in the United States must obtain an SSN.

CAUTION *Do not auto-populate an ITIN into box a.*

Box b—Employer identification number (EIN). Show the EIN assigned to you by the IRS (00-0000000). This should be the same number that you used on your federal employment tax returns (Form 941, Form 941-SS, Form 943, Form 944, Form 944-SS, Form CT-1, or Schedule H (Form 1040)). Do not use a prior owner's EIN. If you do not have an EIN when filing Forms W-2, enter "Applied For" in box b; do not use your SSN. You can get an EIN by applying online at IRS.gov, by calling the toll-free number, 1-800-829-4933, or by filing Form SS-4, Application for Employer Identification Number. Also see *Agent reporting* on page 6.

Box c—Employer's name, address, and ZIP code. This entry should be the same as shown on your Form 941, Form 941-SS, Form 943, Form 944, Form 944-SS, Form CT-1, or Schedule H (Form 1040). The U.S. Postal Service recommends that no commas or periods be used in return addresses. Also see *Agent reporting* on page 6.

Box d—Control number. You may use this box to identify individual Forms W-2. You do not have to use this box.

Boxes e and f—Employee's name and address. Enter the name as shown on your employee's social security card (first name, middle initial, last name). If the name does not fit in the space allowed on the form, you may show the first and middle name initials and the full last name. It is especially important to report the exact last name of the employee. If you are unable to determine the correct last name, use of the SSA's Social Security Number Verification System may be helpful. Separate parts of a compound name with either a hyphen or a blank. Do not join them into a single word. Include all parts of a compound name in the appropriate name field. For example, for the name "John R Smith-Jones", enter "Smith-Jones" or "Smith Jones" in the last name field. If the name has changed, the employee must get a corrected social security card from any SSA office. Use the name on the original card until you see the corrected card. Do not show titles or academic degrees, such as "Dr.," "RN," or "Esq.," at the beginning or end of the employee's name. Generally, do not enter "Jr.," "Sr.," or other suffix in the "Suff." box on Copy A unless the suffix appears on the card. However, the SSA still prefers that you do not enter the suffix on Copy A.

Include in the address the number, street, and apartment or suite number (or P.O. box number if mail is not delivered to a street address). The U.S. Postal Service recommends that no commas or periods be used in delivery addresses. For a foreign address, give the information in the following order: city, province or state, and country. Follow the country's practice for entering the postal code. Do not abbreviate the country name.

Third-party payers of sick pay filing third-party sick pay recap Forms W-2 and W-3 must enter "Third-Party Sick Pay Recap" in place of the employee's name in box e. Do not file the recap Forms W-2 and W-3 electronically. Also, do not enter the employee's SSN in box a. See *Sick Pay Reporting* in section 6 of Pub. 15-A.

Box 1—Wages, tips, other compensation. Show the total taxable wages, tips, and other compensation (before any payroll deductions) that you paid to your employee during the year. However, do not include elective deferrals (such as employee contributions to a section 401(k) or 403(b) plan) except section 501(c)(18) contributions. Include the following.

1. Total wages, bonuses (including signing bonuses), prizes, and awards paid to employees during the year. See *Calendar year basis* on page 11.
2. Total noncash payments, including certain fringe benefits. See *Fringe benefits* on page 8.
3. Total tips reported by the employee to the employer (not allocated tips).
4. Certain employee business expense reimbursements (see *Employee business expense reimbursements* on page 7).
5. The cost of accident and health insurance premiums for 2%-or-more shareholder-employees paid by an S corporation.
6. Taxable benefits from a section 125 (cafeteria) plan if the employee chooses cash.
7. Employee contributions to an Archer MSA.
8. Employer contributions to an Archer MSA if includible in the income of the employee. See *Archer MSA* on page 6.
9. Employer contributions for qualified long-term care services to the extent that such coverage is provided through a flexible spending or similar arrangement.

Form W-2 & W-3 Instructions (Page 13)

10. Taxable cost of group-term life insurance in excess of $50,000. See *Group-term life insurance* on page 8.
11. Unless excludable under *Educational assistance programs* (see page 7), payments for non-job-related education expenses or for payments under a nonaccountable plan. See Pub. 970.
12. The amount includible as wages because you paid your employee's share of social security and Medicare taxes. See *Employee's social security and Medicare taxes paid by employer* on page 7. If you also paid your employee's income tax withholding, treat the grossed-up amount of that withholding as supplemental wages and report those wages in boxes 1, 3, 5, and 7. No exceptions to this treatment apply to household or agricultural wages.
13. Designated Roth contributions made under a section 401(k) plan, a section 403(b) salary reduction agreement, or a governmental section 457(b) plan. See *Designated Roth contributions* on page 7.
14. Distributions to an employee or former employee from an NQDC plan (including a rabbi trust) or a nongovernmental section 457(b) plan.
15. Amounts includible in income under section 457(f) because the amounts are no longer subject to a substantial risk of forfeiture.
16. Payments to statutory employees who are subject to social security and Medicare taxes but not subject to federal income tax withholding must be shown in box 1 as other compensation. See *Statutory employee* on page 17.
17. Cost of current insurance protection under a compensatory split-dollar life insurance arrangement.
18. Employee contributions to a health savings account (HSA).
19. Employer contributions to an HSA if includible in the income of the employee. See *Health savings account (HSA)* on page 8.
20. Amounts includible in income under an NQDC plan because of section 409A. See *Nonqualified deferred compensation plans* on page 9.
21. Payments made to former employees while they are on active duty in the Armed Forces or other uniformed services.
22. All other compensation, including certain scholarship and fellowship grants (see page 9). Other compensation includes taxable amounts that you paid to your employee from which federal income tax was not withheld. You may show other compensation on a separate Form W-2. See *Multiple forms* on page 11.

Box 2—Federal income tax withheld. Show the total federal income tax withheld from the employee's wages for the year. Include the 20% excise tax withheld on excess parachute payments. See *Golden parachute payments* on page 8.

For Forms W-2AS, W-2GU, or W-2VI, show the total American Samoa, Guam, or U.S. Virgin Islands income tax withheld.

Box 3—Social security wages. Show the total wages paid (before payroll deductions) subject to employee social security tax but not including social security tips and allocated tips. If reporting these amounts in a subsequent year (due to lapse of risk of forfeiture), the amount must be adjusted by any gain or loss. See *Box 7—Social security tips* and *Box 8—Allocated tips* on page 14. Generally, noncash payments are considered to be wages. Include employee business expense reimbursements reported in box 1. If you paid the employee's share of social security and Medicare taxes rather than deducting them from wages, see *Employee's social security and Medicare taxes paid by employer* on page 7. The total of boxes 3 and 7 cannot exceed $110,100 (2012 maximum social security wage base).

Report in box 3 elective deferrals to certain qualified cash or deferred compensation arrangements and to retirement plans described in box 12 (codes D, E, F, G, and S) even though the deferrals are not includible in box 1. Also report in box 3 designated Roth contributions made under a section 401(k) plan, under a section 403(b) salary reduction agreement, or under a governmental section 457(b) plan described in box 12 (codes AA, BB, and EE).

Amounts deferred (plus earnings or less losses) under a section 457(f) or nonqualified plan or nongovernmental section 457(b) plan must be included in boxes 3 and/or 5 as social security and/or Medicare wages as of the later of when the services giving rise to the deferral are performed or when there is no substantial forfeiture risk of the rights to the deferred amount. Include both elective and nonelective deferrals for purposes of nongovernmental section 457(b) plans.

TIP *Wages reported in box 3 include:*

- *Signing bonuses an employer pays for signing or ratifying an employment contract. See Rev. Rul. 2004-109, 2004-50 I.R.B 958, available at* www.irs.gov/irb/2004-50_IRB/ar07.html.
- *Taxable cost of group-term life insurance over $50,000 included in box 1. See* Group-term life insurance *on page 8.*
- *Cost of accident and health insurance premiums for 2%-or-more shareholder-employees paid by an S corporation, but only if not excludable under section 3121(a)(2)(B).*
- *Employee and nonexcludable employer contributions to an MSA or HSA. However, do not include employee contributions to an HSA that were made through a cafeteria plan. See* Archer MSA *on page 6 and* Health savings account (HSA) *on page 8.*
- *Employee contributions to a SIMPLE retirement account. See* SIMPLE retirement account *on page 10.*
- *Adoption benefits. See* Adoption benefits *on page 5.*

Box 4—Social security tax withheld. Show the total employee social security tax (not your share) withheld, including social security tax on tips. For 2012, the amount should not exceed $6,826.20 ($110,100 × 6.2%). Include only taxes withheld (or paid by you for the employee) for 2012 wages and tips. If you paid your employee's share, see *Employee's social security and Medicare taxes paid by employer* on page 7.

Box 5—Medicare wages and tips. The wages and tips subject to Medicare tax are the same as those subject to social security tax (boxes 3 and 7) except that there is no wage base limit for Medicare tax. Enter the total Medicare wages and tips in box 5. Be sure to enter tips that the employee reported even if you did not have enough employee funds to collect the Medicare tax for those tips. See *Box 3—Social security wages* on this page for payments to report in this box. If you paid your employee's share of taxes, see *Employee's social security and Medicare taxes paid by employer* on page 7.

General Instructions for Forms W-2 and W-3 (2012) **-13-**

Form W-2 & W-3 Instructions (Page 14)

If you are a federal, state, or local governmental agency with employees paying only the 1.45% Medicare tax, enter the Medicare wages in this box. See *Government employers* on page 8.

Example of how to report social security and Medicare wages. You paid your employee $140,000 in wages. Enter in box 3 (social security wages) 110100.00 but enter in box 5 (Medicare wages and tips) 140000.00. There is no limit on the amount reported in box 5. If the amount of wages paid was $110,100 or less, the amounts entered in boxes 3 and 5 would be the same.

Box 6—Medicare tax withheld. Enter the total employee Medicare tax (not your share) withheld. Include only tax withheld for 2012 wages and tips. If you paid your employee's share of the taxes, see *Employee's social security and Medicare taxes paid by employer* on page 7.

Box 7—Social security tips. Show the tips that the employee reported to you even if you did not have enough employee funds to collect the social security tax for the tips. The total of boxes 3 and 7 should not be more than $110,100 (the maximum social security wage base for 2012). Report all tips in box 1 along with wages and other compensation. Include any tips reported in box 7 in box 5 also.

Box 8—Allocated tips (not applicable to Forms W-2AS, W-2GU, or W-2VI). If you are a food or beverage establishment, show the tips allocated to the employee. See the Instructions for Form 8027, Employer's Annual Information Return of Tip Income and Allocated Tips. Do not include this amount in boxes 1, 3, 5, or 7.

Box 9. Do not enter an amount in box 9.

Box 10—Dependent care benefits (not applicable to Forms W-2AS, W-2GU, or W-2VI). Show the total dependent care benefits under a dependent care assistance program (section 129) paid or incurred by you for your employee. Include the fair market value (FMV) of care in a daycare facility provided or sponsored by you for your employee and amounts paid or incurred for dependent care assistance in a section 125 (cafeteria) plan. Report all amounts paid or incurred (regardless of any employee forfeitures), including those in excess of the $5,000 exclusion. This may include (a) the FMV of benefits provided in kind by the employer, (b) an amount paid directly to a daycare facility by the employer or reimbursed to the employee to subsidize the benefit, or (c) benefits from the pre-tax contributions made by the employee under a section 125 dependent care flexible spending account. Include any amounts over $5,000 in boxes 1, 3, and 5. For more information, see Pub. 15-B.

TIP *An employer that amends its cafeteria plan to provide a grace period for dependent care assistance may continue to rely on Notice 89-111 by reporting in box 10 of Form W-2 the salary reduction amount elected by the employee for the year for dependent care assistance (plus any employer matching contributions attributable to dependent care). Also see Notice 2005-42, 2005-23 I.R.B. 1204, available at www.irs.gov/irb/2005-23_IRB/ar11.html.*

Box 11—Nonqualified plans. The purpose of box 11 is for the SSA to determine if any part of the amount reported in box 1 or boxes 3 and/or 5 was earned in a prior year. The SSA uses this information to verify that they have properly applied the social security earnings test and paid the correct amount of benefits.

Show distributions to an employee from a nonqualified plan or a nongovernmental section 457(b) plan. Also report these distributions in box 1. Make only one entry in this box. Distributions from governmental section 457(b) plans must be reported on Form 1099-R, not in box 1 of Form W-2.

If you did not make distributions this year, show deferrals (plus earnings or less losses) under a nonqualified or any section 457(b) plan that became taxable for social security and Medicare taxes during the year (but were for prior year services) because the deferred amounts were no longer subject to a substantial risk of forfeiture. Also report these amounts in boxes 3 (up to the social security wage base) and 5. Do not report in box 11 deferrals included in boxes 3 and/or 5 and deferrals for current year services (such as those with no risk of forfeiture).

CAUTION *If you made distributions and also are reporting any deferrals in box 3 and/or 5, do not complete box 11. See Pub. 957, Reporting Back Pay and Special Wage Payments to the Social Security Administration, and Form SSA-131, Employer Report of Special Wage Payments, for instructions on reporting these and other kinds of compensation earned in prior years. However,* ***do not file Form SSA-131 if this situation applies but the employee will not be age 62 or older by the end of that year.***

Unlike qualified plans, NQDC plans do not meet the qualification requirements for tax-favored status for this purpose. NQDC plans include those arrangements traditionally viewed as deferring the receipt of current compensation. Accordingly, welfare benefit plans, stock option plans, and plans providing dismissal pay, termination pay, or early retirement pay are not NQDC plans.

Report distributions from NQDC or section 457 plans to beneficiaries of deceased employees on Form 1099-MISC, not on Form W-2.

Military employers must report military retirement payments on Form 1099-R.

TIP *Do not report special wage payments, such as accumulated sick pay or vacation pay, in box 11. For more information on reporting special wage payments, see Pub. 957.*

Box 12—Codes. Complete and code this box for all items described on page 15. Note that the codes do not relate to where they should be entered in boxes 12a through 12d on Form W-2. For example, if you are only required to report code D in box 12, you can enter code D and the amount in box 12a of Form W-2. Report in box 12 any items that are listed as codes A through EE. Do not report in box 12 section 414(h)(2) contributions (relating to certain state or local government plans). Instead, use box 14 for these items and any other information that you wish to give to your employee. For example, union dues and uniform payments may be reported in box 14.

TIP ***On Copy A (Form W-2), do not enter more than four items in box 12.*** *If more than four items need to be reported in box 12, use a separate Form W-2 to report the additional items (but enter no more than four items on each Copy A (Form W-2)). On all other copies of Form W-2 (Copies B, C, etc.), you may enter more than four items in box 12 when using an*

Form W-2 & W-3 Instructions (Page 15)

approved substitute Form W-2. See Multiple forms *on page 11.*

Use the IRS code designated below for the item you are entering, followed by the dollar amount for that item. Even if only one item is entered, you must use the IRS code designated for that item. Enter the code using a capital letter(s). Use decimal points but not dollar signs or commas. For example, if you are reporting $5,300.00 in elective deferrals under a section 401(k) plan, the entry would be D 5300.00 (not A 5300.00 even though it is the first or only entry in this box). Report the IRS code to the left of the vertical line in boxes 12a through 12d and the money amount to the right of the vertical line.

See the *Form W-2 Reference Guide for Box 12 Codes* on page 24. See also the detailed instructions next for each code.

Code A—Uncollected social security or RRTA tax on tips. Show the employee social security or Railroad Retirement Tax Act (RRTA) tax on all of the employee's tips that you could not collect because the employee did not have enough funds from which to deduct it. Do not include this amount in box 4.

Code B—Uncollected Medicare tax on tips. Show the employee Medicare tax or RRTA Medicare tax on tips that you could not collect because the employee did not have enough funds from which to deduct it. Do not include this amount in box 6.

Code C—Taxable cost of group-term life insurance over $50,000. Show the taxable cost of group-term life insurance coverage over $50,000 provided to your employee (including a former employee). See *Group-term life insurance* on page 8. Also include this amount in boxes 1, 3 (up to the social security wage base), and 5.

Codes D through H, S, Y, AA, BB, and EE. Use these codes to show elective deferrals and designated Roth contributions made to the plans listed. Do not report amounts for other types of plans. See the example for reporting elective deferrals under a section 401(k) plan, later.

The amount reported as elective deferrals and designated Roth contributions is only the part of the employee's salary (or other compensation) that he or she did not receive because of the deferrals or designated Roth contributions. Only elective deferrals and designated Roth contributions should be reported in box 12 for all coded plans; except, when using code G for section 457(b) plans, include both elective and nonelective deferrals.

For employees who were 50 years of age or older at any time during the year and made elective deferral and/or designated Roth "catch-up" contributions, report the elective deferrals and the elective deferral "catch-up" contributions as a single sum in box 12 using the appropriate code, and the designated Roth contributions and designated Roth "catch-up" contributions as a single sum in box 12 using the appropriate code.

TIP *If any elective deferrals, salary reduction amounts, or nonelective contributions under a section 457(b) plan during the year are makeup amounts under the Uniformed Services Employment and Reemployment Rights Act of 1994 (USERRA) for a prior year, you must enter the prior year contributions separately. Beginning with the earliest year, enter the code, the year, and the amount. For example, elective deferrals of $2,250 for 2010 and $1,250 for 2011 under USERRA under a section 401(k) plan are reported in box 12 as follows:*

D 10 2250.00, D 11 1250.00. A 2012 contribution of $7,000 does not require a year designation; enter it as D 7000.00. Report the code (and year for prior year USERRA contributions) to the left of the vertical line in boxes 12a through 12d.

The following are not elective deferrals and may be reported in box 14, but not in box 12.
- Nonelective employer contributions made on behalf of an employee.
- After-tax contributions that are not designated Roth contributions, such as voluntary contributions to a pension plan that are deducted from an employee's pay. See the instructions on page 16 for codes AA and BB and on page 17 for code EE for reporting designated Roth contributions.
- Required employee contributions.
- Employer matching contributions.

Code D—Elective deferrals under section 401(k) cash or deferred arrangement (plan). Also show deferrals under a SIMPLE retirement account that is part of a section 401(k) arrangement.

Example of reporting excess elective deferrals and designated Roth contributions under a section 401(k) plan. For 2012, Employee A (age 45) elected to defer $18,300 under a section 401(k) plan. The employee also made a designated Roth contribution to the plan of $1,000, and made a voluntary (non-Roth) after-tax contribution of $600. In addition, the employer, on A's behalf, made a qualified nonelective contribution of $2,000 to the plan and a nonelective profit-sharing employer contribution of $3,000.

Even though the 2012 limit for elective deferrals and designated Roth contributions is $17,000, the employee's total elective deferral amount of $18,300 is reported in box 12 with code D (D 18300.00). The designated Roth contribution is reported in box 12 with code AA (AA 1000.00). The employer must separately report the actual amounts of $18,300 and $1,000 in box 12 with the appropriate codes. The amount deferred in excess of the limit is not reported in box 1. The return of excess salary deferrals and excess designated contributions, including earnings on both, is reported on Form 1099-R.

The $600 voluntary after-tax contribution may be reported in box 14 (this is optional) but not in box 12. The $2,000 nonelective contribution and the $3,000 nonelective profit-sharing employer contribution are not required to be reported on Form W-2, but may be reported in box 14.

Check the "Retirement plan" box in box 13.

Code E—Elective deferrals under a section 403(b) salary reduction agreement.

Code F—Elective deferrals under a section 408(k)(6) salary reduction SEP.

Code G—Elective deferrals and employer contributions (including nonelective deferrals) to any governmental or nongovernmental section 457(b) deferred compensation plan. Do not report either section 457(b) or section 457(f) amounts that are subject to a substantial risk of forfeiture.

Form W-2 & W-3 Instructions (Page 16)

Code H—Elective deferrals under section 501(c)(18)(D) tax-exempt organization plan. Be sure to include this amount in box 1 as wages. The employee will deduct the amount on his or her Form 1040.

Code J—Nontaxable sick pay. Show any sick pay that was paid by a third-party and was not includible in income (and not shown in boxes 1, 3, and 5) because the employee contributed to the sick pay plan. Do not include nontaxable disability payments made directly by a state.

Code K—20% excise tax on excess golden parachute payments (not applicable to Forms W-2AS, W-2GU, or W-2VI). If you made excess "golden parachute" payments to certain key corporate employees, report the 20% excise tax on these payments. If the excess payments are considered to be wages, report the 20% excise tax withheld as income tax withheld in box 2.

Code L—Substantiated employee business expense reimbursements. Use this code only if you reimbursed your employee for employee business expenses using a per diem or mileage allowance and the amount that you reimbursed exceeds the amount treated as substantiated under IRS rules. See *Employee business expense reimbursements* on page 7.

Report in box 12 only the amount treated as substantiated (such as the nontaxable part). Include in boxes 1, 3 (up to the social security wage base), and 5 the part of the reimbursement that is more than the amount treated as substantiated.

Code M—Uncollected social security or RRTA tax on taxable cost of group-term life insurance over $50,000 (for former employees). If you provided your former employees (including retirees) more than $50,000 of group-term life insurance coverage for periods during which an employment relationship no longer exists, enter the amount of uncollected social security or RRTA tax on the coverage in box 12. Also see *Group-term life insurance* on page 8.

Code N—Uncollected Medicare tax on taxable cost of group-term life insurance over $50,000 (for former employees). If you provided your former employees (including retirees) more than $50,000 of group-term life insurance coverage for periods during which an employment relationship no longer exists, enter the amount of uncollected Medicare tax or RRTA Medicare tax on the coverage in box 12. Also see *Group-term life insurance* on page 8.

Code P—Excludable moving expense reimbursements paid directly to employee. Show the total moving expense reimbursements that you paid directly to your employee for qualified (deductible) moving expenses. See *Moving expenses* on page 9.

Code Q—Nontaxable combat pay. If you are a military employer, report any nontaxable combat pay in box 12.

Code R—Employer contributions to an Archer MSA. Show any employer contributions to an Archer MSA. See *Archer MSA* on page 6.

Code S—Employee salary reduction contributions under a section 408(p) SIMPLE plan. Show deferrals under a section 408(p) salary reduction SIMPLE retirement account. However, if the SIMPLE plan is part of a section 401(k) arrangement, use code D. If you are reporting prior year contributions under USERRA, see the *TIP* on page 15.

Code T—Adoption benefits. Show the total that you paid or reimbursed for qualified adoption expenses furnished to your employee under an adoption assistance program. Also include adoption benefits paid or reimbursed from the pre-tax contributions made by the employee under a section 125 (cafeteria) plan. However, do not include adoption benefits forfeited from a section 125 (cafeteria) plan. Report all amounts including those in excess of the $12,650 exclusion. For more information, see *Adoption benefits* on page 5.

Code V—Income from the exercise of nonstatutory stock option(s). Show the spread (that is, the fair market value of stock over the exercise price of option(s) granted to your employee with respect to that stock) from your employee's (or former employee's) exercise of nonstatutory stock option(s). Include this amount in boxes 1, 3 (up to the social security wage base), and 5.

This reporting requirement does not apply to the exercise of a statutory stock option, or the sale or disposition of stock acquired pursuant to the exercise of a statutory stock option. For more information about the taxability of employee stock options, see Pub. 15-B.

Code W—Employer contributions to a health savings account (HSA). Show any employer contributions (including amounts the employee elected to contribute using a section 125 (cafeteria) plan) to an HSA. See *Health savings account (HSA)* on page 8.

Code Y—Deferrals under a section 409A nonqualified deferred compensation plan. It is not necessary to show deferrals in box 12 with code Y. For more information, see Notice 2008-115. However, if you report these deferrals, show current year deferrals, including earnings during the year on current year and prior year deferrals. See *Nonqualified deferred compensation plans* on page 9.

Code Z—Income under section 409A on a nonqualified deferred compensation plan. Enter all amounts deferred (including earnings on amounts deferred) that are includible in income under section 409A because the NQDC plan fails to satisfy the requirements of section 409A. Do not include amounts properly reported on a Form 1099-MISC, corrected Form 1099-MISC, Form W-2, or Form W-2c for a prior year. Also, do not include amounts that are considered to be subject to a substantial risk of forfeiture for purposes of section 409A. For more information, see Regulations sections 1.409A-1 through 1.409A-6 and Notice 2008-115.

The amount reported in box 12 using code Z is also reported in box 1 and is subject to an additional tax reported on the employee's Form 1040. See *Nonqualified deferred compensation plans* on page 9.

For information regarding correcting section 409A errors and related reporting, see Notice 2008-113, Notice 2010-6, and Notice 2010-80.

Code AA—Designated Roth contributions under a section 401(k) plan. Use this code to report designated Roth contributions under a section 401(k) plan. Do not use this code to report elective deferrals under code D. See *Designated Roth contributions* on page 7.

Code BB—Designated Roth contributions under a section 403(b) plan. Use this code to report designated Roth contributions under a section 403(b) plan. Do not use this code to report elective deferrals under code E. See *Designated Roth contributions* on page 7.

-16- **General Instructions for Forms W-2 and W-3 (2012)**

Form W-2 & W-3 Instructions (Page 17)

Code DD—Cost of employer-sponsored health coverage. Use this code to report the cost of employer-sponsored health coverage. **The amount reported with code DD is not taxable.** Additional reporting guidance, including information about the transitional reporting rules that apply, is available on the Affordable Care Act Tax Provisions page of IRS.gov.

Code EE—Designated Roth contributions under a governmental section 457(b) plan. Use this code to report designated Roth contributions under a governmental section 457(b) plan. Do not use this code to report elective deferrals under code G. See *Designated Roth contributions* on page 7.

Box 13—Checkboxes. Check all boxes that apply.

- ***Statutory employee.*** Check this box for statutory employees whose earnings are subject to social security and Medicare taxes but not subject to federal income tax withholding. Do not check this box for common-law employees. There are workers who are independent contractors under the common-law rules but are treated by statute as employees. They are called statutory employees.

1. A driver who distributes beverages (other than milk), or meat, vegetable, fruit, or bakery products; or who picks up and delivers laundry or dry cleaning if the driver is your agent or is paid on commission.
2. A full-time life insurance sales agent whose principal business activity is selling life insurance or annuity contracts, or both, primarily for one life insurance company.
3. An individual who works at home on materials or goods that you supply and that must be returned to you or to a person you name if you also furnish specifications for the work to be done.
4. A full-time traveling or city salesperson who works on your behalf and turns in orders to you from wholesalers, retailers, contractors, or operators of hotels, restaurants, or other similar establishments. The goods sold must be merchandise for resale or supplies for use in the buyer's business operation. The work performed for you must be the salesperson's principal business activity.

For details on statutory employees and common-law employees, see section 1 in Pub. 15-A.

- ***Retirement plan.*** Check this box if the employee was an "active participant" (for any part of the year) in any of the following.

1. A qualified pension, profit-sharing, or stock-bonus plan described in section 401(a) (including a 401(k) plan).
2. An annuity plan described in section 403(a).
3. An annuity contract or custodial account described in section 403(b).
4. A simplified employee pension (SEP) plan described in section 408(k).
5. A SIMPLE retirement account described in section 408(p).
6. A trust described in section 501(c)(18).
7. A plan for federal, state, or local government employees or by an agency or instrumentality thereof (other than a section 457(b) plan).

Generally, an employee is an active participant if covered by (a) a defined benefit plan for any tax year that he or she is eligible to participate in or (b) a defined contribution plan (for example, a section 401(k) plan) for any tax year that employer or employee contributions (or forfeitures) are added to his or her account. For additional information on employees who are eligible to participate in a plan, contact your plan administrator. For details on the active participant rules, see Notice 87-16, 1987-1 C.B. 446; Notice 98-49, 1998-2 C.B. 365; section 219(g)(5); and Pub. 590, Individual Retirement Arrangements (IRAs). You can find Notice 98-49 on page 5 of Internal Revenue Bulletin 1998-38 at *www.irs.gov/pub/irs-irbs/irb98-38.pdf.* Also see Notice 2000-30, which is on page 1266 of Internal Revenue Bulletin 2000-25 at *www.irs.gov/pub/irs-irbs/irb00-25.pdf.*

TIP *Do not check this box for contributions made to a nonqualified or section 457(b) plan.*

- ***Third-party sick pay.*** Check this box only if you are a third-party sick pay payer filing a Form W-2 for an insured's employee or are an employer reporting sick pay payments made by a third party. See *Sick Pay Reporting* in section 6 of Pub. 15-A.

Box 14—Other. If you included 100% of a vehicle's annual lease value in the employee's income, it also must be reported here or on a separate statement to your employee. You also may use this box for any other information that you want to give to your employee. Label each item. Examples include state disability insurance taxes withheld, union dues, uniform payments, health insurance premiums deducted, nontaxable income, educational assistance payments, or a member of the clergy's parsonage allowance and utilities. In addition, you may enter the following contributions to a pension plan: (a) nonelective employer contributions made on behalf of an employee, (b) voluntary after-tax contributions (but not designated Roth contributions) that are deducted from an employee's pay, (c) required employee contributions, and (d) employer matching contributions.

If you are reporting prior year contributions under USERRA (see the *TIP* on page 15 and *Uniformed Services Employment and Reemployment Rights Act of 1994 (USERRA) makeup amounts to a pension plan* on page 10), you may report in box 14 makeup amounts for nonelective employer contributions, voluntary after-tax contributions, required employee contributions, and employer matching contributions. Report such amounts separately for each year. Railroad employers, see page 9.

Boxes 15 through 20—State and local income tax information (not applicable to Forms W-2AS, W-2GU, or W-2VI). Use these boxes to report state and local income tax information. Enter the two-letter abbreviation for the name of the state. The employer's state ID numbers are assigned by the individual states. The state and local information boxes can be used to report wages and taxes for two states and two localities. Keep each state's and locality's information separated by the broken line. If you need to report information for more than two states or localities, prepare a second Form W-2. See *Multiple forms* on page 11. Contact your state or locality for specific reporting information.

Specific Instructions for Form W-3

How to complete Form W-3. The instructions under *How to complete Form W-2* on page 11 generally apply to Form W-3. Use black ink for all entries. Scanners cannot read entries if the type is too light. Be sure to send the entire page of the Form W-3.

General Instructions for Forms W-2 and W-3 (2012) -17-

Form W-2 & W-3 Instructions (Page 18)

TIP *Amounts reported on related employment tax forms (for example, Form W-2, Form 941, Form 941-SS, Form 943, Form 944, or Form 944-SS) should agree with the amounts reported on Form W-3. If there are differences, you may be contacted by the IRS and SSA. Retain your reconciliation information for future reference. See* Reconciling Forms W-2, W-3, 941, 941-SS, 943, 944, 944-SS, CT-1, and Schedule H (Form 1040) *on page 19.*

Box a—Control number. This is an optional box that you may use for numbering the whole transmittal.

Box b—Kind of Payer. Check the box that applies to you. Check only one box. If you have more than one type of Form W-2, send each type with a separate Form W-3. **Note.** The "Third-party sick pay" indicator box does not designate a separate kind of payer.

941 or 941-SS. Check this box if you file Form 941 or Form 941-SS and no other category applies. A church or church organization should check this box even if it is not required to file Form 941, Form 941-SS, Form 944, or Form 944-SS.

Military. Check this box if you are a military employer sending Forms W-2 for members of the uniformed services.

943. Check this box if you are an agricultural employer and file Form 943 and you are sending Forms W-2 for agricultural employees. For nonagricultural employees, send their Forms W-2 with a separate Form W-3, checking the appropriate box.

944 or 944-SS. Check this box if you file Form 944 (or Formulario 944(SP), its Spanish-language version) or Form 944-SS, and no other category applies.

CT-1. Check this box if you are a railroad employer sending Forms W-2 for employees covered under the Railroad Retirement Tax Act (RRTA). Do not show employee RRTA tax in boxes 3 through 7. These boxes are only for social security and Medicare information. If you also have employees who are subject to social security and Medicare taxes, send that group's Forms W-2 with a separate Form W-3 and check the "941" checkbox on that Form W-3.

Hshld. emp. Check this box if you are a household employer sending Forms W-2 for household employees and you did not include the household employee's taxes on Form 941, Form 941-SS, Form 943, Form 944, or Form 944-SS.

Medicare govt. emp. Check this box if you are a U.S., state, or local agency filing Forms W-2 for employees subject only to the 1.45% Medicare tax. See *Government employers* on page 8.

Box b—Kind of Employer. Check the box that applies to you. Check only one box unless the second checked box is "Third-party sick pay."

None apply. Check this box if none of the checkboxes discussed next apply to you.

501c non-govt. Check this box if you are a non-governmental tax-exempt section 501(c) organization. Types of 501(c) non-governmental organizations include private foundations, public charities, social and recreation clubs, and veterans organizations. For additional examples of 501(c) non-governmental organizations, see chapters 3 and 4 of Publication 557, Tax-Exempt Status for Your Organization.

State/local non-501c. Check this box if you are a state or local government or instrumentality that is not a tax-exempt section 501(c) organization. Types of state or local non-501(c) organizations include cities, townships, counties, county hospitals, fire departments, police associations, and public utilities.

State/local 501c. Check this box if you are a dual status state or local government or instrumentality that is also a tax-exempt section 501(c) organization. Types of state or local 501(c) organizations include public schools, colleges, and universities.

Federal govt. Check this box if you are a Federal government entity or instrumentality.

Box b—Third-party sick pay. Check this box if you are a third-party sick pay payer (or are reporting sick pay payments made by a third party) filing Forms W-2 with the "Third-party sick pay" checkbox in box 13 checked. File a single Form W-3 for the regular and "Third-party sick pay" Forms W-2. See *941 or 941-SS* on this page.

Box c—Total number of Forms W-2. Show the number of completed individual Forms W-2 that you are transmitting with this Form W-3. Do not count "Void" Forms W-2.

Box d—Establishment number. You may use this box to identify separate establishments in your business. You may file a separate Form W-3, with Forms W-2, for each establishment even if they all have the same EIN; or you may use a single Form W-3 for all Forms W-2 of the same type.

Box e—Employer identification number (EIN). Enter the nine-digit EIN assigned to you by the IRS. The number should be the same as shown on your Form 941, Form 941-SS, Form 943, Form 944, Form 944-SS, Form CT-1, or Schedule H (Form 1040) and in the following format: 00-0000000. Do not use a prior owner's EIN. See *Box h—Other EIN used this year* below.

If you do not have an EIN when filing your Form W-3, enter "Applied For" in box e, not your social security number (SSN), and see *Box b—Employer identification number (EIN)* on page 12.

Box f—Employer's name. Enter the same name as shown on your Form 941, Form 941-SS, Form 943, Form 944, Form 944-SS, or Form CT-1.

Box g—Employer's address and ZIP code. Enter your address.

Box h—Other EIN used this year. If you have used an EIN (including a prior owner's EIN) on Form 941, 941-SS, Form 943, Form 944, Form 944-SS, or Form CT-1 submitted for 2012 that is different from the EIN reported on Form W-3 in box e, enter the other EIN used. Agents generally report the employer's EIN in box h. See *Agent reporting* on page 6.

Contact person, telephone number, fax number, and email address. Include this information for use by the SSA if any questions arise during processing.

TIP *The amounts to enter in boxes 1 through 19, described next, are totals from only the Forms W-2 (excluding any Forms W-2 marked "VOID") that you are sending with this Form W-3.*

Boxes 1 through 8. Enter the totals reported in boxes 1 through 8 on the Forms W-2.

Form W-2 & W-3 Instructions (Page 19)

Box 9. Do not enter an amount in box 9.

Box 10—Dependent care benefits (not applicable to Forms W-2AS, W-2GU, and W-2VI). Enter the total reported in box 10 on Forms W-2.

Box 11—Nonqualified plans. Enter the total reported in box 11 on Forms W-2.

Box 12a—Deferred compensation. Enter the total of all amounts reported with codes D through H, S, Y, AA, BB, and EE in box 12 on Forms W-2. Do not enter a code.

CAUTION *The total of Form W-2 box 12 amounts reported with Codes A through C, J through R, T through W, Z, and DD is not reported on Form W-3.*

Box 13—For third-party sick pay use only. Third-party payers of sick pay (or employers using the optional rule for Form W-2 described in section 6 of Pub. 15-A) filing third-party sick pay recap Forms W-2 and W-3 must enter "Third-Party Sick Pay Recap" in this box.

Box 14—Income tax withheld by payer of third-party sick pay. Complete this box only if you are the employer and have employees who had federal income tax withheld on third-party payments of sick pay. Show the total income tax withheld by third-party payers on payments to all of your employees. Although this tax is included in the box 2 total, it must be separately shown here.

Box 15—State/Employer's state ID number (territorial ID number for Forms W-2AS, W-2GU, and W-2VI). Enter the two-letter abbreviation for the name of the state or territory being reported on Form(s) W-2. Also enter your state- or territory-assigned ID number. If the Forms W-2 being submitted with this Form W-3 contain wage and income tax information from more than one state or territory, enter an "X" under "State" and do not enter any state or territory ID number.

Boxes 16 through 19 (not applicable to Forms W-2AS, W-2GU, and W-2VI). Enter the total of state/local wages and income tax shown in their corresponding boxes on the Forms W-2 included with this Form W-3. If the Forms W-2 show amounts from more than one state or locality, report them as one sum in the appropriate box on Form W-3. Verify that the amount reported in each box is an accurate total of the Forms W-2.

Reconciling Forms W-2, W-3, 941, 941-SS, 943, 944, 944-SS, CT-1, and Schedule H (Form 1040)

Reconcile the amounts shown in boxes 2, 3, 5, and 7 from all 2012 Forms W-3 with their respective amounts from the 2012 yearly totals from the quarterly Form 941 or 941-SS or annual Form 943, Form 944, Form 944-SS, Form CT-1 (box 2 only), and Schedule H (Form 1040). When there are discrepancies between amounts reported on Forms W-2 and W-3 filed with the SSA and on Form 941, 941-SS, Form 943, Form 944, Form 944-SS, Form CT-1, or Schedule H (Form 1040) filed with the IRS, you will be contacted to resolve the discrepancies.

To help reduce discrepancies on Forms W-2:

- Report bonuses as wages and as social security and Medicare wages on Form W-2, and on Forms 941, 941-SS, 943, 944, 944-SS, and Schedule H (Form 1040).
- Report both social security and Medicare wages and taxes separately on Forms W-2 and W-3, and on Forms 941, 941-SS, 943, 944, 944-SS, and Schedule H (Form 1040).
- Report social security taxes withheld on Form W-2 in box 4, not in box 3.
- Report Medicare taxes withheld on Form W-2 in box 6, not in box 5.
- Do not report a nonzero amount in box 4 if boxes 3 and 7 are both zero.
- Do not report a nonzero amount in box 6 if box 5 is zero.
- Do not report an amount in box 5 that is less than the sum of boxes 3 and 7.
- Make sure that the social security wage amount for each employee does not exceed the annual social security wage base limit ($110,100 for 2012).
- Do not report noncash wages that are not subject to social security or Medicare taxes as social security or Medicare wages.
- If you use an EIN on any quarterly Form 941 or Form 941-SS for the year (or annual Forms 943, 944, 944-SS, CT-1, or Schedule H (Form 1040)) that is different from the EIN reported in box e on Form W-3, enter the other EIN in box h on Form W-3.

To reduce the discrepancies between amounts reported on Forms W-2 and W-3, and Forms 941, 941-SS, 943, 944, 944-SS, CT-1, and Schedule H (Form 1040):

- Be sure that the amounts on Form W-3 are the total amounts from Forms W-2.
- Reconcile Form W-3 with your four quarterly Forms 941 or 941-SS (or annual Forms 943, 944, 944-SS, CT-1, or Schedule H (Form 1040)) by comparing amounts reported for:

1. Income tax withholding (box 2).
2. Social security wages, Medicare wages and tips, and social security tips (boxes 3, 5, and 7). Form W-3 should include Form 941 or 941-SS or Forms 943, 944, 944-SS, or Schedule H (Form 1040) adjustments only for the current year. If the Form 941, Form 941-SS, Form 943, Form 944, or Form 944-SS adjustments include amounts for a prior year, do not report those prior year adjustments on the current year Forms W-2 and W-3.
3. Social security and Medicare taxes (boxes 4 and 6). The amounts shown on the four quarterly Forms 941 or 941-SS (or annual Form 943, Form 944, Form 944-SS, or Schedule H (Form 1040)), including current year adjustments, should be approximately twice the amounts shown on Form W-3.

Amounts reported on Forms W-2 and W-3, and Forms 941, 941-SS, 943, 944, 944-SS, CT-1, or Schedule H (Form 1040) may not match for valid reasons. If they do not match, you should determine that the reasons are valid. Retain your reconciliation information in case you receive inquiries from the IRS or the SSA.

General Instructions for Forms W-2c and W-3c

Applicable forms. Use with the February 2009 revision of Form W-2c and the December 2011 revision of Form W-3c.

Purpose of forms. Use Form W-2c to correct errors on Form W-2, W-2AS, W-2CM, W-2GU, W-2VI, or W-2c filed with the SSA. Also use Form W-2c to provide a corrected Form W-2, W-2AS, W-2CM, W-2GU, W-2VI, or W-2c to employees.

Form W-2 & W-3 Instructions (Page 20)

Corrections reported on Form W-2c may require you to make corrections to your previously filed employment tax returns using the corresponding "X" form, such as Form 941-X, Adjusted Employer's QUARTERLY Federal Tax Return or Claim for Refund; Form 943-X, Adjusted Employer's Annual Federal Tax Return for Agricultural Employees or Claim for Refund; Form 944-X, Adjusted Employer's ANNUAL Federal Tax Return or Claim for Refund; or Form CT-1X, Adjusted Employer's Annual Railroad Retirement Tax Return or Claim for Refund. See section 13 of Pub. 15 (Circular E) for more information. If you are making corrections to a previously filed Schedule H (Form 1040), see Pub. 926, Household Employer's Tax Guide. If an employee repaid you for wages received in a prior year, also see *Repayments* on page 9.

Do not use Form W-2c to report corrections to back pay. Instead, see Pub. 957, Reporting Back Pay and Special Wage Payments to the Social Security Administration, and Form SSA-131, Employer Report of Special Wage Payments.

Do not use Form W-2c to correct Form W-2G, Certain Gambling Winnings. Instead, see the General Instructions for Certain Information Returns for the current reporting year.

Use Form W-3c to send Copy A of Form W-2c to the SSA. Always file Form W-3c when submitting one or more Forms W-2c.

E-filing Forms W-2c and W-3c. The SSA encourages all employers to *e-file* using its secure BSO website. E-filing can save you effort and helps ensure accuracy. See *E-filing* on page 2 for more information.

Where to file paper Forms W-2c and W-3c. If you use the U.S. Postal Service, send Forms W-2c and W-3c to:

Social Security Administration
Data Operations Center
P.O. Box 3333
Wilkes-Barre, PA 18767-3333

If you use a carrier other than the U.S. Postal Service, send Forms W-2c and W-3c to:

Social Security Administration
Data Operations Center
Attn: W-2c Process
1150 E. Mountain Drive
Wilkes-Barre, PA 18702-7997

See Pub. 15 (Circular E) for a list of IRS-designated private delivery services.

TIP *Do not send Forms W-2, W-2AS, W-2GU, or W-2VI to either of these addresses. Instead, see* Where to file paper Forms W-2 and W-3 *on page 4.*

When to file. File Forms W-2c and W-3c as soon as possible after you discover an error. Also provide Form W-2c to employees as soon as possible.

How to complete. If you file Forms W-2c and W-3c on paper, make all entries using dark or black ink in 12-point Courier font, if possible, and make sure all copies are legible. See *How to complete Form W-2* on page 11.

If any item shows a change in the dollar amount and one of the amounts is zero, enter "-0-." Do not leave the box blank.

Who may sign Form W-3c. Generally, employers must sign Form W-3c. See *Who may sign Form W-3* on page 4 for more information.

Special Situations for Forms W-2c and W-3c

HIRE wages and tips paid to qualified employees. Employers who hired a qualified employee under the HIRE Act must report the amount of social security wages and tips paid after March 18, 2010, and before January 1, 2011, for which the employer claimed the payroll tax exemption. A qualified employee is one who:

- Was hired after February 3, 2010, and before January 1, 2011;
- Was not hired to replace another employee unless the other employee separated from employment voluntarily or for cause (including downsizing);
- Was not a family member or other related individual of the employer; and
- Signed Form W-11, Hiring Incentives to Restore Employment (HIRE) Act Employee Affidavit, or other similar statement under penalties of perjury, certifying under penalties of perjury that he or she had not worked more than 40 hours during the 60 days prior to beginning employment.

Report any corrections to the amount of wages and tips paid to the qualified employee for which you claimed the payroll tax exemption in box 12 using code CC. This will include wages and tips paid to the qualified employee from April 1, 2010, through December 31, 2010, for which you claimed the payroll tax exemption, plus wages and tips paid to the qualified employee from March 19, 2010, through March 31, 2010, for which you claimed a payroll tax credit. The amount may not exceed $106,800 (2010 maximum social security wage base). For more information, visit IRS.gov and enter "Payroll Tax Exemption for Hiring Unemployed Workers" in the search box.

Undeliverable Forms W-2c. See *Undeliverable Forms W-2* on page 5 for more information.

Correcting Forms W-2 and W-3

Corrections. Use the current version of Form W-2c to correct errors (such as incorrect name, SSN, or amount) on a previously filed Form W-2 or Form W-2c. File Copy A of Form W-2c with the SSA. To *e-file* your corrections, see *Correcting wage reports* on page 1.

If the SSA issues your employee a replacement card after a name change, or a new card with a different social security number after a change in alien work status, file a Form W-2c to correct the name/SSN reported on the most recently filed Form W-2. It is not necessary to correct the prior years if the previous name and number were used for the years prior to the most recently filed Form W-2.

File Form W-3c whenever you file a Form W-2c with the SSA, even if you are only filing a Form W-2c to correct an employee's name or SSN. However, see *Employee's incorrect address on Form W-2* on page 21 for information on correcting an employee's address. See *Correcting an incorrect tax year and/or EIN incorrectly reported on Form W-2 or Form W-3* on page 21 if an error was made on a previously filed Form W-3.

If you discover an error on Form W-2 after you issue it to your employee but before you send it to the SSA, check the "Void" box at the top of the incorrect Form W-2 on Copy A. Prepare a new Form W-2 with the correct information, and send Copy A to the SSA. Write

Form W-2 & W-3 Instructions (Page 21)

"CORRECTED" on the employee's new copies (B, C, and 2), and furnish them to the employee. If the "Void" Form W-2 is on a page with a correct Form W-2, send the entire page to the SSA. The "Void" form will not be processed. Do not write "CORRECTED" on Copy A of Form W-2.

If you are making a correction for a previously filed Form 941, Form 941-SS, Form 943, Form 944, Form 944-SS, or Form CT-1, use the corresponding "X" form, such as Form 941-X, Form 943-X, Form 944-X, or Form CT-1X for the return period in which you found the error. See section 13 of Pub. 15 (Circular E) for more details. If you are making corrections to a previously filed Schedule H (Form 1040), see Pub. 926. Issue the employee a Form W-2c if the error discovered was for the prior year.

Correcting an employee's name and/or SSN only. If you are correcting only an employee's name and/or SSN, complete Form W-2c boxes d through i. Do not complete boxes 1 through 20. Advise your employee to correct the SSN and/or name on his or her original Form W-2.

If your employee is given a new social security card following an adjustment to his or her resident status that shows a different name or SSN, file a Form W-2c for the most current year only.

Correcting an employee's name and SSN if the SSN was reported as blanks or zeros and the employee name was reported as blanks. If you need to correct an employee's name and SSN, and the SSN was reported as blanks or zeros and the employee's name was reported as blanks, do not use Form W-2c to report the corrections. You must contact the SSA at 1-800-772-6270 for instructions.

Correcting an incorrect tax year and/or EIN incorrectly reported on Form W-2 or Form W-3. To correct an incorrect tax year and/or EIN on a previously submitted Form W-2 or Form W-3, file one Form W-3c along with a Form W-2c for each affected employee. Enter the tax year and EIN originally reported, and enter in the "Previously reported" boxes the money amounts that were on the original Form W-2. In the "Correct information" boxes, enter zeros. Prepare a second Form W-3c along with a second Form W-2c for each affected employee. Enter zeros in the "Previously reported" boxes, and enter the correct money amounts in the "Correct information" boxes. Enter the correct tax year and/or correct EIN.

Correcting more than one Form W-2 for an employee. There are two ways to prepare a correction for an employee for whom more than one Form W-2 was filed under the same EIN for the tax year. You can (1) consider all the Forms W-2 when determining the amounts to enter on Form W-2c or (2) file a single Form W-2c to correct only the incorrect Form W-2.

However, state, local, and federal government employers who are preparing corrections for Medicare Qualified Government Employment (MQGE) employees also must follow the instructions in the *CAUTION* for state, local, and federal government employers on page 22.

Correcting more than one kind of form. You must use a separate Form W-3c for each type of Form W-2 (Form W-2, W-2AS, W-2CM, W-2GU, W-2VI, or W-2c) being corrected. You also must use a separate Form W-3c for each kind of payer/employer combination in box c. If you are correcting more than one kind of form, please group forms of the same kind of payer/employer combination, and send them in separate groups.

Employee's incorrect address on Form W-2. If you filed a Form W-2 with the SSA that reported an incorrect address for the employee, but all other information on the Form W-2 was correct, do not file Form W-2c with the SSA merely to correct the address.

However, if the address was incorrect on the Form W-2 furnished to the employee, you must do one of the following.

- Issue a new, corrected Form W-2 to the employee that includes the new address. Indicate "REISSUED STATEMENT" on the new copies. Do not send Copy A of Form W-2 to the SSA.
- Issue a Form W-2c to the employee that shows the correct address in box i and all other correct information. Do not send Copy A of Form W-2c to the SSA.
- Reissue the Form W-2 with the incorrect address to the employee in an envelope showing the correct address or otherwise deliver it to the employee.

Two Forms W-2 were filed under the same EIN, but only one should have been filed.

Example. Two Forms W-2 were submitted for Mary Smith under the same EIN for the same tax year. One Form W-2 correctly reported social security wages of $20,000. The other Form W-2 incorrectly reported social security wages of $30,000. There are two ways to correct this situation.

- File a Form W-3c along with one Form W-2c, entering $50,000 in box 3 under "Previously reported" and $20,000 in box 3 under "Correct information," or
- File a Form W-3c along with one Form W-2c, entering $30,000 in box 3 under "Previously reported" and $0.00 in box 3 under "Correct information."

Two Forms W-2 were filed under the same EIN, but wages on one were incorrect.

Example. Two Forms W-2 were submitted for Mary Smith under the same EIN for the same tax year. One Form W-2 correctly reported social security wages of $20,000. The other Form W-2 incorrectly reported social security wages of $30,000, whereas $25,000 should have been reported. There are two ways to correct this situation.

- File a Form W-3c along with one Form W-2c, entering $50,000 in box 3 under "Previously reported" and $45,000 in box 3 under "Correct information," or
- File a Form W-3c along with one Form W-2c, entering $30,000 in box 3 under "Previously reported" and $25,000 in box 3 under "Correct information."

Specific Instructions for Form W-2c

Box a—Employer's name, address, and ZIP code. This entry should be the same as shown on your Form 941, 941-SS, 943, 944, 944-SS, CT-1, or Schedule H (Form 1040).

Box b—Employer's Federal EIN. Show the correct nine digit EIN assigned to you by the IRS in the format 00-0000000.

Box c—Tax year/Form corrected. If you are correcting Form W-2, enter all four digits of the year of the form you are correcting. If you are correcting Form W-2AS, W-2CM, W-2GU, W-2VI, or W-2c, enter all four digits of the year you are correcting, and also enter "AS," "CM," "GU," "VI," or "c" to designate the form you are correcting.

General Instructions for Forms W-2 and W-3 (2012) -21-

Form W-2 & W-3 Instructions (Page 22)

For example, "2010" and "GU" shows that you are correcting a 2010 Form W-2GU.

Box d—Employee's correct SSN. You must enter the employee's correct SSN even if it was correct on the original Form W-2. If you are correcting an employee's SSN, you also must complete boxes e through i.

Box e—Corrected SSN and/or name. Check this box only if you are correcting the employee's SSN, name, or both SSN and name. You also must complete boxes d and f through i.

Box f—Employee's previously reported SSN. Complete this box if you are correcting an employee's previously reported incorrect SSN and/or name. If the previous SSN was reported as blanks or not available, then box f should be all zeroes.

Box g—Employee's previously reported name. Complete this box if you are correcting an employee's previously reported incorrect SSN and/or name. You must enter the employee's previously reported full name in box g exactly as it was previously reported.

TIP *For boxes f and g, if the previous SSN and the previous name were reported as blanks, you must show the previous name as blanks.*

CAUTION *For boxes f and g, If both the previous SSN and the previous name were reported as blanks, **do not** use Form W-2c. Contact the SSA at 1-800-772-6270.*

Box h—Employee's first name and initial, Last name, Suff. Always enter the employee's correct name. See *Boxes e and f—Employee's name and address* on page 12 for name formatting information.

Box i—Employee's address and ZIP code. Always enter the employee's correct address. See *Boxes e and f—Employee's name and address* on page 12 for address formatting information.

CAUTION *You must enter the employee's full name in boxes g and h.*

Boxes 1 through 20. For the items you are changing, enter under "Previously reported" the amount reported on the original Form W-2 or on a prior Form W-2c. Enter under "Correct information" the correct amount.

Do not make an entry in any of these boxes on Copy A unless you are making a change. However, see the *CAUTION* for state, local, or federal government employers below.

Box 2—Federal income tax withheld. Use this box only to make corrections because of an administrative error. (An administrative error occurs only if the amount you entered in box 2 of the incorrect Form W-2 was not the amount you actually withheld.) If you are correcting Forms W-2AS, W-2CM, W-2GU, or W-2VI, box 2 is for income tax withheld for the applicable U.S. possession.

Boxes 5 and 6. Complete these boxes to correct Medicare wages and tips and Medicare tax withheld. State, local, or federal government employers also should use these boxes to correct MQGE wages. Box 5 must equal or exceed the sum of boxes 3 and 7.

CAUTION *A state, local, or federal government employer correcting only social security wages and/or social security tips (boxes 3 and/or 7) for an MQGE employee also must complete Medicare wages and tips in box 5. Enter the total Medicare wages and tips, including MQGE-only wages, even if there is no change to the total Medicare wages and tips previously reported.*

Boxes 8 through 11. Use these boxes to correct allocated tips, an advance EIC payment (before 2011), dependent care benefits, or deferrals and distributions relating to nonqualified plans.

Box 12—Codes. Complete these boxes to correct any of the coded items shown on Forms W-2. Examples include uncollected social security and/or Medicare taxes on tips, taxable cost of group-term life insurance coverage over $50,000, elective deferrals (codes D through H, S, Y, AA, BB, and EE), sick pay not includible as income, and employee business expenses. See *Box 12—Codes* on page 14 for the proper format to use in reporting coded items from box 12 of Forms W-2.

Employers should enter both the code and dollar amount for both fields on Form W-2c.

If a single Form W-2c does not provide enough blank spaces for corrections, use additional Forms W-2c.

Box 13. Check the boxes in box 13, under "Previously reported," as they were checked on the original Form W-2. Under "Correct information," check them as they should have been checked. For example, if you checked the "Retirement plan" box on the original Form W-2 by mistake, check the "Retirement plan" checkbox in box 13 under "Previously reported," but do not check the "Retirement plan" checkbox in box 13 under "Correct information."

Box 14. Use this box to correct items reported in box 14 of the original Form W-2 or on a prior Form W-2c. If possible, complete box 14 on Copies B, C, 1, and 2 of Form W-2c only, not on Copy A.

Boxes 15 through 20—State/local taxes. If your only changes to the original Form W-2 are to state or local data, do not send Copy A of Form W-2c to the SSA. Instead, send Form W-2c to the appropriate state or local agency and furnish copies to your employees.

Correcting state information. Contact your state or locality for specific reporting information.

Specific Instructions for Form W-3c

Do not staple or tape the Forms W-2c to Form W-3c or to each other. File a separate Form W-3c for each tax year, for each type of form, and for each kind of payer/employer combination. (The "Third-party sick pay" indicator box does not designate a separate kind of payer or employer.) Make a copy of Form W-3c for your records.

In the money boxes of Form W-3c, total the amounts from each box and column on the Forms W-2c you are sending.

Box a—Tax year/Form corrected. Enter all four digits of the year of the form you are correcting and the type of form you are correcting. For the type of form, enter "2," "2AS," "2CM," "2GU," "2VI," "2c," "3," "3SS," or "3c." For example, entering "2010" and "2" indicates that all the forms being corrected are 2010 Forms W-2.

Box b—Employer's name, address, and ZIP code. This should be the same as shown on your Form 941, Form 941-SS, Form 943, Form 944, Form 944-SS, Form CT-1, or Schedule H (Form 1040). Include the suite, room, or other unit number after the street address. If the Post Office does not deliver mail to the street address

Form W-2 & W-3 Instructions (Page 23)

and you use a P.O. box, show the P.O. box number instead of the street address.

TIP *The IRS will not use Form W-3c to update your address of record. If you wish to change your address, file Form 8822 or Form 8822-B. To get this or any other IRS form, call 1-800 TAX-FORM (1-800-829-3676) or visit IRS.gov.*

Box c—Kind of Payer. Check the box that applies to you. Check only one box. If your previous Form W-3 or Form W-3SS was checked incorrectly, report your prior incorrect payer type in the "Explain decreases here" area below boxes 18 and 19.

941/941-SS. Check this box if you file Form 941 or Form 941-SS.

Military. Check this box if you are a military employer correcting Forms W-2 for members of the uniformed services.

943. Check this box if you file Form 943 and you are correcting Forms W-2 for agricultural employees. For nonagricultural employees, send Forms W-2c with a separate Form W-3c, generally with the 941/941-SS box checked.

944/944-SS. Check this box if you file Form 944 or Form 944-SS.

CT-1. Check this box if you are a railroad employer correcting Forms W-2 for employees covered under the Railroad Retirement Tax Act (RRTA). If you also have to correct forms of employees who are subject to social security and Medicare taxes, complete a separate Form W-3c with the "941/941-SS" box or "944/944-SS" box checked instead.

Hshld. emp. Check this box if you are a household employer correcting Forms W-2 for household employees and you file Schedule H (Form 1040). If you also have to correct forms of employees who are not household employees, complete a separate Form W-3c.

Medicare govt. emp. Check this box if you are a U.S., state, or local agency filing corrections for employees subject only to Medicare taxes.

Box c—Kind of Employer. Check the box that applies to you. Check only one box. If your previous Form W-3 or W-3SS was checked incorrectly, report your prior incorrect employer type in the "Explain decreases here" area below boxes 18 and 19. See *Box b—Kind of Employer* on page 18 for examples of 501(c) organizations.

None apply. Check this box if none of the checkboxes described next apply to you.

501c non-govt. Check this box if you are a non-governmental tax-exempt 501(c) organization.

State/local non 501c. Check this box if you are a state or local government or instrumentality that is not a tax-exempt 501(c) organization.

State/local 501c. Check this box if you are a dual status state or local government or instrumentality that is also a tax-exempt 501(c) organization.

Federal govt. Check this box if you are a Federal government entity or instrumentality.

Box c—Third-party sick pay. Check this box if you are a third-party sick pay payer (or are reporting sick pay payments made by a third party) correcting Forms W-2 with the "Third-party sick pay" checkbox in box 13 of Form W-2c under "Correct information" checked. File a separate Form W-3c for each payer/employer combination reporting "Third-party sick pay" on Form W-2c.

Box d—Number of Forms W-2c. Show the number of individual Forms W-2c filed with this Form W-3c or enter "-0-" if you are correcting only a previously filed Form W-3 or Form W-3SS.

Box e—Employer's Federal EIN. Enter the correct number assigned to you by the IRS in the following format: 00-0000000. If you are correcting your EIN, enter the incorrect EIN you used in box h.

Box f—Establishment number. You may use this box to identify separate establishments in your business. You may file a separate Form W-3c, with Forms W-2c, for each establishment or you may use a single Form W-3c for all Forms W-2c. You do not have to complete this item; it is optional.

Box g—Employer's state ID number. You are not required to complete this box. This number is assigned by the individual state where your business is located. However, you may want to complete this item if you use copies of this form for your state returns.

Box h—Employer's incorrect Federal EIN. Your correct number must appear in box e. Make an entry here only if the number on the original form was incorrect.

Box i—Incorrect establishment number. You may use this box to correct an establishment number.

Box j—Employer's incorrect state ID number. Use this box to make any corrections to your previously reported state ID number.

Boxes 1 through 11. Enter the total of amounts reported in boxes 1 through 11 as "Previously reported" and "Correct information" from Forms W-2c.

Box 9—Advance EIC payment. Enter an amount in box 9 only if you are making a correction for years before 2011.

Box 12a—Deferred compensation. Enter the total of amounts reported with codes D through H, S, Y, AA, BB, and EE as "Previously reported" and "Correct information" from Forms W-2c.

CAUTION *The total of Form W-2c box 12 amounts reported with Codes A through C, J through R, T through W, Z, and DD is not reported on Form W-3c.*

Box 12b—HIRE exempt wages and tips. Enter the total of amounts reported with code CC as "Previously reported" and "Correct information" from Forms W-2c. See *HIRE wages and tips paid to qualified employees* on page 20.

Box 14—Inc. tax w/h by third-party sick pay payer. Enter the amount previously reported and the corrected amount of income tax withheld on third-party payments of sick pay. Although this tax is included in the box 2 amounts, it must be shown separately here.

Boxes 16 through 19. If your only changes to the Forms W-2c and W-3c are to the state and local data, do not send either Copy A of Form W-2c or Form W-3c to the SSA. Instead, send the forms to the appropriate state or local agency and furnish copies of Form W-2c to your employees.

Explain decreases here. Explain any decrease to amounts "Previously reported." Also report here any previous incorrect entry in box c, "Kind of Payer" or "Kind of Employer." Enclose (but do not attach) additional sheets explaining your decreases, if necessary.

General Instructions for Forms W-2 and W-3 (2012) -23-

Form W-2 & W-3 Instructions (Page 24)

Signature. Sign and date the form. Also enter your title, phone number, and the name of a person to contact. If you have a fax number and/or email address, enter them. If you are not the employer, see *Who may sign Form W-3c* on page 20.

Privacy Act and Paperwork Reduction Act Notice. We ask for the information on Forms W-2 and W-3 to carry out the Internal Revenue laws of the United States. We need it to figure and collect the right amount of tax. Section 6051 and its regulations require you to furnish wage and tax statements to employees, the Social Security Administration, and the Internal Revenue Service. Section 6109 requires you to provide your employer identification number (EIN). Failure to provide this information in a timely manner or providing false or fraudulent information may subject you to penalties.

You are not required to provide the information requested on a form that is subject to the Paperwork Reduction Act unless the form displays a valid OMB control number. Books or records relating to a form or its instructions must be retained as long as their contents may become material in the administration of any Internal Revenue law.

Generally, tax returns and return information are confidential, as required by section 6103. However, section 6103 allows or requires the Internal Revenue Service to disclose or give the information shown on your return to others as described in the Code. For example, we may disclose your tax information to the Department of Justice for civil and/or criminal litigation, and to cities, states, the District of Columbia, and U.S. commonwealths and possessions for use in administering their tax laws. We may also disclose this information to other countries under a tax treaty, to federal and state agencies to enforce federal nontax criminal laws, or to federal law enforcement and intelligence agencies to combat terrorism.

The time needed to complete and file these forms will vary depending on individual circumstances. The estimated average times are: Form W-2—30 minutes; Form W-3—28 minutes; Form W-2c—40 minutes; Form W-3c—51 minutes. If you have comments concerning the accuracy of these time estimates or suggestions for making these forms simpler, we would be happy to hear from you. You can write to the Internal Revenue Service, Tax Products Coordinating Committee, SE:W:CAR:MP:T:M:S, 1111 Constitution Ave. NW, IR-6526, Washington, DC 20224. Do not send Forms W-2 and W-3 to this address. Instead, see *Where to file paper Forms W-2 and W-3* on page 4.

Form W-2 Reference Guide for Box 12 Codes (See the box 12 instructions.)

A	Uncollected social security or RRTA tax on tips	K	20% excise tax on excess golden parachute payments	V	Income from exercise of nonstatutory stock option(s)
B	Uncollected Medicare tax on tips	L	Substantiated employee business expense reimbursements	W	Employer contributions (including employee contributions through a cafeteria plan) to an employee's health savings account (HSA)
C	Taxable cost of group-term life insurance over $50,000	M	Uncollected social security or RRTA tax on taxable cost of group-term life insurance over $50,000 (former employees only)	Y	Deferrals under a section 409A nonqualified deferred compensation plan
D	Elective deferrals to a section 401(k) cash or deferred arrangement plan (including a SIMPLE 401(k) arrangement)	N	Uncollected Medicare tax on taxable cost of group-term life insurance over $50,000 (former employees only)	Z	Income under section 409A on a nonqualified deferred compensation plan
E	Elective deferrals under a section 403(b) salary reduction agreement	P	Excludable moving expense reimbursements paid directly to employee	AA	Designated Roth contributions under a section 401(k) plan
F	Elective deferrals under a section 408(k)(6) salary reduction SEP	Q	Nontaxable combat pay	BB	Designated Roth contributions under a section 403(b) plan
G	Elective deferrals and employer contributions (including nonelective deferrals) to a section 457(b) deferred compensation plan	R	Employer contributions to an Archer MSA	CC	HIRE exempt wages and tips (2010 only)
H	Elective deferrals to a section 501(c)(18)(D) tax-exempt organization plan	S	Employee salary reduction contributions under a section 408(p) SIMPLE plan	DD	Cost of employer-sponsored health coverage
J	Nontaxable sick pay	T	Adoption benefits	EE	Designated Roth contributions under a governmental section 457(b) plan

-24- General Instructions for Forms W-2 and W-3 (2012)

Form W-2 & W-3 Instructions (Page 25)

Index

Form W-3

DO NOT STAPLE

33333	a Control number	For Official Use Only ▶ OMB No. 1545-0008

b Kind of Payer (Check one) ▶ 941 ☐ Military ☐ 943 ☐ 944 ☐ CT-1 ☐ Hshld. emp. ☐ Medicare govt. emp. ☐	Kind of Employer (Check one) ▶ None apply ☐ 501c non-govt. ☐ State/local non-501c ☐ State/local 501c ☐ Federal govt. ☐	Third-party sick pay (Check if applicable) ☐

c Total number of Forms W-2	d Establishment number	1 Wages, tips, other compensation	2 Federal income tax withheld
e Employer identification number (EIN)		3 Social security wages	4 Social security tax withheld
f Employer's name		5 Medicare wages and tips	6 Medicare tax withheld
		7 Social security tips	8 Allocated tips
		9	10 Dependent care benefits
g Employer's address and ZIP code		11 Nonqualified plans	12a Deferred compensation
h Other EIN used this year		13 For third-party sick pay use only	12b
15 State	Employer's state ID number	14 Income tax withheld by payer of third-party sick pay	
16 State wages, tips, etc.	17 State income tax	18 Local wages, tips, etc.	19 Local income tax
Contact person		Telephone number	For Official Use Only
Email address		Fax number	

Under penalties of perjury, I declare that I have examined this return and accompanying documents and, to the best of my knowledge and belief, they are true, correct, and complete.

Signature ▶ Title ▶ Date ▶

Form **W-3** Transmittal of Wage and Tax Statements **2013** Department of the Treasury Internal Revenue Service

Send this entire page with the entire Copy A page of Form(s) W-2 to the Social Security Administration (SSA). Photocopies are not acceptable. Do not send Form W-3 if you filed electronically with the SSA.
Do not send any payment (cash, checks, money orders, etc.) with Forms W-2 and W-3.

Reminder

Separate instructions. See the 2013 General Instructions for Forms W-2 and W-3 for information on completing this form.

Purpose of Form

A Form W-3 Transmittal is completed only when paper Copy A of Form(s) W-2, Wage and Tax Statement, is being filed. Do not file Form W-3 alone. Do not file Form W-3 for Form(s) W-2 that were submitted electronically to the SSA (see below). All paper forms **must** comply with IRS standards and be machine readable. Photocopies are **not** acceptable. Use a Form W-3 even if only one paper Form W-2 is being filed. Make sure both the Form W-3 and Form(s) W-2 show the correct tax year and Employer Identification Number (EIN). Make a copy of this form and keep it with Copy D (For Employer) of Form(s) W-2 for your records. The IRS recommends retaining copies of these forms for four years.

E-Filing

The SSA strongly suggests employers report Form W-3 and Forms W-2 Copy A electronically instead of on paper. The SSA provides two free e-filing options on its Business Services Online (BSO) website:

- **W-2 Online.** Use fill-in forms to create, save, print, and submit up to 50 Forms W-2 at a time to the SSA.
- **File Upload.** Upload wage files to the SSA you have created using payroll or tax software that formats the files according to the SSA's *Specifications for Filing Forms W-2 Electronically (EFW2).*

W-2 Online fill-in forms or file uploads will be on time if submitted by March 31, 2014. For more information, go to *www.socialsecurity.gov/employer* and select "First Time Filers" or "Returning Filers" under "BEFORE YOU FILE."

When To File

Mail Form W-3 with Copy A of Form(s) W-2 by February 28, 2014.

Where To File Paper Forms

Send this entire page with the entire Copy A page of Form(s) W-2 to:

Social Security Administration
Data Operations Center
Wilkes-Barre, PA 18769-0001

Note. If you use "Certified Mail" to file, change the ZIP code to "18769-0002." If you use an IRS-approved private delivery service, add "ATTN: W-2 Process, 1150 E. Mountain Dr." to the address and change the ZIP code to "18702-7997." See Publication 15 (Circular E), Employer's Tax Guide, for a list of IRS-approved private delivery services.

For Privacy Act and Paperwork Reduction Act Notice, see the separate instructions.

Cat. No. 10159Y

Form W-2c

DO NOT CUT, FOLD, OR STAPLE THIS FORM

44444 | For Official Use Only ► OMB No. 1545-0008

a Employer's name, address, and ZIP code	c Tax year/Form corrected / W-2
	d Employee's correct SSN
	e Corrected SSN and/or name (Check this box and complete boxes f and/or g if incorrect on form previously filed.) ☐
	Complete boxes f and/or g only if incorrect on form **previously filed** ►
	f Employee's **previously reported** SSN
b Employer's Federal EIN	g Employee's **previously reported** name
	h Employee's first name and initial / Last name / Suff.
Note: Only complete money fields that are being corrected (exception: for corrections involving MQGE, see the Instructions for Forms W-2c and W-3c, boxes 5 and 6).	i Employee's address and ZIP code

Previously reported	Correct information	Previously reported	Correct information
1 Wages, tips, other compensation	1 Wages, tips, other compensation	2 Federal income tax withheld	2 Federal income tax withheld
3 Social security wages	3 Social security wages	4 Social security tax withheld	4 Social security tax withheld
5 Medicare wages and tips	5 Medicare wages and tips	6 Medicare tax withheld	6 Medicare tax withheld
7 Social security tips	7 Social security tips	8 Allocated tips	8 Allocated tips
9 Advance EIC payment	9 Advance EIC payment	10 Dependent care benefits	10 Dependent care benefits
11 Nonqualified plans	11 Nonqualified plans	12a See instructions for box 12 Code	12a See instructions for box 12 Code
13 Statutory employee ☐ Retirement plan ☐ Third-party sick pay ☐	13 Statutory employee ☐ Retirement plan ☐ Third-party sick pay ☐	12b Code	12b Code
14 Other (see instructions)	14 Other (see instructions)	12c Code	12c Code
		12d Code	12d Code

State Correction Information

Previously reported	Correct information	Previously reported	Correct information
15 State	15 State	15 State	15 State
Employer's state ID number	Employer's state ID number	Employer's state ID number	Employer's state ID number
16 State wages, tips, etc.	16 State wages, tips, etc.	16 State wages, tips, etc.	16 State wages, tips, etc.
17 State income tax	17 State income tax	17 State income tax	17 State income tax

Locality Correction Information

Previously reported	Correct information	Previously reported	Correct information
18 Local wages, tips, etc.	18 Local wages, tips, etc.	18 Local wages, tips, etc.	18 Local wages, tips, etc.
19 Local income tax	19 Local income tax	19 Local income tax	19 Local income tax
20 Locality name	20 Locality name	20 Locality name	20 Locality name

For Privacy Act and Paperwork Reduction Act Notice, see separate instructions. **Copy A—For Social Security Administration**

Form **W-2c** (Rev. 2-2009) **Corrected Wage and Tax Statement** Cat. No. 61437D Department of the Treasury Internal Revenue Service

Form W-3c

DO NOT CUT, FOLD, OR STAPLE

55555	a Tax year/Form corrected / W-	For Official Use Only ▶ OMB No. 1545-0008	
b Employer's name, address, and ZIP code	c Kind of Payer (Check one): 941/941-SS ☐ Military ☐ 943 ☐ 944/944-SS ☐ CT-1 ☐ Hshld. emp. ☐ Medicare govt. emp. ☐	Kind of Employer (Check one): None apply ☐ 501c non-govt. ☐ State/local non-501c ☐ State/local 501c ☐ Federal govt. ☐	Third-party sick pay ☐ (Check if applicable)
d Number of Forms W-2c	e Employer's Federal EIN	f Establishment number	g Employer's state ID number
Complete boxes h, i, or j **only** if incorrect on last form filed.	h Employer's **incorrect** Federal EIN	i **Incorrect** establishment number	j Employer's **incorrect** state ID number
Total of amounts previously reported as shown on enclosed Forms W-2c.	**Total of corrected amounts as shown on enclosed Forms W-2c.**	**Total of amounts previously reported as shown on enclosed Forms W-2c.**	**Total of corrected amounts as shown on enclosed Forms W-2c.**
1 Wages, tips, other compensation	1 Wages, tips, other compensation	2 Federal income tax withheld	2 Federal income tax withheld
3 Social security wages	3 Social security wages	4 Social security tax withheld	4 Social security tax withheld
5 Medicare wages and tips	5 Medicare wages and tips	6 Medicare tax withheld	6 Medicare tax withheld
7 Social security tips	7 Social security tips	8 Allocated tips	8 Allocated tips
9 Advance EIC payments	9 Advance EIC payments	10 Dependent care benefits	10 Dependent care benefits
11 Nonqualified plans	11 Nonqualified plans	12a Deferred compensation	12a Deferred compensation
14 Inc. tax w/h by third-party sick pay payer	14 Inc. tax w/h by third-party sick pay payer	12b HIRE exempt wages and tips	12b HIRE exempt wages and tips
16 State wages, tips, etc.	16 State wages, tips, etc.	17 State income tax	17 State income tax
18 Local wages, tips, etc.	18 Local wages, tips, etc.	19 Local income tax	19 Local income tax

Explain decreases here:

Has an adjustment been made on an employment tax return filed with the Internal Revenue Service? ☐ Yes ☐ No

If "Yes," give date the return was filed ▶

Under penalties of perjury, I declare that I have examined this return, including accompanying documents, and, to the best of my knowledge and belief, it is true, correct, and complete.

Signature ▶ Title ▶ Date ▶

Contact person	Telephone number	For Official Use Only
Email address	Fax number	

Form **W-3c** (Rev. 12-2011) **Transmittal of Corrected Wage and Tax Statements** Department of the Treasury Internal Revenue Service

Purpose of Form

Use this form to transmit Copy A of **Form(s) W-2c,** Corrected Wage and Tax Statement (Rev. 2-2009). Make a copy of Form W-3c and keep it with Copy D (For Employer) of Forms W-2c for your records. File Form W-3c even if only one Form W-2c is being filed or if those Forms W-2c are being filed only to correct an employee's name and social security number (SSN) or the employer identification number (EIN). See the 2012 General Instructions for Forms W-2 and W-3 for information on completing this form.

When To File

File this form and Copy A of Form(s) W-2c with the Social Security Administration as soon as possible after you discover an error on Forms W-2, W-2AS, W-2GU, W-2CM, W-2VI, or W-2c. Provide Copies B, C, and 2 of Form W-2c to your employees as soon as possible.

For Paperwork Reduction Act Notice, see separate instructions.

Where To File

If you use the U.S. Postal Service, send Forms W-2c and W-3c to the following address:

Social Security Administration
Data Operations Center
P.O. Box 3333
Wilkes-Barre, PA 18767-3333

If you use a carrier other than the U.S. Postal Service, send Forms W-2c and W-3c to the following address:

Social Security Administration
Data Operations Center
Attn: W-2c Process
1150 E. Mountain Drive
Wilkes-Barre, PA 18702-7997

Cat. No. 10164R

Form I-9

OMB No. 1615-0047; Expires 08/31/12

Department of Homeland Security
U.S. Citizenship and Immigration Services

Form I-9, Employment Eligibility Verification

Read instructions carefully before completing this form. The instructions must be available during completion of this form.

ANTI-DISCRIMINATION NOTICE: It is illegal to discriminate against work-authorized individuals. Employers CANNOT specify which document(s) they will accept from an employee. The refusal to hire an individual because the documents have a future expiration date may also constitute illegal discrimination.

Section 1. Employee Information and Verification *(To be completed and signed by employee at the time employment begins.)*

Print Name: Last	First	Middle Initial	Maiden Name
Address *(Street Name and Number)*		Apt. #	Date of Birth *(month/day/year)*
City	State	Zip Code	Social Security #

I am aware that federal law provides for imprisonment and/or fines for false statements or use of false documents in connection with the completion of this form.

I attest, under penalty of perjury, that I am (check one of the following):

- ☐ A citizen of the United States
- ☐ A noncitizen national of the United States (see instructions)
- ☐ A lawful permanent resident (Alien #) ______
- ☐ An alien authorized to work (Alien # or Admission #) ______ until (expiration date, if applicable - *month/day/year*)

Employee's Signature | Date *(month/day/year)*

Preparer and/or Translator Certification *(To be completed and signed if Section 1 is prepared by a person other than the employee.) I attest, under penalty of perjury, that I have assisted in the completion of this form and that to the best of my knowledge the information is true and correct.*

Preparer's/Translator's Signature	Print Name
Address *(Street Name and Number, City, State, Zip Code)*	Date *(month/day/year)*

Section 2. Employer Review and Verification *(To be completed and signed by employer. Examine one document from List A OR examine one document from List B and one from List C, as listed on the reverse of this form, and record the title, number, and expiration date, if any, of the document(s).)*

	List A	OR	List B	AND	List C
Document title:	______		______		______
Issuing authority:	______		______		______
Document #:	______		______		______
Expiration Date *(if any)*:	______		______		______
Document #:	______				
Expiration Date *(if any)*:	______				

CERTIFICATION: I attest, under penalty of perjury, that I have examined the document(s) presented by the above-named employee, that the above-listed document(s) appear to be genuine and to relate to the employee named, that the employee began employment on *(month/day/year)* ______ **and that to the best of my knowledge the employee is authorized to work in the United States. (State employment agencies may omit the date the employee began employment.)**

Signature of Employer or Authorized Representative	Print Name	Title
Business or Organization Name and Address *(Street Name and Number, City, State, Zip Code)*		Date *(month/day/year)*

Section 3. Updating and Reverification *(To be completed and signed by employer.)*

A. New Name *(if applicable)*	B. Date of Rehire *(month/day/year) (if applicable)*

C. If employee's previous grant of work authorization has expired, provide the information below for the document that establishes current employment authorization.

Document Title: ______ Document #: ______ Expiration Date *(if any)*: ______

I attest, under penalty of perjury, that to the best of my knowledge, this employee is authorized to work in the United States, and if the employee presented document(s), the document(s) I have examined appear to be genuine and to relate to the individual.

Signature of Employer or Authorized Representative	Date *(month/day/year)*

Form I-9 (Rev. 08/07/09) Y Page 4

Form I-9—Instructions (Page 1)

OMB No. 1615-0047; Expires 08/31/12

Department of Homeland Security
U.S. Citizenship and Immigration Services

Form I-9, Employment Eligibility Verification

Instructions

Read all instructions carefully before completing this form.

Anti-Discrimination Notice. It is illegal to discriminate against any individual (other than an alien not authorized to work in the United States) in hiring, discharging, or recruiting or referring for a fee because of that individual's national origin or citizenship status. It is illegal to discriminate against work-authorized individuals. Employers **CANNOT** specify which document(s) they will accept from an employee. The refusal to hire an individual because the documents presented have a future expiration date may also constitute illegal discrimination. For more information, call the Office of Special Counsel for Immigration Related Unfair Employment Practices at 1-800-255-8155.

What Is the Purpose of This Form?

The purpose of this form is to document that each new employee (both citizen and noncitizen) hired after November 6, 1986, is authorized to work in the United States.

When Should Form I-9 Be Used?

All employees (citizens and noncitizens) hired after November 6, 1986, and working in the United States must complete Form I-9.

Filling Out Form I-9

Section 1, Employee

This part of the form must be completed no later than the time of hire, which is the actual beginning of employment. Providing the Social Security Number is voluntary, except for employees hired by employers participating in the USCIS Electronic Employment Eligibility Verification Program (E-Verify). **The employer is responsible for ensuring that Section 1 is timely and properly completed.**

Noncitizen nationals of the United States are persons born in American Samoa, certain former citizens of the former Trust Territory of the Pacific Islands, and certain children of noncitizen nationals born abroad.

Employers should note the work authorization expiration date (if any) shown in **Section 1**. For employees who indicate an employment authorization expiration date in **Section 1**, employers are required to reverify employment authorization for employment on or before the date shown. Note that some employees may leave the expiration date blank if they are aliens whose work authorization does not expire (e.g., asylees, refugees, certain citizens of the Federated States of Micronesia or the Republic of the Marshall Islands). For such employees, reverification does not apply unless they choose to present in Section 2 evidence of employment authorization that contains an expiration date (e.g., Employment Authorization Document (Form I-766)).

Preparer/Translator Certification

The Preparer/Translator Certification must be completed if **Section 1** is prepared by a person other than the employee. A preparer/translator may be used only when the employee is unable to complete **Section 1** on his or her own. However, the employee must still sign **Section 1** personally.

Section 2, Employer

For the purpose of completing this form, the term "employer" means all employers including those recruiters and referrers for a fee who are agricultural associations, agricultural employers, or farm labor contractors. Employers must complete **Section 2** by examining evidence of identity and employment authorization within three business days of the date employment begins. However, if an employer hires an individual for less than three business days, **Section 2** must be completed at the time employment begins. Employers cannot specify which document(s) listed on the last page of Form I-9 employees present to establish identity and employment authorization. Employees may present any List A document **OR** a combination of a List B and a List C document.

If an employee is unable to present a required document (or documents), the employee must present an acceptable receipt in lieu of a document listed on the last page of this form. Receipts showing that a person has applied for an initial grant of employment authorization, or for renewal of employment authorization, are not acceptable. Employees must present receipts within three business days of the date employment begins and must present valid replacement documents within 90 days or other specified time.

Employers must record in Section 2:

1. Document title;
2. Issuing authority;
3. Document number;
4. Expiration date, if any; and
5. The date employment begins.

Employers must sign and date the certification in **Section 2**. Employees must present original documents. Employers may, but are not required to, photocopy the document(s) presented. If photocopies are made, they must be made for all new hires. Photocopies may only be used for the verification process and must be retained with Form I-9. **Employers are still responsible for completing and retaining Form I-9.**

Form I-9 (Rev. 08/07/09) Y

Form I-9—Instructions (Page 2)

For more detailed information, you may refer to the *USCIS Handbook for Employers* (Form M-274). You may obtain the handbook using the contact information found under the header "USCIS Forms and Information."

Section 3, Updating and Reverification

Employers must complete **Section 3** when updating and/or reverifying Form I-9. Employers must reverify employment authorization of their employees on or before the work authorization expiration date recorded in **Section 1** (if any). Employers **CANNOT** specify which document(s) they will accept from an employee.

A. If an employee's name has changed at the time this form is being updated/reverified, complete Block A.

B. If an employee is rehired within three years of the date this form was originally completed and the employee is still authorized to be employed on the same basis as previously indicated on this form (updating), complete Block B and the signature block.

C. If an employee is rehired within three years of the date this form was originally completed and the employee's work authorization has expired **or** if a current employee's work authorization is about to expire (reverification), complete Block B; and:

1. Examine any document that reflects the employee is authorized to work in the United States (see List A **or** C);
2. Record the document title, document number, and expiration date (if any) in Block C; and
3. Complete the signature block.

Note that for reverification purposes, employers have the option of completing a new Form I-9 instead of completing **Section 3.**

What Is the Filing Fee?

There is no associated filing fee for completing Form I-9. This form is not filed with USCIS or any government agency. Form I-9 must be retained by the employer and made available for inspection by U.S. Government officials as specified in the Privacy Act Notice below.

USCIS Forms and Information

To order USCIS forms, you can download them from our website at www.uscis.gov/forms or call our toll-free number at 1-800-870-3676. You can obtain information about Form I-9 from our website at www.uscis.gov or by calling 1-888-464-4218.

Information about E-Verify, a free and voluntary program that allows participating employers to electronically verify the employment eligibility of their newly hired employees, can be obtained from our website at www.uscis.gov/e-verify or by calling 1-888-464-4218.

General information on immigration laws, regulations, and procedures can be obtained by telephoning our National Customer Service Center at 1-800-375-5283 or visiting our Internet website at www.uscis.gov.

Photocopying and Retaining Form I-9

A blank Form I-9 may be reproduced, provided both sides are copied. The Instructions must be available to all employees completing this form. Employers must retain completed Form I-9s for three years after the date of hire or one year after the date employment ends, whichever is later.

Form I-9 may be signed and retained electronically, as authorized in Department of Homeland Security regulations at 8 CFR 274a.2.

Privacy Act Notice

The authority for collecting this information is the Immigration Reform and Control Act of 1986, Pub. L. 99-603 (8 USC 1324a).

This information is for employers to verify the eligibility of individuals for employment to preclude the unlawful hiring, or recruiting or referring for a fee, of aliens who are not authorized to work in the United States.

This information will be used by employers as a record of their basis for determining eligibility of an employee to work in the United States. The form will be kept by the employer and made available for inspection by authorized officials of the Department of Homeland Security, Department of Labor, and Office of Special Counsel for Immigration-Related Unfair Employment Practices.

Submission of the information required in this form is voluntary. However, an individual may not begin employment unless this form is completed, since employers are subject to civil or criminal penalties if they do not comply with the Immigration Reform and Control Act of 1986.

EMPLOYERS MUST RETAIN COMPLETED FORM I-9
DO NOT MAIL COMPLETED FORM I-9 TO ICE OR USCIS

Form I-9 (Rev. 08/07/09) Y Page 2

Form I-9-Lists of Acceptable Documents

LISTS OF ACCEPTABLE DOCUMENTS

All documents must be unexpired

LIST A **Documents that Establish Both Identity and Employment Authorization**	OR	LIST B **Documents that Establish Identity**	AND	LIST C **Documents that Establish Employment Authorization**
1. U.S. Passport or U.S. Passport Card		**1.** Driver's license or ID card issued by a State or outlying possession of the United States provided it contains a photograph or information such as name, date of birth, gender, height, eye color, and address		**1.** Social Security Account Number card other than one that specifies on the face that the issuance of the card does not authorize employment in the United States
2. Permanent Resident Card or Alien Registration Receipt Card (Form I-551)		**2.** ID card issued by federal, state or local government agencies or entities, provided it contains a photograph or information such as name, date of birth, gender, height, eye color, and address		**2.** Certification of Birth Abroad issued by the Department of State (Form FS-545)
3. Foreign passport that contains a temporary I-551 stamp or temporary I-551 printed notation on a machine-readable immigrant visa		**3.** School ID card with a photograph		**3.** Certification of Report of Birth issued by the Department of State (Form DS-1350)
4. Employment Authorization Document that contains a photograph (Form I-766)		**4.** Voter's registration card		**4.** Original or certified copy of birth certificate issued by a State, county, municipal authority, or territory of the United States bearing an official seal
5. In the case of a nonimmigrant alien authorized to work for a specific employer incident to status, a foreign passport with Form I-94 or Form I-94A bearing the same name as the passport and containing an endorsement of the alien's nonimmigrant status, as long as the period of endorsement has not yet expired and the proposed employment is not in conflict with any restrictions or limitations identified on the form		**5.** U.S. Military card or draft record		**5.** Native American tribal document
6. Passport from the Federated States of Micronesia (FSM) or the Republic of the Marshall Islands (RMI) with Form I-94 or Form I-94A indicating nonimmigrant admission under the Compact of Free Association Between the United States and the FSM or RMI		**6.** Military dependent's ID card		**6.** U.S. Citizen ID Card (Form I-197)
		7. U.S. Coast Guard Merchant Mariner Card		**7.** Identification Card for Use of Resident Citizen in the United States (Form I-179)
		8. Native American tribal document		**8.** Employment authorization document issued by the Department of Homeland Security
		9. Driver's license issued by a Canadian government authority		
		For persons under age 18 who are unable to present a document listed above:		
		10. School record or report card		
		11. Clinic, doctor, or hospital record		
		12. Day-care or nursery school record		

Illustrations of many of these documents appear in Part 8 of the Handbook for Employers (M-274)

Form I-9 (Rev. 08/07/09) Y Page 5

Form 1099-MISC

9595 ☐ VOID ☐ CORRECTED

PAYER'S name, street address, city or town, province or state, country, ZIP or foreign postal code, and telephone no.

1 Rents
$

2 Royalties
$

OMB No. 1545-0115

2013

Form 1099-MISC

Miscellaneous Income

3 Other income
$

4 Federal income tax withheld
$

Copy A For Internal Revenue Service Center

PAYER'S federal identification number

RECIPIENT'S identification number

5 Fishing boat proceeds
$

6 Medical and health care payments
$

File with Form 1096.

RECIPIENT'S name

7 Nonemployee compensation
$

8 Substitute payments in lieu of dividends or interest
$

For Privacy Act and Paperwork Reduction Act Notice, see the **2013 General Instructions for Certain Information Returns.**

Street address (including apt. no.)

9 Payer made direct sales of $5,000 or more of consumer products to a buyer (recipient) for resale ▶ ☐

10 Crop insurance proceeds
$

City or town, province or state, country, and ZIP or foreign postal code

11 Foreign tax paid
$

12 Foreign country or U.S. possession

Account number (see instructions)

2nd TIN not. ☐

13 Excess golden parachute payments
$

14 Gross proceeds paid to an attorney
$

15a Section 409A deferrals
$

15b Section 409A income
$

16 State tax withheld
$
$

17 State/Payer's state no.

18 State income
$
$

Form **1099-MISC** Cat. No. 14425J www.irs.gov/form1099misc Department of the Treasury - Internal Revenue Service

Do Not Cut or Separate Forms on This Page — Do Not Cut or Separate Forms on This Page

Form 1099-MISC—Instructions to Recipients

Instructions for Recipient

Recipient's identification number. For your protection, this form may show only the last four digits of your social security number (SSN), individual taxpayer identification number (ITIN), or adoption taxpayer identification number (ATIN). However, the issuer has reported your complete identification number to the IRS and, where applicable, to state and/or local governments.

Account number. May show an account or other unique number the payer assigned to distinguish your account.

Amounts shown may be subject to self-employment (SE) tax. If your net income from self-employment is $400 or more, you must file a return and compute your SE tax on Schedule SE (Form 1040). See Pub. 334 for more information. If no income or social security and Medicare taxes were withheld and you are still receiving these payments, see Form 1040-ES (or Form 1040-ES(NR)). Individuals must report these amounts as explained in the box 7 instructions on this page. Corporations, fiduciaries, or partnerships must report the amounts on the proper line of their tax returns.

Form 1099-MISC incorrect? If this form is incorrect or has been issued in error, contact the payer. If you cannot get this form corrected, attach an explanation to your tax return and report your income correctly.

Box 1. Report rents from real estate on Schedule E (Form 1040). However, report rents on Schedule C (Form 1040) if you provided significant services to the tenant, sold real estate as a business, or rented personal property as a business.

Box 2. Report royalties from oil, gas, or mineral properties, copyrights, and patents on Schedule E (Form 1040). However, report payments for a working interest as explained in the box 7 instructions. For royalties on timber, coal, and iron ore, see Pub. 544.

Box 3. Generally, report this amount on the "Other income" line of Form 1040 (or Form 1040NR) and identify the payment. The amount shown may be payments received as the beneficiary of a deceased employee, prizes, awards, taxable damages, Indian gaming profits, or other taxable income. See Pub. 525. If it is trade or business income, report this amount on Schedule C or F (Form 1040).

Box 4. Shows backup withholding or withholding on Indian gaming profits. Generally, a payer must backup withhold if you did not furnish your taxpayer identification number. See Form W-9 and Pub. 505 for more information. Report this amount on your income tax return as tax withheld.

Box 5. An amount in this box means the fishing boat operator considers you self-employed. Report this amount on Schedule C (Form 1040). See Pub. 334.

Box 6. For individuals, report on Schedule C (Form 1040).

Box 7. Shows nonemployee compensation. If you are in the trade or business of catching fish, box 7 may show cash you received for the sale of fish. If the amount in this box is SE income, report it on Schedule C or F (Form 1040), and complete Schedule SE (Form 1040). You received this form instead of Form W-2 because the payer did not consider you an employee and did not withhold income tax or social security and Medicare tax. If you believe you are an employee and cannot get the payer to correct this form, report the amount from box 7 on Form 1040, line 7 (or Form 1040NR, line 8). You must also complete Form 8919 and attach it to your return. If you are not an employee but the amount in this box is not SE income (for example, it is income from a sporadic activity or a hobby), report it on Form 1040, line 21 (or Form 1040NR, line 21).

Box 8. Shows substitute payments in lieu of dividends or tax-exempt interest received by your broker on your behalf as a result of a loan of your securities. Report on the "Other income" line of Form 1040 (or Form 1040NR).

Box 9. If checked, $5,000 or more of sales of consumer products was paid to you on a buy-sell, deposit-commission, or other basis. A dollar amount does not have to be shown. Generally, report any income from your sale of these products on Schedule C (Form 1040).

Box 10. Report this amount on Schedule F (Form 1040).

Box 11. Shows the foreign tax that you may be able to claim as a deduction or a credit on Form 1040. See the Form 1040 instructions.

Box 12. Shows the country or U.S. possession to which the foreign tax was paid.

Box 13. Shows your total compensation of excess golden parachute payments subject to a 20% excise tax. See the Form 1040 (or Form 1040NR) instructions for where to report.

Box 14. Shows gross proceeds paid to an attorney in connection with legal services. Report only the taxable part as income on your return.

Box 15a. May show current year deferrals as a nonemployee under a nonqualified deferred compensation (NQDC) plan that is subject to the requirements of section 409A, plus any earnings on current and prior year deferrals.

Box 15b. Shows income as a nonemployee under an NQDC plan that does not meet the requirements of section 409A. This amount is also included in box 7 as nonemployee compensation. Any amount included in box 15a that is currently taxable is also included in this box. This income is also subject to a substantial additional tax to be reported on Form 1040 (or Form 1040NR). See "Total Tax" in the Form 1040 (or Form 1040NR) instructions.

Boxes 16–18. Shows state or local income tax withheld from the payments.

Future developments. For the latest information about developments related to Form 1099-MISC and its instructions, such as legislation enacted after they were published, go to *www.irs.gov/form1099misc*.

Form 1099-MISC—Instructions for Payers

Instructions for Payer

General and specific form instructions are provided separately. You should use the 2013 General Instructions for Certain Information Returns and the 2013 Instructions for Form 1099-MISC to complete Form 1099-MISC. A chart in the general instructions gives a quick guide to which form must be filed to report a particular payment. To order these instructions and additional forms, go to *www.irs.gov/form1099misc* or call 1-800-TAX-FORM (1-800-829-3676).

Caution: *Because paper forms are scanned during processing, you cannot file with the IRS Forms 1096, 1097, 1098, 1099, 3921, 3922, or 5498 that you print from the IRS website.*

Due dates. Furnish Copy B of this form to the recipient by January 31, 2014. The due date is extended to February 18, 2014, if you are reporting payments in boxes 8 or 14.

File Copy A of this form with the IRS by February 28, 2014. If you file electronically, the due date is March 31, 2014. To file electronically, you must have software that generates a file according to the specifications in Pub. 1220, Specifications for Filing Forms 1097, 1098, 1099, 3921, 3922, 5498, 8935, and W-2G Electronically. The IRS does not provide a fill-in form option.

Need help? If you have questions about reporting on Form 1099-MISC, call the information reporting customer service site toll free at 1-866-455-7438 or 304-263-8700 (not toll free). Persons with a hearing or speech disability with access to TTY/TDD equipment can call 304-579-4827 (not toll free). The hours of operation are Monday through Friday from 8:30 a.m. to 4:30 p.m., Eastern time.

Form SS-8 (Page 1)

Form **SS-8**
(Rev. August 2011)
Department of the Treasury
Internal Revenue Service

Determination of Worker Status for Purposes of Federal Employment Taxes and Income Tax Withholding

OMB. No. 1545-0004
For IRS Use Only:
Case Number:
Earliest Receipt Date:

Name of firm (or person) for whom the worker performed services		Worker's name	
Firm's mailing address (include street address, apt. or suite no., city, state, and ZIP code)		Worker's mailing address (include street address, apt. or suite no., city, state, and ZIP code)	
Trade name	Firm's email address	Worker's daytime telephone number	Worker's email address
Firm's fax number	Firm's website	Worker's alternate telephone number	Worker's fax number
Firm's telephone number (include area code)	Firm's employer identification number	Worker's social security number	Worker's employer identification number (if any)

Note. If the worker is paid for these services by a firm other than the one listed on this form, enter the name, address, and employer identification number of the payer. ▶ ______________________

Disclosure of Information

The information provided on Form SS-8 may be disclosed to the firm, worker, or payer named above to assist the IRS in the determination process. For example, if you are a worker, we may disclose the information you provide on Form SS-8 to the firm or payer named above. The information can only be disclosed to assist with the determination process. If you provide incomplete information, we may not be able to process your request. See *Privacy Act and Paperwork Reduction Act Notice* on page 6 for more information. **If you do not want this information disclosed to other parties, do not file Form SS-8.**

Parts I–V. All filers of Form SS-8 must complete all questions in Parts I–IV. Part V must be completed if the worker provides a service directly to customers or is a salesperson. If you cannot answer a question, enter "Unknown" or "Does not apply." If you need more space for a question, attach another sheet with the part and question number clearly identified. Write your firm's name (or workers' name) and employer identification number (or social security number) at the top of each additional sheet attached to this form.

Part I General Information

1 This form is being completed by: ☐ Firm ☐ Worker; for services performed ______________ (beginning date) to ______________ (ending date).

2 Explain your reason(s) for filing this form (for example, you received a bill from the IRS, you believe you erroneously received a Form 1099 or Form W-2, you are unable to get worker's compensation benefits, or you were audited or are being audited by the IRS). ______________________

3 Total number of workers who performed or are performing the same or similar services: ______________.

4 How did the worker obtain the job? ☐ Application ☐ Bid ☐ Employment Agency ☐ Other (specify) ______________

5 **Attach copies of all supporting documentation (for example, contracts, invoices, memos, Forms W-2 or Forms 1099-MISC issued or received, IRS closing agreements or IRS rulings).** In addition, please inform us of any current or past litigation concerning the worker's status. If no income reporting forms (Form 1099-MISC or W-2) were furnished to the worker, enter the amount of income earned for the year(s) at issue $ ______________.
If both Form W-2 and Form 1099-MISC were issued or received, explain why. ______________________

6 Describe the firm's business. ______________________

For Privacy Act and Paperwork Reduction Act Notice, see page 6. Cat. No. 16106T Form **SS-8** (Rev. 8-2011)

Form SS-8 (Page 2)

Form SS-8 (Rev. 8-2011) Page 2

Part I **General Information** (continued)

7 If the worker received pay from more than one entity because of an event such as the sale, merger, acquisition, or reorganization of the firm for whom the services are performed, provide the following: Name of the firm's previous owner: ____________

Previous owner's taxpayer identification number: ____________ Change was a: ☐ Sale ☐ Merger ☐ Acquisition ☐ Reorganization

☐ Other (specify) ____________

Description of above change: ____________

Date of change (MM/DD/YY): ____________

8 Describe the work done by the worker and provide the worker's job title. ____________

9 Explain why you believe the worker is an employee or an independent contractor. ____________

10 Did the worker perform services for the firm in any capacity before providing the services that are the subject of this determination request?
☐ **Yes** ☐ **No** ☐ **N/A**

If "Yes," what were the dates of the prior service? ____________

If "Yes," explain the differences, if any, between the current and prior service. ____________

11 If the work is done under a written agreement between the firm and the worker, attach a copy (preferably signed by both parties). Describe the terms and conditions of the work arrangement. ____________

Part II **Behavioral Control** (Provide names and titles of specific individuals, if applicable.)

1 What specific training and/or instruction is the worker given by the firm? ____________

2 How does the worker receive work assignments? ____________

3 Who determines the methods by which the assignments are performed? ____________

4 Who is the worker required to contact if problems or complaints arise and who is responsible for their resolution? ____________

5 What types of reports are required from the worker? Attach examples. ____________

6 Describe the worker's daily routine such as his or her schedule or hours. ____________

7 At what location(s) does the worker perform services (for example, firm's premises, own shop or office, home, customer's location)? Indicate the appropriate percentage of time the worker spends in each location, if more than one. ____________

8 Describe any meetings the worker is required to attend and any penalties for not attending (for example, sales meetings, monthly meetings, staff meetings). ____________

9 Is the worker required to provide the services personally? . . . . ☐ **Yes** ☐ **No**

10 If substitutes or helpers are needed, who hires them? ____________

11 If the worker hires the substitutes or helpers, is approval required? . . . . ☐ **Yes** ☐ **No**

If "Yes," by whom? ____________

12 Who pays the substitutes or helpers? ____________

13 Is the worker reimbursed if the worker pays the substitutes or helpers? . . . . ☐ **Yes** ☐ **No**

If "Yes," by whom?

Form **SS-8** (Rev. 8-2011)

Form SS-8 (Page 3)

Form SS-8 (Rev. 8-2011) Page **2**

Part I **General Information** (continued)

7 If the worker received pay from more than one entity because of an event such as the sale, merger, acquisition, or reorganization of the firm for whom the services are performed, provide the following: Name of the firm's previous owner: ____________

Previous owner's taxpayer identification number: ____________ Change was a: ☐ Sale ☐ Merger ☐ Acquisition ☐ Reorganization

☐ Other (specify) ____________

Description of above change: ____________

Date of change (MM/DD/YY): ____________

8 Describe the work done by the worker and provide the worker's job title. ____________

9 Explain why you believe the worker is an employee or an independent contractor. ____________

10 Did the worker perform services for the firm in any capacity before providing the services that are the subject of this determination request?

☐ **Yes** ☐ **No** ☐ **N/A**

If "Yes," what were the dates of the prior service? ____________

If "Yes," explain the differences, if any, between the current and prior service. ____________

11 If the work is done under a written agreement between the firm and the worker, attach a copy (preferably signed by both parties). Describe the terms and conditions of the work arrangement. ____________

Part II **Behavioral Control** (Provide names and titles of specific individuals, if applicable.)

1 What specific training and/or instruction is the worker given by the firm? ____________

2 How does the worker receive work assignments? ____________

3 Who determines the methods by which the assignments are performed? ____________

4 Who is the worker required to contact if problems or complaints arise and who is responsible for their resolution? ____________

5 What types of reports are required from the worker? Attach examples. ____________

6 Describe the worker's daily routine such as his or her schedule or hours. ____________

7 At what location(s) does the worker perform services (for example, firm's premises, own shop or office, home, customer's location)? Indicate the appropriate percentage of time the worker spends in each location, if more than one. ____________

8 Describe any meetings the worker is required to attend and any penalties for not attending (for example, sales meetings, monthly meetings, staff meetings). ____________

9 Is the worker required to provide the services personally? . . . . . ☐ **Yes** ☐ **No**

10 If substitutes or helpers are needed, who hires them? ____________

11 If the worker hires the substitutes or helpers, is approval required? . . . . . ☐ **Yes** ☐ **No**

If "Yes," by whom? ____________

12 Who pays the substitutes or helpers? ____________

13 Is the worker reimbursed if the worker pays the substitutes or helpers? . . . . . ☐ **Yes** ☐ **No**

If "Yes," by whom?

Form **SS-8** (Rev. 8-2011)

Form SS-8 (Page 4)

Form SS-8 (Rev. 8-2011) Page 4

Part V **For Service Providers or Salespersons.** Complete this part if the worker provided a service directly to customers or is a salesperson.

1 What are the worker's responsibilities in soliciting new customers?

2 Who provides the worker with leads to prospective customers?

3 Describe any reporting requirements pertaining to the leads.

4 What terms and conditions of sale, if any, are required by the firm?

5 Are orders submitted to and subject to approval by the firm? . . . ☐ Yes ☐ No

6 Who determines the worker's territory?

7 Did the worker pay for the privilege of serving customers on the route or in the territory? . . . ☐ Yes ☐ No

If "Yes," whom did the worker pay?

If "Yes," how much did the worker pay? . . . $

8 Where does the worker sell the product (for example, in a home, retail establishment)?

9 List the product and/or services distributed by the worker (for example, meat, vegetables, fruit, bakery products, beverages, or laundry or dry cleaning services). If more than one type of product and/or service is distributed, specify the principal one.

10 Does the worker sell life insurance full time? . . . ☐ Yes ☐ No

11 Does the worker sell other types of insurance for the firm? . . . ☐ Yes ☐ No

If "Yes," enter the percentage of the worker's total working time spent in selling other types of insurance . . . %

12 If the worker solicits orders from wholesalers, retailers, contractors, or operators of hotels, restaurants, or other similar establishments, enter the percentage of the worker's time spent in the solicitation . . . %

13 Is the merchandise purchased by the customers for resale or use in their business operations? . . . ☐ Yes ☐ No

Describe the merchandise and state whether it is equipment installed on the customers' premises.

Sign Here

Under penalties of perjury, I declare that I have examined this request, including accompanying documents, and to the best of my knowledge and belief, the facts presented are true, correct, and complete.

▶ Type or print name below signature. Title ▶ Date ▶

Form **SS-8** (Rev. 8-2011)

Form SS-8 (Page 5)

Form SS-8 (Rev. 8-2011) Page **5**

General Instructions

Section references are to the Internal Revenue Code unless otherwise noted.

Purpose

Firms and workers file Form SS-8 to request a determination of the status of a worker for purposes of federal employment taxes and income tax withholding.

A Form SS-8 determination may be requested only in order to resolve federal tax matters. If Form SS-8 is submitted for a tax year for which the statute of limitations on the tax return has expired, a determination letter will not be issued. The statute of limitations expires 3 years from the due date of the tax return or the date filed, whichever is later.

The IRS does not issue a determination letter for proposed transactions or on hypothetical situations. We may, however, issue an information letter when it is considered appropriate.

Definition

Firm. For the purposes of this form, the term "firm" means any individual, business enterprise, organization, state, or other entity for which a worker has performed services. The firm may or may not have paid the worker directly for these services.

CAUTION *If the firm was not responsible for payment for services, be sure to enter the name, address, and employer identification number of the payer on the first page of Form SS-8, below the identifying information for the firm and the worker.*

The Form SS-8 Determination Process

The IRS will acknowledge the receipt of your Form SS-8. Because there are usually two (or more) parties who could be affected by a determination of employment status, the IRS attempts to get information from all parties involved by sending those parties blank Forms SS-8 for completion. Some or all of the information provided on this Form SS-8 may be shared with the other parties listed on page 1. The case will be assigned to a technician who will review the facts, apply the law, and render a decision. The technician may ask for additional information from the requestor, from other involved parties, or from third parties that could help clarify the work relationship before rendering a decision. The IRS will generally issue a formal determination to the firm or payer (if that is a different entity), and will send a copy to the worker. A determination letter applies only to a worker (or a class of workers) requesting it, and the decision is binding on the IRS. In certain cases, a formal determination will not be issued. Instead, an information letter may be issued. Although an information letter is advisory only and is not binding on the IRS, it may be used to assist the worker to fulfill his or her federal tax obligations.

Neither the Form SS-8 determination process nor the review of any records in connection with the determination constitutes an examination (audit) of any federal tax return. If the periods under consideration have previously been examined, the Form SS-8 determination process will not constitute a reexamination under IRS reopening procedures. Because this is not an examination of any federal tax return, the appeal rights available in connection with an examination do not apply to a Form SS-8 determination. However, if you disagree with a determination or you have additional information concerning the work relationship that you believe was not previously considered, you may request that the determining office reconsider the determination.

Completing Form SS-8

Answer all questions as completely as possible. Attach additional sheets if you need more space. Provide information for **all** years the worker provided services for the firm. Determinations are based on the entire relationship between the firm and the worker. Also indicate if there were any significant changes in the work relationship over the service term.

Additional copies of this form may be obtained on IRS.gov or by calling 1-800-TAX-FORM (1-800-829-3676).

Fee

There is no fee for requesting a Form SS-8 determination letter.

Signature

Form SS-8 must be signed and dated by the taxpayer. A stamped signature will not be accepted.

The person who signs for a corporation must be an officer of the corporation who has personal knowledge of the facts. If the corporation is a member of an affiliated group filing a consolidated return, it must be signed by an officer of the common parent of the group.

The person signing for a trust, partnership, or limited liability company must be, respectively, a trustee, general partner, or member-manager who has personal knowledge of the facts.

Where To File

Send the completed and signed Form SS-8 to the address below for the firm's location. Faxed, photocopied, or electronic versions of Form SS-8 are not acceptable for the initial request for the Form SS-8 determination. However, only for cases involving federal agencies, send Form SS-8 to the Internal Revenue Service, Attn: CC:CORP:T:C, Ben Franklin Station, P.O. Box 7604, Washington, DC 20044. **Do not submit Form SS-8 with your tax return as that will delay processing time.**

Firm's location:	Send to:
Alaska, Arizona, Arkansas, California, Colorado, Hawaii, Idaho, Illinois, Iowa, Kansas, Minnesota, Missouri, Montana, Nebraska, Nevada, New Mexico, North Dakota, Oklahoma, Oregon, South Dakota, Texas, Utah, Washington, Wisconsin, Wyoming, American Samoa, Guam, Puerto Rico, U.S. Virgin Islands	Internal Revenue Service Form SS-8 Determinations P.O. Box 630 Stop 631 Holtsville, NY 11742-0630
Alabama, Connecticut, Delaware, District of Columbia, Florida, Georgia, Indiana, Kentucky, Louisiana, Maine, Maryland, Massachusetts, Michigan, Mississippi, New Hampshire, New Jersey, New York, North Carolina, Ohio, Pennsylvania, Rhode Island, South Carolina, Tennessee, Vermont, Virginia, West Virginia, all other locations not listed	Internal Revenue Service Form SS-8 Determinations 40 Lakemont Road Newport, VT 05855-1555

Form **SS-8** (Rev. 8-2011)

Form SS-8 (Page 6)

Form SS-8 (Rev. 8-2011) Page **6**

Instructions for Workers

If you are requesting a determination for more than one firm, complete a separate Form SS-8 for each firm.

CAUTION *Form SS-8 is not a claim for refund of social security and Medicare taxes or federal income tax withholding.*

If the IRS determines that you are an employee, you are responsible for filing an amended return for any corrections related to this decision. A determination that a worker is an employee does not necessarily reduce any current or prior tax liability. For more information, call 1-800-829-1040.

Time for filing a claim for refund. Generally, you must file your claim for a credit or refund within 3 years from the date your original return was filed or within 2 years from the date the tax was paid, whichever is later.

Filing Form SS-8 does not prevent the expiration of the time in which a claim for a refund must be filed. If you are concerned about a refund, and the statute of limitations for filing a claim for refund for the year(s) at issue has not yet expired, you should file Form 1040X, Amended U.S. Individual Income Tax Return, to protect your statute of limitations. File a separate Form 1040X for each year.

On the Form 1040X you file, do not complete lines 1 through 22 on the form. Write "Protective Claim" at the top of the form, sign and date it. In addition, enter the following statement in Part III: "Filed Form SS-8 with the Internal Revenue Service Office in (Holtsville, NY; Newport, VT; or Washington, DC; as appropriate). By filing this protective claim, I reserve the right to file a claim for any refund that may be due after a determination of my employment tax status has been completed."

Filing Form SS-8 does not alter the requirement to timely file an income tax return. Do not delay filing your tax return in anticipation of an answer to your Form SS-8 request. In addition, if applicable, do not delay in responding to a request for payment while waiting for a determination of your worker status.

Instructions for Firms

If a **worker** has requested a determination of his or her status while working for you, you will receive a request from the IRS to complete a Form SS-8. In cases of this type, the IRS usually gives each party an opportunity to present a statement of the facts because any decision will affect the employment tax status of the parties. Failure to respond to this request will not prevent the IRS from issuing a determination letter based on the information he or she has made available so that the worker may fulfill his or her federal tax obligations. However, the information that you provide is extremely valuable in determining the status of the worker.

If you are requesting a determination for a particular class of worker, complete the form for one individual who is representative of the class of workers whose status is in question. If you want a written determination for more than one class of workers, complete a separate Form SS-8 for one worker from each class whose status is typical of that class. A written determination for any worker will apply to other workers of the same class if the facts are not materially different for these workers. Please provide a list of names and addresses of all workers potentially affected by this determination.

If you have a reasonable basis for not treating a worker as an employee, you may be relieved from having to pay employment taxes for that worker under section 530 of the 1978 Revenue Act. However, this relief provision cannot be considered in conjunction with a Form SS-8 determination because the determination does not constitute an examination of any tax return. For more information regarding section 530 of the 1978 Revenue Act and to determine if you qualify for relief under this section, visit IRS.gov.

Privacy Act and Paperwork Reduction Act Notice. We ask for the information on Form SS-8 to carry out the Internal Revenue laws of the United States. This information will be used to determine the employment status of the worker(s) described on the form. Subtitle C, Employment Taxes, of the Internal Revenue Code imposes employment taxes on wages, including income tax withholding. Sections 3121(d), 3306(a), and 3401(c) and (d) and the related regulations define employee and employer for purposes of employment taxes imposed under Subtitle C. Section 6001 authorizes the IRS to request information needed to determine if a worker(s) or firm is subject to these taxes. Section 6109 requires you to provide your taxpayer identification number. Neither workers nor firms are required to request a status determination, but if you choose to do so, you must provide the information requested on this form. Failure to provide the requested information may prevent us from making a status determination. If any worker or the firm has requested a status determination and you are being asked to provide information for use in that determination, you are not required to provide the requested information. However, failure to provide such information will prevent the IRS from considering it in making the status determination. Providing false or fraudulent information may subject you to penalties. Generally, tax returns and return information are confidential, as required by section 6103. However, section 6103 allows or requires the IRS to disclose or give the information shown on your tax return to others as described in the Code. Routine uses of this information include providing it to the Department of Justice for use in civil and criminal litigation, to the Social Security Administration for the administration of social security programs, and to cities, states, the District of Columbia, and U.S. commonwealths and possessions for the administration of their tax laws. We also may disclose this information to other countries under a tax treaty, to federal and state agencies to enforce federal nontax criminal laws, or to federal law enforcement and intelligence agencies to combat terrorism. We may provide this information to the affected worker(s), the firm, or payer as part of the status determination process.

You are not required to provide the information requested on a form that is subject to the Paperwork Reduction Act unless the form displays a valid OMB control number. Books or records relating to a form or its instructions must be retained as long as their contents may become material in the administration of any Internal Revenue law.

The time needed to complete and file this Form SS-8 will vary depending on individual circumstances. The estimated average time is: Recordkeeping, 23 hrs., 55 min.; Learning about the law or the form, 1 hr., 48 min.; Preparing the form, 5 hrs., 03 min.; and Sending the form to the IRS, 48 min. If you have comments concerning the accuracy of these time estimates or suggestions for making this form simpler, we would be happy to hear from you. You can write to the Internal Revenue Service, Tax Products Coordinating Committee, SE:W:CAR:MP:T:M:S, 1111 Constitution Ave. NW, IR-6526, Washington, DC 20224. Do not send the tax form to this address. Instead, see *Where To File* on page 5.

Final Examination (Optional)

MASTERING PAYROLL

Instructions: Detach the Final Examination Answer Sheet on page 317 before beginning your final examination. Select the correct letter for the answer to each multiple choice question below, then fill it in on the Answer Sheet. Allow approximately two hours.

1. As of December 6, Joe's year-to-date wages are $112,400. On December 7, 2013, he is due wages of $2,000. How much FICA tax should the employer withhold from this payment?

a. $128.20 b. $153.00 c. $109.60 d. $83.60

2. How many days after a full-time employee starts to work does an employer have to complete the I-9?

a. 4 b. 1 c. 5 d. 3

3. Which form does an employee need to submit to obtain a Social Security card?

a. W-4 b. I-9 c. 1099 d. SS-5

4. An employee works 48 hours in the workweek and is paid $9.00 per hour. How much premium pay is due this employee under federal law?

a. $36.00 b. $72.00 c. $108.00 d. $48.00

5. Which form does an employer use to obtain an Employer Identification Number for depositing employment taxes?

a. 8109 b. 941 c. SS-4 d. I-9

6. If, on April 17, 2013, a state's minimum wage is $6.95 per hour, what is the minimum rate that employers in that state must pay employees?

a. $5.15 b. $6.95 c. $5.85 d. $7.25

7. At what rate must federal income tax be withheld for an employee who has not properly completed a W-4?

a. married with two allowances
b. married with one allowance
c. single with zero allowances
d. single with one allowance

8. FUTA tax must be deposited as soon as the quarterly tax liability exceeds:

a. $100 b. $3,000 c. $1,500 d. $500

9. Employers can file the employment tax return annually (Form 944) if they anticipate their federal employment tax liability will not exceed:

a. $50,000
b. $500
c. $2,500
d. $1,000

10. Carla earns $110,300 from January through November 2013, before resigning to work for a new employer who pays her $3,000 for December 2013. How much FICA would be withheld on the $3,000?

a. $229.50 b. $43.50 c. $169.50 d. $186.00

11. On August 10, 2013 Chen is paid a weekly gross of $300 for a 38-hour workweek. If he works 39 hours in week 1 and 38 hours in week 2, how much pay is he due for the two weeks?

a. $600.00 b. $599.64 c. $611.84 d. $615.79

12. State unemployment returns are filed:

a. weekly b. monthly c. annually d. quarterly

13. Form 1099 informational statements must be furnished to recipients no later than:

a. January 31
b. February 28
c. January 15
d. January 1

14. In general, how often employees are paid and the method of payment are regulated by:

a. IRS b. FLSA c. state laws d. SSA

15. Francesca is paid $1,000 semimonthly. If she works a 40-hour week, what is her hourly rate under federal law?

a. $25.00 b. $12.50 c. $11.54 d. $15.00

16. Charlie is paid biweekly at a rate of $7.60 per hour. If he works 35 hours in week 1 and 45 hours in week 2, how much should his gross wages be on his next paycheck?

a. $608.00 b. $627.00 c. $646.00 d. $665.00

17. In 2012, Aretha receives a salary advance against 2013 wages. Which year's wage base is used to calculate Social Security tax on the advance?

a. 2012 b. 2013

18. Lawrence received a salary advance of $50. He plans to repay this advance from his gross wages of $450 to be paid on September 15. What is his taxable income for the September 15 paycheck?

a. $500 b. $400 c. $450 d. $350

19. Gail works 32 hours Monday through Thursday. On Friday, she is out with the flu and receives 8 hours' sick pay under her employer's policy. She returns to work for 4 hours on Saturday. If she earns $8.00 per hour and the federal minimum requirements for overtime pay apply, how much pay will she receive?

a. $352.00 b. $320.00 c. $368.00 d. $288.00

20. Juan works on a holiday for which he receives 8 hours' regular pay and 8 hours' holiday pay. During the rest of the workweek he works 32 hours. If his normal pay rate is $8.00 per hour, how much pay must he receive under federal law?

a. $416.00 b. $320.00 c. $448.00 d. $384.00

21. When employers are subject to both federal and state laws, they must observe the law that:

a. is the more recent one
b. is more favorable to the employer
c. is more favorable to the employee
d. has the bigger penalties

22. Which year's Social Security tax rate and wage limit apply to employee bonus checks dated January 20, 2013, but received on December 30, 2012?

a. 2012 b. 2013

23. The final due date for the 4th quarter 941 for employers that have paid all taxes on time is:

a. December 31
b. February 10
c. January 31
d. February 1

24. What should be withheld from a bonus in the year it is paid?

a. FIT
b. FICA
c. FIT and FICA
d. FIT, FICA and FUTA

25. On Friday, March 5, Dynamic Manufacturing's payroll resulted in a deposit obligation of $2,600. Under the semiweekly deposit rule, this deposit must be made by:

a. March 10
b. April 15
c. March 12
d. March 8

26. Abigail's normal work hours are Monday through Friday, 8:00 A.M. to 5:00 P.M. On Saturday, Abigail flies to a temporary work site between 9:00 A.M. and 7:00 P.M. An overnight stay is required. How many hours, if any, must Abigail be paid for travel time?

a. 8 b. 10 c. 0 d. 7

27. The correct entry for the withholding of an employee's contribution to a pension plan is:

a. Salary Expense
    Pension Plan Payable
b. Salary Expense
    Cash
c. Pension Plan Payable
    Cash
d. Salary Expense
    Pension Plan Expense

28. How many days does an employer have to process data on a revised W-4?

a. 30 days b. 90 days c. 60 days d. 10 days

29. An employer is subject to FUTA requirements when its wages paid for the quarter exceed:

a. $51,300 b. $5,000 c. $1,500 d. $3,000

30. Employees must receive a copy of their W-2 no later than:

a. December 31
b. January 31
c. February 28
d. January 15

31. When paychecks are distributed to employees on December 30, 2012, George is ill and does not claim his check until January 4, 2013. For what year must this income be reported?

a. whichever year George requests
b. 2012
c. 2010
d. 2013

32. On which form do employers report employees' gross taxable income?

a. W-2 b. 1099 c. SS-8 d. W-4

33. On which form do employers report income for nonemployees?

a. W-4 b. SS-8 c. 1099 d. W-2

34. Retail businesses that began operation prior to April 1, 1990, must abide by federal wage and hour law if gross annual sales exceed:

a. $500,000 b. $250,000 c. $362,500 d. $0

35. The hourly rate for an employee who earns $400 per week for a normal 38-hour workweek is:

a. $10.00 b. $10.53 c. $10.50 d. $9.53

36. Employers are required to turn unclaimed wages over to the state under:

a. the enterprise coverage
b. FLSA
c. escheat law
d. consumer protection law

37. Wages paid in May are reported on the Form 941 that is filed by:

a. December 30
b. January 31
c. June 30
d. July 31

38. How many years is an employer required to retain records of wages paid employees under federal wage and hour law?

a. 3 b. 5 c. 1 d. 4

39. How many years does the IRS require an employer to retain a Withholding Allowance Certificate?

a. 3 b. 5 c. 1 d. 4

40. The entry to record the employee's portion of FICA tax is:

a. FICA Payable
    Cash
b. FICA Payable
    Salary Expense
c. Cash
    FICA Payable
d. Salary Expense
    FICA Payable

41. The entry to record remittance of the employer's portion of FICA tax is:

a. Payroll Taxes Payable—FICA
   Cash
b. FICA Payable
   Payroll Taxes Payable—FICA
c. Cash
   FICA Payable
d. Payroll Taxes Payable—FICA
   FICA Payable

42. Total undeposited taxes for Wednesday, May 12, are $2,600. Under the semiweekly rule, this deposit must be made no later than:

a. May 19   b. May 11   c. June 15   d. May 12

43. Which of the following forms must be completed for every new employee?

a. W-2   b. SS-4   c. I-9   d. 1099

44. Federal copies of Forms W-2 are sent to the:

a. SSA   b. IRS   c. OMB   d. FLSA

45. Which of the following documents substantiates the employee's identity and authorization to work for I-9 purposes?

a. Social Security card
b. driver's license
c. birth certificate
d. U.S. passport

46. Which of the following categories of employees are not exempt from the overtime pay requirements under federal law?

a. administrative
b. professional
c. blue collar
d. executive

47. The entry to record deductions from employee pay for health insurance is:

a. Health Insurance Expense
    Health Insurance Payable
b. Salary Expense
    Health Insurance Withheld Payable
c. Health Insurance Expense
    Cash
d. Cash
    Health Insurance Payable

48. Which of the following is not an option on the W-4?

a. additional allowances
b. withholding no tax
c. additional withholding
d. a flat tax

49. Tax withheld from an independent contractor is known as:

a. Social Security tax
b. federal income tax
c. federal unemployment tax
d. backup withholding tax

50. An employer whose quarterly employment tax liability is under $2,500 deposits the taxes . . .

a. monthly
b. quarterly
c. semi-weekly
d. annually

Final Examination Answer Sheet

MASTERING PAYROLL

Instructions: Detach this sheet before starting the Final Exam. For each question, check the box beneath the letter of the correct answer. Use a #2 pencil to make a dark impression. When completed, return to: AIPB Continuing Education, Suite 500, 6001 Montrose Road, Rockville, MD 20852. If you attain a grade of at least 70, you will receive the Institute's *Certificate of Completion*. Answer Sheets are not returned.

Certified Bookkeeper applicants: If you attain a grade of at least 70, and become certified you will be eligible to register seven (7) Continuing Professional Education Credits (CPECs) toward your *Certified Bookkeeper* CPEC requirements.

1. a ☐ b ☐ c ☐ d ☐	14. a ☐ b ☐ c ☐ d ☐	27. a ☐ b ☐ c ☐ d ☐	39. a ☐ b ☐ c ☐ d ☐
2. a ☐ b ☐ c ☐ d ☐	15. a ☐ b ☐ c ☐ d ☐	28. a ☐ b ☐ c ☐ d ☐	40. a ☐ b ☐ c ☐ d ☐
3. a ☐ b ☐ c ☐ d ☐	16. a ☐ b ☐ c ☐ d ☐	29. a ☐ b ☐ c ☐ d ☐	41. a ☐ b ☐ c ☐ d ☐
4. a ☐ b ☐ c ☐ d ☐	17. a ☐ b ☐	30. a ☐ b ☐ c ☐ d ☐	42. a ☐ b ☐ c ☐ d ☐
5. a ☐ b ☐ c ☐ d ☐	18. a ☐ b ☐ c ☐ d ☐	31. a ☐ b ☐ c ☐ d ☐	43. a ☐ b ☐ c ☐ d ☐
6. a ☐ b ☐ c ☐ d ☐	19. a ☐ b ☐ c ☐ d ☐	32. a ☐ b ☐ c ☐ d ☐	44. a ☐ b ☐ c ☐ d ☐
7. a ☐ b ☐ c ☐ d ☐	20. a ☐ b ☐ c ☐ d ☐	33. a ☐ b ☐ c ☐ d ☐	45. a ☐ b ☐ c ☐ d ☐
8. a ☐ b ☐ c ☐ d ☐	21. a ☐ b ☐ c ☐ d ☐	34. a ☐ b ☐ c ☐ d ☐	46. a ☐ b ☐ c ☐ d ☐
9. a ☐ b ☐ c ☐ d ☐	22. a ☐ b ☐	35. a ☐ b ☐ c ☐ d ☐	47. a ☐ b ☐ c ☐ d ☐
10. a ☐ b ☐ c ☐ d ☐	23. a ☐ b ☐ c ☐ d ☐	36. a ☐ b ☐ c ☐ d ☐	48. a ☐ b ☐ c ☐ d ☐
11. a ☐ b ☐ c ☐ d ☐	24. a ☐ b ☐ c ☐ d ☐	37. a ☐ b ☐ c ☐ d ☐	49. a ☐ b ☐ c ☐ d ☐
12. a ☐ b ☐ c ☐ d ☐	25. a ☐ b ☐ c ☐ d ☐	38. a ☐ b ☐ c ☐ d ☐	50. a ☐ b ☐ c ☐ d ☐
13. a ☐ b ☐ c ☐ d ☐	26. a ☐ b ☐ c ☐ d ☐		

Name ____________________ Title ____________________

Company ____________________ Street Address ____________________

City ____________________ State __________ Zip __________ Phone Number ____________________

For *Certified Bookkeeper* applicants only: #____________________
Membership or Certification (nonmember) ID Number

Course Evaluation for
MASTERING PAYROLL

Please complete and return (even if you do not take the Final Examination) to: AIPB Continuing Education, 6001 Montrose Road, Suite 500, Rockville, MD 20852. **PLEASE PRINT CLEARLY.**

Circle one

1. Did you find the instructions clear? Yes No
Comments: ______________________________

2. Did you find the course practical? Yes No
Comments: ______________________________

3. Is this course what you expected? Yes No
Comments: ______________________________

4. Would you recommend this course to other accounting professionals? Yes No
Comments: ______________________________

5. What did you like most about *Mastering Payroll*? ____________

6. What would have made the course even more helpful? ________

7. May we use your comments and name in advertising for the course? Yes No

8. Would you be interested in other courses? Yes No

Please indicate what subject areas would be of greatest interest to you:

1. ______________________ 4. ______________________
2. ______________________ 5. ______________________
3. ______________________ 6. ______________________

Name (optional) ____________ Title ____________

Company ____________ Street Address ____________

City ____________ State ____________ Zip ____________ Phone Number ____________